I0560726

The Manifestation Frequency

Hidden Ancient Secrets Revealed to Awaken the Power Within
—by Roy Waugh

Shava Books, Phoenix, AZ, USA

The Manifestation Frequency
Copyright © 2025 by Roy Waugh
All rights reserved

No part of this publication may be reproduced, distributed, or transmitted in any form or by any means, including photocopying, recording, or other electronic or mechanical methods, without the prior written permission of the publisher, except in the case of brief quotations used in critical reviews and specific other noncommercial uses permitted by copyright law. For permission requests, write:

Shava Books
22433 N. 30th St.
Phoenix, AZ 85050

First Edition Published by Shava Books
Phoenix, AZ, USA.

Cover design by: Roy Waugh

Hardcover ISBN: 979-8-9997069-1-1
Paperback ISBN: 979-8-9997069-0-4
eBook ISBN: 979-8-9997069-2-8
Audiobook ISBN: 979-8-9997069-3-5

Library of Congress Cataloging-in-Publication Data has been applied for.
eCO: 1-14980078111
For more information, visit: shavabooks.com.
Printed in the United States of America.

Table of Contents

Introduction 7

Part I—Tuning the Frequency Within 11
—Awakening the Power Within

Part II—Raising Your Resonance 149
—Becoming a Vibrational Match for What You Seek

INTRODUCTION

The Manifestation Frequency: *Hidden Ancient Secrets Revealed to Awaken the Power Within*

You did not find this book by accident.
Something drew you here—a whisper, a pull, a frequency long buried beneath the noise of the world.

This is not another typical book on Manifestation; it is a sacred unveiling. Once protected, the truths within these pages were guarded as sacred wisdom, hidden because they were considered too powerful for the masses.

For centuries, this knowledge was reserved for the few: the most pious and the influential among us, the mystics, sages, and kings and queens of the world. It was woven into scrolls, scriptures, chants, and oral traditions —crossing deserts and temples, veiled in plain sight across nearly every spiritual path. And now, it is being placed in your hands for the first time —not as a secret to protect, but as a birthright to reclaim.

From the deserts of the Middle East to the mountains of Tibet, from Hebrew psalms to Vedic chants, from Sufi poetry to Buddhist sutras, this divine technology of creation has always been here—encoded, protected, whispered.

But this knowledge is no longer hidden; it's being revealed now because it belongs to all of us.

Within these pages lies a revelation long hidden in plain sight: No matter what name you call the Higher Power—God, Allah, Yahweh, Brahman, the Universe, the Almighty, or Source—it doesn't change the truth of who YOU are; you are created in the image of that very power.

And because you are created in its likeness, you carry that same divine, creative force within you.

It lives in your thoughts, speaks through your voice, and breathes in and out of you with every inhale and exhale.

You are not separate from the Divine.
You are an extension of it.

And here is a more profound truth still:
Everything is energy. Everything already exists.

You are not trying to manifest something out of nothing.
You are aligning with what already is—what already vibrates in the field of infinite potential. Energy cannot be created or destroyed; it only shifts, moves, and rearranges. That means the love, abundance, healing, opportunity, and clarity you seek are not missing—they are present, waiting for resonance and to find their way to you.

The illusion of lack is one of the greatest deceptions humanity has inherited. We were taught there isn't enough—that blessings are scarce and only a select few are worthy of receiving them.

But the truth is: the universe is infinite. There is no shortage in Spirit.

Your thoughts and words carry frequency.
Those frequencies draw to you what vibrates at that same frequency.
You are not creating from scratch—you are accessing, attuning, aligning.

Manifestation is not about reaching outward. It's about resonating inward. And when your energy, intention, and words align, what you seek begins to move toward you—by spiritual law.

When you finally awaken to this truth, you will stop reaching for miracles as if they are outside of you.

You begin to embody them.

This book will not just teach you how to manifest.
It will reveal the forgotten laws of creation—hidden in the sacred

teachings of the Bible, the Qur'an, the Torah, the Vedas, and the teachings of Buddha.

I will help you weave together the knowledge I have learned—blending spirit, science, story, and ancient wisdom—so you do not just understand manifestation.

You will become it.

You were never meant to sit back and wish.
You were born to speak with power and co-create with the divine.
You haven't been lost—you have just been sleeping.

But now it is time to wake up.

So, take a deep breath and turn the page.

Allow me to share these ancient, sacred truths I have learned, experienced, and lived.

Let me show you how to unlock what is already inside you and to help you find your power, awaken your divine frequency, and most of all,

To help you remember who you really are.

Part I—Tuning Your Inner Frequency
—Awakening the Power Within

Before manifestation becomes visible, it begins within. Part I is about laying the foundation—not through external action but internal alignment. These chapters help you discover the truth that your words, your energy, your thoughts, and your faith all emit a frequency—and that frequency shapes your reality.

In this section, you will learn how belief forms the root of everything you create. You will understand the spiritual science of how words carry power, how gratitude magnetizes what you desire, and how your energy isn't just a mood—it's a message. You will begin to see yourself not just as a hopeful participant, but as an active co-creator.

Whether you have never explored manifestation or have been walking this path for years, these chapters will help you tune your inner instrument to the frequency of divine alignment so that everything you create flows from truth, clarity, and deep spiritual resonance.

This is where the shift begins—from thinking to tuning in.

Here, we explore the core truths of manifestation—faith, speech, energy, and spiritual identity. These chapters help you tune into your divine nature and set the energetic stage for what will come.
Are you ready?

Chapter 1: The Call to Create
—Awakening to the Power Within

Opening Reflection

"Every word you speak becomes a seed, a seed of infinite potential. When given the power of your intention, truth to root it in, time—and a touch of love—the harvest is inevitable."
—Roy Waugh

Introduction

Before science gave it language and modern thinkers reimagined it, the ancients knew that creation begins with recognition.

You are not a passive participant in this life—you are a co-creator in the image of the Divine. The moment you honestly remember this, your entire story begins to shift. You stop waiting for permission and start walking with purpose.

This chapter isn't just about words—it's about alignment. You were made in the image of the Creator, which means that the sacred creative force spoken of in ancient texts is not separate from you. It lives within you. It is speaking through your voice, moving through your belief, and responding to your vibration.

When you speak, you plant.
When you believe, you water.
When you act in alignment, you harvest.

The seed does not question whether it will grow. It simply surrenders to the mystery—trusting the light, the soil, the unseen forces, and divine timing. And so must you.

You were never meant to live life on mute, you were born to echo the ancient power spoken by prophets, sages, and mystics—to speak mountains into motion—to declare light amid darkness and to co-author miracles with the Divine.

This is the call to create.

And it begins now—with your next thought, your next word, and your next breath.

Hidden Teachings from Ancient Traditions
—The Creative Power of Word, Thought, and Frequency

Across the ancient world, sacred texts carried a hidden thread that taught humanity that creation begins not in matter, but in vibration: sound, thought, intention. These teachings were often veiled in parables, chants, or poetic metaphor, but they held the same essential truth: what is spoken and believed becomes. When aligned with the Divine, your words are not mere language. They are creative acts.

What follows are five echoes of this sacred law—preserved across traditions and now revealed again, for your remembering, your awakening.

✧Christian Faith

In Christian scripture, creation begins not with hands, but with a word. **"And God said, 'Let there be light,' and there was light**." (Genesis 1:3) The world as we know it emerged from the voice of God—not from effort or labor, but from divine command. The spoken word was not symbolic—it was generative.

Jesus, too, demonstrated the creative authority of words. He healed with them, calmed storms with them, and raised the dead by calling them forth. When He said, "**Out of the abundance of the heart the mouth speaks**" (Matthew 12:34), He reminded us that what is inside—when spoken—shapes what is outside.

Even Paul writes in Romans 4:17 that **"God calls into being things that were not**." This shows a pattern: words aligned with faith don't just describe reality—they create it.

To speak is to sow. And when your words align with divine will, you are not just praying—you are planting.

✧Jewish Wisdom

In Jewish tradition, the creative force of the spoken word is deeply woven into both scripture and practice. The Hebrew language itself is considered sacred—each letter believed to carry divine energy, and each word capable of shaping reality. Creation in the Jewish telling isn't constructed—it's spoken. **"By the word of the Lord the heavens were made, their starry host by the breath of His mouth**." (Psalm 33:6, Tanakh) The cosmos was not built with tools, but uttered into being through sacred breath and sound.

The Hebrew word ruach means both "spirit" and "breath," reminding us that what we speak is never neutral—it carries spirit. This belief is not metaphorical; it's mystical and foundational. Words create worlds.
Proverbs 18:21 affirms this sacred power: **"Death and life are in the power of the tongue, and those who love it will eat its fruits**." (Proverbs 18:21, Tanakh) In other words, speech isn't simply expressive— it's formative. To speak is to direct energy, plant seeds, and release frequency into the fabric of the world.

In the mystical tradition of Kabbalah, the divine light that sustains creation flows through the vessels of language. The Zohar teaches that speech aligned with truth becomes a channel through which divine energy flows into form.

In the Jewish worldview, speaking with intention is to co-create with the Divine. Every word carries weight, and every breath echoes the first breath that gave life to everything.

✧Islamic Teaching

The Qur'an speaks of a divine creative word: **"When He decrees a matter, He only says to it, 'Be,' and it is."** (Qur'an 2:117) The word "Kun"—meaning "Be"—is considered a sacred vibrational command. In Islam, God does not labor or negotiate—He speaks, and creation obeys.

This vibrational principle echoes how the Prophet Muhammad (peace be upon him) lived. Aisha described him as *"a walking Qur'an."* His life embodied the divine message—demonstrating that sacred speech is not only what you say, but how you live.

The Qur'an itself is spoken aloud—recited rhythmically and melodically. Its sound carries more than meaning. It carries power.

In Islam, words are not casual. They are aligned with truth and mercy, or they carry weight before God. To speak is to take responsibility for what you shape.

When your intention is pure and your voice is aligned with divine will, your speech becomes a vessel through which the unseen becomes real.

✧ Buddhist Practices

Buddhism teaches that the world is shaped from within. Reality, as we perceive it, begins in the mind—and the thoughts we entertain become the life we live. The Dhammapada opens with this timeless verse: **"We are what we think. All that we are arises with our thoughts. With our thoughts, we make the world."** (Verse 1) This verse isn't mere optimism—it's energetic law. Your internal dialogue becomes your external experience. The vibrations of your mind ripple out and return to you as form.

In practice, Buddhist mantras are repeated not simply for mental focus, but to shape consciousness. The vibration of the chant aligns mind, body, and energy. Thought becomes frequency, and frequency becomes form.

Even silence in Buddhism is filled with sacred presence. The absence of words becomes a space where awareness sharpens, and truth rises.

To think with clarity is to speak with power. And to speak with awareness is to create with grace.

✧Hindu Traditions

In Hindu cosmology, the universe itself was born of sound—specifically, the sacred vibration **Om**. This syllable is not a symbol—it is a frequency. It represents the divine source pulsing through all of existence. The Vedas say, "**In the beginning was the Word, and the Word was with Brahman, and the Word was Brahman**." (Rig Veda 10.125, interpreted) When chanted with awareness, the spoken word is believed to carry Shakti, or divine energy. Mantras aren't incantations. They are vibrational alignments. Each one attunes the soul to a specific aspect of the Divine.

One of the most sacred declarations in the Upanishads is "Aham Brahmasmi"—"**I am Divine**." To speak this truth is not arrogance. It is awakening.

In Hindu tradition, the voice is a gateway. When used with love, truth, and devotion, it becomes the bridge between the inner self and universal creation.

These ancient voices were never meant to compete—they were meant to harmonize. Across continents and centuries, each tradition held a piece of the same sacred technology: creation begins with frequency. Whether it is breath, chant, prayer, mantra, or holy decree—the power to shape reality begins with vibration.

And that frequency lives in you.

Wisdom From Contemporary Spiritual Leaders

Before modern science caught up with the language of creation, spiritual teachers were already pointing us inward. They reminded us that the voice within is not powerless—it is divine, creative, and encoded with the frequency to shape reality.

Even our language carries spiritual weight, and few words reveal this more clearly than the word "*future*."

Future (n.): **The time or a period of time following the moment of speaking or writing; time regarded as still to come.**

Your future isn't just something that happens to you—it responds to you. Every belief you hold in this moment sends instructions ahead. Speak hope now, and hope is what greets you there. Speak with intention, and your intention is what meets you there. What you believe now determines what has permission to exist later.

Across traditions and generations, the mystics and mentors of our time have echoed the ancient call: creation begins with belief, intention, and voice.

So, let us go and revisit some of their guiding wisdom.

—Joyce Meyer reminds us that "**words are containers for power.**" When we speak in faith, we are not simply expressing hope—we are activating a force that calls things into being. Her teaching affirms the biblical principle that creation responds to voice when that voice aligns with belief.

—Deepak Chopra teaches, "**Intention is the starting point of every dream**." In his spiritual and scientific explorations, he bridges the unseen with the seen—revealing that consciousness itself is creative power, and our words are extensions of that force.

—Esther Hicks, through the Abraham teachings, explains that "**you are the creator of your own reality, and so you are the initiator of the vibration that creates it**." Her voice reminds us that manifestation begins with the frequency we emit.

—Iyanla Vanzant once said: "**Words are the voice of the heart. Speak with intention, because every word you utter plants a seed in the world—and in you.**" This reminder is clear: speech is never neutral. It imprints on the soul, it plants in the unseen, and it creates conditions for what will later grow.

—Roy Waugh, "**Every word you speak becomes a seed—planted in the soil of your reality. If you want a sacred harvest, you must speak with sacred intent.**" These words carry the resonance of both wisdom and personal testimony, revealing the divine nature of human expression.

When we tune into the voices of these spiritual leaders, we hear a unifying thread: Your words are not decoration, they are declarations. They do not just describe your world—they design it. *You were created to speak light into form and possibility into motion.*

Scientific Perspectives on Thought and Creation
—The Mind as a Manifesting Instrument

We often think of science and spirituality as separate languages, but they speak in harmony when it comes to manifestation. The deeper we look into neuroscience, epigenetics, and quantum physics, the clearer it becomes: your thoughts are not just fleeting impulses. They are the first ingredients in your reality.

The power to create is not somewhere out there—it is already wired within you. And science is finally catching up to what faith has always known: the mind is a divine instrument, capable of reshaping both biology and the world around it.

✧Neuroscience of Thought

Neuroscience confirms that repetition shapes the brain. Every time you think a thought, you strengthen a neural pathway. The more a thought is repeated, the more it becomes a default route—easier to travel, harder to unlearn. This is how beliefs are biologically formed. It's not just philosophy—it is neuroplasticity.

You rewire your brain by choosing what you think, again and again.

✧ Epigenetics and Belief

The groundbreaking field of epigenetics shows that genes are not your fate. They are influenced—switched on or off—by your environment, emotions, and even your belief system.

As Dr. Bruce Lipton teaches, perception has the power to alter cellular activity. In other words, your biology responds to your beliefs. You are not a prisoner of your DNA—you are a partner with it, shaping its expression through the thoughts you allow and the energy you embody.

✧ Quantum Physics and Attention

Quantum physics brings the mystery full circle: at the subatomic level, the observer influences the outcome. This means consciousness itself plays a role in shaping matter. The famous double-slit experiment revealed that particles behave differently when observed. Why? Because energy follows attention.

When you focus your thoughts and intentions, you collapse possibility into form. You are not just watching life happen—you are participating in its unfolding.

✧ Vibrational Effects on Matter

In addition to modern physics and biology, the work of Dr. Masaru Emoto offers a striking visual metaphor for how consciousness might influence form. Emoto's controversial experiments with water showed that molecules exposed to words like "love" or "gratitude" formed stunning, symmetrical crystals—while those exposed to hateful or chaotic speech became disordered. Though debated in scientific circles, his work remains a powerful illustration of the potential relationship between vibration, intention, and physical reality—especially given that the human body is composed of over 70% water.

So, what does it all mean? It means that belief is not just a feel-good mantra. It is a measurable force. It means that your mind is not passive—it is participatory. Every thought you think sends ripples through your body, energy field, and the fabric of the world around you. And when those thoughts align with truth, vision, and divine intention, they carry the frequency of creation itself.

Science does not replace faith—it confirms its brilliance. You are not imagining your power. You are awakening it.

Personal Story
—The Song That Saved a Life

Early in my singing career, I was invited to perform at a church I had never visited. I was eager, grateful, and ready to share. But the moment I stepped on stage, I felt something was off.

The room was silent—too silent. No applause. No smiles. Just blank stares and folded arms. I questioned everything. Should I even be here? Did I miss something? Is this touching anything or anyone?

But I kept going. I finished the concert, even though inside, I felt like I had failed.

As people left, a few shook my hand and politely said thank you.

Then, near the end of the line, a young woman approached, crying.
She could barely speak but managed to whisper, "You have no idea what you have done." Then she walked away.

Right then, I said a quiet prayer for her, released the weight of it, and moved on.

Two years later, that same church invited me back. I thought about declining the invitation. I had thought my first visit had no impact. But I went, arrived early, as always, and began setting up.

A young woman walked in relatively early. Radiant. Glowing. Peaceful. Smile from ear to ear. She said, "I don't know if you remember me...", I knew immediately who she was. I said, "I do. You told me, 'You have no idea what you have done.'" She smiled and nodded. "That's all I could say that night. But now I can tell you the rest."

She told me that during my previous concert, I sang a song called Keep Believing. She remembered every word. Keep believin'. It had stayed with her.

The next morning, she was scheduled for an abortion. But something within her shifted during that song. Then, I learned that she had canceled the appointment.

Suddenly, her mother walked in, carrying the most beautiful little girl I had ever seen. She had curly blonde hair, bright blue eyes, and the biggest, brightest smile I had ever seen.

I burst into tears.

I ran and scooped her into my arms and wept—not only for the life that was spared, but also because I did not know I had planted a seed during the concert that night.

And it grew.

Practical Applications

—Activating the Creator Within

Knowing you are powerful is not enough—you must practice it. Creation responds to consistency, not just intention. These practical applications are not just habits—they are holy rituals. They help you move from inspiration into embodiment, from revelation into reality. The following steps are designed to activate the creator within you. They will train your mind, align your voice, and ground your energy in the daily practice of manifestation because power without direction is scattered. But power with intention? **That is where miracles grow**.

1. **What is you intention**?
   Think before you speak. Before you start planting, decide your intention while planting the seeds of your tongue.

2. **Identify what you are planting**.
   Ask yourself daily: What thoughts am I sowing? What energy am I watering? What harvest am I calling in?

3. **Chose your soil wisely**.
   Surround yourself with environments and voices that nourish your growth.

4. **Speak the harvest, not the fear**.
   Speak from the future you're growing into. "I am becoming." "I am aligned." "My harvest is on the way."

5. **Nurture daily**.
   Don't wait for motivation. Show up like a farmer—consistent, committed, faithful.

6. **Honor divine timing**.
   Seeds take time. Just because you don't see growth yet, this does not mean it is not happening. Trust the unseen.

The act of creation is not reserved just for mystics or masters—it is your daily birthright. Each intention you set, each word you speak, each thought you nurture is a sacred gesture of divine authorship.

These practices are not small. They are how you rewire your reality from the inside out. By tending to your inner garden with consistency, clarity, and care, you begin to live not as a passive observer of life, but as its deliberate co-creator.

Remember: the seeds you plant today are already listening. Water them with faith. Align your voice with your vision. And trust that what you're building in the unseen will bloom in perfect, divine time.

Affirmation

"I am a living seed of divine potential. I plant my words and thoughts with intention, water them with faith, and trust waits in expectation: the harvest is already on the way."

Guided Meditation
—Awakening the Garden

Place your attention at the center of your chest. Breathe in through your nose slowly and exhale slowly.

Now, imagine a small seed resting in the soil of your heart. It holds everything—your dreams, gifts, and purpose. With each breath, light shines down, warming the soil. The seed gently cracks—not in pain but in possibility. Roots stretch downward. A sprout rises upward.

You are the seed. You are the soil. You are the light that allows it to grow. To visualize is to remember the truth of your being: that the Divine lives within you, and through your thoughts, devotion, and aligned action, you shape the life you are here to live.

Open your mind and breathe in your potential and exhale the bounty of your intention.

Conclusion

Creation begins with recognition.

You're not a passive participant in this life—you're a co-creator. The moment you awaken to the power within you, the entire story begins to shift. You stop waiting for permission and start walking with purpose.
But this chapter has not only been about words—it has been about *remembrance*. A sacred remembrance of who you truly are and what has always lived within you.

You were made in the image of the Creator. That means the same power that once hovered over the waters and that spoke galaxies into motion, now hums beneath your breath. *It moves through your thoughts, your voice, and your vibration—and it responds.*

You are not separate from creation. You are part of the creative force itself.

The ancients knew this, the mystics taught it, and now it is returning to your awareness.

When you speak, you plant. **When you believe, you water**. **When you act in alignment, you harvest**.

The seed does not demand proof or beg to grow but simply trusts the mystery. It leans into the unseen and surrenders to the sacred rhythm of light, soil, and divine timing.

It does not strive—it knows. And so must you.

You were never meant to live life on mute, you were born to echo the divine frequency of creation. To speak the unspoken, to declare light in the midst of darkness, to shake the silence with sacred sound, and to co-author miracles with the Source of all that is.

There is a sound waiting to rise through you. There is a future waiting to unfold through your voice. There is a divine frequency calling you home to your power.

This is the call to create. And it begins now—with your next thought, your next word, your next breath.

Chapter 2: The Law of Belief
—According to Your Faith

Opening Reflection

"Whether you think you can, or whether you think you can't—you're right."
—Henry Ford (Paraphrased)

Introduction

Across every ancient tradition—from desert prophets to Himalayan sages—there has always been one unshakable truth: **what you believe is what you will achieve**.

Belief was *never* treated as wishful thinking. It was law. A spiritual force. A sacred technology that shaped reality long before science dared to measure it.

The mystics knew it, the healers lived by it, and the scriptures whispered it in every language under heaven: *"According to your faith... it shall be done unto you."*

And this truth has not faded. It still echoes in our time. Even Henry Ford, a man not known for mysticism, said plainly: *"Whether you think you can, or whether you think you can't—you're right."*

Belief is not passive. It's generative. It's the hidden code behind every breakthrough and every breakdown. What you accept as truth—especially about yourself—becomes the lens through which your entire life takes shape.

This chapter invites you to uncover what has been running beneath the surface: your inner belief system, quiet convictions, inherited scripts, and subtle agreements you have made with fear or faith.

Because here is the truth the ancients understood—and that modern seekers are just beginning to reclaim.

You do not get what you want. You get what you believe.
And the voice you believe the most—especially your own—is the one that sets the frequency of your future.

Hidden Teachings from Ancient Traditions
—Belief as the Engine of Manifestation Across the Sacred Texts

The Law of Belief is not a modern discovery—it is a timeless spiritual law, whispered through the sacred writings of prophets, mystics, sages, and seers. Long before neuroscience measured thought patterns or psychology studied the subconscious, the ancients already understood that *belief shapes reality*. What you carry in the heart, you project into the world.

What you believe about life, God, and yourself becomes the energetic blueprint for everything that follows.

These five traditions carry this truth in distinct but harmonizing tones, each revealing that belief is not just a thought—it's power in motion.

✧Christian Faith

In the teachings of Jesus, belief is not an accessory to faith—it is its foundation. When two blind men came seeking healing, Jesus asked if they believed He could do it. And then He said, "**According to your faith let it be done to you**." (Matthew 9:29, NIV) He didn't measure effort, status, or merit—only belief.

Time and again, Jesus made this principle clear: "**Everything is possible for one who believes**." (Mark 9:23, NIV) Belief was the spiritual currency that unlocked the miraculous.

Even Peter, when walking on water, began to sink only when his belief wavered. It wasn't the storm that overwhelmed him—it was his inner doubt.

The message is unmistakable: belief either opens the door to the miraculous or shuts it.

In the Christian tradition, to believe is to give divine permission for the impossible to become possible.

✧Jewish Wisdom

In Jewish thought, belief resides not just in the intellect but in the heart—the deepest seat of identity and intention. "**As a man thinketh in his heart, so is he.**" (Proverbs 23:7, KJV) This verse from the Hebrew Bible reflects a mystical truth: your internal beliefs shape your lived experience.

The Hebrew word lev (heart) represents the core of one's being, not just emotion, but will, thought, and essence. In this tradition, belief isn't an abstract idea but a generative force.

Kabbalistic wisdom teaches that thought is the first stage of creation. Before action, before form—there is intention. And intention, when sustained with belief, shapes the energetic pathways of life.

To believe is to create—first in spirit, then in substance. Jewish teachings remind us that the world responds not to who we appear to be, but to who we truly believe we are.

✧Islamic Teaching

In Islam, belief—iman—is a living force. It's not static dogma, but a dynamic alignment of the heart, mind, and actions with the will of Allah. The Qur'an teaches, "**Indeed, those who believe and do righteous deeds—the Most Merciful will appoint for them affection.**" (Surah Maryam 19:96, Sahih International)

Here, belief draws divine response. It magnetizes favor, connection, and unfolding peace. It's both an internal conviction and a vibrational prayer. Another verse affirms, "**Whoever believes in Allah—He will guide his heart.**" (Surah At-Taghabun 64:11) In other words, belief becomes the compass of the soul. It doesn't simply hope for guidance—it receives it.

The Prophet Muhammad (peace be upon him) said, "**Verily, Allah does not look at your appearance or wealth, but rather He looks at your hearts and deeds**." (Sahih Muslim 2564) Belief, then, becomes the inward mirror that determines divine response.

In Islam, belief isn't just trust in God—it's surrender to a divine unfolding that meets you at the level of your faith.

❖**Buddhist Practices**

Buddhism teaches that the mind is the maker of reality. Thought is not neutral—it's formative. The Dhammapada 2 says, "**Mind precedes all mental states. Mind is their chief; they are all mind-wrought. If with an impure mind a person speaks or acts, suffering follows him like the wheel that follows the foot of the ox. If with a pure mind a person speaks or acts, happiness follows him like his never-departing shadow**." (The Dhammapada verse 2) This is not metaphor—it's metaphysics. Belief isn't just an idea floating in the mind; it's the architect of perception, the shaper of karma, the seed of samsara or liberation.

In Buddhist practice, this is embodied in mindfulness—the moment-to-moment awareness of one's thoughts, beliefs, and assumptions. What you hold onto becomes your lens. What you repeatedly believe becomes your experience.

Chanting, meditation, and mental discipline are not rituals of control but pathways to clarity. They help you become aware of your beliefs—and through that awareness, you gain the power to choose differently.

To believe in Buddhism is to recognize that every thought emits a frequency—and that frequency echoes back as your life.

❖**Hindu Traditions**

In Hinduism, belief isn't merely mental—it is vibrational. The Bhagavad Gita declares, **"Man is made by his belief. As he believes, so he is."** (Bhagavad Gita 17:3) This is not poetic—it's instructional. Belief, in the Vedic worldview, is creative energy in motion.

The Sanskrit term shraddha means faith or belief, but it goes deeper—it implies a heartfelt trust in the unseen, a surrender to the Divine order. What you believe becomes your bhava—your inner state—which shapes your actions, your vibration, and your destiny.

Yogic traditions teach that the subtle body responds to belief the way soil responds to seed. Belief is what activates spiritual energy—kundalini, prana, and shakti. It determines what will rise and what will remain dormant.

In Hindu cosmology, the self (atman) is already divine. But until you believe that truth, you live as if you are separate from it. To believe is to remember. And in remembering, you rise.

The ancients did not need brain scans to prove what they already knew: belief is reality in seed form. Whether it is whispered in Sanskrit, chanted in Pali, spoken in Hebrew, Arabic, or Aramaic—the sacred truth is the same. You are not shaped by what you wish for. You are shaped by what you believe.

And the moment your belief aligns with truth, your entire frequency begins to rise—calling your reality to meet it.

Wisdom from Contemporary Spiritual Leaders

When ancient truths echo in modern voices, something powerful happens —we remember. We remember that belief is not outdated or abstract. It's alive. It's the pulse of prophets and poets, mystics, and motivators.

Today's spiritual leaders may use different language, but the message is the same: belief shapes reality. It forms the inner frequency that determines what you allow, what you expect, and what you create. Here are voices who have lived that truth.

—Maya Angelou once said, "**I believed that I was born to do something. That belief has made all the difference.**" To her, belief was not passive—it was power. It was the fire that burned through injustice, fear, and limitation. Maya didn't just teach us to hope. She showed us how to stand tall in the knowing that our existence matters, that our presence has purpose, and that belief is the bridge between pain and transformation.

—Iyanla Vanzant "**You cannot expect to live a positive life with a negative mind.**" She teaches that belief systems are more than thoughts. They are blueprints. Either they trap us in a cycle of limitation, or they crack open the walls that hold our greatness hostage. Belief is a decision that becomes a pattern, and patterns become destiny.

—Rhonda Byrne, author of The Secret, writes: "**When you truly believe that you are worthy of receiving, and feel it as your truth, you become magnetic to the manifestation.**" This isn't metaphor—it's mechanics. The universe responds not just to want, but to belief, not just to prayer, but to alignment. When belief and desire vibrate in harmony, manifestation isn't luck. It is law.

—Roy Waugh, "**Belief isn't just a mindset—it's the spiritual DNA of everything you're manifesting.**" I've learned that belief doesn't wait for evidence—it creates it. Every time you affirm your worth, even when the world is silent, you're rewriting the script. You're tuning your soul to the frequency of the life you are meant to live. You don't need permission. You don't need perfection. You need one thing: a belief bold enough to speak before the blessing arrives. Because the world does not bend to what you hope for. It bends to what you believe is already yours.

These modern-day spiritual voices aren't separate from the sacred traditions—they are a continuation of them.

The vibration of belief is timeless. And when you choose to believe, even in the absence of proof, you are joining a lineage of light-bearers who understood: faith is the seed. Belief is the soil. And creation begins when both come alive.

Scientific Perspectives on Belief and the Brain
—Rewiring Reality—The Sacred Science of Belief

What you believe does not just shape your mindset—it literally reshapes your brain. Belief isn't some wispy idea floating above your life. It is a neurological structure, a pattern, a frequency—something you carry in your biology. In the world of science, *belief is measurable*. And what science is discovering only echoes what the spirit already knows: *belief has the power to sculpt reality*.

✧Neuroscience of Belief

Every belief you hold is encoded in the brain as a neural network—a physical pattern that gets stronger with repetition. The more you repeat a belief, the more your brain defaults to it as truth.

This means that limiting beliefs, like "I'll never be enough," are not just emotional—they are structural. But here is the miracle: your brain is programmable. It can rewire. You can choose a new belief, repeat it with conviction, and over time, it becomes your new default.

✧Confirmation Bias

Your brain is constantly scanning your environment for evidence to support what you already believe. This is known as confirmation bias. If you believe the world is dangerous, your brain filters reality to highlight threats. If you believe you are worthy of love, your brain helps you notice kindness and connection.

Your belief system does not just interpret the world—it edits it. As the ancient proverb says, **"As a man thinks in his heart, so is he."** (Proverbs 23:7)

✧The Placebo Effect

One of the most powerful scientific validations of belief is the placebo effect. In countless clinical trials, patients who receive a sugar pill—but believe it is medicine—often show real, measurable healing. Their belief triggers the body's own capacity to restore itself. Studies have documented pain relief, improved mood, even tumor regression—not because of the substance, but because of the belief. This isn't trickery. It's biology responding to inner conviction.

✧Belief as Energy

From an energetic perspective, belief isn't just a mental stance—it's a vibration. When you believe deeply in something, you emit a frequency that shapes your field. Think of belief like a tuning fork. Whatever frequency you hold, you begin to attract matching experiences. That's not magic. That's resonance. The universe responds not just to your thoughts, but to the energy behind them.

Belief is not a wish. It's a force. It rewires your brain, reorients your focus, alters your body, and shifts your frequency. Whether you believe in lack or in abundance, your mind and energy will shape your world to reflect that conviction. So, choose your beliefs with reverence—because they are not just shaping your future, they are shaping you.

Personal Story
—The Mirror in the Dressing Room

I stood in front of the mirror, fully dressed, fully prepared, and completely undone.

The room was silent, but inside my head, a storm raged. That old voice—the one that had followed me for years—showed up like an uninvited guest. It didn't yell. It whispered.

"Who do you think you are... You do not belong here."

I looked at myself—not just my clothes or my hair, but deeper. And I saw it. The smallness. The self-doubt. The quiet agreement I had made somewhere along the way that I was never enough.

I had the credentials. I had the talent. But in that moment, none of it mattered because belief had the final word. And mine was still catching up.

Then—right in the middle of that internal unraveling—something shifted. Not loud. Not dramatic. Just a still, undeniable presence that rose from within like a flame catching breath.

A new voice spoke. Not from my ego, but from my spirit.
"You're not here by accident. You were sent. You don't just belong here—you were born for this."

And in that moment, I remembered.

I remembered the truth that had always been buried beneath the noise. That belief does not come from the outside. It does not wait for applause. It's forged in silence, in fire, in moments like this.

I took one last look in that mirror and nodded—not to the fear, but to the part of me that had finally stood up and taken its place.

I walked out on stage with a smile on my face, not because the fear was gone, but because something greater had taken its place. Faith. Not the kind that floats in theory—but the kind that anchors you in truth.

The kind that burns through excuses. The kind that changes the atmosphere before you say a word.

That mirror became more than a reflection. It became sort of an altar. A place where I laid down who I thought I was and picked up the frequency of who I was created to be.

Practical Applications
—Strengthening the Power of Belief

Belief is more than a feeling—it is a muscle. And like any muscle, it grows stronger with daily use. These practical applications are not just tips; they are tools to retrain your mind, rewire your language, and realign your actions with the frequency of faith. If belief is the blueprint, then these practices are how you build. They will help you uproot limiting patterns, speak with power, and walk in the direction of what you say you believe. Because belief does not just wait for the miracle—it prepares for it. Daily.

1. **Examine your beliefs.**
   Ask: "What do I really believe about love, abundance, healing, and purpose?" Write it out. You cannot change what you will not confront.

2. **Challenge the lies.**
   When you uncover a limiting belief like, "I'm not good enough," ask: "Whose voice is this? Is it true? Does it serve me?" Then choose to release it.

3. **Speak what you want to believe.**
   Even if it feels unfamiliar, declare it aloud: "I am worthy." "Good things are unfolding for me." "I trust divine timing."

4. **Repetition creates roots.**
   The more you repeat a belief, the more familiar it becomes. Keep choosing it until it becomes your baseline.

5. **Act in alignment.**
   Belief without action is fragile. Move like the door is already open. Act like what you seek is already seeking you.

Belief is not wishful thinking—it is a conscious construction, built word by word, action by action, day by day. These practices are the scaffolding of a new reality, one where your faith is not passive but participatory. When you speak differently, you live differently. And when your actions align with your declarations, the universe responds in kind.

So keep showing up. Keep declaring what you choose to believe. Because every time you challenge a lie, plant a new truth, or act from your highest knowing, you are strengthening the frequency that builds worlds. Belief is not just the beginning of the journey. It is the journey.

Affirmation

"I believe in what I cannot yet see. My faith is the magnet that draws divine goodness into my life."

Guided Meditation
—Anchoring Belief

Breathe deeply.

Imagine yourself standing before a wide-open door. Beyond it lies the life you are calling in—peace, purpose, abundance, love.

Now, take a step forward.

With every breath, repeat silently: "I believe." Feel belief settle into your body—your chest, your core, your heart.

The door does not open because you force it. It opens because you know you belong on the other side.

Conclusion

Belief is not just a mindset. It's a frequency.

It sends a signal to the universe, to God, to your own soul: This is who I am. This is what I expect. This is what I accept.

And what you believe—deeply, silently, even unconsciously—becomes the blueprint your life starts building upon. Not because you are being rewarded or punished, but because your belief is the blueprint from which your reality reads. It sets the tone, the vibration, and the invitation for what comes next.

The ancients understood this long before we had language for it. They did not wait to believe after things got better—they believed so that things could change. They aligned their hearts with truth, their speech with power, and their lives with a faith that refused to settle.

You can do the same.

Belief isn't only for the spiritually elite, and it's not something you earn—it's something you reclaim. It's already alive in you. It's what kept you going. It's what brought you here. And now it's what is calling you to rise.

The real question is: **What are you believing right now—about yourself, your future, your worth**?

Because sometimes, the beliefs that limit us do not sound like fear; they sound like reason, like protection, or like "just being realistic."

But buried beneath them is a deeper truth trying to rise—one that says: **You were made for more**.

The Law of Belief isn't waiting to activate—it's already working. The only question is:

Is it working for you or against you?

This chapter was not just about shifting your thoughts. It was about shifting your identity.

It was about waking up to the truth that faith is not soft—it's fire. It burns through excuses, stretches possibility, and calls forth what your eyes cannot yet see.

So, speak to yourself with the authority of someone who knows who they are. Speak to your life as someone who knows the power within them is not small, not silent, and not done yet.

Because your words have weight and your beliefs have frequency.

The moment you decide to believe something new, The Universe starts to rearrange itself to match it.

This is not just theory. It is law.

And anything is possible—if you just believe.

Chapter 3: The Power of Words
—Speaking Life and Shaping Reality

Opening Reflection

"By the word of the Lord the heavens were made, their starry host by the breath of His mouth."
—Psalm 33:6

Introduction

Your words are not empty. They are not background noise. They are not merely descriptions of reality—they are instruments of creation.

From the beginning of time, the spoken word has carried power. Long before psychology studied affirmations or science proved the impact of sound on matter, the ancients understood this simple, sacred truth: *to speak is to shape.*

What you declare becomes the architecture of your experience. What you repeat becomes the rhythm of your reality. The spoken word is not just sound vibrating through the air—it is energy infused with intention. It's a seed. It's an instruction. It's a summons.

This chapter explores the hidden technology of speech—one found in scrolls and chants, scripture, and sound-waves. From ancient texts to modern science, you will uncover why your words do not just reflect what is; they create what will be.

This is more than "positive thinking." This is a call to become intentional with your voice—to speak from alignment, to prophesy your path, and to remember: you are always speaking truth into your life—whether you realize it or not.

Hidden Teachings from Ancient Traditions
—The Creative Power of Speech Across Sacred Paths

The power of the spoken word is not a modern discovery. Long before microphones, affirmations, or sound healing apps, ancient texts whispered a divine law: **words shape worlds**. In nearly every spiritual tradition, speech is treated not as a casual expression, but as a sacred creation. To speak is to align, to activate, to direct. Words carry vibration, and vibration carries form. What follows are five sacred echoes of this truth—carried through the scrolls, sutras, and scriptures of the ages.

✧ Christian Faith

In Christian teaching, words are not just tools for communication—they are vessels of power. Jesus repeatedly used spoken declarations to realign reality. He said to the sea, *"Peace, be still,"* and the storm surrendered. He said, *"Lazarus, come forth,"* and the dead man rose. His words did not describe a situation—they transformed it.

This divine principle is explicitly taught in Mark 11:23: **"Truly I tell you, if anyone says to this mountain, 'Go, throw yourself into the sea,' and does not doubt in their heart but believes that what they say will happen, it will be done for them."** (Mark 11:23, NIV) Here, speech isn't passive—it's a creative act charged with belief and authority.

Paul echoes this same spiritual law when he writes that God **"calls those things which are not as though they were."** (Romans 4:17, KJV)
And Proverbs affirms: **"Death and life are in the power of the tongue, and those who love it will eat its fruits."** (Proverbs 18:21, ESV)

Speech, in the Christian worldview, isn't descriptive—it is directive. When your words are aligned with faith and divine intention, they become a living instrument of manifestation. The tongue, though small, is a mighty force that carries the frequency of creation itself.

✧ Jewish Wisdom

In Jewish tradition, speech is more than communication—it is creation. Psalm 33:6 tells us, **"By the word of the Lord the heavens were made, their starry host by the breath of His mouth**." (Tanakh)

The universe, according to Jewish scripture, was spoken into being. The word davar in Hebrew means both "word" and "thing"—what is spoken becomes real.

The Ten Commandments are not referred to as "commands" in Hebrew, but as Aseret haDibrot— "The Ten Sayings." Creation and law were both delivered through speech, not by decree, but by divine utterance.

Jewish mysticism teaches that each letter of the Hebrew alphabet carries vibrational energy—frequencies that shaped creation itself. And the ethical concept of lashon hara—the "evil tongue"—warns that words can destroy as powerfully as they can create.

To speak in Jewish wisdom is to engage in the act of manifestation. Words are sacred tools, and when used with reverence, they reveal the hidden light behind the seen world.

✧ Islamic Teaching

In Islam, the creative power of speech is embedded in the concept of Kun fa-yakūn—**"Be, and it is**." (Qur'an 36:82, Sahih International) Allah does not build creation with hands—He commands it into being. The very vibration of divine will becomes manifest through spoken intent.

The Qur'an is not merely a book—it is a recitation. Its verses are meant to be heard, felt, and spoken. Words are sound, and sound is sacred.

The Prophet Muhammad (peace be upon him) said, **"Let whoever believes in Allah and the Last Day speak good or remain silent**." (Sahih al-Bukhari and Muslim) In this teaching, speech is not neutral—it is a spiritual act with consequences.

The Islamic practice of dua, or supplication, demonstrates that voicing your prayer is more than asking—it is aligning. To speak your needs before the Divine is to step into the current of divine intention.

Words, in Islam, are bridges between heaven and earth. And when spoken in sincerity, they open unseen doors.

✧ Buddhist Practices

In Buddhism, the voice is a tool of either liberation or bondage. Right Speech is one of the Noble Eightfold Path's essential disciplines—calling for language that is truthful, kind, timely, and purposeful.

Though often silent in nature, Buddhist practice reveres the spoken word.

Chanting sacred phrases like Nam Myoho Renge Kyo or repeating mantras is not ritual for ritual's sake—it is a vibrational act of spiritual alignment.

The Dhammapada opens with the teaching: "**All that we are is the result of what we have thought. It is founded on our thoughts; it is made up of our thoughts**." (The Dhammapada Verse 1) While silence is honored in many Buddhist traditions, when words are used, they are to be sacred, intentional, and kind. Words, when true and loving, have the power to shift consciousness.

Speaking in Buddhism means shaping karma. Speech is not just vibration —it is an energetic imprint. And it leaves ripples in the fabric of your reality.

✧ Hindu Traditions

In Hindu thought, speech is never seen as ordinary. Words are vessels of shakti—divine energy—that ripple outward into both the seen and unseen worlds. To speak is to participate in the very act of creation, for sound is believed to carry the same force that sustains the cosmos. The tongue is thus a sacred instrument, and every utterance carries responsibility.

The Bhagavad Gita affirms this when Lord Krishna teaches: **"Austerity of speech consists in speaking words that are truthful, pleasing, beneficial, and not agitating to others**." (Gita 17:15)

Mantras, spoken with devotion, are understood as vibrational codes that unlock higher states of consciousness and alignment with the divine. Each syllable resonates as a thread in the great fabric of existence, weaving harmony between self and source.

In the Hindu worldview, speech is not symbolic—it is reality-shaping. Words direct energy, call forth transformation, and embody the power of intention. The ancients did not speak casually; they invoked, they declared, they aligned.

Across these five sacred paths, one truth is echoed again and again: words are not empty. They are energy, intention, and frequency. They do not simply describe reality—they direct it.

The ancients did not casually speak—they invoked, they declared, they aligned. And now, you are invited to do the same—not just to talk, but to speak as one who remembers:

Your voice carries the same divine spark that once said, "Let there be..."

Wisdom from Contemporary Spiritual Leaders

If words are the seeds, then belief is the water. Every sacred tradition reminds us that the world was spoken into being—not wished, not imagined, but declared. And today, spiritual voices across the globe echo this truth: your voice is not decoration. It is a creative force. When you speak, you do not just express—you activate.

What follows are insights from leaders who have harnessed the sacred vibration of language and understand that speech is not random—it is revelation.

—Maya Angelou: "**Words are things, I'm convinced...Someday we'll be able to measure the power of words. I think they are things. They get on the walls. They get in your wallpaper. They get in your rugs, in your upholstery, and your clothes, and finally into you**." Maya Angelou's words are a sacred reminder that language is not neutral—it leaves residue. Every word we speak carries energetic weight, embedding itself into our environment, our relationships, and eventually, our identity. This is why conscious speech is not just a spiritual practice—it's a creative force. When we speak with intention, we don't just describe reality—we shape it.

—Iyanla Vanzant teaches, "**Your words create your world**." She calls us to speak what calls us higher—to declare the direction we want to grow, not the fear we are trying to escape. Your words are not for describing your life. They are for designing it.

—Oprah Winfrey once said, "**You become what you believe, not what you want**." Desire without declaration is dormant. Oprah reminds us that when you speak with conviction—not from desperation but from alignment—you pull the future toward you. Your words begin to gather matter around your mission. They are not just communication. They are creation.

—Denise Woods, one of the most respected voice coaches in the world, teaches that "**Your voice carries more than words—it carries your energy**." Your breath, your tone, your intention—they speak even when your lips do not. Denise reminds us that your voice is not just a sound. It is a signature. It reveals how deeply you believe what you say, and how clearly you trust what you carry.

—Abraham Hicks affirms this same truth: "**When you speak your desires aloud with conviction, you align your vibration with the reality you seek.**" Speaking affirmations is not for the universe's benefit —it is for yours. It sharpens your frequency. It calibrates your inner compass. When words and energy match, manifestation is no longer a question of if—it is a matter of when.

—Roy Waugh, "**Your words are like a boomerang. Be careful what you throw out there—it might come back and hit you in the forehead**." Why? Because your words always return. Every declaration carries momentum. Every complaint, prophecy, praise, or curse is a seed launched into the soil of your life. And that soil is always listening.

So, if you want joy, speak joy. If you long for peace, send out peace. If you are praying for abundance—speak abundance aloud, not as a wish, but as a truth in motion. Because you cannot speak bitterness and expect sweetness, you cannot curse your path and expect it to bloom. And you cannot plant a tomato seed and expect a watermelon to grow.

Speak like the universe is echoing back your exact words—because it is. And when your voice aligns with your belief, you will not just change your world, you will create it.

Scientific Perspectives on Speech and Vibration
—The Energetics and Neuroscience of Spoken Words

The words we speak are not just sounds—they are vibrational codes, energetic pulses, and biological activators. Science confirms what scripture and ancient wisdom have always whispered: your voice holds creative power. In this section, we explore how speech shapes your brain, your biology, your energy, and even the world around you.

✧ Cymatics and Sound Vibration

Cymatics is the study of visible sound vibrations. When sound frequencies are played through a metal plate covered with sand or water, intricate geometric patterns emerge—each tone creating a distinct shape. This isn't metaphor—it's physics.

Just as sound shapes matter on a plate, your spoken words shape the atmosphere of your life. You are constantly imprinting reality with your frequency. As Psalm 33:6 declares, "By the word of the Lord the heavens were made, their starry host by the breath of his mouth."

✧ Neuroscience and Self-Talk

In psychology and neuroscience, self-talk is more than a habit—it is a feedback loop that reprograms the brain. When you consistently speak affirming truths, you activate neuroplasticity: the brain's ability to rewire itself.

This is not just theory—it is transformation. Repeated affirmations, whether aloud or internally, strengthen neural pathways that support confidence, joy, and forward motion. As Dr. Joe Dispenza notes, "**Nerve cells that fire together, wire together.**" Speak life, and your brain begins to believe it.

✧ Quantum Physics and the Observer Effect

Quantum science tells us that the observer affects the observed. But the language you use while observing also matters. Words frame perception, and perception channels energy. When you describe your life with language of possibility, peace, or abundance, you tune your frequency to match.

In the quantum field, energy responds to alignment—and alignment begins with intention. Speech becomes the conductor of your focus, and focus is the gateway of manifestation.

✧ The Biological Impact of Spoken Intention

Scientific studies in psycholinguistics show that vocalized intention impacts heart rate, cortisol levels, and immune response.

Kind words lower stress.

Loving affirmations elevate emotional resilience. Speaking with purpose is not just spiritual—it is somatic. Your body listens. Every word you speak sends instructions—not only into the universe, but directly into your nervous system. Proverbs 18:21 affirms this with simplicity and weight: **"Death and life are in the power of the tongue."**

When you understand that your words are not empty—they are energetic, electrical, and embodied—you begin to speak with reverence.

When you stop filling the air with fear or doubt and start declaring truth with intention, your voice becomes a vessel for transformation. Because you are not just describing your life—you are designing it, frequency by frequency.

Personal Story
—When I Changed What I Said, Everything Changed

I did not realize how destructive my words had become—not toward others, but toward myself. They were not loud. They were not dramatic. They were quiet, familiar, and constant.

It was so constant; in fact, I did not even notice them. I thought I was just being realistic, saying things like; "I'm always a day late and a dollar short.", "Things never work out for me.", "I could never afford that."

I said things like that without a second thought—half-laughing, half-serious—but over time, they became my inner soundtrack. A low, steady hum of self-imposed limitation. And the more I said them, the more they echoed. The more they echoed, the more my world seemed to prove them true.

Then one day, I casually said, "Well, I guess I'll always be the one who gets the short end of the stick." And a friend—gentle but bold—looked me in the eye and said: **"Do you hear what you are declaring over your life? That is not just a complaint, that is a prayer, a prophecy."**

It hit me like a bolt of lightning.

I had never thought of my words that way.
A prayer.
A prophecy.
Yikes!

Suddenly, I realized: **I was shaping my life with every sentence I spoke**. The weeds I kept tripping over were growing from seeds I had unknowingly planted with my own voice.

From that moment on, I started paying attention. I swapped "I'm always behind" with "I'm right on time." I changed "Nothing ever works out for me." to "Everything is aligning in divine timing."

I caught myself mid-sentence sometimes and redirected the story.
Was it easy? No. Old patterns do not die quietly. But I kept speaking differently—even when I did not feel it yet. And over time, things began to shift.

My energy shifted, my relationships changed, and suddenly opportunities started showing up. My outer world started reflecting the new language I was living by.

It was like turning a frequency dial—my voice became tuned to a different station, and life began to respond accordingly.

The biggest transformation came in a moment of quiet. I was sitting in meditation, asking God for clarity, when I felt a gentle whisper stir in my spirit: *"Stop asking. Start speaking it as if it is done."*

That was the shift.

Not begging. Not hoping. Not describing what was not working. **But declaring. Naming. Calling it forth. Speaking as a creator—not a victim**.

My grandmother used to say, *"If you don't have anything good to say, don't say anything at all."* I used to think she spoke about being polite.

Now I realize—she was talking about spiritual law.
Because what you speak becomes what you live.

Practical Applications
—Speaking with Creative Intention

It is one thing to understand the power of the spoken word—it is another to use it on purpose. Your voice is not just for commentary; it is for creation. These daily practices will help you become intentional with your speech, retrain your subconscious, and align your words with the life you are manifesting.

You are not just affirming—you are activating. Each time you speak with clarity, faith, and vision, you send energy into the field of possibility.

These are not just phrases—they are frequencies. Speak them like your future depends on it.

1. **Speak what you want to see.**
   Stop narrating the problem. Start declaring the outcome. Speak peace. Speak healing. Speak provision.

2. **Bless yourself out loud.**
   Every morning, affirm something aloud to yourself. Train your nervous system to respond to your voice.

3. **Replace negative self-talk.**
   Swap "I'm always broke" with "I'm learning abundance. "Swap, "I'll never be that lucky," with "Things are working out perfectly for me."

4. **Use "I Am" with intention.**
   The words you place after "I am" become your identity. Be careful what you attach to it.

5. **Speak into the unseen**.
   Call it before you see it. "Doors are opening." "Help is on the way." "I am rising."

Speak as though it is already happening. Your words are not just reflections of your reality—they are instruments that shape it. When you speak with intention, you are not begging the universe for change; you are declaring alignment with what already exists in the unseen.

This is not performance—it is participation in creation.

Every time you choose empowering language, you are rewriting your internal programming and tuning your energy to the life you desire. Speak with faith. Speak with purpose. Because the moment your voice matches your vision, the manifestation begins.

Affirmation

"My words are sacred. I speak with power, alignment, and love. What I declare, I create."

Guided Meditation
—The Creative Voice

Sit quietly and bring your awareness to your breath.

Now, imagine your words as golden threads, weaving the fabric of your future. Each phrase is a stitch. Each sentence is a song.

Say quietly to yourself: "I speak life. I speak peace. I speak purpose."

Feel the vibration of those words moving through your chest, your throat, your entire being.

Do you feel that?

You are aligning. You are creating. You are calling it forth.

Conclusion

Your words matter.

They are not just reactions to life—they are instructions to life. They do not simply describe what is—they begin to declare what will be.
Every sentence is a seed. Every phrase has a frequency, and every declaration, a doorway.

You may think you are just venting, joking, or "telling it like it is"—but in the unseen realm, your voice is planting something. And everything you plant will grow. Because your words are not just sound—**they are a creative force.**

Scripture did not say the universe was built with bricks. It says, "By the word of the Lord the heavens were made, their starry host by the breath of His mouth." (Psalms 33:6 NIV) The same breath that spoke stars into existence lives in you. And your words are never empty—they are either building or breaking, blessing, or blocking.

So, speak carefully. Speak consciously. Speak boldly. Whether about your body or your future, your relationships, or your dreams—**only speak what you are ready to harvest**.

Because you cannot plant bitterness and expect joy, you cannot curse yourself and expect peace. And like I always say; **You cannot plant a tomato seed and expect a watermelon to grow**.

I think of it like this: your voice is the remote control of your reality. It changes the channel. It changes the atmosphere. It changes you.

So, if you want peace, speak peace. If you want clarity, speak light. If you want favor, speak gratitude, alignment, and divine timing.

Your words do not just echo; they create, they calibrate, and they call things into being.
And if you just believe,

Your voice will build the life you were born to live.

4: Vibration and Energy
—The Frequency of Faith

Opening Reflection

"Everything in life is vibration."
—Albert Einstein

Introduction

Everything is energy.

This is not just a spiritual metaphor—it is a scientific reality, echoed in ancient wisdom and now confirmed by quantum physics.

You are not merely a body moving through time—you are a living frequency. A walking field of vibration. A dynamic current of thought, feeling, and intention. And the quality of that energy—the tone of your inner frequency—determines what flows into your life.

You do not attract what you say you want. You attract what your energy is calibrated to receive.

Long before modern science discovered this truth, it was hidden in sacred teachings and secret scrolls. Woven through scripture, prayer, and ritual, ancient traditions understood that vibration is creation. The tone of your being either aligns you with the divine or sends static into your future.

This chapter reveals how manifestation is not powered by words alone—but by vibration. The energy behind the words. The emotion beneath the thought. The silent frequency that precedes the natural world.
We will explore how to shift your energetic posture and become a vibrational match for what you are truly ready to receive—not just in theory, but in practice.

Because faith is more than belief—it is a frequency.

Hidden Teachings from Ancient Traditions
—Vibration as Divine Alignment Across Sacred Paths

Long before "vibration" was explored in science or echoed in self-help circles, ancient traditions were already attuned to it—sometimes literally. Through sacred chants, breathwork, mantra, ritual, and emotion, spiritual elders across the world recognized that energy is everything. This was not a metaphor. It was mystical technology.

From scriptures to scrolls, sutras to songs, they taught that the essence of creation is frequency—that what you carry in your spirit shapes what you attract. These were not just poetic insights.

They were energetic blueprints.

Let us revisit their truths.

✧ Christian Faith

In the Gospel of John, it is written: **"In the beginning was the Word, and the Word was with God, and the Word was God... Through Him all things were made."** (John 1:1–3, NIV) Speech and spirit, vibration and substance—were one.

Jesus did not only heal through touch—He healed through tone. **"Your faith has made you whole,"** He said, not simply referring to belief, but to the energetic alignment between faith and divine flow.

In Galatians 5, Paul describes the *"fruit of the Spirit"*—love, joy, peace, patience, kindness—not as fleeting moods, but as sustained frequencies of a Spirit-aligned life. To live in these states is to vibrate with the Spirit of God. It is to become a resonance point for miracles.

✧ Jewish Wisdom

In Jewish mysticism, existence itself is understood as the flow of divine energy. The Kabbalistic sefirot are ten emanations through which God interacts with the world—Chesed (lovingkindness), Gevurah (strength), Tiferet (beauty)—each one a vibrational expression of the Divine.

The Hebrew word nefesh, meaning "*soul*," is intimately linked to breath. **"Then the Lord God formed man from the dust of the earth. He blew into his nostrils the breath of life, and man became a living being.**" (Genesis 2:7, Tanakh) Breath is not symbolic—it is vibration. To breathe is to harmonize with the Creator's rhythm.

Prayer (tefillah) is not mere recitation—it is sacred tuning. When prayer is offered with sincerity, it becomes a frequency of spiritual elevation. Even time, in Jewish tradition, is energetic. The Sabbath is more than rest—it is a portal. When observed with reverence, it invites the soul into a higher state of wholeness—shalom—the completeness of divine vibration.

✧ Islamic Teaching

In Islam, rhythm and vibration are woven into the cadence of daily devotion. The five daily prayers (salat) are not rituals of repetition—they are intentional resets, anchoring the soul in divine frequency.

The Qur'an reveals: **"Verily, in the remembrance of Allah do hearts find rest.**" (Qur'an 13:28, Sahih International) This remembrance—zikr—is not intellectual. It is vibrational. The repeated utterance of the names of God—Ar-Rahman (The Merciful), As-Salam (The Source of Peace), Al-Haqq (The Truth)—resonates with the soul and recalibrates the heart.

Even acts like fasting during Ramadan, giving zakat (charity), or practicing sabr (patience) are not merely moral—they are energetic. Each one clears interference and elevates the soul's frequency toward divine harmony.

To remember God in Islam is not only to think of Him—it is to vibrate in rhythm with His names.

✧ Buddhist Practices

In Buddhism, vibration is not metaphor—it is the fabric of reality. Meditation is not an escape—it is frequency awareness. A chaotic mind emits one energy. A still mind another.

Practices like loving-kindness meditation (metta bhavana) are used to generate compassionate energy, which radiates outward like ripples. Mantras such as Om Mani Padme Hum are not symbolic—they are sacred tones. Each syllable is said to dissolve lower vibrations and awaken higher states of awareness.

Karma itself is vibrational: every thought, every word, every action carries energy, and that energy returns. The Dhammapada teaches: **"What we are today comes from our thoughts of yesterday, and our present thoughts build our life of tomorrow."** (Dhammapada, Verse 1)

In this view, your mind is a transmitter. Your thoughts are your tuning fork. And your life is the echo.

✧ Hindu Traditions

In Hinduism, the universe is not only created through sound—it is sound. Nāda Brahma means *"Sound is God."* The sacred syllable Om is understood to be the primal vibration from which all of time, space, and consciousness arise.

When chanted with awareness, Om is more than a sound—it is a recalibration of the soul to its source. It aligns the practitioner with the heart of creation.

The Bhagavad Gita reveals: **"Those who are free from anger and all material desires... who are self-disciplined and constantly**

striving for perfection... are assured of liberation." (Bhagavad Gita 5:26, ESV) Liberation, in this context, is not a destination. It is vibrational alignment with the true Self.

Practices like mantra, mudra, pranayama (breath control), and dhyana (meditation) are not just spiritual exercises—they are tools for energetic refinement. They help the practitioner match the frequency of divine consciousness.

To raise your vibration is to remember your divinity. Every sacred path— from Torah to Qur'an, from Dhammapada to Vedas—teaches the same hidden truth: You are energy, and you are frequency. The power to manifest does not begin with effort. It begins with alignment.

These ancient teachings do not contradict modern science—they anticipated it. Where science measures, the mystics already knew:
Your vibration is your signature. And when that signature resonates with divine truth, you do not just experience life.

You become a living frequency of the Divine.

Wisdom from Contemporary Spiritual Leaders

Long before we had the language of vibration and frequency, many spiritual teachers were already living it. They may have used different words—energy, presence, spirit, intention—but the essence was always the same: what you put out is what comes back.

Today, these voices help bridge ancient knowing with modern understanding. They remind us that you do not attract what you want. You attract what you are.

— Esther Hicks says, "**You are a vibrational being in a vibrational universe**." Her message is simple but profound: Creation does not begin with hustle—it begins with harmony. When your thoughts are tuned to lack, you attract more lack. But when you live in gratitude, generosity, and joy, you magnetize abundance, not by force, but by frequency.

—Dr. Joe Dispenza teaches, **"The moment you feel abundant and worthy, you are generating wealth. The moment you feel empowered, you are stepping into your destiny."** To him, elevated emotions are not just pleasant states—they are energy signals. Joy, love, inspiration—these are frequencies that begin to shape reality in real time. Manifestation happens not when you chase your future, but when you begin to feel it now.

—Louise Hay reminded us, **"What I give out comes back to me."** She was not warning us—she was handing us the formula. Every thought, every affirmation, every feeling you carry is a seed of energy. Louise taught that the energy behind your words is the force behind your life. Speak healing, and healing begins. Speak love, and love expands.

—Albert Einstein, though a scientist and not a spiritual teacher, delivered one of the most quoted truths in manifestation: **"Everything is energy, and that is all there is to it. Match the frequency of the reality you want, and you cannot help but get that reality."** He was not speaking metaphorically. He was speaking scientifically. Your vibration is not poetry—it's physics. Every desire has a frequency. Every person, a signal. When you become the match, manifestation becomes inevitable.

—Roy Waugh I tell people all the time: **"If your energy is off, it doesn't matter how gorgeous your vision board looks—you're just sending glittery desperation into the universe."** It is not enough to say the right words if your soul is saying something else. The universe is not picking up what is on your lips. It is tuning in to what's underneath them.

You cannot chant your way into abundance if your core frequency is still laced with fear. You cannot pretend joy into being if your emotional undercurrent is resentment or scarcity. Manifestation begins with a calibration—not of your vision board—but of your vibration.

When your energy aligns with your essence, your words become power, and your life begins to resonate with what you were always meant to become.

Scientific Perspectives on Energy and Frequency
—The Physics of Faith—How Energy Aligns with Intention

You are energy. Every thought you think, every emotion you feel, every word you speak carries a measurable frequency. Science is now affirming what mystics have known for centuries: your vibration shapes your experience. Understanding the energetic nature of your being is not just enlightening—it is empowering. If everything is frequency, then faith, intention, and alignment are not just spiritual—they are scientific.

✦ Quantum Physics and the Frequency Field

Quantum mechanics tells us that all matter is energy vibrating at specific frequencies. Your body, your voice, your thoughts—they are not solid objects but vibrating waves.

The quantum field responds to coherence: when your intention, emotion, and belief are in sync, your vibration becomes a magnet. As Albert Einstein famously said, "Everything is energy, and that is all there is to it. Match the frequency of the reality you want, and you cannot help but get that reality."

✦ The Heart's Electromagnetic Power

The HeartMath Institute has found that the human heart produces an electromagnetic field up to 60 times greater than the brain's. This field is not just passive—it changes based on your emotional state. Emotions like gratitude, compassion, and joy create smooth, coherent wave patterns that improve cognitive function and well-being.

In contrast, fear and stress produce erratic, disharmonious signals that disrupt internal systems. Your emotional frequency is not just felt—it is broadcast.

✧ Neuroscience and Emotional Conditioning

Your brain is constantly mapping your internal and external environment. When you dwell in states of fear, stress, or worry, those emotional patterns become hardwired. Your nervous system adapts to expect danger, and your body prepares for it—even when it is not there. But neuroplasticity means that with intention, you can rewire those patterns.

Practicing elevated emotions like joy or love begins to reset your baseline vibration and literally shifts your biology. As Dr. Bruce Lipton teaches, *"The moment you change your perception is the moment you rewrite the chemistry of your body."*

✧ Energy Psychology and Embodied Resonance

Fields like energy psychology and somatic therapy confirm that your vibration affects both internal regulation and external outcomes. Muscle tension, hormonal output, and immune response all shift based on an energetic state. Even simple practices like breathwork or spoken affirmations can raise your frequency and affect your physical health. Alignment radiates. Coherence heals.

When you realize that frequency is not just a concept—it is your current—everything changes. You are not stuck with the energy you have been given. You can shift it. Attune it. Elevate it. The same way you tune an instrument, you can tune your life. And when your frequency matches faith, love, and purpose, you become a beacon for the very reality you were born to manifest.

Personal Story
—The Day I Became the Frequency

I used to believe that hard work was everything. That if I just pushed harder, success would come. But no matter how much I did, I kept hitting invisible walls. My effort was high—but my energy was off.

One afternoon, while preparing for an important performance, I felt that wall again. I had rehearsed the song endlessly. Every note was in place. But the joy was gone. My spirit felt tight. I couldn't explain it, but something was off.

So, I paused. I sat in silence and asked God—Source, Spirit—for clarity. What I sensed was clear and gentle: "It's not the song. It's your frequency. And your frequency is being shaped by your intention. What is your intention in singing this song?"

In that moment, it all made sense.

My intention, though subtle, was rooted in fear—fear of failure, fear of how I would be perceived. And that energy was affecting everything.

Intention always gives birth to energy.

If your intention is rooted in love, your energy is magnetic. If it's rooted in fear, your energy sends out static. I had been doing the right thing—but from the wrong frequency.

So, I changed it. I turned on music that lifted me. I breathed. I whispered affirmations like prayers: "I am at peace. I am full of joy. I am already enough."

When I walked on that stage later, I did not perform because of pressure; I expressed myself from alignment.

After the show, a woman came up and said, "Wow, you didn't just sing; you were radiating something. I could feel it before you even opened your mouth."

That moment changed me forever.

You do not manifest what you want.
You manifest what you are a vibrational match for.
And intention sets the tone.

Practical Applications
—Raising Your Frequency

Understanding vibration is powerful—but living in alignment with it is where transformation happens. The following practices are designed to help you raise your frequency from the inside out. These are not just habits; they are energetic rituals.

Each one is a choice to step out of survival mode and into spiritual alignment. You will learn how to tune your emotional state, elevate your environment, and consciously shift the energy you bring into every room, relationship, and request.

Because your vibration is not fixed—it is formed, moment by moment, by how you think, feel, speak, and move. And when you begin to live as energy in motion, the universe moves with you.

1. **Emotional Awareness**.
    Check in throughout the day. What are you feeling? What frequency are you radiating?

2. **Use music and movement**.
    Dance, walk in nature, and play music that lifts your spirit. When your body moves, your vibration rises.

3. **Surround yourself with good vibes**.
    Energy is contagious. Be intentional with your people, places, and content.

4. **Meditate into alignment**.
    Just five minutes of breathwork or visualization can recalibrate your field.

5. **Speak what you want to radiate**.
    Declare aloud: "I am aligned." "I am magnetic." "I am love." "I am at peace." Let your words match your vibration.

6. **Do not plant what you do not want to grow**.
Be mindful of your conversations. Words carry energy. An apple seed will never grow an orange tree. Speak what aligns with the harvest you desire.

Raising your frequency is not a one-time event—it is a daily devotion to your highest self. With each conscious breath, each intentional word, each shift in your environment or emotion, you are choosing alignment over autopilot.

These practices are more than routines—they are energetic recalibrations that call your power back into the present moment. As you embody higher states of love, clarity, peace, and joy, you don't just change your own life—you begin to elevate the field around you. Because when you move in frequency, the universe can't help but move in harmony.

Affirmation

"I am energy in motion. I align with the frequency of love, abundance, peace, and purpose. I attract what I am ready to receive."

Guided Meditation
—Vibrational Alignment

Bring attention to your breath.

With each inhale, feel light entering your body—cleansing, calming, realigning. With each exhale, release resistance.

Now, imagine your body as a tuning fork. Begin to hum inwardly the energy of peace. Let it grow. Let it vibrate through your chest, your throat, your being.

Say inwardly: "I am aligned. I am magnetic. I am ready." Stay here a while —radiating, receiving, remembering who you are.

Conclusion

You are not just matter—you are movement. Not just a body—you are breath, rhythm, and radiant frequency. You are a living field of energy, and everything around you is listening.

Your life is not happening to you. It is responding to you. Not to your words alone. Not even to your thoughts alone. But to your **vibration**— your inner resonance, your emotional signature, your unseen posture of spirit.

Manifestation does not occur because you tried harder or wished louder. It occurs because you aligned more clearly. It happens when your internal world vibrates in harmony with the life you are ready to receive.

If you want peace, do not chase it. **Become it**.
If you want abundance, do not strive endlessly; **radiate worthiness**.
If you want love, do not search the earth; **embody it with every breath**.

Your vibration is the invitation. It is the silent song the universe responds to. It does not answer desperation. It answers resonance. And when your energy matches the truth of what is meant for you, what is meant for you flows effortlessly.

This is not fantasy. This is divine law. As sure as gravity, frequency shapes your reality.

You were never meant to force life into alignment. You were meant to tune your soul to its divine pitch—and let life rise to meet you.

So, rise, attune, and live like the sacred instrument you were created to be.

And trust this: **When your vibration harmonizes with love, faith, and truth— everything begins to move in time, with you.**

Chapter 5:
Faith; The Substance of Things Hoped For
—Faith as a Manifesting Force

Opening Reflection

"...**Faith is the substance of things hoped for, the evidence of things not seen.**"
—Hebrews 11:1

Introduction

Faith is not wishful thinking. It is not naive optimism. It is not crossing your fingers and hoping the universe is in a good mood. Faith is substance. It is a force. It is the spiritual blueprint of what has not yet come into form. It is evidence of what the eyes cannot see—but what the soul already knows is real.

It is the root of manifestation. Not because it guarantees immediate results, but because it keeps you aligned in the waiting, steady in the unseen, and expectant in the unknown.

In this chapter, we explore faith as the invisible infrastructure of creation. We will look at what faith really is—not a religious cliché, but a manifesting energy that calls things into being. You do not have to know how. You just have to hold what you believe with deep enough clarity that heaven begins to move in your direction.

You will learn that faith is the hand that reaches into the invisible and pulls the vision forward.

Faith is the tuning fork of creation—the frequency that causes unseen things to resonate into form.

Hidden Teachings from Ancient Traditions
—Faith as Sacred Frequency Across Ancient Paths

Faith has never been just an idea—it is a vibration, a frequency of trust that reverberates across every sacred tradition. Long before modern science confirmed the power of belief to influence biology and reality, the sages, prophets, and mystics of the world already knew: faith builds unseen bridges between intention and manifestation.

It is not passive acceptance—it is spiritual momentum. These ancient teachings show that to walk in faith is to align your energy with the Source of all creation.

Let us return to the wisdom they preserved:

✧ Christian Faith

The New Testament defines faith not as a concept, but as substance: **"Now faith is the substance of things hoped for, the evidence of things not seen."** (Hebrews 11:1, KJV) Faith here is not a feeling—it is the invisible architecture of manifestation.

Jesus repeatedly linked healing to belief. **"According to your faith be it unto you,"** He said in Matthew 9:29 (KJV). The miracle did not begin with His hands—but with their alignment.

Paul echoes this principle: **"For we walk by faith, not by sight."** (2 Corinthians 5:7, KJV)

This is not blindness—it is deeper vision. Christian faith teaches that what is believed in spirit becomes visible in time. Faith is the tuning fork that draws heaven into earth.

✧ Jewish Wisdom

In Judaism, emunah—translated as "faith"—goes far beyond belief. It implies unwavering trust, spiritual steadiness, and alignment with divine will. "**Commit your way to the Lord; trust in Him, and He will act**." (Psalm 37:5, Tanakh) This is not superstition—it is sacred cooperation.

In Kabbalah, faith is energetic connectivity. The ten sefirot—divine emanations—Yesod (Foundation) symbolizes the bridge between the unseen and the seen. Faith here is the frequency through which divine intention becomes physical expression.

When the Israelites stood at the edge of the Red Sea, they did not wait for the waters to part—they walked forward. And the sea responded. Faith was the signal that moved the sea.

✧ Islamic Teaching

In Islam, īmān (faith) is one of the five pillars. It includes belief in the unseen (ghayb), trust in divine wisdom, and surrender to sacred timing. "**Indeed, those who have said, 'Our Lord is Allah' and then remained steadfast—the angels will descend upon them...**" (Qur'an 41:30, Sahih International)

Faith is rewarded not always with ease—but with presence.
In Sufism, the mystical path of Islam, faith becomes vibration through dhikr—the remembrance of God's names. Names like Al-Fattāḥ (The Opener), Al-Mujīb (The Responder), and Al-Ḥayy (The Ever-Living) carry frequency. When spoken with reverence, they transform the energetic field.

To have faith in Islam is not to wait passively—it is to become a magnet for divine flow.

Faith is not an idea—it is a spiritual current.

✧ Buddhist Practices

In Buddhism, saddhā (faith) is the first of the Five Spiritual Powers. It is the seed from which all practice blooms. Faith in this tradition is not blind belief—it is trust in the unseen transformation that spiritual discipline awakens.

The Buddha taught that faith sustains you through uncertainty. You sit not because clarity has arrived—but because you trust that it will. **"Just as the great ocean has one taste—the taste of salt—so too, this Dhamma and Discipline has one taste—the taste of liberation."** (Udāna 5.5)

Faith tastes like freedom—even before it arrives.

To meditate is to believe your stillness is working. To practice mindfulness is to affirm that each breath reshapes your reality. Faith is the inner fire that warms the journey.

✧ Hindu Traditions

In Hinduism, śraddhā is sacred faith—not based on proof, but on inner knowing. It is the heart's resonance with divine intelligence, and the soul's trust in cosmic design. **"A man is made by his belief. As he believes, so he is".** (Bhagavad Gita 17:3, ESV) In this verse, belief is not a filter—it is formation. You become what you hold in faith.

Faith energizes bhakti (devotion), empowers karma yoga (action without attachment), and sustains the path of jñāna (wisdom). Whether chanting Om, offering mantras, or entering silent meditation, each act of trust raises the vibrational field.

Liberation (moksha) is not something earned—it is something remembered.

Faith aligns you with who you already are.
Every sacred tradition, each in its own voice, reveals the same truth:

Faith is not weakness—it is the spiritual voltage that powers manifestation. It is the frequency of the unseen. The architecture of the possible. And the pulse of divine reality flowing into form.

Faith does not begin when you see the miracle. It begins when you align with it—before it appears. And when your faith resonates from spirit, not fear, you awaken the ancient technology of becoming.

Let your faith be bold, let it be grounded, and let it be the echo of the Divine moving through you—unseen, but unmistakable.
The future listens not to what you fear, but to what you believe.

Wisdom from Contemporary Spiritual Leaders

The great spiritual voices of our time have echoed the ancient truth that faith is not mere belief—it is creative power. These teachings, across backgrounds and philosophies, remind us that when faith becomes frequency, it shifts not only what we expect—but what becomes possible.

—Joyce Meyer teaches that faith is action before evidence: "**Faith is not believing that God can—it's knowing that He will**." To her, faith is the key that unlocks spiritual authority and supernatural manifestation.

—Rhonda Byrne, author of The Secret, emphasizes that "**Faith is trusting in the unseen and being certain of what you hope for**." She connects faith directly with vibrational alignment—explaining that belief is the signal, and doubt is the static.

—Eckhart Tolle offers this clarity: "**Faith is the substance of surrender**." He speaks of it not as passivity, but as powerful presence— the kind that magnetizes miracles when resistance falls away.

—Iyanla Vanzant reminds us that "**Faith is the light that guides you through the darkness—not away from it, but through it**." Her words reveal faith not as escape, but as sacred endurance that carries the soul through transformation.

—Roy Waugh shares: "**Faith is not crossing your fingers—it is opening your heart to what has not yet arrived. You do not manifest by wishing. You manifest by trusting it is already on the way.**" This message is a call to energetic agreement—to live as though the answer is already unfolding.

These leaders, in their own language and legacy, illuminate the same divine law: *Faith is frequency, and belief is energy; and when you align with trust, the unseen begins to materialize.*

These voices join the ancient ones, pointing us back toward the source— reminding us again that "Anything is possible, if you just believe."

Scientific Perspectives on Faith and Expectation
—The Energetics and Biology of Belief

Faith is more than a feeling—it is a measurable force. In the body, in the brain, and in the field around us, belief creates changes that science continues to observe.

When you hold a strong expectation—especially when it is emotionally charged—it sends signals throughout your nervous system, influences perception, and shapes the outcomes you move toward. In short: what you believe has power, not just in spirit, but in science.

✧ The Placebo Effect: The Body Responds to Belief

The placebo effect remains one of the most documented phenomena in medical literature. Patients who believe they are receiving real treatment —when in fact they are not—often experience real, measurable healing. Heart rate changes. Pain decreases. Symptoms lessen. All because the body responds to the belief that healing is taking place.

This shows us something profound: *your biology listens to your expectations.*

✧ Neuroscience: Predictive Processing and Expectation

The brain is a prediction machine. It does not just interpret reality—it constantly forecasts it. Based on what you believe and expect, your brain prepares your body to respond. This process, known as predictive coding, means that your belief system shapes how you perceive the world, what you notice, and how you react.

Optimism and confidence are not just positive thinking—they are neural signals that create patterns of possibility.

✧ Cognitive Bias and Selective Attention

Belief filters perception. Through a mechanism called confirmation bias, your brain prioritizes information that matches what you already believe. If you expect rejection, your brain will notice signs that support it. If you believe in opportunity, you are more likely to see doors open.

Your expectations create a lens. And through that lens, reality begins to mirror your internal state.

✧ Quantum Observation: Influence Through Attention

In quantum physics, the observer effect demonstrates that the act of observing can influence the outcome of a quantum event. Though still debated in its implications, this principle reveals a connection between consciousness and matter. At the subatomic level, attention appears to affect how particles behave.

This suggests that focused intention may play a more active role in shaping reality than we once believed.

Belief is not just emotional—it's neurological.
Expectation is not just hopeful—it's biological.
And attention is not just passive—it's participatory.

When you align your thoughts and emotions with a consistent expectation, your brain, body, and energy begin to synchronize. That synchronization becomes a signal—clear, measurable, and powerful enough to influence the world around you. Not through magic. But through mechanism.

This is how faith becomes frequency.

Personal Story
—When I Chose to Believe Anyway

I found myself standing in the space between what I believed and what I could prove. It was the kind of season where everything looked still on the outside, but inside, you were carrying a hope so fragile you were almost afraid to say it out loud.

I had a vision—a quiet knowing of something I was meant to do. I could not explain it fully, and there was no physical evidence that it would ever come to pass. But it lived in me like a heartbeat. I would wake up thinking about it. I would fall asleep seeing glimpses of it. Still, every attempt to move toward it seemed to be met with resistance. Closed doors. No answers. Delays that made no sense.

At one point, I nearly gave up. I remember sitting on the edge of my bed one evening, staring at the floor, exhausted by my own hope. I did not want to keep getting excited only to be disappointed. But in that silence, I felt something stir. Not loud. Not dramatic. Just a whisper that said:

"What if you believed anyway?"

That was the moment I realized—faith is not always loud or confident. Sometimes, faith is choosing to hold the vision even when your hands are empty. It is saying yes without seeing the outcome. It is walking toward the thing without knowing the route.

So, I did.

I stopped begging the Universe for proof and started acting like the proof was already unfolding. I showed up differently. I spoke differently. I carried myself as if what I had been believing for was already forming behind the scenes.

And it was.

Bit by bit, signs began to appear. A random connection that turned into a meaningful opportunity. A door that had once been closed quietly swinging open. A moment of divine timing I could not have orchestrated on my own. And eventually, what I had once only seen in my imagination became something I could touch, live, and share.

That experience taught me something I hold close:

Faith is not passive. It is creative.

It builds. It carries. It sends out a signal that heaven responds to. Not because you earned it, but because you aligned with it.

Faith is not the absence of doubt—it is the refusal to let doubt be the loudest voice in the room.

So now, whenever I face something that seems bigger than me, I return to that place—not the fear, but the whisper.

What if you believed anyway?

Practical Applications
—Activating Faith as a Force

Faith is not just a belief you carry—it is a frequency you live from. These practices are designed to help you move from passive hope into active trust. They are not about forcing outcomes, but about aligning your thoughts, actions, and energy with the reality you believe is already forming.

When you speak faith, move with faith, and visualize with faith, you create a current that draws the unseen into the seen. Use these tools to build that current daily—because faith is not waiting for evidence. It is walking like it is already done.

1. **Speak Your Faith**.
   Declare what you believe—not just in quiet hope, but out loud. Say it. Speak it. Anchor it in language.

2. **Act as If.**
   Faith moves. Take steps that reflect trust. Make the call. Write the book. Show up for the vision.

3. **Catch the Doubt Early**.
   Doubt will come. But you do not have to entertain it. When it whispers, ask: "Is this faith, or fear?" Then return to your belief.

4. **Visualize with Certainty**.
   Do not just hope—see it done. Visualize your desired reality as if it already exists. Feel the gratitude. This is faith in motion.

5. **Trust the Timing**.
   Faith means allowing space. Some things take time to manifest—not because they are delayed, but because they are developing. Trust the unfolding.

Faith is not fragile—it is a force, and when practiced daily, it becomes your default posture toward life. These tools are not just spiritual exercises; they are energetic declarations that you trust what you cannot yet see.

With every word you speak, step you take, and vision you hold, you are reinforcing the bridge between the invisible and the inevitable. Faith is not passive waiting—it is powerful becoming. And the more you move in faith, the more reality moves to meet you.

Affirmation

"My faith is a force. I trust what I cannot yet see. I walk in alignment, knowing the unseen is already forming in my favor."

Guided Meditation
—The Energy of Faith

Sit in stillness. Breathe gently.

Imagine your heart as a glowing space—open, calm, and expectant. Feel the presence of faith—not as pressure, but as peace.

Now picture something you have been believing for. Do not see it as far away. See it as coming closer. It is forming. It is finding you.

Say softly within: "I believe, I receive, I trust the unfolding." Let that energy wash over you like light and breath it in. Then. Exhale and receive.

Conclusion

Faith is the bridge between vision and manifestation.

It is not denial of reality—it is alignment with a higher one. It does not ignore the facts—it just refuses to be ruled by them.

Faith is spiritual sight. It speaks when the evidence is missing. It walks when the path is unclear. It sows when the soil is dry. It celebrates before the harvest.

Because faith is not a feeling—it is also a frequency. It does not wait for things to look possible. It vibrates as if they already are. Faith is the vibration that heaven responds to. Not because you earned it—but because you dared to align with it.

You do not need certainty to move forward. You just need willingness. You do not need the whole staircase. You just need to take the next step.

Faith is not pretending. It is preparing. It is speaking in the direction of what you believe. It is making space for what is coming—even when you do not know the exact hour of its arrival.

So, let your faith be more than a whisper. Let it be a declaration. A vibration. A force.

You are not waiting for proof—you are walking as proof. You do not have to know how. You just have to believe deep enough, steady enough, and long enough for the unseen to take form.

Because the moment you do—Heaven starts moving. And what was once only a seed of hope—Becomes the substance of your now.

Chapter 6: Desire as Divine Direction
—Honoring the Sacred Pull Within

Opening Reflection

"Your heart knows the way. Run in that direction."
—Often attributed to Rumi; paraphrased by Roy Waugh

Introduction

Desire has been misunderstood.

It has been dismissed as selfish, suppressed as sinful, or diluted into shallow consumerism. But true desire—the deep, soul-born kind—is not a distraction from your spiritual path. It is your spiritual path.

Desire is divine direction. It is the inner compass that points you toward your purpose, the whisper of the life you were designed to live. It is not greed, it is guidance.

It is not an impulse, it is an invitation. When honored with wisdom and alignment, desire becomes one of the most powerful forces in the manifesting process.

This chapter reclaims desire as sacred—a divine signal long buried beneath layers of fear, guilt, and cultural distortion. We will explore how longing is not something to shame or ignore, but something to listen to with reverence.

Because your desire did not come out of nowhere—it came out of you. And what comes from within you is holy.

You are not wrong for wanting more. You are remembering that you were made for it.

Hidden Teachings from Ancient Traditions
—Desire as Divine Direction—Honoring the Sacred Pull Within

Desire, at its root, is not rebellion against the Divine—it is a response to it. In every major spiritual tradition, we find that longing—when aligned—is not dismissed but revered. Beneath the surface of scripture and ancient wisdom lies a hidden thread: your desire is a divine signal, not a distraction.

When we approach it with reverence, it becomes a compass, a coded invitation back to the Source. The traditions below reveal this secret clearly—when read with an awakened heart.

✧ Christian Insight

Desire in Christian tradition is not condemned—it is consecrated through alignment with God. **"Delight yourself in the Lord, and He will give you the desires of your heart."**(Psalm 37:4) This scripture, often misread as transactional, is actually transformational. When we delight in God—when our heart becomes attuned to Divine rhythm—our desires shift from ego to essence.

Jesus Himself honored desire by asking, **"What do you want me to do for you**?" (Mark 10:51) He invited people to name their longing, because *desire awakens faith*. Even creation itself began with desire—God's longing to give, express, and love. And since we were made in God's image, that divine longing continues in us.

✧ Jewish Wisdom

In Jewish tradition, desire is not feared—it is refined. The teachings of yetzer ha-tov (good inclination) and yetzer ha-ra (evil inclination) remind us that desire is neutral until directed. The Talmud says, **"Were it not for the yetzer ha-ra, no man would build a house, take a wife, or beget children**." (Genesis Rabbah 9:7) In other words, without desire, life would not move forward.

Desire, when channeled through justice and truth, becomes holy. Jewish mysticism adds that longing is a sign that the soul remembers something higher. The yearning within us is not lack—it is the echo of divine connection, calling us home.

✧ Islamic Teaching

In Islam, desire is examined—not erased. The Qur'an warns of nafs (the lower self) but also honors the purification of desire through remembrance. **"Perhaps you love a thing, and it is bad for you; and perhaps you hate a thing, and it is good for you. Allah knows while you know not."** (Qur'an 2:216)

This verse teaches that desire is not the enemy—misalignment is. When our hearts are purified through dhikr (remembrance of God), our desires shift from self-serving to soul-serving. The Prophet Muhammad (peace be upon him) longed for justice, unity, and divine nearness. His desires did not lead him away from God—they were fulfilled through Him.

✧ Buddhist Practices

Buddhism distinguishes between craving (tanha) and wholesome desire. The Buddha taught that suffering comes from clinging—not from longing itself. Pure desire—such as the aspiration for wisdom, compassion, or liberation—is the very spark behind the spiritual path.

Bodhicitta, the sincere wish to attain enlightenment for the benefit of all beings, is revered as the highest motivation. It is not suppressed. It is cultivated.

As the Itivuttaka says: **"All that we are arises with our thoughts. With our thoughts, we make the world."** (Itivuttaka 1.1) This verse mirrors the truth that what we focus our desire upon begins to shape our reality.

In Buddhist wisdom, when desire is unbound from ego and aimed at awakening, it becomes sacred momentum. It is no longer a grasping—it is a guiding light toward freedom.

✧ Hindu Insights

In Hinduism, desire (kāma) is not a sin—it is a sacred aim. It is listed among the four purusharthas, or goals of life: dharma (duty), artha (prosperity), kāma (desire), and moksha (liberation). Desire, when rooted in dharma, becomes a divine force—not a distraction.

As Lord Krishna says: "**I am the desire in beings which is not opposed to dharma**." (Bhagavad Gita 7:11) This teaching redefines desire not as a temptation but as a transmission—one that flows from the Divine when grounded in truth.

Through practices like mantra, devotion (bhakti), and sankalpa (sacred intention), desire becomes a bridge to union, not separation.

Across traditions, the message is clear: *true desire*—when purified, examined, and honored—*is a sacred impulse*. It is not a flaw to fix. It is a flame to follow.

These ancient teachings whisper a shared truth: the longing that stirs within you is not against the Divine—it is the Divine, pulling you back into remembrance. Trust it. Honor it. Let it lead.

Wisdom from Contemporary Spiritual Leaders

So many people have been taught to suppress their desires—as if wanting something deeply was selfish or somehow a sign of spiritual immaturity. But the most profound spiritual teachers remind us that desire is not the problem—disconnection is. The soul knows what it came here to do, and desire is often its first language.

What follows are powerful insights from those who have walked paths of wisdom, each echoing the truth that desire, when honored with reverence, becomes holy direction.

—Abraham Hicks teaches: "**Desire is the beginning of all new creation**." This truth reminds us that nothing manifests without it. Desire is not just a passing feeling—it is the spiritual spark that ignites alignment. When you feel it stir within you, pay attention. That stirring is the evidence of something real already forming in the unseen.

—Oprah Winfrey has often said, "**Every right decision I've ever made has come from my gut**." She teaches that the body's internal compass —our gut, our heart, our longing—is not to be ignored but embraced. She does not describe desire as a craving, but as an intuitive pull. When we lean into that inner wisdom, we are not being impulsive—we are being guided.

—Elizabeth Gilbert, in Big Magic, writes: "**Your curiosity is a clue. Follow it**." She reframes desire as sacred curiosity. The quiet nudge. The question you cannot stop asking. The gentle urge that will not let go. That is not restlessness. That is a holy invitation. Sometimes, it does not shout —it just whispers until you follow.

—Deepak Chopra offers this reminder: "**The desire to improve your life, to grow spiritually, to love more deeply—is a divine impulse**." He views desire not as something we generate but as something we receive. It is a frequency—a divine prompting—that rises up when we are ready to expand.

—Roy Waugh, "**The desire that will not let go of you—that quiet pull that returns in your stillest moments—is not a distraction. It is direction. It is the soul tapping you on the shoulder saying, 'Remember why you came.'**" I have come to realize that the desires we try to silence are often the ones most aligned with who we are becoming. Not every want is sacred, but the ones that echo across seasons—that show up again and again in your spirit—those are not just wants. Those are callings.

Desire is not a flaw to correct—it is a compass to follow. These teachers remind us that honoring your desire is not giving in to ego, but giving voice to purpose. When you stop resisting the pull within and start walking with it, you do not just move toward your calling—you become it.

Scientific Perspectives on Motivation and Inner Drive
—The Sacred Science of Longing—How Desire Fuels Transformation

Desire is not just a poetic notion or spiritual metaphor—it is measurable. It lives in the body. It activates the brain. It shifts the nervous system. In other words, desire is not just mystical—it is biological, neurological, and energetic. And when we view it through the lens of science, we begin to see that our soul's longing is not only sacred—it is built into the very wiring of who we are.

✧ Psychological Research

The self-determination theory, developed by psychologists Edward Deci and Richard Ryan, reveals that intrinsic motivation—desire that comes from within rather than from external rewards—is essential for human thriving.

When a person is moved by inner desire (for meaning, growth, connection, contribution), they are more likely to experience fulfillment, creativity, and resilience. In other words, people flourish when they listen to the quiet pull inside.

✧ Neuroscience of Desire

From a neurological standpoint, desire activates the brain's dopaminergic pathways, which govern anticipation, focus, and reward. Dopamine is not just a "pleasure" chemical—it is a motivation molecule. It surges when we pursue something meaningful, not just when we get it.

This means the very act of honoring your desire—taking even one step toward it—releases energy and clarity into your system. It tells the brain: "This matters."

✧ Quantum Perspective

Quantum physics reminds us that everything is energy—and energy responds to frequency. The moment you desire something with sincerity and clarity, you shift your vibrational output. You begin to resonate with the reality you long for. That resonance is not wishful thinking—it is a measurable field.

The heart's electromagnetic field, for instance, is over 60 times stronger than the brain's and can influence the environment around it.

When your desire is felt deeply in the heart, it becomes a magnetic signature—calling back to you the essence of what you seek.

✧ Energetic Alignment

Desire in its purest form is not a craving from lack—it is a frequency of alignment. It carries the signal of who you are becoming. When your desire aligns with belief, emotion, and embodiment, it generates a powerful current. That current becomes a bridge between the unseen and the seen. And manifestation begins—not from desperation—but from coherence.

So yes, science validates what the spirit already knows: Desire is not weakness. It is not a symptom of lack. It is the engine of purpose moving through you.

When you let your longing live—not just in your imagination, but in your biology and energy—you awaken the divine design written into your very being.

Personal Story
—The Whisper That Would Not Let Go

There was a moment in my life when everything looked fine from the outside. I had a steady rhythm, a familiar routine, and all the signs of stability. But something inside me felt unsettled. Not in a loud, chaotic way—but in a quiet, pulsing kind of way. Like something was calling from within me, just beneath the surface.

It was not a shout. It was a whisper: You are meant to be creating.
Not just producing or showing up for others—but pouring from your soul. Making something lasting.

At first, I did not fully understand what that meant. But I felt the pull—especially when I let myself be still. Thoughts would come. Phrases. Sentences. Sometimes, just a single word that carried weight. I would scribble them down on napkins, in journals, on the backs of receipts—never fully knowing why. The trials I had gone through, over the years, those fragments added up.

And still, I doubted it.

Who was I to write anything meaningful? What if it did not matter? What if I was wrong about what I was feeling?

I tried to talk myself out of it more than once. But desire—true, soul-level desire—is persistent. It does not fade. It waits. And it whispers again.

One night, I sat alone in my kitchen. A warm mug of tea in my hands. The house was quiet. I opened an old journal and flipped through the pages—fragments of thoughts I had jotted down over the years. And suddenly, it hit me: This book I am now writing began a long time ago. Not when I sat down to start it, but in all those in-between moments. In the questions. In the quotes I could not forget. In the midnight downloads, I had scribbled and shelved. Desire had been gathering, layering, and waiting for me to finally say yes.

That night was not a beginning—it was a realization: This is what I was being prepared for all along. And once I said yes—once I stopped analyzing the desire and started honoring it—things began to move. Not always quickly. Not without resistance. But with unmistakable alignment. Doors opened. Words flowed.

And page by page, what was once just longing became something real.

Now, every time I sit to write a chapter, I do not do it just for the sake of writing. I do it because I am finally answering the sacred pull I have felt for years.

Desire brought me here.

And what I have come to know is this:
When a desire lives in you that long—when it echoes across seasons and whispers in the quiet—it is not a distraction. It is divine direction.

So, I listen. I write. I follow the pull.

Because what began as a single word has become a sacred work to me. And I know it is not just for me. It is for whoever is open and meant to receive it.

Practical Applications
—Honoring Desire as Sacred Direction

Desire is not enough on its own—it must be honored, examined, and moved through. The following practices are designed to help you engage with your deepest longings in a sacred, intentional way.

These steps are not about chasing empty wants—they are about listening to your soul, aligning your actions with divine guidance, and taking steps toward the life that is calling you. When desire meets clarity and movement, manifestation begins.

1. **Listen to the longing**.
   What are you drawn to—even if it does not make sense yet? Journal the desires that keep showing up. They are not random.

2. **Let desire be ok**.
Do not shame yourself for wanting more love, freedom, success, or peace. If the desire is pure, it is pointing to your soul's expansion.

3. **Refine, do not deny**.
Ask: "Is this desire coming from love or fear? Is it about expression or validation?" Purify the desire without discarding it.

4. **Feed it with action**.
Desire without motion withers. Take one small step toward it. Desire grows stronger with participation.

5. **Speak it into the universe**.
Declare it. Whisper it in prayer. Hold it in meditation. Let the desire breathe in sacred space.

Desire is not a distraction from your path—it is the path. When honored with discernment and aligned with love, it becomes divine direction encoded in longing. These practices are not about indulgence—they are about remembrance: remembering the dreams seeded in your soul for a reason.

When you stop silencing your desires and start moving with them, you awaken the energy of purpose, passion, and possibility. So let your desire speak. Let it guide. And most of all, let it lead you closer to the life your spirit already knows is yours.

Affirmation

"My desires are sacred signals. I honor what I long for, and I move in alignment with divine direction."

Guided Meditation
—Tuning Into the Sacred Pull

Sit quietly. Breathe into your chest.

Now ask yourself gently: "What do I truly desire right now?"

Let the answer rise without judgment. Feel the pull—not as pressure, but as a path. See it glowing ahead of you, warm and inviting.

Whisper inwardly: "I trust what I feel. I follow where I am drawn." Breathe again, deeper this time. The way is already opening.

Conclusion

Desire is not the enemy of your spiritual journey. It is the beginning of it.

We have been taught to mistrust longing, to downplay the ache for more as selfish or foolish. But the truth is—your desire was never random. It was never misplaced. It was encoded in you for a reason.

When you feel the gentle pull of a dream that will not let go, or when a quiet voice rises within you saying, "There's more for you than this," that is not your ego talking. That is your soul remembering.

The whisper that keeps returning? The longing that will not be silenced? That is not a distraction from your spiritual path—it is your spiritual path. And that yearning you feel? It is sacred because within every holy desire lives the blueprint of your becoming.

You do not have to explain it to everyone. You do not have to justify why you want what you want. You only have to listen.

Desire is the Divine reaching through you, reminding you that something is unfolding. You are not here just to survive—you are here to create. To answer the call. To follow the pull. To say yes to the holy hunger placed in your heart before time began.

What you want, when purified by truth, becomes a compass toward destiny. It is not greedy to want more peace, more purpose, more presence. That is God in you wanting to be made manifest through you.

So, listen when your soul stirs. Listen when your heart leaps. Trust that your desire is not asking for too much. It is revealing just how much more is already within you.

The call is already in motion.
The path is already forming.
All that is left to do now—is follow the fire.

Chapter 7: The Kingdom Within

—Manifesting from the Inside Out

Opening Reflection

"Do you not know that your bodies are temples of the Holy Spirit, who is in you...?"
—1 Corinthians 6:19

Introduction

We have been taught to look outward for answers. To reach, to chase, to climb toward something greater—believing that power, purpose, or peace are somewhere out there waiting to be earned or summoned. But manifestation, in its truest and most sacred form, does not come from reaching out. It comes from returning inward.

The Kingdom is not above the clouds or tucked away in a holy book. It is not hidden in a mountaintop monastery or a faraway temple. It is within you—closer than your breath, louder than your fear, deeper than your striving.

This is the sacred reversal the mystics and prophets understood: You do not need to become something else to manifest. You only need to remember who you already are. The spark of the Divine is not something you visit. It is something you carry. Always.

Your body is not separate from Spirit—it is the very dwelling place of the sacred. The manifestation you seek is not a far-off dream. It begins right here, in the sanctuary of your own being. This chapter is an invitation to come home to that truth—and to manifest not by force, but by frequency.

In this chapter, we turn our gaze inward, exploring the truth that the Kingdom we seek is not found in the distance, but carried within our very being.

Hidden Teachings from Ancient Traditions
—Ancient Wisdom on the Sacred Space Within

Across every sacred tradition, there is a thread—a quiet but undeniable truth: the Divine is not far off. It is not locked behind temple walls, and it is not reserved for mountaintops or mystics. It is here within you. Always has been.

These ancient teachings weren't just meant to elevate the holy—they were meant to awaken the holiness already inside of you. They do not point you outward. They gently, persistently, turn you inward because that is where the real work of creation begins.

✧ Christian Faith

Jesus did not say the Kingdom of God was coming to you; He said it was already in you (Luke 17:21), and that alone changes everything. And Paul echoed it, writing, **"Don't you know that you yourselves are God's temple and that God's Spirit dwells in your midst?"** (1 Corinthians 3:16). That is not poetic language—that's divine architecture. John 14:23 reminds us that those who love God do not have to go searching—God makes His home in them.

The message?

You do not have to reach toward heaven to manifest miracles. You just have to awaken to the fact that heaven lives inside your very breath.

✧ Jewish Wisdom

In Judaism, the soul—the neshama—is understood as the actual breath of God inside of us. Genesis 2:7 says God formed man and breathed life into his nostrils. That word, breathe—neshima—is from the same root as neshama.

So, every breath you take is not just survival—it is sacred memory. Kabbalistic teachings say each of us is a mikdash me'at—a small sanctuary, a walking temple. Exodus 25:8 says, "**Have them build a sanctuary for me, and I will dwell among them**." But the deeper invitation is this: build the sanctuary within, and God will meet you there. You do not have to go anywhere else to find the Divine.

✧ Islamic Teaching

The Qur'an says, "**We are closer to them than their jugular vein**." (Surah Qaf 50:16). That is not metaphor—that's truth. Islam teaches that the center of spiritual perception is the qalb, the heart.

The Prophet Muhammad (peace be upon him) said, "**There is a piece of flesh in the body—if it is sound, the whole body is sound... it is the heart**." (Sahih al-Bukhari 52).

Practices like dhikr, the remembrance of God, are not about pulling the Divine down from the sky—they are about waking up to what is already living in your chest.

Surah Al-Baqarah 2:186 says, "**I am near. I respond to the call of the caller when he calls upon Me**." The distance was never real. And manifestation begins the moment your heart remembers that.

✧ Buddhist Practices

Buddhism does not teach you to run from life. It teaches you to return to yourself. The Dhammapada opens with this: "**All that we are is the result of what we have thought**." (Verse 1). The Buddha's last teaching was, "**Be a lamp unto yourself**." Not because the world has no light—but because the truest light is already burning in you.

Through meditation, mindfulness, and loving-kindness (metta), you stop grasping and start allowing. The more you still your mind, the clearer your center becomes.

In this path, manifestation is not about effort—it is about alignment. When you clear what is in the way, what you desire begins to rise naturally from within.

✧ Hindu Insights

Hinduism teaches that the Self (Atman) is not separate from the Divine (Brahman)—it is one and the same. **"Tat Tvam Asi"**— **"Thou art That**." (Chandogya Upanishad 6.8.7). That is not just ancient wisdom—it is a direct reminder. The Bhagavad Gita says, **"The Lord dwells in the hearts of all beings**." (18:61). The sacred does not just visit you. It lives in you.

Through practices like meditation (dhyana), breathwork (pranayama), and devotion (bhakti), Hindu tradition teaches us not to chase enlightenment—but to uncover it. Your body is not an obstacle—it is a holy vessel. And when you live from the inside out, creation begins to move through you.

Across every tradition, the message is the same: the Divine is already within. It is not something you earn, or reach, or chase. It is something you remember. The moment you stop searching outside yourself and begin to honor what is already alive inside, you do not just manifest—you become the manifestation.

Wisdom from Contemporary Spiritual Leaders

Throughout the ages, the most profound spiritual teachers have echoed a sacred truth: the journey to divine power is not an ascent—it is a return. The wisdom you seek, the power you chase, and the presence you pray for are already pulsing within you.

These voices remind us that the most transformative manifestation begins not with reaching outward, but with turning inward and remembering who we are.

—Dr. Joe Dispenza teaches that "**When you change your internal state, you change your external reality**." His work explores how brainwave patterns, heart coherence, and personal energy fields create our lived experience. Your internal world does not just influence your life; it designs it.

—Joyce Meyer often says, "**You cannot have a positive life and a negative mind**." Her teachings drive home the truth that your thoughts are the atmosphere in which your faith breathes. Renewing your inner world is the beginning of seeing miracles unfold in your outer world.

—Maya Angelou offered this radiant reminder: "**Nothing can dim the light that shines from within**." Her life modeled how to carry grace, dignity, and power not because of circumstances—but in spite of them. She lived from the light within, not the approval without.

—Tara Brach, a renowned meditation teacher, speaks of "**the sacred pause**"—that gentle, present moment when we return to our essence. She reminds us that our wholeness is not something to earn, but something to remember.

—Roy Waugh, "**You do not need to go mountain climbing to find God. Sometimes the holiest place is the quiet corner of your own mind—right between your last doubt and your next breath**." Here, the truth is simple: God's presence is as close as your own breath.

Too often, we think the sacred requires ceremony, distance, or spectacle. But these teachers remind us of a deeper truth: the most powerful miracles are born in stillness. When you pause, breathe, and come home to yourself, you are not stepping away from the divine—you are stepping into it. You are already the sacred space. And the power that moves mountains begins with the one who believes from within.

Scientific Perspectives on the Inner State
—The Temple Within—Science Confirms What Spirit Already Knows

Modern science continues to affirm what spiritual wisdom has whispered for centuries: that your inner world powerfully shapes your outer reality. From neuroscience to quantum physics to heart-based studies, research now reveals that the body is not just a physical shell—it is a dynamic temple of energy, thought, and potential.

Science does not replace the sacred. It reflects it. Here is what the data shows about the divine design within.

✧ Neuroscience

The reticular activating system (RAS) in the brain filters incoming information based on what you consistently think, believe, and feel. When your internal narrative changes, so does what your brain chooses to notice and prioritize.

In other words, if you dwell on fear or lack, your brain will seek confirmation of it. But if you dwell on peace, gratitude, and divine alignment, your brain begins scanning for opportunities, insights, and possibilities that match that frequency.

Repeated internal focus actually restructures your neural pathways through neuroplasticity. Thought patterns, especially when paired with emotion, can physically rewire the brain—shaping your perception, behavior, and even your biology.

✧ Quantum Physics

Quantum theory affirms that the observer affects the observed. While interpretations vary, the consistent conclusion is this: focused intention changes outcomes. You are not a passive witness—you are an active participant in shaping what unfolds.

The energy of your attention, especially when directed inward with clarity and intention, creates a resonance that shifts not only your perception, but the field around you. Just as light behaves differently when observed, so too does your life respond when you approach it from inner alignment.

✧ Heart-Based Research

Studies from the HeartMath Institute reveal that the heart emits an electromagnetic field up to 60 times greater than that of the brain. This field is not static—it changes based on your emotional state. Love, compassion, gratitude, and inner coherence create a stable, harmonious frequency. Stress, fear, and anxiety create incoherence and internal chaos.

This electromagnetic field does not just influence your own body—it has measurable effects on others. The state of your heart, quite literally, radiates. When you return to your sacred center, you do not just shift your health—you shift your atmosphere.

Your body is not a boundary—it is a beacon.

Science now tells the same story the mystics have always told: When you align your inner world, the outer world begins to mirror that resonance.

Manifestation is not a mystery—it is a map encoded in your biology, your energy, and your awareness. You are the temple. And when you honor that truth, you activate the divine circuitry already alive within you.

Personal Story
—Playing David, Becoming Me

When I was cast to play King David in the national touring musical "David: A Man After God's Own Heart" by Cam Floria, I said yes with my mouth—but inside, I was scared.

It was the kind of role people dream about. The lead. A powerful, complex character. A man with a legacy of songs, mistakes, battles, and blessings. David was not just a figure in history—he was a force. A shepherd, a king, a warrior, a poet. A man known for chasing after the very heart of God.
And I was supposed to embody him?

I started preparing the only way I knew how—by diving into the scriptures. I read everything I could about David's life. I studied the

Psalms not as a performer, but as someone searching for clues to a soul. I wanted to feel his humanity, understand his flaws, absorb his hunger for the Divine. The more I read, the more I admired him. And the more I admired him, the more unworthy I felt.

I began to question why I was chosen at all.
Who was I to portray a man like this? A legend? A king?
Someone who danced with such abandon before the Lord, who faced giants, who carried the Ark of the Covenant, who heard God's voice so clearly?

I convinced myself that I could not do it without something supernatural overtaking me. I did not just want to play the part—I needed to be overtaken by something holy. I prayed relentlessly, "God, I cannot do this without You. If YOU do not embody this performance, I will fall flat. I will fail. I will misrepresent someone sacred."

What I did not realize then was that I had already started manifesting from lack. I was reaching outward for what I believed I did not yet have. I was treating God's presence like a visitor I had to summon rather than a presence I already carried.

Rehearsals began, and the pressure built. I memorized the lines, studied the blocking, and shaped my voice to meet the music. But underneath it all, I was still waiting for a "moment"—some unmistakable surge of power that would make me worthy to stand in David's sandals.

That moment never came—at least not in the way I expected.

Instead, something quieter happened.
One day during rehearsal, I was alone on stage practicing a solo scene—one of the more vulnerable moments in the production. There were no lights, no audience, no music. Just me and a quiet, empty stage. I sat down, heart pounding, and closed my eyes. I had no performance left. No act. No script. Just breathe.

And in that stillness, I heard something within me—simple but undeniable:

"You are not pretending to carry My presence. You already do. David was a man after my heart. But so are you."

That realization—**tore—me—up**.

Not because it was grand, but because it was true.
I did not need to become someone else to be worthy of the role. I needed to remember who I already was.

I had spent so much time preparing the outer—my voice, my expression, the staging, the delivery—that I had forgotten the most sacred part of the performance: the inner alignment.

The Kingdom of God was not something I had to pull down from heaven. It was already within me, waiting to be released.
From that day on, everything shifted.

When I stepped into David's role, I was not performing; I was embodying. I was not chasing presence—I was carrying it. And the audience felt it. Not because I was flawless. But because I was fully anchored in something deeper than script or spotlight.

That experience did not just shape my career. It shaped my theology. It taught me that manifestation does not begin with effort. It begins with embodiment. The light we search for is not up there or out there—it is within us, waiting for stillness, waiting for belief, waiting to be remembered.

Now, whenever I step on stage—or into any sacred space—I do not ask for God to come down.

I remind myself: He already lives here. And give thanks because this temple is enough.

Practical Applications
—Returning to the Inner Temple

It is one thing to *know* the Kingdom is within—it is another to live like it. Inner alignment does not happen by accident. It happens through practice. Through small, intentional moments that ground you in your own sacred center. The following steps are not rituals for summoning something outside of you—they are gentle reminders to return to what is already inside. These practices help you quiet the noise, honor your temple, and manifest from the inside out.

1. **Create daily stillness**.
   Make time to be with yourself—not your phone, your tasks, or your worries. Just you. Even five minutes of breath and presence can recalibrate your inner space.

2. **Speak to the inner you**.
   Before asking for anything, say inwardly: "I trust the power within me." Begin with gratitude for what already lives in you.

3. **Walk in inner identity**.
   When you move through the world, carry the awareness: "I am a temple. I carry light. I co-create." This shifts your posture, your energy, and your choices.

4. **Ask from alignment, not lack**.
   Desire is holy—but desperation is a sign of disconnection. Go inward first. Align. Then ask. You will speak from authority, not anxiety.

5. **Guard the gate**.
   Your inner world is sacred ground. Be careful what you allow in. Words, media, energy—they all affect your temple. Choose what honors your spirit.

Your inner temple is not a place you visit once—it is a sanctuary you return to daily. These practices are not just spiritual exercises; they are acts of remembrance. Each breath of stillness, each word of alignment, each choice to protect your inner world is a declaration that you know where your true power resides.

The Kingdom is not a far-off destination—it is the quiet strength within you, always available, always sacred. When you live from this center, you don't just manifest differently—you move through life with divine authority.

Affirmation

"I carry the Kingdom within. I align with the power, peace, and presence that already lives in me. I manifest from my sacred center."

Guided Meditation
—Return to the Temple Within

Breathe.

Imagine your body as a cathedral of light. Your heart, a glowing altar. Your mind is a sanctuary of peace.

Inhale deeply. Say inwardly, "I am home." See the space within you expanding—soft, warm, alive. Feel divine presence not above you, but within you.

Sit here for a moment, in reverence. In wholeness. In truth.

You are the dwelling place, you are the co-creator, and you are the light.

Conclusion

We spend so much of life searching—searching for answers, for healing, for a breakthrough. We reach outward, hoping that something "out there" will finally shift our reality. But the true shift—the one that changes everything—begins within.

The Kingdom is not a place you arrive at. It is a presence you awaken to.

Your body is not just skin and bone—it is a living, breathing sanctuary. A vessel for divine energy. A holy dwelling.
And manifestation does not begin when the outer conditions are perfect—it begins the moment you remember what already lives in you.

We have been trained to chase, to grasp, to beg the heavens for what we already carry in seed form. But no amount of striving can replace the power of stillness. It is in the silence—beneath the noise of fear and striving—that you rediscover your sacredness.

That is where manifestation takes root.

When you align with your inner world, you do not need to wait for a sign. You become the sign. You become the answer to the prayer you were about to pray.

Because this Kingdom? It is not somewhere far off. It is not behind a locked door. It is right here—within your breath, your being, your belief.

So, the next time you feel lost, unsure, or disconnected from your power, do not look up. Do not look around. Look in.

That is where the real miracle is waiting. It is where the light never left. And where manifestation begins.

Go inward. Stay anchored. Let the world reflect what you now remember to be true.

Chapter 8: Gratitude as Magnetic Energy
—Receiving Before It Arrives

Opening Reflection

"Gratitude is the bridge between your desire and its arrival. Give thanks as if it is already yours, and the Universe has no choice but to respond."
—Roy Waugh, Inspired by Abraham Hicks

Introduction

Gratitude is not a reaction—it is a frequency. A magnetic field that goes before you and reshapes the unseen.

It is more than saying "thank you" when something good happens. Gratitude is a way of being. A sacred resonance that tells the universe, the Divine, and your inner self: I am aligned. I trust. I receive.

In the frequency of manifestation, gratitude is the tuning fork that draws your desires out of the invisible and into form. It collapses the distance between what is and what can be. It is not a delayed celebration—it is the sound that calls the miracle forth.

When you express gratitude before the blessing appears, you speak the language of Divine certainty. You are not pleading—you are preparing. You are not guessing—you are guiding the frequency of your life into deeper coherence. Gratitude becomes the vibrational signature of trust.

This chapter invites you to see gratitude not as a feeling that comes and goes—but as a field you live in. A sacred rhythm that places you in resonance with abundance, healing, favor, and peace. When the soil of your spirit becomes grateful, manifestation begins to move.

Because gratitude is not just part of the journey—it is the journey.
And when you embody it, the whole frequency changes.

Hidden Teachings from Ancient Traditions

—The Sacred Frequency of Gratitude—Ancient Pathways to Divine Increase

Gratitude is not just a polite practice—it is a spiritual current. Across every major tradition, we see the same ancient law: when you give thanks, you align with abundance. When you bless what is, you create a path for what is next.

These sacred teachings do not treat gratitude as reactive, but as generative —a force that shifts energy, opens the heart, and welcomes miracles. Let us return to the wisdom of the ancients, who understood long before us that thanksgiving is not the result of favor; it is often the reason it arrives.

✧ Christian Faith

In Christian tradition, gratitude is more than a gesture—it is a gateway. Psalm 100:4 declares, **"Enter his gates with thanksgiving and his courts with praise; give thanks to him and praise his name."** Gratitude, here, is not optional—it is a portal. In the story of the ten lepers (Luke 17:11–19), only one returns to thank Jesus. His gratitude does more than acknowledge healing—it completes it.

Jesus says, **"Your faith has made you whole."** (Luke 17:19). Paul echoes this energetic truth in 1 Thessalonians 5:18: **"Give thanks in all circumstances..."**—reminding us that thanksgiving is not based on what has happened. It is a frequency that invites what can happen.

✧ Jewish Wisdom

Judaism holds gratitude as a foundational rhythm of life. The morning begins with the Modeh Ani prayer: **"I thank You, living and eternal King, for returning my soul within me with compassion; abundant is Your faithfulness."** (Siddur). This daily acknowledgment sanctifies the breath itself. The Hebrew word todah does not just mean thanks—it means recognition.

Gratitude in Jewish thought is about seeing the divine in the details, even in hardship. At funerals, the blessing Baruch Dayan HaEmet— **"Blessed is the True Judge."** (Talmud Bavli, Berakhot 59b)—is spoken, affirming that even sorrow is held in sacred perspective. The Psalms, filled with thanksgiving uttered in the midst of struggle, teach that gratitude is not the result of joy—it is the path to it.

✧ **Islamic Teaching**

In Islam, gratitude (shukr) is a divine amplifier. The Qur'an promises: **"If you are grateful, I will surely increase you [in favor]."** (Qur'an 14:7). Gratitude here is not only a virtue—it is cause and effect. The Prophet Muhammad (peace be upon him) prayed through the night, even when all was well. When asked why, he replied, **"Should I not be a grateful servant?"** (Sahih al-Bukhari, Book 76, Hadith 478).

Gratitude was his worship, not just his response. In Sufism, it is said that gratitude polishes the heart like a mirror, so it can reflect divine light. A thankful soul becomes a vessel through which increase flows—not because they beg for more, but because they already honor what is.

✧ **Buddhist Practices**

In Buddhism, gratitude arises naturally from awareness. To be mindful is to notice the miracle of now. While a commonly cited quote attributed to the Buddha says, **"Let us rise and be thankful..."** (source unverified in canonical texts), the spirit of the teaching remains clear: even the smallest grace is worthy of reverence.

Practices like metta bhavana (loving-kindness meditation) and mudita (rejoicing in others' joy) cultivate an inner field of gratitude—not just toward people, but toward life itself. In this tradition, gratitude is not clung to—it is lived. It flows from presence. And when you live gratefully, you align yourself with the gentle joy that always was.

✧ Hindu Traditions

In Hinduism, gratitude is a sacred offering—not something you feel, but something you do. Lord Krishna teaches, "**Whatever you do... offer it to Me.**" (Bhagavad Gita 9:27). Acts of devotion—lighting lamps, chanting mantras, sharing meals—are all expressions of thanks, not for transaction, but for transformation.

The concept of prasad teaches that every blessing, every breath, is a divine gift. And in the Rig Veda, we find this beautiful duality: "**Let us be grateful to the light... let us be grateful to the darkness.**" (Rig Veda 1.50.10, paraphrased). Gratitude here embraces both joy and trial as part of sacred unfolding. It does not wait for things to get better—it blesses them into becoming.

Gratitude, across every faith, is more than polite prayer. It is spiritual electricity. A signal that says, "I am open. I am aware. I am ready." And the moment you give thanks—not for what has happened, but for what is happening now—you step into divine alignment. You match the frequency of abundance. And the Universe, God, Source, responds—not because you earned it, but because you finally recognized that it was always on the way.

Wisdom from Contemporary Spiritual Leaders

Gratitude is more than polite behavior—it is a profound energetic tool recognized by spiritual leaders, scientists, and visionaries alike. These voices remind us that gratitude is not a response to good fortune—it is a frequency we tune into that creates the very conditions for transformation. True spiritual power begins when gratitude becomes your default vibration.

—Dr. Joe Dispenza teaches that elevated emotions like gratitude signal to the body and brain that the future you desire is already happening. In his words: "**Gratitude is the ultimate state of receivership.**" By expressing thanks in advance, you align your neurochemistry with the timeline where your desire already exists.

—Oprah Winfrey has long championed the practice of gratitude journaling, calling it the tool that changed her life. She says: "**Be thankful for what you have; you'll end up having more.**" Oprah teaches that when you focus on the good, you draw more of it toward you.

—Louise Hay believed that gratitude is a healing frequency. She wrote: "**The universe loves gratitude. The more grateful you are, the more goodies you get.**" She encouraged readers to bless even their challenges, because doing so sends a signal of worthiness and trust.

—Esther Hicks (Abraham) emphasizes that feeling good is the foundation of manifestation, and nothing raises your vibration faster than appreciation. "**Appreciation in advance brings everything you want to you.**" It is not wishful thinking—it is vibrational alignment.

—Deepak Chopra teaches that gratitude expands your awareness of abundance. He writes: "**Gratitude opens the door to...the power, the wisdom, the creativity of the universe.**" Gratitude connects the individual to the whole and allows intention to flow freely through that channel.

—Albert Einstein, who viewed the mysteries of life with reverent awe, once said: "**There are only two ways to live your life. One is as though nothing is a miracle. The other is as though everything is a miracle.**" He thanked the universe daily—for every insight, equation, and moment of clarity. For Einstein, gratitude was not a sentiment. It was a sacred perspective.

—Roy Waugh, "**When you say thank you before the blessing shows up, you are not pretending—it is prophecy.** Gratitude is the voice of someone who already knows they are heard." Gratitude is not just polite—it is prophetic. It is not performance. It is presence. When you give thanks in advance, you align yourself with the timeline where the prayer is already answered, the door is already open, and the blessing is already yours. It is not about faking faith—it is about feeling the frequency of fulfillment now.

Whether through journaling, meditating, blessing meals, or simply pausing to give thanks for breath—these teachers agree: the vibration of gratitude is not a final step in manifestation. It is the starting point. It is the invitation. It is the alignment.

Gratitude is not waiting for good things to arrive. It is recognizing that you are already standing in the stream of blessing, and your thankfulness opens the floodgates wider.

Scientific Perspectives on Gratitude and the Brain

—The Frequency of Thanks—How Gratitude Rewires Body, Brain, and Field

Gratitude is not just a feeling—it is a frequency that transforms your inner chemistry. It has a measurable impact on the way your brain fires, the way your heart beats, and even the way your genes express themselves. Science is finally catching up to what the soul has always known: gratitude is a healer, a harmonizer, and a manifesting force.

✧ Neuroscience: Gratitude Rewires the Brain

Studies in neuroscience show that when we feel and express gratitude, the brain activates the prefrontal cortex and releases dopamine and serotonin —chemicals associated with joy, reward, and connection. The more often you feel grateful, the easier it becomes. Neural pathways are strengthened through repetition. Gratitude becomes a mental habit, not just an emotional experience.

The Reticular Activating System (RAS)—your brain's personal filter— begins to tune in to whatever you are focused on. When you train your mind to look for what is good and what's working, the RAS will begin to reveal more of it. You literally start to see more opportunities, blessings, and synchronicities, not because they suddenly appear, but because you've attuned your awareness to them.

Gratitude does not just shift your mindset. It shifts your mental architecture.

✧ Epigenetics: Gratitude and Gene Expression

In the field of epigenetics, researchers have found that elevated emotional states—like love, compassion, and gratitude—can influence which genes get activated or suppressed. In other words, the way you feel and think can directly affect how your DNA operates.

One study published in Psychoneuroendocrinology found that practicing gratitude and other heart-centered emotions can downregulate inflammatory genes and upregulate genes involved in immune function. Gratitude becomes a biological intervention. You are not just raising your vibe—you are rewriting the script your cells follow.

Gratitude, in this sense, becomes a cellular frequency. It signals the body to heal, to regenerate, and to align with vitality.

✧ Psychophysiology: Vibration, Resonance, and Heart-Brain Coherence

Gratitude does not stay locked in your chest—it echoes through your body's electromagnetic field. The HeartMath Institute has shown that feelings of gratitude and appreciation bring the heart and brain into a state of coherence—a smooth, harmonic rhythm where all systems are working in sync.

This heart-brain coherence creates a state of resonance, similar to striking a tuning fork and causing another fork of the same frequency across the room to begin vibrating. Your body is an instrument. When you strike the frequency of gratitude, everything in your field that matches that note begins to vibrate with you.

That is not just metaphor—it is measurable. Instruments can detect the electromagnetic waves your heart emits when you are in a grateful state. Those waves influence not just your own body, but also the people and energy fields around you.

When you practice gratitude consistently—especially before the evidence shows up—you are doing more than nurturing your spirit. You are tuning your biology, your neurology, your frequency, and your field. You are becoming the magnet. And as science now confirms, the vibration you live in is the life you start to see.

Personal Story
—The Project I Could Not Afford, But Received Anyway

Years ago, after being named Best Male Vocalist in a prestigious, global Christian Artist Competition with over 4,000 participants, I was awarded professional studio time with a legendary gospel music producer—someone whose songs had shaped the very soundtrack of my faith.
It felt like walking into the pages of a dream I had barely dared to speak aloud.

Initially, I planned to keep it simple: a few familiar cover songs that I could breeze through without too much cost or stress. This was my first professional recording, and I figured the less complicated, the better. But after hearing my voice, the producer had other ideas.

"You know," he said, "a friend of mine and I write a lot of original material—and I think your voice would be perfect for some of it."

He played me a few tracks, and as soon as I heard the first verse of the first song, I knew. These songs were not just good—they fit. They spoke to the kind of singer and messenger I longed to be. I told him I would be honored to record them.

Wanting to be financially responsible, I reached out to some friends from a band I had once performed with and asked if they would help lay down the instrumental tracks. They agreed graciously, and we all headed into the studio together. It was a labor of love, and after several weeks, we were finally mixing the project and nearing the finish line.
That is when everything changed.

The owner of the studio walked in—an icon in the industry. A mega-superstar. A legend I had admired for most of my singing life. His presence filled the room. I was both humbled and stunned that he would even take the time to listen to my work.

After a while, he turned to me and said, "You've got a fantastic voice. May I make a suggestion?"

I nodded, breathless, heart pounding.

He said, "These musicians—wonderful live players, clearly—but I can tell they are not studio musicians. They do not quite match your energy or the level of professionalism we need to capture on a recording like this. If it is alright with you, I would like to bring in a few guys I normally work with."

Without hesitation, I said yes.

The project was scrapped and completely re-recorded. He brought in Garth Brooks' guitarist, John Cougar Mellencamp's drummer, and Sandi Patty's pianist. These were not just musicians—they were masters. What had taken nearly two months to build before was now laid down in just eight hours. And it was glorious. Crisp, powerful, alive.

I re-recorded all my vocals. We layered the harmonies. Mixed and refined every detail. The project was becoming everything I had hoped for—more, actually.

But quietly, behind the scenes of my celebration, I was panicking.
This new level of production far exceeded the original prize package I had won. I had already used all the time awarded to me. I knew this caliber of work did not come cheap—and I had about two hundred dollars to my name. No backup plan. No safety net.

I needed the finished product in order to make CDs, sell them, and start repaying, but I could not get the CDs until the master was paid for. I felt completely stuck. The math did not work. The logic fell apart.

But something deeper whispered: "You did not open this door. Trust the one who did."

So, I did. I took a deep breath, and instead of spiraling into fear, I began silently thanking God. Not begging. Not bartering. Just thanking. For the project. For the provision. For the people who would be blessed by it.

I offered up gratitude—not for what I hoped might come, but for what I knew was already working behind the scenes.

Just before we completed the final mix, the studio owner called and invited me to join him and his wife for lunch at their home down the road. My heart raced. I was sure he was going to bring up the cost, and I had no idea what to say. I did not want to go. But I went.

The lunch was warm and gracious. They asked me about my story, about my hopes for the music. And when they asked what I intended to do with the project, I told them the truth: "This music is a piece of my heart. I want it to reach people. I want it to bring peace, hope, healing—whatever they need. I want to use it for good."

They looked at each other and smiled, then stood up and held hands across the table. With tears in their eyes, they said:

"We give this to you in the name of our Lord. Use it for His glory. You do not owe us a penny."

I sat stunned. Speechless. Tears spilled over.

In that moment, I understood something I had only believed in theory before: Gratitude opens gates that hustle never could.

That experience became a living parable for me. Gratitude was the key that unlocked provision I could not see, a currency that paid for what my pockets could not. When I chose to thank God before the answer came— when I aligned with the energy of already receiving—the doors flew open.

Gratitude did not just prepare the way; it became the way. That moment was more than a personal breakthrough. It was a spiritual blueprint: whatever you are facing, whatever you need, meet it first with thanks. The miracle responds to the music of your thankfulness.

Practical Applications
—Activating the Energy of Gratitude

Gratitude is more than a positive attitude—it is a frequency. A divine signal. A sacred practice that tunes your entire being to the vibration of abundance, wholeness, and receiving. When you embody gratitude before the blessing arrives, you become a magnet for divine flow.

These practices are not meant to be complicated. They are meant to rewire your energy field, shift your perception, and open the gates for grace to move. Gratitude, when lived daily, becomes more than a reaction. It becomes the resonance of your spirit.

1. **Start and end with thanks**.
   Before your feet hit the ground, whisper three things you are grateful for. End your day the same way. Make gratitude your bookend.

2. **Gratitude journaling**.
   Commit to writing five things each day. Do not repeat them. Stretch your awareness. Notice the sacred in the simple.

3. **Give thanks before it arrives**.
   Choose something you are calling in—abundance, healing, clarity. Say, "Thank You" as if it is already yours. Speak it. Feel it. Believe it.

4. **Bless what you have**.
   Even what seems small. "I bless this home." "I bless this job." "I bless this breath." Gratitude transforms ownership into stewardship.

5. **Shift in the moment**.
   When fear, worry, or doubt arise, stop and list three blessings aloud. This immediately shifts your vibration from scarcity to receiving.

6. **Gratitude Walks**.
   As you walk, thank life with each step. "Thank you for my feet. Thank you for this sky. Thank you for this breath." Turn movement into meditation.

7. **Teach it to Others**.
   Model gratitude to your children, your friends, and your partner. Invite others to join you. Gratitude magnifies when shared.

Gratitude is not just something you feel after life blesses you—it is the frequency that invites the blessing in. These daily practices are portals, rewiring your energy to receive, recognize, and resonate with abundance before it arrives.

When gratitude becomes your default posture, miracles no longer feel like surprises—they feel like alignment. The more you live in thankfulness, the more life gives you to be thankful for. Let your gratitude not just be a reaction, but your sacred rhythm—an offering, a vibration, a way of walking in constant communion with the divine.

Affirmation

"**I am grateful now. I bless what is and welcome what is becoming. Gratitude is my divine frequency. Abundance flows through me with ease. I receive with joy, I give with love, and I align with the rhythm of sacred receiving.**"

Guided Meditation:
—Receiving Through Gratitude

Breathe gently, and draw your awareness into your chest.

Let each breath soften the space around your heart. With each inhale, feel your spirit expand.

With each exhale, let tension melt away. Now, remember a recent moment that sparked joy—a kind word, a deep breath, a moment of awe. Let it rise gently within you. Feel the warmth of gratitude blooming like light in your chest.

Ok, now, turn your attention toward something you are calling in. See it—not as a hope, but as a reality already forming. Visualize it as though it is complete.

Let the energy of fulfillment surround you. Feel the relief, the peace, the quiet joy of having received. Whisper to yourself, "Thank you. I receive this with grace. I welcome this with joy."

Let that gratitude pour through your body like golden light, radiating through your cells, rippling outward into the room around you.

Conclusion

Gratitude is not the reward at the end of the journey—it is the road that leads you there. It is not the applause after the miracle—it is the song that calls the miracle forth.

When you embody gratitude before anything has arrived, you shift from being a seeker to a receiver. You stop waiting for proof and begin vibrating with faith. You stop pleading and start preparing. Gratitude is not weakness—it is alignment. It does not ignore reality—it reshapes it.

Every moment you choose to give thanks, especially when there seems to be nothing obvious to be thankful for, you are declaring to the universe: I trust. I believe. I am open to receive. That declaration changes your energy. And when your energy changes, so does your atmosphere.

This is not just emotional. It is energetic. It is spiritual law.

Gratitude is a magnet because it draws to itself whatever reflects its frequency. A grateful heart creates space for more. It expands your capacity. It speaks a language that blessing understands.

You do not need to see the finish line to celebrate. You do not need the harvest in hand to bless the soil. You just need to speak from faith instead of fear. You just need to thank your way forward.

What you appreciate—appreciates.
What you honor—expands.
And what you give thanks for, even in the unseen, begins to move toward you with divine timing.

So today, do not just wait for a reason to be grateful—be the reason. Let gratitude be your atmosphere. Your intention. Your silent prayer and your spoken praise. Let it rise from your breath like incense, invisible but powerful.

Gratitude will never leave you empty. It will multiply what you already have. It will illuminate what you thought was ordinary. It will make room for what your soul has been waiting for.

So, give thanks—not just after the blessing, but before, not just for what is visible, but for what is on its way, and not just for what has happened, but for what is unfolding right now.

Gratitude is not an echo of what has been—it is the vibration that calls forth what is yet to come.

Chapter 9: The Law of Alignment
—Becoming a Match for What You Desire

Opening Reflection

"When you want something, the universe conspires to deliver it. But it is not your wanting that unlocks the flow—it is your alignment. When your heart, mind, and energy say yes in harmony, manifestation becomes motion."
—Roy Waugh, Inspired by Paulo Coelho's The Alchemist.

Introduction

Manifestation does not respond to pressure—it responds to resonance.
You do not have to chase what is meant for you. You do not have to scream to be heard by the Divine. What you desire is already reaching for you—it is just waiting for you to match its vibration.

This is the law of alignment: you receive not what you want, but what you are in harmony with.

Desire alone is not enough. Visualization alone is not enough. Faith without embodiment is like tuning the dial but never turning the volume up. The real question is not just "What do I want?"—but "Who am I becoming to match that desire?"

Alignment means your thoughts, emotions, actions, and energy all say yes. It is when your inner world becomes a mirror of what your outer world is trying to manifest.

In this chapter, we will explore how aligning yourself with what you seek is the sacred missing link in most manifestation practices—and how you can enter vibrational agreement with the future that is already calling your name.

Hidden Teachings from Ancient Traditions
—Spiritual Alignment—Becoming a Vessel for Divine Flow

Across every sacred tradition, we find the same divine pattern: what appears in your life first begins within your spirit. Whether called surrender, obedience, mindfulness, or dharma, the principle is clear: true manifestation flows from alignment. Not just alignment of action, but of heart, intention, and energy.

When inner harmony is reached, outer change begins. These traditions did not just teach about aligning with God—they taught how to become a vessel through which divine power could move freely.

✧ Christian Faith

In Christianity, alignment is often described as walking in the Spirit—living in harmony with divine purpose rather than the pull of the flesh. Paul writes, **"Since we live by the Spirit, let us keep in step with the Spirit"** (Galatians 5:25, NIV). This imagery is not passive—it is rhythmic, calling the believer to match their steps with God's.

Jesus modeled perfect alignment: rising early to pray, withdrawing to quiet places, and acting from divine timing rather than human pressure. He often said, "My time has not yet come" (John 2:4), reminding us that manifestation is not just about what we want—but about becoming ready to hold it. In this faith, alignment is about surrender, obedience, and being led—not driven.

✧ Jewish Wisdom

Jewish tradition views alignment as wholehearted devotion—where every layer of being is united in love for the Divine. The Shema declares, **"You shall love the Lord your God with all your heart, with all your soul, and with all your might"** (Deuteronomy 6:5, Tanakh). This is not compartmentalized faith—it is embodied integrity.

The Talmud teaches, "**Words that come from the heart enter the heart**" (Berakhot 6b), reflecting the power of sincere alignment between speech and spirit. In Jewish mysticism, alignment is found in kavannah—spiritual intention. Without it, rituals become empty. But with it, even ordinary acts can become sacred channels of divine flow.

✧ Islamic Teaching

The entire concept of Islam means *"surrender,"* pointing directly to alignment with divine will. The Qur'an instructs, "**And establish prayer and give zakat and obey the Messenger—so that you may receive mercy**" (Qur'an 24:56, Sahih International). Each practice—prayer, charity, fasting—is not only a ritual but a tool for harmonizing the self with God.

The Prophet Muhammad (peace be upon him) said, "**There is a piece of flesh in the body—if it is sound, the whole body is sound... it is the heart**" (Sahih al-Bukhari 52). Alignment, in Islam, begins in the heart. It is an inner purity that overflows into action. In Sufism, alignment is called fana—the annihilation of the ego so that only divine will remains.

When heart, tongue, and deed align with the Divine, manifestation becomes movement within sacred flow.

✧ Buddhist Practices

Buddhism teaches that suffering arises when the inner self is out of alignment with truth. The Eightfold Path offers a framework for realignment—through Right View, Right Thought, Right Action, and more. "**We are what we think. All that we are arises with our thoughts**" (Dhammapada 1:1).

Mindfulness practice brings the scattered mind into unity with the breath, the body, and the present moment. In this stillness, the self begins to align with clarity, compassion, and truth. Metta (loving-kindness) meditation does not just change how we feel—it alters the vibration we carry into the world. When intention, attention, and action are unified, suffering lessens, and freedom rises.

✧ Hindu Traditions

In Hinduism, alignment is called dharma—one's sacred path and inner truth. As the Bhagavad Gita teaches, **"It is better to live your own dharma imperfectly than to live another's perfectly"** (Bhagavad Gita 3:35). This powerful verse calls us not to imitation, but to integrity.

Yoga is not merely physical—it is union. Karma yoga (selfless action), bhakti yoga (devotion), and jnana yoga (wisdom) are all paths to aligning the self with divine essence. In this tradition, alignment is less about trying and more about remembering. You are already one with the Divine —your work is to clear what blocks that truth.

When inner and outer life reflect the same sacred rhythm, the universe does not resist—it responds.

Alignment is the sacred permission slip for manifestation.

When your thoughts, actions, beliefs, and emotions all say yes to what your soul already knows, the universe echoes that yes. Across every lineage, the truth is revealed again and again: alignment is not perfection —it is coherence. It is the silent chord struck in the soul that tells the world, "I am ready." And in that readiness, everything begins to move.

Wisdom from Contemporary Spiritual Leaders

Every generation has its messengers—those who carry ancient truths in modern tongues. These leaders speak from lived experience, blending spiritual insight with practical wisdom. Their words are not just teachings; they are invitations. Invitations to align, to awaken, to embody what you say you believe.

In the sacred rhythm of alignment, these voices echo what the sages have always known: You become what you are in harmony with.

—Abraham Hicks teaches, "**You cannot have what you are not willing to become**." If you are longing for something—whether it is love, wealth, peace, or purpose—start by checking your vibration. Are you radiating the energy of what you are asking for, or are you resonating with the absence of it? Alignment is not a wish—it is a frequency shift.

—Iyanla Vanzant often says, "**You must master you, before you can master manifestation**." The first law of alignment is self-honesty. Before you try to change your world, take a look in the mirror. Are your thoughts congruent with your desires? Is your energy rehearsing victory or sabotage? Master yourself, and the rest begins to move.

—Dr. Joe Dispenza explains, "**When your thoughts and feelings are out of sync, you send mixed signals to the universe**." Your body does not know whether to brace for fear or celebrate the future. Manifestation responds to your dominant vibration. When your mind, heart, and body agree, life follows suit.

—Maya Angelou once said, "**When you know better, do better**." But the deeper lesson is in the doing. You do not shift your life by collecting wisdom—you shift it by applying it. When your knowledge turns into daily choices, alignment happens. And with alignment comes movement. Growth. Manifestation.

—Roy Waugh: "**You can't manifest what your mouth says yes to if your spirit keeps whispering no. Alignment isn't performance— it's permission**." Too often, we chase dreams that were never ours or accept roles that no longer fit. Just because something looks right on paper does not mean it is right in your spirit. When you stop forcing and start listening—when your energy, your actions, and your truth all say yes —that's when manifestation flows like breath.

These quotes and teachings remind us that alignment is not a destination —it is a daily devotion. You do not get there by striving—you get there by syncing. The power you seek is not waiting outside you. It is activated the moment you remember who you truly are and dare to live from that frequency.

Scientific Perspectives on Alignment and Coherence
—Sacred Symmetry—The Measurable Power of Inner Agreement

Alignment is not just a spiritual idea—it has a foundation in science. What spiritual teachers have known for centuries, modern researchers are beginning to confirm: when your thoughts, emotions, and physiology are in harmony, your external world begins to reflect that inner coherence.

✧ Neuroscience and Alignment

Neuroscientists have found that the brain is constantly interpreting internal and external stimuli to create a sense of reality. Dr. Joe Dispenza's work emphasizes that when we repeatedly think and feel in alignment with a desired outcome, we rewire the brain to expect it.

Through neuroplasticity, the brain begins to fire as if the future we envision is already real. When thought and emotion are congruent—when you not only think abundance but feel abundant—you shift from a state of separation to a state of unity. The mind and body begin to act as one.

✧ Heart-Brain Coherence

The HeartMath Institute has done groundbreaking work on what they call "heart-brain coherence." When we enter a state of gratitude, compassion, or peace, the heart begins to beat in a more ordered, rhythmic pattern.

This, in turn, signals the brain to enter a state of coherence. In this state, the nervous system calms, cortisol levels drop, and the body becomes more efficient at healing and processing information. More importantly, we become energetically aligned—resonating with clarity, peace, and higher-order thinking. This alignment is not theoretical—it is measurable.

✧ Epigenetics and Internal Agreement

Epigenetics explores how our thoughts and environment can influence gene expression. Researchers like Dr. Bruce Lipton have shown that genes are not static blueprints. They respond to the biochemical signals sent by our emotions and beliefs. In other words, if your internal world is out of alignment—if you are thinking positively but feeling afraid—your biology registers the conflict. But when you experience internal harmony, your genes are more likely to express health, vitality, and resilience.

This reveals a profound truth: alignment does not just shape your circumstances—it shapes your cells.

✧ Psychophysiology of Resonance

The study of psychophysiology has revealed that humans operate like tuning forks. We are constantly resonating with the energy around us and the signals within us.

When your thoughts, breath, posture, emotions, and intentions are unified, your entire being emits a coherent frequency. Others feel it. Opportunities respond to it. You become magnetic not because of effort, but because of harmony. And when dissonance occurs—when parts of you are misaligned—your frequency scatters, and so does your focus and manifestation potential.

The science affirms what the soul has always known: coherence is power. Alignment is not just a spiritual nicety—it is a biological, neurological, and energetic truth. When your mind, body, and spirit move as one, the universe does not just hear you—it harmonizes with you.

Personal Story
—The Offer I Had to Turn Down

A few years ago, I was invited to help develop, write, and potentially host a new television show. The concept was fresh and engaging—a single expert managing all the details for overwhelmed brides as they planned their weddings. It combined logistics, creativity, design, and emotion into one beautifully orchestrated event. On paper, it was perfect for me. I had officiated weddings as a minister. I had done pre-marital counseling, created floral arrangements, baked wedding cakes, sewn gowns, done hair and makeup, and managed large-scale productions from start to finish. My skillset did not just match—it mirrored the role entirely.

Everyone around me agreed: "You were made for this." And for a moment, I believed it too.

So, I said yes.

The production team was excited. I began sketching out treatments and branding ideas. Late nights were filled with outlines and strategy meetings. Everything on the outside looked aligned. But inside?
Something was off.

It was not fear or doubt. It was a quiet ache—a dissonance I could not explain. The truth was, I was not doing it from a place of soul resonance. I was doing it because it looked like favor. Because it sounded impressive and because it seemed like the "next big step."

But my spirit knew better. The energy did not match. I began dreading phone calls. I sat in meetings nodding politely while feeling disconnected from my own voice. I was not just tired—I was misaligned.

Then came the moment.

After one particular meeting, I drove home in silence—no music, no phone, just the hum of my breath and a knowing in my chest. I pulled into my garage, turned off the engine, and sat in stillness. And then, with no prompting, no performance, I whispered out loud: "This doesn't feel right."

It was not dramatic or emotional. It was just—honest.

That moment became a spiritual turning point. I realized I had been chasing a manifestation that did not match my inner truth. I had said yes with my resume, but no with my spirit. I was not afraid of the opportunity —I just was not aligned with it.

So, I let it go.

The title, the exposure, and the affirmation. Not because I was shrinking, but because I was finally choosing to expand—into alignment.

I had to ask myself the deeper question: Does this match who I truly am now, or just who I have been trying to prove I still need to be?

And that is when everything changed.

I understood something sacred: Just because something aligns with your talents does not mean it aligns with your truth. And just because you are qualified does not mean you are called.

Alignment is not about chasing every open door—it is about discerning which ones carry your frequency. It is about moving but not with force, with faith. And when the yes in your spirit and soul matches the yes in your life, that's when true manifestation flows—not from effort, but from ease.

That day, I did not just turn down a role. I turned toward resonance.
And if any part of you is whispering no—listen. That whisper may be the only honest voice in the room.

Practical Applications
—Becoming a Match

Alignment is not a single moment—it is a sacred rhythm. A lived expression of who you are becoming. It is how you walk, speak, and believe—even in unseen places.

These practices are not about performance; they are about inner resonance. When your thoughts, emotions, and actions all hum in agreement with your desire, manifestation becomes less of a mystery and more of a natural unfolding.

You are not chasing after something—you are manifesting.

1. **Define your desired identity**.
    Ask: "Who do I need to become to receive this?" If you want peace, are your thoughts peaceful? If you want success, are your habits aligned?

2. **Check for internal conflicts**.
    Do you say you want love but fear vulnerability? Want abundance but carry guilt about money? Identify and shift the contradictions.

3. **Move as if**.
    Do not wait to become aligned—practice it now. Walk, speak, and show up as the version of you who already has it.

4. **Elevate your environment**.
    Your space reflects your standards. If you are manifesting expansion, make room for it—spiritually and physically.

5. **Embody the energy**.
    Feel now what you expect to feel then. If you want joy, find ways to live joyfully now. If you want confidence, practice it now.

6. **Speak only what aligns**.
    Your words shape your vibration. Speak from faith, not fear. Speak the outcome, not the obstacle.

7. **Meditate and recalibrate**.
    When you are out of alignment, do not judge. Pause. Breathe. Return. Meditation is your alignment tool.

You are not simply manifesting goals—you are embodying your soul's agreement. Every small choice, every new thought, every aligned action is a note in the frequency you are transmitting to the universe.

As you practice these applications, remember: you are not striving to become someone else—you are remembering who you truly are. And when that remembrance becomes your rhythm, your reality will rise to meet it.

Affirmation

"I am aligned with my highest vision. My thoughts, emotions, actions, and energy are in perfect harmony with what I am creating."

Guided Meditation
—Tuning the Frequency of Me

Sit still. Breathe deeply.

Visualize yourself as a tuning fork. With each breath, bring your thoughts into focus—aligned with love.

With the next breath, align your emotions—breathe in peace.

Now, see your body relaxed and your posture confident.

Say inwardly: "I am ready. I am in harmony. I am aligned." Feel the vibration of your entire being, tuning into the frequency of your desired life.

You are the channel. You are the receiver. You are the match.

Conclusion

Alignment is not a luxury reserved for the spiritually elite—it is the sacred, everyday practice of bringing every part of you into agreement with what your soul knows to be true.

It is where manifestation shifts from striving to surrender and from performance to presence. When you become the frequency of your desire, the life you are calling in can finally recognize your signal.

So many people ask, "Why hasn't it happened yet?" And often, the answer is gentle, but honest: "Because the version of you that is asking—is not yet resonating with what you are asking for."

This is not a delay as punishment—it is a delay as preparation. The Divine is not withholding from you; it is waiting for your full alignment. Waiting for your thoughts to echo your prayers and for your daily habits to echo your highest vision. For your emotional energy to carry the same charge as your spoken affirmations.

We do not manifest what we wish for—we manifest what we are ready to sustain. Alignment means your outer life is anchored in the architecture of your inner wholeness. It means checking in with your soul before checking another box. It means becoming still enough to hear when your yes is real—and when it is not. There is no true manifestation without integrity and no lasting magnetism without coherence.

When your energy sends mixed messages, the field reflects confusion.
But when every part of you—mind, body, voice, and spirit—sings in harmony with your truth, the frequency becomes undeniable. Doors open. Timing aligns. The unseen begins to form in your favor.

Alignment is not about perfection—it is about participation. Not in the performance of spirituality but in surrendering to it. Not in getting everything right, but in becoming the person who no longer needs to prove their worth.

Let this be the day your energy, intention, and soul say yes—together. Not just with your words, but with your walk. Because what you are meant to manifest is not waiting for your effort.
It is waiting for your resonance.

And when your whole being rings with yes, creation responds in kind.

Chapter 10: Trusting Divine Timing
—Manifestation in the Waiting

Opening Reflection

"For I know the plans I have for you," declares the Lord, "plans to prosper you and not to harm you, plans to give you a future and a hope."
—Jeremiah 29:11

Introduction

Divine timing rarely looks divine while you are in it.

It can feel like silence. Like delay. Like the door that never opens. But when you begin to tune your inner frequency to the sacred rhythm of who you are becoming, you realize that delay is not denial—it is design.

Manifestation is not always instant. And it is not meant to be. The waiting is part of the weaving. It refines your readiness and strengthens your surrender. In the unseen space between your desire and its arrival, something holy is happening.

God is not withholding. God is aligning. The timing you resist is often the protection you needed.

To trust divine timing is to stop fighting the flow. To believe that the manifestation frequency is more powerful than the pressure of a deadline. When you live from that space—of inner alignment and sacred trust—you no longer chase manifestations. You magnetize them.

In this chapter, we learn how to rest in the rhythm of divine timing, where every pause carries purpose.

Hidden Teachings from Ancient Traditions
—The Rhythm of Right Timing—Trusting the Sacred Unfolding

Every spiritual path teaches it in one way or another: that there is a divine unfolding at work—one we cannot rush, delay, or bypass. Across continents and centuries, ancient wisdom reminds us that everything happens not on our schedule, but on sacred time.

Whether we call it surrender, mo'ed, tawakkul, karma, or trust, the invitation is the same: to stop forcing and start flowing. The divine clock is not ticking against you. It is ticking for you. Let us return to the timeless truth these traditions have preserved.

✧ Christian Faith

In Christianity, divine timing is woven into every miracle. The story of Lazarus being raised from the dead reveals a powerful principle—Jesus deliberately waited. Not because He lacked power, but because the timing would unveil a greater glory. As scripture says, "**He has made everything beautiful in its time**." (Ecclesiastes 3:11, NIV)

Over and over again, the Bible affirms that God moves precisely—never too early, never too late. To "*wait on the Lord*" is not a passive stance—it is a spiritual readiness. Isaiah 40:31 says, "**They that wait upon the Lord shall renew their strength**." Waiting becomes a sacred act—an inner alignment with divine orchestration.

✧ Jewish Wisdom

In Judaism, time itself is holy. The Hebrew word mo'ed means "*appointed time*," and it forms the foundation of the entire Jewish calendar. From Sabbaths to festivals, nothing is scheduled by convenience —only by divine rhythm.

The psalmist writes, "**My times are in Your hands**." (Psalm 31:15, Tanakh) This is not resignation—it is reverence.

In the Talmud, the rabbis caution that blessings received too early can become burdens.

The Sabbath is perhaps the greatest example of spiritual timing in practice—a day set apart not by productivity, but by trust. When we honor time as sacred, we begin to walk in step with something higher than our plans.

✧ Islamic Teaching

In Islam, trust in divine timing is central to faith. The Qur'an says, **"For every nation is a [specified] term. So, when their time has come, they will not remain behind an hour, nor will they precede [it]."** (Qur'an 10:61–62, Sahih International) This teaching affirms that everything unfolds at its destined moment. The concept of tawakkul—complete trust in Allah—guides the believer to act with faith, but release attachment to outcome.

The Prophet Muhammad (peace be upon him) reminded his followers that even when results are delayed, it may be God's mercy at work. In Islam, the timing of manifestation is never accidental—it is precise, purposeful, and always in your favor.

✧ Buddhist Practices

Buddhism teaches that urgency is often rooted in illusion. Enlightenment cannot be forced—it arises in presence. **"A fool is not known by the moment of speaking, but time reveals the wise."** (Dhammapada 5:2) This verse echoes the principle that truth, growth, and insight all have their own pace.

The lotus blooms in its season—not because of pressure, but because of alignment.

Buddhist meditation cultivates stillness so we can hear the timing of our own becoming. When we stop clinging to control, we begin to move with the current of life—and discover that the universe was never in a rush.

✦ Hindu Traditions

In Hinduism, time (kāla) is seen as divine in itself. Lord Krishna proclaims, **"I am Time, the great destroyer of the worlds."** (Bhagavad Gita 11:32) This awe-inspiring statement reminds us that time is not just a backdrop—it is a force of sacred transformation.

The law of karma works not only through cause and effect, but through timing. What you plant today may bloom lifetimes from now. The practice of vairāgya—spiritual detachment—is a conscious release of timing to the Divine. When you act from truth and let go of outcome, you step into harmony with the greater flow.

These ancient voices agree: You were never meant to push your way into purpose. You were meant to trust the unfolding. When your soul is ready, what you have asked for will not be delayed. It will arrive with precision, with grace, and right on time.

Wisdom from Contemporary Spiritual Leaders

There comes a point on every spiritual journey where belief must become patience, and patience must become peace. That point is called divine timing. It is the sacred space between asking and receiving, sowing and harvest, vision, and fulfillment. While the ego wants proof, the soul is learning to trust the process.

The following teachers each remind us in their own way that delay is not denial—it is often divine choreography. Timing, when guided by Spirit, is never random. It is refinement. It is rhythm. And the waiting season is not wasted—it is where faith is forged.

—Joyce Meyer says, **"God is never late, but He's also rarely early. He is always right on time."** She teaches that trust in timing is a form of spiritual maturity—learning to wait with expectation, not anxiety.

—Rhonda Byrne writes in The Power that trusting the process is part of allowing. "**When you believe, you know. You are calm, you are at peace**." That energy draws things in faster than frantic effort.

—Eckhart Tolle reminds us that resistance to the present moment creates suffering. "**Realize deeply that the present moment is all you ever have**." The more you dwell in presence, the more gracefully you align with divine timing.

—Iyanla Vanzant teaches that "**Everything that happens is exactly what needs to happen to bring us into the next moment of our evolution**." Trust is not always comfortable—but it is always holy.

—Roy Waugh: "**Trust that God knows what He is doing. He sees the whole map—we are just staring at the next hill. What feels like a detour to us is often perfect direction from above**." From our limited view, delays can feel like obstacles. But from God's vantage point, they are assisting you in alignment. The Almighty sees what is coming long before we do.

The sacred art of surrender is not passive—it is powerful. When you learn to walk in rhythm with divine timing, you no longer chase what is meant for you. You prepare for it. You vibrate with it. You trust that every pause has purpose, every delay holds direction, and that what is yours will arrive not a moment too soon or too late—but exactly when your spirit is ready to hold it.

Scientific Perspectives on Timing, the Brain, and Trust

—Sacred Delay—The Brain, the Field, and the Frequency of Trust

Trusting divine timing may sound like a spiritual concept, but neuroscience and quantum theory suggest it is more than just faith—it is frequency. Modern science reveals that the human brain is wired to seek certainty and immediate outcomes, yet paradoxically, it is in the pause— in the waiting—that the deepest rewiring and transformation take place.

What we call "waiting" is often the hidden space where alignment happens at a cellular and energetic level. Let us explore what science has to say about surrendering to the rhythm of when.

✧ The Neuroscience of Delay and Reward

The prefrontal cortex—the region of the brain responsible for decision-making and long-term planning—plays a central role in how we experience time and anticipate outcomes.

Studies show that when we learn to delay gratification, we strengthen neural pathways related to self-regulation, resilience, and emotional maturity.

The famous "marshmallow experiment" revealed that children who could wait for a second marshmallow tended to have higher success rates in various areas of life later on.

But here is the deeper truth: waiting is not just a psychological discipline —it changes the architecture of your brain. When you learn to trust timing instead of resisting it, you reduce anxiety, increase clarity, and create space for divine flow.

✧ Quantum Possibility and Divine Delay

Quantum physics has shown us that time is not linear—it is vibrational. Possibilities exist in superposition until observed or aligned with. This means that what we perceive as delay may not be a denial but an unfolding. Energy must match. The observer effect in quantum mechanics suggests that what we focus on influences the outcome.

If we observe our life through the lens of lack or fear, we collapse the potential into anxiety. But when we trust, stay present, and align with peace, we collapse time around us in favor of flow. In other words, faith alters the field.

✧ Chronobiology and Rhythmic Alignment

Chronobiology is the study of biological rhythms. Just like the Earth has cycles of day and night, our bodies and cells are governed by circadian rhythms. Disruption of these natural patterns leads to dis-ease. Trusting divine timing is not just spiritual—it is biological. When we live in harmony with nature's timing, our bodies heal better, our minds function more clearly, and our emotions stabilize. Trusting the rhythm of life means stepping out of urgency and back into coherence.

The wisdom of science reminds us that surrendering to divine timing is not weakness—it is intelligent alignment. Your brain is not your enemy in waiting—it is being trained to hold more peace. Your cells are not being punished—they are syncing with something higher. And your energy is not stagnant—it is tuning to the exact vibration of your answered prayer. The delay is not a void—it is the womb of manifestation.

Personal Story
—The Mailbox Miracle

I remember a moment in my life when trusting divine timing taught me more than any sermon, any lecture, or any book ever could.

I was in college—a private Christian university—with a deadline looming over me like a storm cloud. I was short on tuition; two thousand dollars short. The kind of "short" that does not bend. No grace period. No payment plan. No polite conversation. Just a firm and final: You are out.

I had exactly $100 left in my pocket and only enough in my bank account to keep it open (which was about $5.00). And I was holding onto it like a life preserver. It was all I had—for food, for gas, for survival. Every part of me said, "Keep it." But in the quiet hush of prayer, I felt something unexpected rise up inside me. A nudge. A whisper. A strange, holy instruction: *Give it away.*

I wrestled with it. I reasoned with it. But the feeling only grew stronger. Later that night, I had a dream.

In it, I saw a house—one I recognized immediately. It was near campus. I had once considered renting it before deciding to stay in student housing. In the dream, I saw myself walking to it in the dark and placing something inside its mailbox.

When I woke up around 2:00 a.m., the dream was still vivid, and the pull on my heart was unmistakable. I did not ask questions, I just moved.

I slipped on my shoes, snuck out of my dorm (because we were not allowed out after 10:00 p.m.), took that last $100 in my wallet, and walked through the quiet streets toward the house I had seen.

It looked exactly as it did in the dream. I stood there in the dark, unsure if anyone even lived there. It felt empty, still, and silent. And yet—something in me knew I was supposed to be there.

So, with trembling hands and a strange sense of peace, I slipped the $100 into the mailbox. No name. No note. Just trust.

I walked back to campus with empty pockets but a strangely full heart. I did not know why. I just knew it was right.

About a week later, I went to a campus meet-up. The room was buzzing—students laughing, telling stories, connecting.

Then a young couple stood up—holding a newborn in their arms. They said they had just moved into a house near campus. The husband had gotten a job, but his car broke down right before his first day. They used the last of their money to get it fixed. They explained the baby needed diapers and formula and they had no local family, no backup to help them.

So, they did the only thing they could: they prayed.

And the next morning, they found $100 in their mailbox.

I froze.

The blood left my face. I had chills from head to toe. I knew that house, I knew that mailbox, and I knew that $100. I stood there in silence.

Their answered prayer was my act of obedience. I was Gobsmacked.

But God was not finished.

A few days later, I got a message from my bank. One of the tellers I had become friendly with asked me to come in. When I arrived, she handed me a check, upside down—ready to be deposited into my account. The only condition? I could not know who sent it. I just had to sign the back.

The amount? (Drumroll) Exactly $2,000. Not a penny more. Not a penny less.

That was divine timing, divine alignment, and divine mathematics.

It taught me something I will never forget: *When you let go in faith, you do not lose anything—you make room.*

When you give from alignment, heaven meets you in the place of your release. And what you thought was the end, becomes the doorway to your miracle.

Practical Applications
—Living in Trust

Trusting divine timing does not mean doing nothing. It means doing the right things—internally and energetically—while the bigger picture unfolds.

These practices are not about forcing results; they are about preparing your heart, your space, and your frequency for what is already aligning behind the scenes.

When you move through the waiting with intention, you do not just hold on—you rise up. You co-create with God in the stillness between the seed and the bloom. Stop measuring your miracle by days or deadlines. Say: "This or something better, in divine timing."

1. **Release the timeline**.
   Every day, declare: "I trust the process. What is meant for me is finding me now."

2. **Affirm the unseen**.
   Use the waiting to grow, build, organize, and heal. Do not just wait passively—get ready.

3. **Visualize Calmly**.
   Instead of anxious manifesting, sit in peaceful visualization. Smile as if it is done.

4. **Reflect on the past**.
   Think of something that worked out beautifully in hindsight. Let it remind you: things always align.

5. **Speak gratitude for the process**.
   Say, "Thank You" even in uncertainty. It tells the Universe you are already in agreement with the outcome.

Each of these small acts is a sacred agreement with the unseen. They remind your spirit that waiting is not wasting—it is womb time. The manifestation is not being delayed; it is maturing.

Stay faithful. Stay grounded. The divine is never rushed, but never late. What is yours is not passing you by—it is preparing to arrive, right on time.

Affirmation

"I trust divine timing. What is meat for me is already in motion. I am not late. I am right on time, on path, and on purpose."

Guided Meditation
—Sitting in the Sacred Timeline

Breathe deeply.

Imagine yourself sitting beside a stream. You are not rushing the water, you are not controlling the flow; you are present and trusting. Let the current carry what belongs to you.

Whisper inwardly: "Everything I need is finding me. I am aligned. I am at peace." Feel the timing settling into your bones like rest. You are not late. You are in rhythm.

Conclusion

Divine timing is not the absence of movement—it is the presence of precision. It is not a sign that you have been forgotten, but sacred evidence that something greater is being orchestrated on your behalf.

When your timeline does not unfold the way you imagined, the human response is to push, to panic, or to question everything. But manifestation is not measured by speed—it is measured by alignment. And alignment is often revealed in the stillness. In that holy stretch between planting and harvest—where faith is no longer a feeling but a conscious choice.

It takes inner strength to trust what you cannot yet see. And it takes wisdom to hold the vision while releasing the deadline.
But this is the sacred practice: to wait without shrinking, to rest without retreating, to remain open even when you have no evidence—because you know: the Universe is never late.

The Creator wastes nothing. Every pause holds a purpose. Every setback is folded into the setup. What feels slow from your view is unfolding right on time—according to a rhythm greater than your own.

You may not see over the next hill—but the Divine sees the entire map.

You may not understand the wait, but the way is being prepared.

You may feel still—but heaven is in motion.

So, do not confuse quiet with disconnection. And never let waiting distort your worth.

The path is not stagnant—it is sacred. The timing is not off—it is divine. And your readiness is the signal.

So, stay grounded, stay grateful and stay in flow.

When what is meant for you arrives, it will not be rushed, it will not be forced; it will arrive in divine perfection.

And it will feel like it was always meant to be.

Frequency: Activated
—The End of Part I

Well, here we are.

The end of Part I—and the beginning of something else entirely.
If you have made it to this moment, I want you to pause and really take that in. Because this is not just the closing of this section—it is a sacred milestone. A turning point. A spiritual echo reminding you that something in you has already shifted.

Perhaps you do not even realize it.
But your frequency is already changing.

As I told you earlier, you did not find this book by accident.
You were drawn here—by a whisper, a pull, a sacred current running beneath the noise of everyday life. Something in you already knew. And that part of you—the ancient, eternal part—has been remembering more with each page.

This first section wasn't about doing; it was about tuning.
You have been aligning and awakening. You have been peeling back the layers of forgetfulness and stepping into the sacred truth that was never really lost—just hidden beneath the static of striving, shame, or silence.

You have learned that your voice carries divine vibration, your thoughts are frequencies, and faith is not passive—it is a force. That energy does not lie—it creates.

You have been given ancient tools, once protected in scrolls and scriptures of oral traditions:

✧ **How belief initiates creation**

✧ **How words sculpt reality**

✧ **How energy becomes invitation**

✧ **How gratitude becomes magnetism**

✧ **How alignment becomes embodiment**

You have begun to understand that manifestation is not about begging the Universe to bless you—it is about becoming a vibrational match for what is already yours.

And most importantly, YOU have remembered something vital: You are not separate from the Divine; you are made of it.

It speaks through your voice, through your breath, and it echoes in your being.

You are not here to merely hope. You are here to harmonize and to speak, align, and awaken. This is the rhythm of receiving. The melody of faith. The song of co-creation.

Part II will build upon this sacred foundation.

It will take you deeper into the embodiment of these truths—into divine timing, surrendered action, spiritual identity, and the art of living in flow with what you have already called in.

But for now—pause.

Let the frequencies of these first ten chapters settle into your bones.
Let them recalibrate your inner instrument.
Let them become not just something you know—but something you are.

So, take a breath, honor this moment, and when your spirit is ready, turn the page.

The frequency ahead is not a destination—it is an invitation.

Part II — Raising Your Resonance

—Becoming a Vibrational Match for What You Seek

Once your inner frequency is tuned, the next step is expansion.

Part II is where belief becomes behavior, and intention becomes embodiment. It is no longer about simply knowing you are powerful—it is about living as if you are. These chapters guide you into alignment not just in thought, but in action, energy, and emotion.

Here, you will discover how worthiness plays a central role in receiving, how to let go of control and trust the flow, and how to focus your attention like a laser beam toward the life you are calling in.

You will learn how to persist when doubt creeps in, and how to move with divine rhythm rather than forcing outcomes.

Each chapter offers sacred tools to help you embody the version of yourself that your highest manifestation requires.

This section is about vibrational integrity—living in alignment with what you say you believe.

Because when your actions, emotions, and energy all resonate with your vision, that vision becomes inevitable.

This is where manifestation becomes momentum.

Chapter 11: Worthiness
—The Sacred Key to Receiving

Opening Reflection

"You were never meant to beg for what is already in your spiritual inheritance. You were born worthy. The moment you believe it, the gates open."
—Roy Waugh

Introduction

Manifestation is not just about what you want but about what you believe is already yours.

You can visualize every day, speak affirmations, write goals, and remain spiritually consistent—but if, deep down, you do not feel worthy of receiving what you have asked for, you will unknowingly block or delay its arrival.

Worthiness is not a luxury emotion—it is the sacred gatekeeper of manifestation. Without it, blessings may hover around you but never land. With it, even the seemingly impossible finds its way into your life. Not because the universe suddenly decides you are enough—but because you do.

We have been conditioned to believe that worth must be earned through effort, perfection, and performance, that we must strive to deserve peace, and that we must prove ourselves to merit love. Earn our way into abundance or healing. But divine worth is not performance-based. It is presence-based. It is the birthright stamped upon your soul before taking your first breath.

You are not manifesting to become worthy. You are manifesting because you already are.

This chapter is your sacred return. A call to stop begging for what has already been given. To remember your spiritual inheritance and to realign with the truth that worthiness is not a goal to reach—but a state to receive.

Hidden Teachings from Ancient Traditions

—The Sacred Inheritance—Ancient Wisdom on Worthiness and Divine Identity

Across every sacred tradition, we find a divine echo that transcends doctrine: You are not here to earn love—you are here to remember that you are love.

Worthiness is not granted by status, perfection, or performance. It is inscribed in the soul, whispered through scripture, and reflected in ritual. These ancient teachings remind us that spiritual worth is not earned—it is revealed.

Let us return to the sacred truths that affirm who you already are.

✧ Christian Faith

The Christian tradition is rich with declarations of divine worth. "**For we are God's masterpiece. He has created us anew in Christ Jesus, so we can do the good things He planned for us long ago**." (Ephesians 2:10, NLT) You are not an afterthought—you are intentional, designed, and precious.

Romans 8:17 goes even further: "**Now if we are children, then we are heirs—heirs of God and co-heirs with Christ**." Worthiness is not something you strive toward—it is an inheritance you awaken to.

Jesus often healed not based on merit, but on faith. The woman with the issue of blood, considered unclean by society, reached for His garment— and He turned to her and said, "**Daughter, your faith has made you well; go in peace and be healed of your affliction**." (Mark 5:34, NKJV)

He did not question her past. He affirmed her identity. Worthiness, in Christ's teachings, is not about being perfect—it is about knowing you are already seen, already loved, and already worthy.

✧ Jewish Wisdom

In Judaism, every soul carries the Tzelem Elohim—the image of God. You were not made to prove your worth—you were made as a reflection of the Divine.

One of the most beloved teachings comes from Rabbi Zusya, who said on his deathbed: **"In the world to come, they will not ask me, 'Why were you not Moses?' They will ask me, 'Why were you not Zusya?'"** (Rabbi Zusya of Hanipol 1718–1800) The lesson: your worth is in being fully yourself—not a copy, but a creation.

The High Holy Days, especially Yom Kippur, are not about shaming the self, but about teshuvah—returning to your divine nature. The soul is already whole. Already clean. Already worthy. Psalm 139 affirms: **"I praise You because I am fearfully and wonderfully made."** (Psalm 139:14, NIV)

Gratitude for your worthiness is not arrogance—it is alignment.

✧ Islamic Teaching

The Qur'an affirms inherent dignity in all humanity: **"And We have certainly honored the children of Adam..."** (Qur'an 17:70, Sahih International) This karamah—honor—is not conditional. It is a birthright. You carry the divine breath that alone affirms your sacred value.

The mercy of God—rahmah—is described as vast, boundless, and not based on perfection. The Prophet Muhammad (peace be upon him) reminded his followers: **"None of you will enter Paradise solely by your deeds."** (Sahih al-Bukhari 5673; Muslim 2816)

Worthiness, in Islam, is not transactional. It is relational. You are beloved not because you have earned it, but because the Divine loves first.
Practices like dhikr—remembrance—are not ways to become worthy. They are ways to return to the truth that you always have been.

✧ Buddhist Practices

Buddhism teaches that every being possesses Buddha-nature—an inherent potential for awakening. As the Dhammapada says: "**All that we are is the result of what we have thought**." (Verse 1) But underneath thought is the truth: you are already whole.

The practice of metta bhavana—loving-kindness meditation—often begins with this gentle invocation: "**May I be well. May I be happy. May I be at peace**." (Karaniya Metta Sutta, Sutta Nipata 1.8) You do not speak these words to become deserving—you speak them because you already are.

A modern echo of this truth comes from the Udana: "**You yourself, as much as anybody in the entire universe, deserve your love and affection**." (Paraphrased from Udana 5.1, Pali Canon) Worthiness in

Buddhism is not about the ego. It is about remembering the radiance that has always been inside.

✧ Hindu Traditions

In Hindu philosophy, the Atman—the divine self—is never unworthy. It is a spark of Brahman, the eternal Source. Beneath every illusion of brokenness lies your original wholeness.

The Bhagavad Gita says: "**I am seated in the heart of all living beings**." (Bhagavad Gita 15:15) This indwelling presence affirms that worth is not something to be earned. It is something to be remembered.

The path of bhakti yoga—devotion—is not rooted in shame but in sacred relationship. You are not begging to be seen—you are simply showing up in the presence of a God who already sees you.

In darshan, the act of seeing and being seen by the Divine, the soul is mirrored back in love. There is no fixing, no striving, just full acceptance.

You are not too late. You are not too flawed. You are the embodiment of sacred potential. And when you remember this, manifestation is no longer something you chase. It becomes something you receive.

Wisdom from Contemporary Spiritual Leaders

Across generations, spiritual teachers, healers, and transformational voices have returned again and again to the same truth: worthiness is not something you earn—it is something you remember.

The words that follow are not just affirmations; they are reminders. Reminders that you are already enough, you are already equipped, and you are already worthy of the life you are praying for.

These leaders, each in their own way, reveal what happens when you stop trying to prove your value and start living from it. Their wisdom holds the frequency of truth—and when you tune into it, something inside you begins to rise.

—Louise Hay taught that low self-worth was at the root of almost every disease she encountered. Her core message: "**You've been criticizing yourself for years, and it hasn't worked. Try approving of yourself and see what happens.**"

—Iyanla Vanzant says, "**Your willingness to look at your darkness is what empowers you to manifest your light.**" Worthiness is not about perfection. It is about truth.

—Abraham Hicks teaches that resistance to receiving is often based on unworthiness. They say, **"You are worthy because you exist. You don't need to prove or earn—it is your birthright**."

—Denise Woods, vocal coach to stars, emphasizes the power of self-approval. She says, **"Your voice is shaped by your self-perception**." If you believe you are worthy, your sound carries confidence. Your message carries energy.

—Roy Waugh: **"You're not waiting on the blessing—the blessing is waiting on you to remember who you are**." So often, we think we have to strive, earn, or chase in order to receive. But the truth is, what we are asking for is already aligned and available. The gap is not in the timing —it is in our belief. When you stop disqualifying yourself and start showing up as someone who is already worthy, the doors begin to open. Because the moment you believe it, is the moment you are ready to receive it.

These voices remind us that faith without self-worth is like asking without hands open. You are not behind. You are not disqualified. You are already loved, already held, and already chosen. And when you live from that frequency, everything begins to respond.

Scientific Perspectives on Worthiness and Self-Perception

—The Worthiness Frequency—Rewiring the Brain to Receive

Science is beginning to catch up with what spiritual traditions have long known: the way you see yourself changes the way the world responds to you. Worthiness is not just an emotional concept—it has a biological footprint.

Your sense of deservingness, or lack thereof, affects how your brain perceives opportunity, regulates your emotions, and influences your ability to manifest. You are not just thinking your life into being—you are wiring it.

✧ The Neuroscience of Self-Worth

Studies in neuroscience show that self-worth is deeply tied to activity in the prefrontal cortex and limbic system—regions responsible for decision-making, motivation, and emotional regulation.

When you believe you are worthy, your brain is more likely to interpret neutral or ambiguous situations as positive and inviting. This shapes your actions, risk-taking, and openness to possibility. On the other hand, low self-worth activates the brain's threat response, creating patterns of avoidance, self-sabotage, and scarcity thinking

✧ Self-Fulfilling Prophecies and Cognitive Bias

Psychologists have long observed the power of self-fulfilling prophecy: people who believe they are undeserving often unconsciously reinforce that belief by rejecting opportunities or attracting relationships that mirror their inner doubt. This is not just psychological—it is energetic.

Your brain seeks congruence between belief and experience. If you believe you are unworthy, your subconscious filters out evidence that contradicts that narrative. But the opposite is also true: the moment you shift into self-acceptance, your mind begins scanning for alignment with your new identity.

✧ Heart-Brain Coherence and Receptivity

HeartMath Institute research reveals that feelings of appreciation, compassion, and self-love create physiological coherence between the heart and brain. This state enhances intuition, emotional clarity, and energetic receptivity.

When you feel worthy, your internal systems move into harmony. That coherence sends out a measurable electromagnetic field that affects not only your biology, but the environment around you. In this sense, worthiness becomes a frequency—one that literally makes you a match for miracles.

Worthiness is more than a mindset—it is a neurological stance, a vibrational signature, and a physiological rhythm. When you embody the belief that you are worthy, your brain fires differently. Your energy flows differently. Your life opens differently.

The science affirms what the spirit already knows: you do not receive because you have earned it, you receive because you are aligned with it. And the moment you believe you are enough, the universe begins to echo back the same.

Personal Story
—Learning to Receive Love I Did Not Think I Deserved

I did not question whether love existed—I just did not believe it had my name on it, especially not that kind of love.

When I met my partner, now my husband, I felt unworthy almost instantly. Not because of how he treated me—he was kind, open, and gracious. But because of who I believed I was.

He was a respected physician, accomplished, deeply rooted in his culture, and came from a prominent family with a legacy that spanned generations.

He was the baby of eight. His father and grandfather were both lawyers. When his parents were married, they were given bars of gold, jewelry, and elephants. Yes—actual elephants.

And then, there was me.

I was the oldest of six kids. Raised in poverty so deep it shaped my bones.

My parents were so poor they could barely pay attention, let alone pay the bills. I did not grow up asking for toys at Christmas; I asked for socks and underwear. Essentials, most children never even think to lack. But I had none. If it were not for food pantries, we would have gone hungry. Often, we did anyway.

My mother, a woman of quiet strength, was born deaf and trapped in an abusive marriage. My father was addicted to drugs and alcohol, a man drowning in his own unhealed pain. Our home was chaos. Survival was the goal. Tenderness was rare.

So, when someone like him came into my life—gentle, loving, secure—I did not feel lucky. I felt terrified.

Who was I to deserve someone like this?
Who was I to be loved by someone who came from gold and elephants, when I came from secondhand shoes and shame?

What could I possibly offer that was not broken?

I remember lying awake at night, rehearsing all the reasons he would eventually leave: all the things about me that made me "less than." The education I had to fight for. The pain I carried in my voice, and the rooms, I still did not feel worthy of entering.

But what I have learned is this:
The Universe does not gift you something to embarrass you. It brings you what matches the healing you are ready for.

He did not see my lack—he saw my light. He did not look for my pedigree —he felt my presence.

Slowly, I began to see myself through his eyes, the eyes of someone who had come to love me as I was and invited me to love myself the same way.

It was not easy. Worthiness rarely is. But every time I stayed, every time I softened, every time I allowed myself to receive the love I kept thinking I had to earn—I healed a little more.

And I came to understand something sacred:
It is not that I was not worthy of that kind of love. It was that I had never believed I could be worthy of that kind of love.

You are not "unworthy" because of where you come from. You are powerful because of what you have survived.

And love does not ask you to be perfect. It just asks you to show up—fully, and freely—as yourself.
Because worthiness was never the problem.

It was the belief that I had to earn what was already mine.
I was not being tested—I was being invited; invited to simply receive.

Practical Applications
—Living Worthy Now

Realizing your worth is not a one-time revelation—it is a daily practice. It is a choice to show up, to receive, and to remember that you no longer have to beg for what you were born to carry.

The following practices are designed to help you embody that truth, to anchor your energy in worthiness, and to shift your vibration from striving to allowing. Because when you know you are enough, you do not chase—you attract.

1. **Start your day with worthiness**.
   Before checking your phone or rushing into action, pause and say: "I am enough. I am worthy of all that is good."

2. **Question the inner critic**.
   When a voice says, "You can't," or "You're not ready," ask: "Whose voice is that? Is it true?" Replace it with truth.

3. **Stop deferring joy**.
   Do not wait until the goal is reached to feel happy. Worthiness means enjoying now. Celebrate the small. Bless the in-between.

4. **Dress and speak from value**.
   Wear what makes you feel powerful. Speak with the confidence of someone who belongs in the room, because you do.

5. **Receive complements fully**.
   Do not deflect. Do not downplay. Say "Thank you." Let it land. Let it rewire your nervous system.

6. **Treat yourself as sacred space**.
   How would you treat a temple? Clean it. Feed it. Honor it. Speak love into it. Your body and spirit are no less holy.

The more you practice worthiness, the more natural it becomes. What once felt foreign will begin to feel like home. Because you are not becoming someone new—you are returning to who you have always been beneath the doubt, the shame, and the noise.

Let these small sacred actions realign you with that truth. You were not created to shrink or apologize for your light. You were created to receive fully. Freely. Unapologetically. Not someday. Now.

Affirmation

"I am worthy of love, abundance, healing, and joy—not because I have earned it, but because I am. I receive with ease. I allow what is mine."

Guided Meditation
—Returning to Worth

Sit in stillness. Let your breath anchor you.

Imagine your heart glowing softly, pulsing with divine light.

Now hear these words: "You are worthy." Whisper them to yourself. "I am worthy." Let that phrase settle in your bones.

See yourself receiving, not because you hustled—but because you are aligned.

Let the light grow.

Let the worthiness become the energy you carry forward.

Conclusion

Worthiness is not a finish line you cross—it is the sacred truth that has been whispering your name since the beginning. Not something to be earned, but something to be remembered.

For so many of us, the act of receiving feels uncomfortable, even foreign. We have been conditioned to hustle for approval, to strive for belonging, to wear exhaustion like a badge of honor.

So, when grace arrives—when love, favor, or opportunity appears—we hesitate. We question. We wonder: Could this really be for me?

But manifestation does not respond to doubt. It responds to frequency. And worthiness is a frequency.

The life you long for is not waiting for a future version of you to show up. It is waiting for you to return to the truth of who you are beneath the noise: not broken. Not behind. Not too late. Just beloved. Radiant. Ready.

You are not disqualified by your past, you are not defined by your pain, and you are not required to earn what has already been written in your spiritual inheritance.

You are worthy.

Worthy of love, worthy of peace, worthy of joy, worthy of Abundance, and worthy of a life that feels like home.

Manifestation is not about shouting into the universe in desperation—it is about softening into your truth, aligning your energy with Divine remembrance, and making space for the miraculous to land because you no longer push it away.

Let this be your sacred remembering: *You are already enough; you do not have to fix yourself to be chosen, and you are already favored.*
You only have to believe what the Divine has always known: *That you are worthy, you always have been.*

And now, you are finally ready to receive like it.

Chapter 12: The Power of Spoken Words
—Manifesting with the Power of Your Voice

Opening Reflection

"Words mean more than what is set down on paper. It takes the human voice to infuse them with deeper meaning."
—Maya Angelou

Introduction

Maya Angelou reminds us that words don't live on paper alone — they come alive when carried by the human voice. What you speak over your life carries weight. Words are vibrations dressed in syllables. They echo through the atmosphere, imprint the soul, and send ripples into the unseen. Every sentence is more than sound; it is an instruction to your future, a seed carrying the DNA of what will grow.

Think about it: the same voice that can soothe a child to sleep can also ignite nations into action. The words you speak daily — over your health, your finances, your relationships, your dreams — are far from casual. They are currents of energy, either reinforcing what limits you or empowering what frees you. When you declare, "I can't," the universe aligns with that command. When you affirm, "I will," creation begins shifting in your favor.

This chapter is about moving from theory into practice. You have studied the power of thought, belief, and intention — now you will give that power a voice. When thought is unspoken, it remains potential; but when spoken, it becomes motion. Words are how the invisible takes form. They are how spirit bends matter.

The truth is, you are already a creator. With every word, you are painting the canvas of your reality. The only question is: are you painting with colors of fear, doubt, and limitation — or with faith, hope, and possibility? It's time to train your tongue to match your vision, to align your speech with the destiny already written within you. This is not just about being careful with words. It's about being intentional — choosing language that elevates, affirms, and creates.

As we step into this chapter, don't approach it as more information. Approach it as an activation. This is where you begin to embody the truth that your words are not just sounds in the air, but frequencies shaping your world.

Hidden Teachings from Ancient Traditions
—The Sacred Frequency of the Voice — Power to Speak Life into Being

Across every sacred tradition, one truth resounds: speech is not ordinary. The ancients understood what modern thinkers are only rediscovering — that words are forces of creation. They vibrate, they shape, they direct energy. To speak is to activate reality. To declare aloud is to imprint the unseen into form.

Whether whispered in reverence, proclaimed in prayer, or sung in chant, the voice is a sacred instrument of manifestation. The hidden teachings of the ancients remind us that speech is not passive communication — it is divine participation in creation itself.

✧ Christian Faith

In the Christian tradition, words are not merely sounds but spiritual currents with eternal impact. Proverbs teaches, **"The words of the reckless pierce like swords, but the tongue of the wise brings healing."** (Proverbs 12:18, NIV). Words can wound or they can restore, destroy or breathe life.

From the opening of Genesis, God speaks creation into being: **"And God said, 'Let there be light,' and there was light".** (Genesis 1:3). And in the Gospels, Jesus demonstrates this same authority — commanding storms into silence (Mark 4:39), calling Lazarus out of the grave (John 11:43), and healing with a spoken word (Matthew 8:8–13).

Romans affirms that our own voices carry this same creative bridge: **"For it is with your heart that you believe and are justified, and it is**

with your mouth that you profess your faith and are saved." (Romans 10:10). Speech is the point where belief touches reality.

✧ Jewish Wisdom

In Jewish mysticism, words are sparks of divine energy. Kabbalistic teaching holds that the cosmos itself was shaped through the utterance of holy letters. The Tanakh reminds us: "**Whoever guards his mouth and tongue keeps his soul from troubles.**" (Proverbs 21:23, Tanakh).

The Talmud compares words to arrows — once loosed, they cannot be recalled. Jewish tradition warns against lashon hara (the evil tongue), teaching that careless speech fractures spiritual alignment. Yet blessing and prayer create pathways of light. In this path, speech itself is holy stewardship — either a weapon of harm or an instrument of healing.

✧ Islamic Teaching

Islam elevates the spoken word as an act of devotion and manifestation. The very word Qur'an means "recitation," revealing its destiny to be voiced aloud, vibrating through human breath. In Surah Ibrahim, God describes: "**A good word is like a good tree, whose root is firmly fixed and its branches reach to the sky.**" (Qur'an 14:24, Sahih International).

The Prophet Muhammad (peace be upon him) instructed, "**Whoever believes in Allah and the Last Day should speak good or remain silent.**" (Sahih al-Bukhari 6136; Sahih Muslim 47). Through dhikr (remembrance), God's names are repeated in rhythm, attuning heart and tongue to divine frequency. In this tradition, every word becomes a seed planted for eternity — either rooted in light or cast into shadow.

✧ Buddhist Practices

Buddhism regards speech as a sacred discipline. The Eightfold Path teaches Right Speech as a core practice. The Sutta Nipāta counsels:

"Speak only the speech that neither torments self nor does harm to others. That speech is truly well spoken." (Sn 451).

Chanting sutras and mantras is not ritual alone — it is vibrational recalibration. Every syllable aligns the practitioner with clarity, compassion, and awakening. Silence itself is considered powerful — not absence, but presence. When words are spoken from stillness and wisdom, they transform both the speaker and the listener, becoming echoes of enlightenment.

✧ Hindu Traditions

Hinduism teaches that creation was not built but sounded into existence. The sacred syllable Om is regarded as the seed vibration of the universe. The Manusmriti instructs: **"One should utter speech that is truthful, agreeable, and beneficial, and should abstain from speech that causes excitement**." (Manusmriti 4.138).

Speech is even personified in Vak, the goddess of speech, honored as divine power. The Bhagavad Gita declares: **"Speech that is not offensive, is truthful, pleasant, and beneficial, and the regular recitation of the Vedas — these are declared as the austerity of speech**." (Bhagavad Gita 17:15). Mantra and sacred recitation are not performance, but transformation — reshaping consciousness and infusing creation with divine sound.

Across every path — Christian, Jewish, Islamic, Buddhist, Hindu — the message is one: your words are sacred. They are not neutral. They are vibrational currents that design destiny. When you whisper in prayer, speak in faith, or chant in devotion, you are not simply filling the air with sound. You are shaping the atmosphere.

So guard your tongue. Speak with reverence. Declare with faith. Align your voice with love, with truth, and with light. Then watch as the very fabric of reality bends to the frequency you release.

Wisdom from Contemporary Spiritual Leaders

Before modern science caught up with the language of creation, spiritual teachers were already pointing us inward. They reminded us that words are not powerless—they are divine, creative, and encoded with the frequency to shape reality. Across generations, the mystics and mentors of our time have echoed the ancient call: creation begins with belief, intention, and voice.

—Howard Thurman says: **"There is something in every one of you that waits and listens for the sound of the genuine in yourself. It is the only true guide you will ever have."** This reminds us that words without authenticity are empty echoes. The true power of speech is not in eloquence but in genuineness—when what we say rises from the core of who we are. It is the sound of the genuine that carries weight, transforms atmospheres, and awakens others to truth.

—Oprah Winfrey has echoed this power of voice, declaring, **"You have the ability to change somebody's life with your words."** This challenges us to consider the weight of even our smallest conversations. A sentence offered at the right moment can heal, encourage, or redirect the trajectory of another's life. Words are never neutral—they are always planting seeds.

—Iyanla Vanzant speaks directly to this same truth: **"Your words are your wand. They create your reality."** Here we are reminded that words are not mere descriptions of life; they are instruments of creation. With every declaration, you are either aligning with abundance or reinforcing limitation. Your tongue is a tool of transformation.

—Dannion Brinkley affirms: **"Every thought and word is energy. Once released, it continues to exist. Words can heal or harm, uplift or destroy."** His testimony pulls back the veil to show us that language carries eternal consequence. What we release into the world through our speech doesn't vanish—it continues to ripple through lives, shaping outcomes long after the sound has faded.

—Roy Waugh, "**Silence holds potential, but speech activates creation. What you dare to speak, you give permission to exist.**" This is the crossroads of manifestation. Potential rests in quiet possibility, but it is only when the voice dares to call it forth that the unseen becomes seen. Speaking is a sacred act of faith.

Together, these voices form a chorus across time and tradition. They teach us that our words are not filler for silence—they are catalysts for creation. Each sentence we speak either builds or breaks, blesses or diminishes. When we begin to honor the weight of our words, we realize that speech itself is a spiritual practice. And when aligned with love and intention, it becomes one of the greatest forces for transformation we possess.

Scientific Perspectives on Speech and Manifestation
— The Psychology and Neuroscience of Spoken Words

Science has only recently begun to measure what ancient traditions proclaimed centuries ago: words are frequencies that enter the body and shift reality itself. They are not simply sounds; they are signals—coded with the power to instruct the brain, move the heart, and direct the body's energy. Every phrase we utter sparks chemical changes, activates neural networks, and alters perception.

In this way, modern neuroscience and psychology are not breaking new ground but rediscovering what sages and mystics always knew: speech is creation.

✧ Neuroscience: The Brain on Words

Brain imaging studies reveal that negative words activate the amygdala, releasing stress hormones like cortisol that narrow focus and increase fear. In contrast, positive words stimulate the prefrontal cortex, enhancing problem-solving, creativity, and emotional balance.

Neuroscientists Andrew Newberg and Mark Robert Waldman show that compassionate words literally rewire the brain toward resilience and peace.

The brain doesn't just hear your words—it reshapes itself around them.

✧ Psychology: The Self-Fulfilling Power of Speech

In social psychology, the Pygmalion Effect illustrates how expectations spoken aloud can become reality. Rosenthal and Jacobson's famous study showed that when teachers were told certain students had higher potential (though chosen at random), those students excelled—solely because of the words spoken over them.

What you say to others—and to yourself—becomes the soil in which destiny grows.

✧ Health and Medicine: Words as Healing Agents

Psychoneuroimmunology demonstrates that language affects the immune system and healing. James Pennebaker's research found that people who expressed emotions through writing or speaking experienced reduced stress and stronger immune responses.

Spoken prayer, affirmations, and verbal expression act as catalysts for inner healing, sending signals of safety and renewal through the body.

Words are prescriptions you write for your own body—speak wisely.

✧ Quantum Linguistics: Language Shapes Perception

The Sapir-Whorf Hypothesis proposes that language forms the boundaries of thought. Words don't simply describe reality; they shape how we see it. Cultures with multiple words for shades of blue literally perceive those shades differently.

In our lives, reframing "I can't" to "I'm learning" shifts perception, opening space for new outcomes.

Change your words, and the world you see changes with them.

Taken together, these fields—neuroscience, psychology, medicine, and linguistics—converge on a single truth: words matter more than we realize. They don't simply float into the air and vanish. They leave imprints—on our biology, on our relationships, and on our perception of reality itself. Science may frame it in data and experiments, but the wisdom is timeless: to speak is to shape. The real question, then, is not whether words have power—it's whether we will choose to use that power with intention.

Personal Story
—When Words Come Alive

I will never forget the day my grandfather came to one of my early performances. He had been a singer himself—a country musician with a raw, soulful voice—and he knew what it meant to pour yourself into a song. Afterward, he pulled me aside, looked me straight in the eye, and said something that hit me harder than I expected.

He admitted that when I was a little boy, he used to joke that I "probably couldn't carry a tune in a bucket." And then, standing there years later, he shook his head and said, "I was wrong." He told me he could see that I really did have something special. But then he gave me advice I have carried ever since.

He said, "The songs you sing—they're not just notes or words on a page. If all you do is say them, they'll fall flat. But if you feel them, if you let the words live inside you first, then when you open your mouth, people will feel them too. You have to make the people in your audience feel what you're feeling through the words that are coming out of your mouth. Words only matter if you breathe life into them. That's when they carry power—that's when you can move people."

That moment changed me.

I realized my voice was not just about sound—it was about spirit. My grandfather was reminding me that words are more than syllables strung together. They are vessels. They carry emotion. They carry energy. They carry life—or they carry nothing at all.

After that, I could never sing the same way again. Before I stepped on stage, I would take a moment to let the lyrics touch me, to feel them resonate in my own heart before I ever released them into the room. And something shifted. My voice didn't just fill the space—it carried something deeper. People weren't just hearing me; they were feeling me.

Now I know what my grandfather was really teaching me: words don't create impact until they're alive in you. If you don't believe them, if you don't embody them, they won't land. But when you give your words breath, faith, and feeling—they can move mountains.

Practical Applications

—Training Your Voice to Shape Reality

Words are not neutral—they are energetic tools of creation. Every sentence you speak is either planting seeds of possibility or scattering weeds of doubt. This chapter has reminded you that your voice is not simply sound—it is frequency, it is force, it is spiritual fire. But revelation only becomes transformation when you put it into practice.

These exercises are not about performance. They are about presence. About tuning your everyday speech so that your words begin to carry truth, conviction, and creative power. When your voice aligns with your vision, your life begins to echo what you declare.

1. **Speak the outcome, not the obstacle**.
   Instead of "I'm exhausted," say "I'm being renewed." Instead of "I'll never get ahead," say "I am walking into increase." Shift your words to announce the destination, not the detour.

2. **Bless your day aloud**.
   Each morning, declare out loud: "Today is a day of favor, peace, and possibility." Give your day its assignment before it begins.

3. **Feel the frequency**.
   When you speak affirmations, don't just recite—embody them. Let your tone, your breath, your posture carry the truth. Words are only powerful when you feel them first.

4. **Catch and correct**.
   If you hear yourself speaking lack or fear, pause. Say, "Cancel. What I mean is..." Then reframe it. Don't let careless words linger—redirect them on the spot.

5. **Practice the sacred yes and the holy no**.
   Speak "yes" boldly to what ignites your spirit. Speak "no" with grace where boundaries are needed. Every yes and every no becomes a building block for your destiny.

6. **Journal your language.**
   At the end of each day, write down the phrases you repeated most—about money, relationships, or your future. Ask: do these words match the life I want to create? Rewrite them if they don't.

You don't need louder words—you need aligned ones. These practices are not about pretending; they are about planting. Every word is a seed. And when you speak them with clarity, belief, and feeling, they carry the frequency of manifestation.

So begin today. Don't just read about the power of words—live it. The more you honor your voice, the more the universe rises to echo your vibration.

Affirmation

"My words are alive with power. Every sentence I speak plants a future I am ready to live. I align my voice with truth, with love, and with creation—and I call my destiny into being now."

Guided Meditation
—Breathing Life into Words

Close your eyes and take a slow breath. Notice the words you often speak about yourself. Do they lift you—or weigh you down?

Whisper softly: "Cancel." Let the old words dissolve.

Now, speak a new phrase of truth—one filled with hope and possibility. Say it aloud, not flatly, but with feeling. Let it vibrate through your chest, your spirit, your being.

Repeat it once more, stronger this time. Feel it take root inside you.

Place your hand on your heart and affirm: "My words carry life. I speak with power. I speak with love."

Open your eyes knowing—every word you give life to is a seed of creation.

Conclusion

Your words are not background noise. They are front-row builders of your reality. Every sentence you speak is either a seed of destiny or a chain to your past. Too often we speak on autopilot—repeating old wounds, old fears, or careless habits of speech.

But your voice was never meant to echo yesterday. It was meant to create tomorrow.

You don't need to shout to be powerful. You need to be clear. Clear in your intention, clear in your energy, and clear in the truth you are willing to feel and embody.

Yes, we have all spoken words we regret. But here is the grace: your voice is renewable. Redeemable. You can reclaim it today. Because your mouth is not just where language lives—it is where manifestation begins.

So speak words that carry life. Speak the future as if it is listening—because it is. Let your words become invitations instead of limitations. Let them echo faith, not fear. Let them carry feeling, conviction, and clarity.

Stop rehearsing your fear and start declaring your vision. Speak like your life depends on it—because it does.

Your words are not commentary—they are prophecy. They are not just sound—they are blueprints. The moment you stop speaking doubt and start declaring destiny, the atmosphere begins to shift.

Doors open.
Healing rises.
Heaven leans in.

This is your call to action: don't just believe the power of words—live it. Speak your life into being, daily. Because the miracle you've been waiting for may be waiting on the sound of your own voice.

Chapter 13: The Energy of Belief
—Fueling Your Faith for Manifestation

Opening Reflection

"Anything is possible... if you just believe."
—Roy Waugh

Introduction

Belief is the engine of manifestation. But not passive belief—you know, the kind that agrees quietly in theory but hesitates in practice. What moves mountains is activated belief—alive, energetic, rooted in the soul, and radiating through the body. The kind of belief that breathes power into your prayers and clarity into your actions.

This chapter is about the energy of belief—how it works, how it feels, and how it manifests. Not just what you think in your mind, but what you vibrate in your frequency. Your belief sends out a signal—clear or conflicted—and the universe, like a mirror, reflects it back.

Here, we will explore how sacred traditions have long understood belief not just as a thought, but as a force. We will look at what it means to embody belief with your words, emotions, imagination, and action. Because belief is not just about hoping—it is about aligning with what is already true in the spiritual realm.

The universe responds not to what you say you want, but to what you believe is already yours.

Hidden Teachings from Ancient Traditions
—The Engine of the Unseen — How Belief Initiates Manifestation Across Faiths

All across the sacred texts of the world's oldest traditions, belief has never been treated as something passive. It is not just agreement—it is ignition.

A force that initiates movement in the unseen. Whether it is called emunah, iman, shraddhā, or simply faith, belief is honored as the spark that brings divine potential into motion. These ancient teachings still speak, reminding us: what you hold as true within you begins to shape what unfolds around you.

✧ Christian Faith

In the teachings of Jesus, belief was never just theory—it was power. "**If you believe, you will receive whatever you ask for in prayer**." (Matthew 21:22, NIV). That was not said as a suggestion—it was an invitation into alignment with divine reality.

There is a moment in Mark's Gospel when a father pleads for his child's healing. Jesus says, "**Everything is possible for one who believes**," and the father, with raw honesty, cries out, "**I believe; help my unbelief**." (Mark 9:23–24, NIV). That vulnerability did not disqualify him—it moved heaven.

Even Abraham, often called the father of faith, was not flawless—but his belief aligned him with promise. "**Abraham believed God, and it was credited to him as righteousness**." (Romans 4:3, NIV).
In Christian scripture, belief does not whisper—it declares. It moves. It manifests.

✧ Jewish Wisdom

In Jewish teaching, emunah is not just believing that God exists—it is walking with that belief like it is a heartbeat. The Midrash Tanchuma teaches: "**The measure of belief is the measure of blessing**." (Vayishlach 6). That is not about earning favor—it is about expanding your capacity to hold what is already yours.

At the center of Jewish life is the Shema: "**Hear, O Israel: The Lord our God, the Lord is One**." (Deuteronomy 6:4, Tanakh). It is more than a declaration—it is an invitation to return to divine alignment. To gather up every fragmented piece of the self and center it in oneness.

Jewish mysticism holds emunah as one of the highest spiritual virtues. It is not blind. It is rooted in something deeper than logic. It says, *"I don't need to see the blessing to believe it's already in motion."* Belief, here, is not waiting—it is preparing. You are not chasing miracles. You are clearing space to receive them.

✧ Islamic Teachings

In Islam, iman—faith—is the very foundation of life aligned with divine order. It is not just about believing in God—it is about trusting His wisdom, His nearness, and His perfect timing. The Qur'an says: **"Indeed, those who believe and do righteous deeds will have gardens beneath which rivers flow..."** (Surah Al-Baqarah 2:25, Sahih International). Belief here is living—it breathes, it acts, it transforms.

Look at Prophet Ibrahim (Abraham). When thrown into the fire for refusing to deny his faith, he simply said, **"Hasbunallahu wa ni'mal wakeel"**— **"Allah is sufficient for me, and He is the best disposer of affairs**." (Surah Al-Imran 3:173, Sahih International). That is not passive—that has surrendered power.

The Prophet Muhammad (peace be upon him) taught: **"Call upon God while being certain of being answered."** (Tirmidhi 3479). Faith, in this tradition, is certainty wrapped in reverence. You do not beg—you believe. And that belief carries vibration. It moves through every prayer, every breath, every moment of surrender.

✧ Buddhist Practices

In Buddhism, belief—called saddhā—is not about clinging. It is about clarity. It is the confidence to walk even when the path ahead is foggy. It is not blind—it is deeply rooted in lived experience.

The Dhammapada opens with this teaching: **"All that we are is the result of what we have thought. The mind is everything. What we think, we become."** (Dhammapada 1:1). Belief here is creative. It is not an idea—it is a vibration that shapes reality. In stillness, in silence, in every return to breath, belief takes form, not through striving, but through presence.

Buddhist mindfulness practice does not require proof to believe—it requires practice. Each breath is an act of sacred trust. Belief, in this tradition, is not loud. It is steady. It does not push—it aligns.

✧ Hindu Traditions

In Hinduism, belief is a sacred current. It is not abstract—it is energy. The Rig Veda says, "**In the beginning was Brahman. With Him was the Word. And the Word was Brahman.**" (Rig Veda 10.114.8). That Word—Vak—is speech, sound, vibration. And in Hindu tradition, that sound is sacred. It creates.

The Bhagavad Gita teaches: "**Austerity of speech consists in speaking truthfully and beneficially and in avoiding speech that offends.**" (Bhagavad Gita 17:15, ESV). Belief is not separate from speech—it moves through it. In this tradition, to chant a mantra is to align yourself with the structure of the universe.

And shraddhā, or faith-filled devotion, is not about effort—it is about resonance. Through mantra, through prayer, through the honoring of divine rhythm, belief becomes something you vibrate, not just something you think.

Across these faiths, one unified insight remains: belief is not passive. It is participatory. It initiates. It aligns you with what is already seeking to be born through you. The scriptures do not call belief a theory—they call it a seed. One that holds the frequency of the future inside it. When you believe—not out of fear, but out of truth—you do not force your future. You activate it.

You are not waiting for proof. You are becoming the proof.
And belief is the frequency that starts it all.

Wisdom from Contemporary Spiritual Leaders

Belief is not just an inner feeling—it is a force that takes shape through repetition, conviction, and voice. Across time and culture, spiritual teachers have echoed this sacred truth: what you believe is not separate from what you receive. Belief is the energetic blueprint from which your future is drawn. And when belief is spoken—when it becomes language, declaration, mantra, or affirmation—it activates a frequency that reshapes reality.

In this section, we gather voices from modern spiritual guides whose lives and teachings affirm one shared revelation: your belief, when expressed, becomes a bridge between the invisible and the inevitable.

—Dr. Joe Dispenza teaches that your belief system is the software running your life. "**To change your life, you have to change your beliefs**." He shows how belief impacts the brain, the body, and the quantum field.

—Abraham Hicks says: "**A belief is just a thought you keep thinking**." The more you repeat it, the more it becomes your energetic baseline.

—Iyanla Vanzant encourages radical self-belief. "**The only thing keeping you from your next level is what you believe you can't have**." When you shift your belief, your entire vibration changes.

—Louise Hay often reminded readers: "**I am open and receptive to all the good and abundance in the Universe**." She taught belief as energy—not a wish, but a welcome mat.

—Maya Angelou lived her belief out loud. "**I believed I could speak truth and that it would matter. And so, I did**." She didn't just believe—she embodied belief as action, giving voice to truth with unwavering conviction.

—Roy Waugh: "**Your voice does not just describe your life—it designs it**." The truth is, it is about realizing that your words are not passive—they are creative. Most people use their voice to report what they see. "I am tired. I am stuck. I never get a break." And they wonder why nothing changes. But when you shift from describing your life to designing it with intention—something happens. You stop narrating lack, and you start declaring overflow. You stop repeating fear, and you start reinforcing faith. Your voice becomes a tool, not just a trait.

The words you speak shape the frequency you live in. And the frequency you live in? That is what calls your future forward. So, speak what you want to build. Speak what you want to walk into. Speak from where you are headed—not where you have been. Because your voice is not just telling your story—it is writing the next chapter.

Scientific Perspectives on Belief and Energy
—From Thought to Form — Scientific Proof That Belief Creates Reality

Modern science continues to unveil what the ancients already knew: belief is not a passive internal state—it is a dynamic energy that shapes both biology and reality. What you believe determines how your brain fires, how your body responds, and how the field around you organizes itself. In this way, belief becomes more than a feeling—it becomes a frequency that communicates with the very fabric of the universe.

Below are three scientific perspectives that affirm the unseen power belief holds over creation.

✧ The Placebo Effect: Belief as Medicine

One of the most documented phenomena in medical science is the placebo effect. People who believe they are receiving healing—whether through a sugar pill or a fake treatment—often experience real, measurable improvements in health. Studies show that belief alone can stimulate the brain's release of endorphins, modulate pain response, and activate self-healing mechanisms.

It is not about deception—it is about perception. The body responds to what the mind believes is true. This is not magic; it's the biology of belief.

✧ Neuroplasticity: Rewiring Your Reality

In neuroscience, belief is not stored as a single idea—it is wired into the brain's neural networks. Every time you affirm a belief—whether empowering or limiting—you strengthen that neurological pathway. But the miracle of neuroplasticity is this: those pathways can be changed.

Through intentional repetition, visualization, and emotionally charged affirmations, the brain begins to prune old thought patterns and form new ones. In this way, belief becomes a sculptor—reshaping your mental architecture and, by extension, your life.

✧ Quantum Mechanics: The Observer Effect

In the realm of quantum physics, the act of observation influences outcomes. Known as the observer effect, this principle reveals that particles behave differently when they are being watched. The implication is profound: consciousness interacts with the field of possibility.

When you believe something will happen, you are not simply waiting— you are engaging. Your focus collapses potential into form. Your belief is not passive attention—it is participatory alignment with energy and outcome.

When science and spirit meet, a deeper truth emerges: belief carries frequency. It changes brain waves. It moves molecules. It rearranges patterns in both body and field. Whether through a sugar pill or a spoken affirmation, belief has the power to turn thought into form.

You are not simply reacting to reality—you are co-creating it. And every time you choose faith over fear, alignment over doubt, you send a signal to the universe: I am ready. I believe. I receive.

Personal Story
—I Don't Receive That

From the time I was about ten years old, I had a dream: I wanted to be an Olympic gymnast.

Not just a childhood whim—a soul-deep calling. I could see it. Feel it. Every cell in me was wired for it. But dreams like that are not cheap. And I came from a family so poor we did not ask for toys at Christmas—we asked for socks and underwear.

And as I said earlier in this book, if it were not for food pantries, we would not have eaten. My mother, born deaf, was a survivor of abuse. My father struggled with addiction. We lived with lack in every direction.

But still—I began.

I scraped together every dollar I could. I mowed lawns. Babysat. Cleaned houses, garages—whatever anyone needed. I was a kid with a purpose. And the people around me knew it. They saw the grit, the hunger, the spark. And many of them, quietly, helped me along the way.

I trained hard. Every spare moment. Every spare cent. And by the time I turned twenty, I had clawed my way to the edge of something extraordinary: I had a shot at Nationals—the competition that would determine who advanced toward a place on the U.S. gymnastics team.

I was that close to the dream I had been chasing since childhood.
And then—everything changed.

I was working as an account representative at a lending agency when someone announced over the loudspeaker: "If we have any able-bodied people, please help in the mailroom." They needed help lifting and loading boxes of maintenance due statements onto a truck. I was young, strong, and eager to help. I stood up, grabbed a heavy tray of mail, and as I lifted it, I heard it—A loud pop.

In a single second, every disc in my lower spine ruptured.

By the next morning, I could barely move my legs.

My parents rushed me to the hospital. After a series of scans and tests, the neurosurgeon came in with eyes heavy and almost tearful.
"Son," he said, "I am so sorry. I do not want to be the one to have to tell you this, but whatever you do from this point forward, you will have to be in a wheelchair. There is nothing we can do."

I wailed.

Not cried—wailed. It came from somewhere so deep I did not even know it existed.

I saw my entire life flash before me—every yard I had mowed, every scraped knee, every quiet prayer. All those years of working, believing, and hoping were now shattered.

And for a year and a half, that was my life. Some days I was in a wheelchair. Other days, I hobbled on crutches. Some days, I could not move at all.

I saw every kind of specialist imaginable. Orthopedic surgeons. Neurosurgeons. Acupuncturists. Psychologists. Each one gave the same answer: "There's nothing we can do."

People around me—well-meaning, compassionate people—began suggesting changes: lower your counters, install ramps, get used to this new normal.

But I could not accept it.

Something inside me pushed back.

And every time someone tried to hand me that reality, I would say:
"I don't receive that."

They did not understand what I meant. I am not sure I fully did, either. But I knew one thing: *I was not going to sign a contract for a sentencing I did not believe belonged to me.*

Then, one day, my grandmother—who never backed down from anything or anyone—took me back to the last orthopedic surgeon I had seen. She barged into his office and said, "This poor boy is in pain. Please—just do something."

After some hesitation, the doctor agreed to try exploratory surgery. And that surgery changed everything.

While I was under, he found damage that had never shown up on any MRI or scan—something hidden, but fixable. He corrected what he could. And when I woke up, something miraculous happened: I moved my big toe on my right foot.

Not a flicker. Not a twitch. A clear, steady, controlled movement, and I wept.

Not because I was fully healed—but because I saw proof. A spark. A crack of light. The beginning of a breakthrough.

That moment reminded me that belief is not just a mindset—it is a frequency. And mine had never stopped calling in the healing.

There is one more moment I will never forget during this time in my life.

While I was still in that hospital bed, curtain drawn, legs numb, future uncertain—I heard a soft voice from the other side of the room. "Excuse me," the man said gently. "You don't know me... but I know who you are."

Confused, I responded, "How?"

He explained that I had sung at his church during a revival. He remembered my voice. And then he said something that pierced my soul: "Even if you are in a wheelchair... You can still sing."

In that moment, it was like God whispered through a stranger to say:
Even if the "how" changes... your calling does not.

My healing journey was not over. There were more surgeries, more rehab, more moments that tested everything in me. But I never went back to the wheelchair. And today—if you saw me walking down the street—you would never guess I was once told I would never walk again.

Because when the world handed me a sentence,
I handed it back with a whisper of belief: "I don't receive that."

And that belief? That was the energy that began to heal me—mind, body, and spirit. That was the current that carried me forward.

Belief did not erase the pain, it rewrote the outcome.

Practical Applications
—Raising the Energy of Your Belief

Belief is more than a thought—it is an energy. And like all energy, it can rise, expand, and gain momentum when nurtured. Whether your faith feels strong or faint, it can be strengthened through intention and practice.

The tools that follow are designed to help you raise the energy of your belief—to move from hoping to knowing, from wishing to receiving. Because the moment you start vibrating in alignment with your desire, the universe begins to respond.

1. **Catch and replace doubting thoughts**.
   When a limiting belief arises ("I can not," "It is not for me"), pause and consciously reframe: "I'm learning to believe it's possible."

2. **Use "because" statements**.
   Say: "I believe this is coming to me because I'm aligned, because I'm ready, because I'm worthy." This gives your mind a reason to agree.

3. **Visualize the full sensory immersion**.
   See it. Smell it. Hear it. Feel it. Let your entire body experience the manifestation in your imagination.

4. **Believe in steps if you cannot yet believe the whole**.
   If "I believe I'm a millionaire" feels fake, start with: "I believe I am opening up to greater financial flow." Build the muscle gradually.

5. **Surround yourself with proof**.
   Listen to stories of others who have manifested what you are calling in. Let their belief fuel yours.

6. **Speak it daily**.
   Say aloud: "I believe something good is happening for me. I believe I am walking in favor. I believe the universe is on my side."

Every belief you nurture is a current you send out into the field—an energetic agreement with the life you are calling in. These practices are not about pretending or forcing faith; they are about choosing to tune into a higher frequency—again and again—until it becomes your default setting.

Even the smallest shift in belief can move mountains in motion.

So, be patient with yourself, be bold with your declarations, and above all, be faithful to the vision seeded in your spirit.

The universe is listening—not just to what you say, but to what you believe. Speak it. Feel it. Live it. The rest will meet you there.

Affirmation

"I believe in my vision. I believe in divine timing. I believe in the power within me. My belief is my energy—and my energy is creating my reality."

Guided Meditation
—Sitting in the Energy of Belief

Breathe slowly. Settle into your body.

Now, imagine one thing you deeply desire. Bring it to the forefront of your mind. See it, feel it, smell it, touch it. Imagine you are already living it.

Hear yourself saying: "I believe. I receive. I allow."

Let that belief fill your chest like light—warm, alive, expansive. Let it settle in your belly, in your shoulders, and in your voice.

You are not asking. You are believing. Sit with that vibration.

Now—bring it back with you into your natural world.

Conclusion

Belief is not passive. It is not polite. It is not a whisper in the back row. Belief is power in motion. It is the moment you stop begging and start becoming. It is the internal shift that moves the heavens, the earth, and everything in between.

You cannot fake this energy. You cannot say one thing and believe another. The universe does not respond to your wish—it responds to your witness. To what your spirit is testifying to behind the scenes. To what your body, your thoughts, your habits, and your emotions are vibrating in agreement with.

And yes, belief can be hard, especially when life has handed you reasons to doubt, when the past echoes louder than your vision, and when the doors seem slow to open.

But belief doesn't ask you to be perfect. It asks you to be present. To return again and again to that inner knowing: "Something good is on its way. And I am ready to receive it."

Because your belief is not just a wish—it's a blueprint. It tells the universe what to build. It shapes the atmosphere around you. It magnetizes the people, the provision, the timing, and the path.

So, let your belief stretch. Let it get louder than your fear. Let it live in your language. Let it breathe through your actions. Let it interrupt your doubt and rewrite your future.

Because belief does not just see what is possible; it starts walking toward it. And the moment you align with that kind of belief, your life will rise to meet you.

So, believe boldly. Believe beyond what you can see. Believe when it is easy and believe when it is not.

Because the truth is: **Your belief is your superpower**.
And it is already creating the world you are about to walk into.

Chapter 14: Letting Go of Control
—Surrendering to the Flow of Manifestation

Opening Reflection

"The weight you carry was never yours. Let go—and the path will rise to meet you."
—Roy Waugh

Introduction

There is a moment in every manifestor's journey when the most sacred act is not to push harder—but to release. Not to strive—but to soften.

Control is the burden we carry when fear tells us we are not safe. It convinces us that if we do not micromanage the outcome, nothing will happen. But manifestation does not arrive through force—it flows through surrender.

Letting go is not defeat. It is a sacred exchange: your grip for grace, your burden for flow, and your fear for faith.

This chapter is an invitation to loosen your hold, to unclench your heart, and to stop strangling the blessings already making their way toward you.

Because often, the thing you are trying to control was never meant to be carried by you in the first place. It was meant to arrive, not be wrestled into place.

Hidden Teachings from Ancient Traditions
—Letting Go Through Action—When Surrender Takes a Step Forward

Across every sacred tradition, surrender is not portrayed as weakness—it is a holy strength. But surrender does not always mean stillness.

Sometimes, it takes the shape of sacred movement—an action made not from striving, but from trust.

The wisdom keepers of every lineage teach that manifestation unfolds most powerfully when we act in alignment with divine flow rather than personal control. These are the steps we take not to force—but to follow.

The following sacred teachings remind us: true surrender does not mean doing nothing. It means doing only what is ours to do and letting the rest move through Spirit.

✧ Christian Faith

In Christianity, surrender often looks like obedient motion—not passive waiting, but faith-filled release. Jesus Himself modeled this in Gethsemane, saying, "**Yet not my will, but Yours be done.**" (Luke 22:42, NIV). It was not resignation—it was active yielding.
Paul echoes this flow in Romans: "**Offer your bodies as a living sacrifice, holy and pleasing to God—this is your true and proper worship**." (Romans 12:1, NIV)

Here, surrender is not stillness—it is embodied devotion. A willing release of control in order to become a vessel. The disciples were often called to move before clarity came—to cast nets again, to walk on water, to go where they were sent. In this tradition, letting go is not giving up. It is stepping forward with open hands, trusting that God fills what we cannot force.

✧ Jewish Wisdom

In Judaism, surrender is woven into the rhythm of life through practices like Sabbath and sabbatical rest—acts of stopping as spiritual obedience. Yet even in moments of movement, surrender is key. The Exodus itself required action steeped in trust. The Israelites walked into an unknown wilderness—not with answers, but with obedience.

The prophet Micah beautifully captures the surrendered posture of the soul: "**He has shown you, O mortal, what is good. And what does the Lord require of you? To act justly and to love mercy and to walk humbly with your God**." (Micah 6:8, Tanakh)

This is not performance—it is humble participation. Walking, not running. Trusting, not controlling. In Jewish thought, bitachon (deep trust) and hishtadlut (effort) dance together. You do your part—not in grasping, but in grace—and allow God's hand to meet you in motion.

✧ Islamic Teachings

In Islam, surrender is the very meaning of the word: Islam itself derives from silm—peace through submission. Yet this submission is not passive —it is actively lived. The Qur'an teaches: "**And whoever relies upon Allah—then He is sufficient for him. Indeed, Allah will accomplish His purpose**." (Surah At-Talaq 65:3, Sahih International) But relying on Allah does not mean you do nothing.

The Prophet Muhammad (peace be upon him) said: "**If you hear of a plague in a land, do not enter it; and if it occurs in a land you are already in, do not leave it**." (Sahih al-Bukhari 5728) Even divine trust includes wise, intentional response. And of course, his timeless teaching: **"Tie your camel and trust in Allah." (Tirmidhi 2517)**
In this tradition, to surrender is to act from alignment—not anxiety. You release the outcome, not the responsibility. The path forward is walked in submission, but it is still walked.

✧ Buddhist Practices

In Buddhism, surrender is practiced through non-attachment—releasing clinging to outcomes while remaining present in right action. The Buddha taught: "**Do not dwell in the past, do not dream of the future, concentrate the mind on the present moment**." (Dhammapada 18:248) This is not avoidance—it is awareness. Action becomes sacred when it flows from mindfulness, not from fear. The Eightfold Path teaches

Right Effort—a gentle perseverance born not of force, but of clear intention.

Metta meditation, walking meditation, and mindful service are examples of movement born of surrender. They are not goal-driven but rooted in presence. In this path, you release control not by freezing, but by flowing —with compassion, clarity, and calm.

✧ Hindu Traditions

Hinduism teaches that to act in alignment with one's dharma—without attachment to results—is the highest form of surrender. This is the essence of karma yoga.

Krishna teaches Arjuna in the Bhagavad Gita: "**You have a right to perform your prescribed duties, but you are not entitled to the fruits of your actions. Never consider yourself to be the cause of the results of your activities**." (Bhagavad Gita 2:47, Swami Prabhupada translation)

This does not mean inaction. It means sacred action. To do your part, fully, lovingly, and then to let go. In this tradition, action becomes a spiritual offering.

The flow of surrender is not passive—it is pulsing. It is spanda, the divine vibration that moves through all things. And when we move in rhythm with it, even the simplest act becomes infused with the power of the Source.

Across every tradition, the message is this: *Surrender is not the absence of movement—it is the presence of trust within the movement.*

When your actions are not fueled by control but by sacred openness, they become bridges between spirit and form.

Wisdom from Contemporary Spiritual Leaders

In every generation, spiritual pioneers emerge to remind us of the power within. These voices—rooted in science, soul, and sacred truth—echo a consistent message: your words carry energy. They are not passive. They are purposeful. Whether spoken in faith or fear, every syllable shapes the vibrational field around you.

The teachers below have devoted their lives to awakening humanity to this truth: what you speak becomes your atmosphere. What you declare becomes your direction.

—Louise Hay wrote: "**I do not fix problems. I fix my thinking. Then problems fix themselves**." That is surrender.

—Esther Hicks (Abraham) teaches: "**Manifestation becomes effortless when we stop '*efforting*.'**" When we stop trying to force the outcome and simply align, the energy of attraction handles the rest.

—Oprah Winfrey has spoken often about learning to let go: "**I let go and trusted that life would unfold as it was meant to**." Oprah's words remind us that surrender is not weakness—it's a powerful act of trust in divine timing.

—Dr. Wayne Dyer once said, "**Let go and let God**." He reminded us that ego wants control, but the spirit wants flow.

—Joyce Meyer echoes the same truth in her own way: "**You can't cast your cares on God and keep worrying about them at the same time**." Wisdom calls us to release control fully—faith and worry cannot occupy the same space.

—Roy Waugh says, "**Letting go is not losing... it is making space for what is already yours**." When we hold on too tightly—whether to outcomes, people, timelines, or fears—we create resistance. Our grip becomes a barrier. But the very thing we fear losing is often waiting patiently on the other side of surrender.

Letting go is not waving a white flag—it is clearing the runway. It is telling the universe, "*I trust you. I am ready. I am open.*" And in that open space, grace moves. What is meant for you does not have to be chased. It only needs a place to land.

Words are not ornaments—they are instruments of transformation. What these leaders understand is that the voice is not just a way of communicating—it is a way of creating. When you speak with alignment, you are not just expressing thoughts—you are casting spiritual architecture into form.

These are not just quotes. They are keys. And when used with clarity and intention, they unlock the frequency of manifestation already encoded within you.

Scientific Perspectives on Surrender and Flow
—When Science Meets Surrender—The Measurable Power of Letting Go

Surrender is not giving up—it is giving over. In the realm of science, what we call "surrender" is often seen as the state of alignment with natural flow, the sweet spot where resistance drops and coherence rises. This state—far from passive—activates some of the most powerful mechanisms in the body, brain, and energetic field.

From neuroscience to quantum physics, modern research affirms what the mystics have always taught: when we stop fighting reality and start flowing with it, life begins to move through us in remarkable ways. Surrender, at its core, is a physiological and energetic opening—one that invites harmony between thought, body, and the unseen forces shaping our path.

✧ Neuroscience of Letting Go

From a neurological standpoint, surrender activates the parasympathetic nervous system—commonly known as the "rest and digest" response. When we release control or let go of obsessive overthinking, the brain shifts from survival mode (fight-or-flight) to a state of peace and repair.

Dr. Judson Brewer, a neuroscientist and mindfulness researcher, explains that "letting go" reduces activity in the brain's default mode network—associated with rumination and egoic self-narratives. This shift enhances clarity, decision-making, and emotional resilience. In other words, when you stop grasping, your mind becomes more available to receive insight.

✧ Flow State and Peak Performance

Psychologist Mihaly Csikszentmihalyi coined the term "flow" to describe the optimal state of consciousness where we feel and perform our best. In flow, the sense of self fades, time dilates, and action and awareness merge. Interestingly, this state arises not from control but from surrender—releasing conscious effort and trusting the body and mind to work in harmony.

Flow is often experienced by athletes, artists, and meditators, and studies show it enhances creativity, productivity, and happiness. Surrender, then, is not the absence of effort—but the alignment of energy. It is the moment when your intention stops pushing and starts partnering with something greater.

✧ Heart-Brain Coherence

Research from the HeartMath Institute shows that when we enter a state of inner alignment—often through practices like meditation, gratitude, or prayer—the heart and brain begin to synchronize. This state is called "heart-brain coherence," and it leads to greater emotional regulation, intuition, and a stronger immune response.

Surrender plays a key role in initiating this coherence. When we stop resisting our current reality and drop into acceptance, our physiology follows. The heart rhythm smooths, the brain waves calm, and the body enters coherence—and from that state, we make better decisions, connect more deeply, and manifest with greater ease.

✧ Quantum Observations and Allowing

In quantum physics, the observer effect reveals that particles behave differently when they are being watched. Observation changes outcomes. But it is not just the act of observing—it is the energy behind it. The more we grasp or try to force a specific outcome, the more we introduce chaos into the field. But when we release attachment and simply hold a clear intention, we allow the universe to organize around that frequency.

This is the science of allowance. Surrender doesn't mean abandoning your vision. It means trusting the timing, the unfolding, and the intelligence of the field to deliver in the right way.

✧ The Biology of Trust

From a biological standpoint, the body responds to trust and surrender with healing. Cortisol levels decrease. Oxytocin and dopamine increase. Muscles relax. Digestion improves. Immune function strengthens. These are not small effects—they are measurable shifts in the terrain of the body. Dr. Bruce Lipton, a cellular biologist, teaches that belief and environment shape genetic expression. A surrendered mindset—rooted in trust rather than fear—creates a biological environment of openness, receptivity, and growth. Surrender, in this light, becomes an energetic yes to life, which the body echoes in return.

Science now confirms what spiritual traditions have long whispered: surrender is not weakness—it is wisdom. It is the sacred recalibration where striving gives way to stillness, and control transforms into trust.

From the neurons in your brain to the rhythms of your heart, your entire being responds when you shift from resistance to release. In that shift, the energy begins to move. Doors begin to open.

The frequency of flow becomes your new normal. And what once felt out of reach begins to arrive—not through force, but through the quiet, intelligent power of surrender.

Personal Story
—The Moment I Let Go and Music Found Me

I did not grow up hearing worship music or bedtime prayers. Sundays were not for church—they were for watching wrestling on TV and trying to forget how empty the house felt. My mother, born deaf and scarred by years of abuse, did her best to hold it all together. My father, locked in addiction, often chose alcohol and drugs over food for his six children. We were not just poor—we were worn out and worn thin, invisible, trying to survive in a world that did not seem to notice.

By the time I was fifteen, the weight of it all had become too much. I had already started working—thanks to a state policy that allowed children of disabled parents to begin working early—and I had saved enough to buy a little car. I did not have a license yet, but I had something more powerful than a license. I had a plan.

I did not know exactly where I was going or what I was going to do, but I knew **this was not my life**. If I stayed, I would be stuck going nowhere and eventually just disappear. All I could think was, "God, get me out of here."

So, one morning, I packed some of my things, skipped school, and slid behind the wheel. As I pulled out of town—tears clouding my eyes—my best friend spotted me. He flagged me down, jumped in the passenger seat, and asked, "Where are you going?" "I don't know, but I have to get out," I whispered. He said, "Well, I'm going with you."

We drove across states—two kids with next to nothing but desperation — chasing something we could not name. We made it all the way to San Diego, hoping to find my friend's brother at a military base. But when we got there, the guards told us he had been transferred to Georgia. We were out of gas, out of money, and out of hope.

Desperate, we broke down sobbing right there at the gate.
And then, a stranger overheard us. "Wait, there are a few men by that name on this base," he said. "Let me make a call." Twenty minutes later,

my friend's brother showed up in disbelief. He took us in, fed us, and gave us a place to rest. Later that night, he handed us an envelope.
"You need to go home," he said gently. "My platoon took up a collection. Use this for gas and food. This is not where you are supposed to be."

The next morning, we turned around and headed back.
When I dropped my best friend off, his parents were waiting on the porch —two people I had never met. As he ran into their arms, I sat in the car, unsure of what to do. My friend had run into the house, but their eyes stayed on me, warm and unwavering.

I tried to leave, but I could not gather the strength. So, I stepped out.
They walked toward me and embraced me like I was theirs. "God loves you," they said. "Do you know angels have been watching over you. You are not alone. You never have been."

Something inside me cracked open in that moment.

That weekend, I walked into church for the first time in my life.
A few weeks later, my friend's father—the pastor—handed me a cassette tape and said, "There is a revival coming up. I want you to sing this."
I blinked, my eyes wide open. "I do not sing. I have never sung in my life, especially not in front of people."

He smiled and said, "Just try. Do it for me."
So, I did. I practiced for hours.

The night of the revival, I stood in front of a crowd of people from several churches, voice trembling, knees shaking, and sang. When it was over, people clapped. Some cried. And one by one, pastors came up to me, asking, "Will you come and sing that song at our church?"
Without hesitation, I said, "Yes."

One invitation turned into another. Then another. Soon, I was singing nearly every weekend. They gave me small offerings—just enough to cover gas and a meal—but it added up. They did not just support my singing—they helped pay for my gymnastics training. They became part of the very answer to the prayer I had whispered on my way out of town: "God, please get me out of here."

I did not know I had a gift. I did not know I had a calling.
The life I thought I had to chase was waiting patiently for me the whole time.

Letting go does not always look like a perfect plan. Sometimes, it looks like breaking down at a gate in a city where you do not belong. Sometimes, it sounds like a song you never knew you could sing.

But when you stop gripping the reins, grace takes the wheel.
And what you never could have imagined for yourself begins to unfold right in front of you.

Practical Applications
—Learning the Art of Letting Go

That chapter of my life taught me something I've never forgotten: letting go is not weakness—it is wisdom. It is trusting the river more than your oars.

When we release control, we are not giving up on the dream—we are giving it space to breathe, to stretch, to arrive in its own divinely-timed way. What flowed into my life after I surrendered could not have been forced, planned, or predicted. It had to come through grace.

And now, I invite you to experience that same shift—from gripping to opening. From fear to flow. Here is how you begin to practice the sacred art of letting go.

1. **Surrender statements**.
   Say out loud: "I have done my part. Now I trust divine timing." Let that be your release ritual.

2. **Create space for flow**.
Declutter your schedule. Your home. Your mind. Make space for something new to flow in.

3. **When in doubt, breathe**.
When anxiety creeps in, pause. Inhale peace and exhale control. Repeat until your grip loosens.

4. **Use visual let-go rituals**.
Write your worry on a piece of paper. Burn it. Or tie it to a balloon and release it into the sky.

5. **Practice "no more forcing" days**.
Dedicate a day to not forcing anything. Flow, not fight. Let life lead.

6. **Bless and release others**.
If you are waiting on someone to change or respond, say: "I bless them and release them. I surrender the outcome."

Letting go is not the end of your manifestation journey—it is the moment it begins to unfold without resistance. When you loosen your grip, you shift from striving to receiving. You move from pressure into peace.

These practices are not about giving up—they are about opening up. And as you release, trust that what is truly meant for you is already on its way. The flow knows. And now, so do you.

Affirmation

"I let go of control. I trust the unfolding. I surrender with peace and open hands. What is meant for me flows freely toward me now."

Guided Meditation

—Releasing the Grip

Find stillness. Feel your shoulders soften. Inhale deeply.

As you exhale, imagine opening your hands. Let them rest palms up.

Whisper within: "I release the need to control. I trust the greater plan. I am open to receive."

Visualize a river flowing gently through your life. You are floating. Carried. Held. Not steering—but trusting. Feel the tension melt.

Let surrender become your sanctuary.

Conclusion

Letting go is not weakness—it is sacred wisdom. It is the moment you stop wrestling with the current and allow yourself to be carried by something greater.

So many of us spend years gripping tightly—clutching timelines, forcing outcomes, praying with one hand open and the other clenched in fear. But manifestation does not thrive in tension. It flows where there's room to move.

We confuse control with faith. We call it planning, but often, it is panic wearing a mask. The deeper truth? Some of the most divine movements begin the moment we stop needing to know how the story ends.

Surrender is not giving up—it is stepping aside so grace can move. It is Moses raising his staff without a plan. It is Jesus, heart heavy, whispering, **"Not my will, but Yours."** (Luke 22:42) And it is you, knees to the floor, saying, "I can't do this alone," and hearing heaven whisper back, "You were never meant to."

Letting go is not abandoning your dream—it is releasing your grip on how it has to happen. It is making space for surprise. For alignment. For the divine choreography that only unfolds when you stop trying to micromanage the sacred.

When you release what was never yours to control, everything shifts.
Your spirit softens, your nervous system calms, your frequency rises, and suddenly, what felt blocked begins to move.

Letting go does not mean you stop believing—it means you believe enough to stop forcing. You trust the current. You open your hands and say with your whole being: *"I surrender to the flow that knows more than I do.*

And in that surrender, the miracle makes its move.

So, breathe, loosen your grip, and unclench your soul.
You are not falling. You are finally being carried, and the moment you trust that truth, is often the moment your entire life begins to unfold in divine rhythm.

Chapter 15: Embodying the Vision
—Becoming the Energy of What You Seek

Opening Reflection

"Don't wait to receive it. Become the energy of what you've asked for, and let your life rise to match the frequency of your desire."
—Roy Waugh

Introduction

Manifestation is not just about hoping or believing—it is about becoming.

To truly call in what you desire, you must begin to carry its energy, walk in its essence, and vibrate at its frequency. This is the sacred embodiment of vision. It means feeling the outcome so completely that your very being becomes its home—before the world ever sees it.

So often, we treat our dreams like distant visitors—something to wait for or chase. But the truth is, what you seek is waiting for you to align. Not to watch from afar, but to mirror its vibration. To live as if it is already true. Not to pretend—but to become.

This chapter is about embodiment—the holy act of bringing the vision into your bones. It is about tuning your energy to match the frequency of your future.

When your breath, your voice, your decisions, and your presence all begin to hum with the reality of what you desire, manifestation is not delayed. It is magnetized.

Because manifestation does not happen when you receive, it happens when you become.

Hidden Teachings from Ancient Traditions

—Living the Prayer—Embodiment as a Spiritual Practice Across Traditions

Across every major spiritual tradition, embodiment is not just encouraged —it is essential. It is the movement of belief into action, the transformation of inner truth into outer expression.

To embody is to allow the divine to dwell not just in your mind or heart, but in your very being. When your body, your breath, and your choices begin to echo your prayers, you become a living manifestation of what you believe.

These sacred lineages teach us that to manifest is not only to ask—but to become.

✧ Christian Faith

In Christianity, embodiment is an extension of living faith. "**Faith without works is dead**." writes the apostle James (James 2:17, NRSV). True belief cannot remain still—it must move, act, and take form in the world.

Jesus was the ultimate example of embodiment: "**The Word became flesh and dwelt among us**." (John 1:14, KJV). He did not simply speak peace—He became it. His healing was not just in His words—it was in His presence.

The Apostle Paul reminds us, "**Do you not know that your bodies are temples of the Holy Spirit, who is in you**?" (1 Corinthians 6:19, NIV). Your body is not just a shell—it is a sanctuary.

And David, as he stepped forward to face Goliath, didn't speak from fear. He declared, "**This day the Lord will deliver you into my hand**." (1 Samuel 17:46, ESV). He embodied the outcome before it arrived.

In this tradition, embodiment is not about pretending. It is about walking in what your spirit already knows is true.

✧ Jewish Wisdom

In Judaism, the body is a sacred vessel of divine expression.

The Hebrew word nefesh speaks of the soul as breath, showing that body and spirit are one. **"Then the Lord God formed man from the dust of the ground and breathed into his nostrils the breath of life..."** (Genesis 2:7, ESV). With that breath, we became carriers of the divine.

In Kabbalah, the mystical branch of Jewish teaching, divine light flows through every created thing—including the human form. Our actions and posture become pathways for that light.

When Moses asked for God's name, the answer came: **"Ehyeh Asher Ehyeh"**— **"I Am That I Am."** (Exodus 3:14, ESV). This was not just a name. It was a statement of being.

The Talmud echoes this idea: **"Great is study, for it leads to action."** (Kiddushin 40b).

Knowledge in Judaism is never complete until it is embodied. Truth must take form.

✧ Islamic Teaching

In Islam, embodiment is worship in motion. Prayer (salah) is a full-body expression of surrender—standing, bowing, prostrating. Faith is never limited to thought. It moves.

The Prophet Muhammad (peace be upon him) was called **"a walking Qur'an."** by his wife Aisha (Hadith, Musnad Ahmad 24601). His teachings were not just recited—they were lived.

The Qur'an says, "**Indeed, those who have said, 'Our Lord is Allah' and then remained steadfast—the angels will descend upon them...**" (Surah Fussilat 41:30, Sahih International). This istiqamah—steadfastness—is not only spiritual. It is physical, emotional, and behavioral alignment.

And the Prophet also said, "**Actions are judged by intentions**." (Sahih Bukhari, Book 1, Hadith 1).

In this tradition, faith must move through the limbs. Intention must be carried by action. The vision must live in how we walk, speak, and serve.

✧ Buddhist Practices

In Buddhism, embodiment is the heart of practice. "**What you think, you become. What you feel, you attract. What you imagine, you create." (Dhammapada, Verse 1).** The mind is not a separate tool—it is the sculptor of being.

Mindfulness grounds that truth. Walking meditation, for example, turns each step into a sacred practice. Thich Nhat Hanh said, "**Walk as if you are kissing the Earth with your feet**." (Peace Is Every Step, 1992). That is not poetry alone—it is practice.

Mantras, too, are a form of embodiment. The chant Om Mani Padme Hum is not just sound—it is vibration that shapes the body and soul into compassion.

In Buddhism, to embody is to awaken, not in theory, but in the living breath of each moment. You become what you consistently bring your awareness to.

✧ Hindu Insights

In Hinduism, embodiment is spiritual alignment realized. "**A person is what he believes himself to be**." (Bhagavad Gita 6:5). You are not becoming—you already are.

The Upanishads remind us, **"Tat Tvam Asi"** — **"Thou art That**
(Chandogya Upanishad 6.8.7). This is the essence of the Atman—the inner
Self that is not separate from the Divine.

Through the practice of bhava (emotional embodiment), you do not just
believe in a truth—you feel it in your being. If you desire abundance, walk
in the feeling of abundance. If you seek divine union, live in remembrance
that it is already yours.

The mantra Aham Brahmasmi means **"I am Divine**." (Brihadaranyaka
Upanishad 1.4.10). It is not arrogance. It is sacred memory. In this path,
embodiment is not pretending—it is remembering who you really are.

Across every tradition, one message echoes: Embodiment is the bridge.
Between desire and reality. Between belief and becoming. Between the
sacred and the seen.

When you walk in the vibration of what you have asked for, you are not
just calling in the vision; you are becoming it.

And the Divine meets you there—not because you were waiting, but
because you were already walking.

Wisdom from Contemporary Spiritual Leaders

True manifestation is not just conceptual—it is experiential. The most
powerful teachers of our time remind us that to receive what you desire,
you must become it. Not in imagination alone, but in energy, in posture,
in vibration.

These voices have echoed the truth that the frequency you emit is the
future you attract. Embodiment, they teach, is the living signal of faith in
motion.

—Dr. Joe Dispenza teaches that to manifest your future, you must
emotionally feel it before it arrives. **"The body must experience it as
real now,"** he says. **"The future is drawn to the one who already**

feels it." This is not mere visualization—it is a physiological rehearsal of your destiny.

—Neville Goddard taught, "**Assume the feeling of the wish fulfilled**." He did not mean to pretend—he meant to enter the state of consciousness where your desire is already true, and dwell there. The body becomes the container of faith when the feeling becomes real.

—Abraham Hicks teaches that manifestation begins with vibration: "**You must become a vibrational match to what you want**." And how do you match it? By feeling it now. The vibrational frequency of what you want must first resonate from within you.

—Louise Hay shared, "**What you think and what you believe will create your reality. If you want to change your life, change the way you think—and feel**." She emphasized that the body and mind are not separate in the process of creation—they are unified instruments of divine frequency.

—Maya Angelou; I*n her stillness and strength, embodied a lived sacredness. She did not just speak truth—she walked it.* She moved through the world with the grace of someone who had seen darkness and still chose to be light. **That is embodiment**.

—Roy Waugh: "Become **the vibration of your vision, and the universe will respond—echoing your frequency back to you in the same form**." Manifestation is not about pursuing something outside of yourself—it is about matching the internal with the eternal. Once you align your energy, reality has no choice but to mirror it.

Embodiment is the sacred bridge between belief and becoming. These teachers—each in their own language—remind us that manifestation is not something we chase. It is something we live into. When you feel it, move like it, speak from it, and breathe with it—your vision is no longer just a possibility. It becomes a present frequency, and the world must rise to meet it.

Scientific Perspectives on Embodiment and Energy

—When Energy Becomes Identity—Scientific Evidence for Living Your Vision Now

Modern science is beginning to confirm what ancient traditions have known for centuries: your body is not just a shell—it is an energetic instrument of creation.

The thoughts you think, the emotions you embody, and the frequency you carry all shape your physiological state and influence your reality. Manifestation is not just spiritual poetry—it is a biological, neurological, and quantum process of becoming.

✧ Neuroscience and Mental Rehearsal

Research shows that the brain does not clearly distinguish between real experience and vividly imagined experience. When you visualize your desired outcome while engaging the emotions associated with it, your brain lights up as if it is actually happening. This process, known as mental rehearsal, strengthens neural pathways and conditions the mind and body to believe a new reality.

In the words of Dr. Joe Dispenza, "Nerve cells that fire together wire together," which means you can train your brain to embody your future before it arrives.

✧ Embodiment and the Nervous System

Your nervous system responds to emotional states as real data. When you embody calm, confidence, gratitude, or joy, your body enters a state of coherence. Heart rate, brain waves, and hormonal output begin to synchronize. Studies in psychoneuroimmunology show that such emotional states reduce stress hormones like cortisol and increase immunity-supporting hormones like DHEA.

In essence, the way you feel directly instructs the body on how to function. Embodiment is health. Embodiment is alignment.

✧ Quantum Physics and Resonance

In the quantum field, everything is energy—including you. The law of resonance states that frequencies attract like frequencies. Just as tuning forks vibrate in harmony when matched, your energetic signature draws in matching realities.

When you carry the vibration of your vision—when your thoughts, feelings, and actions align—you become a magnet for that reality. Energy does not lie. It reflects. And it responds to coherence.

✧ Behavioral Science and Embodied Identity

Research in behavioral science reveals that people who adopt the identity of their desired outcome (e.g., "I am healthy," "I am confident," "I am worthy") are significantly more likely to act in alignment with that identity. This psychological principle—known as self-perception theory—shows that belief-based behaviors can create a feedback loop, where embodying the trait leads to becoming the trait.

Identity is not fixed. It is formed through repetition, emotion, and intention.

When science and spirit agree, pay attention. Embodiment is not just a poetic metaphor—it is a living biological truth. You are wired to become what you consistently feel, believe, and behave as. The moment you feel the future in your bones, your body begins to adapt to it. And the world around you starts to shift in response.

Personal Story
—Seeing The House Before It Existed

I have taught for years that when you pray—when you ask, when you believe—you must be specific. If you are asking for a car, do not just say "a car." What kind of car? What year? What color? What does the interior look like? Can you smell the leather? Feel the steering wheel? I would tell people again and again: **"Clarity brings power. The Universe responds to detail**."

But when it came to my own life, especially my dream home, I was stuck.

We were house hunting and had been for a while. Nothing felt quite right. I would scroll endlessly through listings—dozens a day. Some were beautiful, but they did not feel like home. Some were close, but something was always missing. I kept saying, "I'll know it when I see it," but the truth was—I did not know what I was even looking for. And that was the problem.

One day, it hit me: I was not following my own teaching.
I had asked vaguely. I had hoped generally. But I had not embodied the vision.

I had not given the Universe a clear blueprint. I had not told the Creator what I actually desired.

So, I stopped searching, and I went inward.

I sat down with a journal and started writing. Not a list of requirements—but a love letter to the home I knew was waiting for me. I described the roof—arched and strong, like it had shoulders to carry peace. I pictured the walls—painted in warm, natural tones that felt like a soft exhale. I felt my feet sink into the floors—rich hardwood under rugs woven with memory. I saw the kitchen—light-filled and spacious, the kind of place where laughter and aroma fill every corner. I walked out into the yard in my mind—green, private, peaceful, a place to pray, to breathe, to simply be.

I did not just see it. In my mind, I stepped into it. I began to imagine myself waking up in that home. Pouring tea at the window. Lighting a candle in the entryway. Hosting dinners. Laughing in the living room. I felt what it would feel like to be there.
Then I gave thanks for it—before I ever held the keys.
Something began to shift.

I was not begging for a home anymore—I was becoming the person who lived in it. I started embodying the version of me who had already moved in. My energy aligned. My prayer became posture. My faith became form.

And not long after, we found it.
The house did not just match the vision—it was the vision, almost to the detail. It felt like it had been waiting for me to remember it. To call it in. To become its match.

That is the power of embodiment.

It was not about forcing the process. It was not about demanding a timeline. It was about aligning myself with the energy of what I said I wanted—and living in that energy now.

Because the Universe does not just hear what you say, it responds to what you become.

And once I walked as the vision, the vision opened its doors.

Practical Applications
—Becoming the Energy of Your Vision

This is where embodiment begins—not with force, but with frequency. To embody your desire is to become a living resonance of the thing you seek. It is like preparing the guest room before the guest arrives—setting the table, lighting the candles, pouring the wine—because you know it is coming. It is about living today in the vibration of tomorrow's fulfillment.

In the steps that follow, you will practice aligning your thoughts, posture, words, and decisions with the reality you are calling in. Not someday—but now.

Because when you walk as if it is already yours, you are no longer chasing the vision—you are hosting it. You become the invitation. You become the magnet. You become the match.

1. **Feel it fully in meditation**.
   When you meditate on your desire, do not just imagine it. Feel it. See it. Smell it. Hold it. Let every sense engage.

2. **Dress for the energy you are calling in**.
   You do not have to buy anything new. Just show up daily in a way that reflects the version of you who already has it.

3. **Speak from the fulfilled place**.
   Say things like: "I am already supported." "I feel so thankful for this new opportunity." Let your language match your future.

4. **Move with purpose**.
   How would you walk if you were already living in the answered prayer? How would you carry yourself? Begin now.

5. **Create an embodiment anchor**.
   Choose a scent, a song, or an item that symbolizes your vision. When you engage with it, let it reconnect you to the energy of becoming.

6. **Make decisions as that version of yourself**.
   When you face a choice, ask: "What would the version of me who already has this choose right now?"

You are not waiting to become—you are already becoming.

Every embodied act, every aligned step, every word you speak from the frequency of your future sends a signal to the universe: I am ready now. This is not pretending. This is prophetic living.

When you honor your desire by living its energy, you collapse the distance between longing and reality. The outer world begins to mirror the inner truth.

Because manifestation is not about reaching forward—It is about rising inward. And the moment you live it in your bones, it begins to arrive at your door.

Affirmation

"I embody the energy of my vision. I feel it, live it, and walk in it now. I am aligned and ready to receive."
Guided Meditation:

Guided Meditation
—Living the Vision Now

Take a breath. Now another.

Picture your desire in vivid detail. Do not just see it—step into it. You are there. Right now.

Feel it in your hands. Smell the space around you. Hear the sounds. Taste the moment. Feel the lightness, the gratitude, the joy.

This is your now. Let it rise in your chest. Let it settle in your body.

Say softly, "This is who I am. I am the one who lives this." Sit in that energy.

Let it anchor you. Now, bring it back into your natural world.

Conclusion

To embody is to prepare before the door ever opens.

It is the sacred, unseen act of becoming a match for what you desire—not by force, but by frequency. When you walk, breathe, speak, and move in the rhythm of your vision, the Universe no longer sees you as someone hoping. It recognizes you as someone already aligned. Someone ready.
This is not pretense. It is not performance. It is alignment. It is an energetic truth, and it is vibrational faith in motion.

To embody is to remember what your soul already knows—that the frequency of your future already lives within you.

When you step into resonance with the life you have prayed for, longed for, and imagined in your highest self, you stop chasing your dreams and start living them ahead of schedule.

You are not just calling the future toward you. You are becoming the version of you who already lives inside it, and you are embodying the answer before it arrives.

And as you do, everything begins to respond. People shift, doors open, opportunities accelerate. Life begins to arrange itself around your new signal.

You are not just attracting the vision—You are becoming the vision, made visible.

So, live it now, walk in it now. Let your energy tell the truth before your circumstances do.

Because when your life becomes the echo of your desire, manifestation is no longer a distant hope. It is a sacred inevitability.

And when you walk as the vision, the Universe will answer—not with hesitation, but with harmony.

It will move in rhythm with your becoming. Because what you embody is what will arrive.

Chapter 16: The Rhythm of Receiving
—Opening to the Sacred Flow of What You've Asked For

Opening Reflection

"When the heart is open and the hands release control, the gifts of the universe flow like water."
—Roy Waugh, inspired by Buddhist wisdom and universal flow

Introduction

There is a rhythm to manifestation—and its final, most sacred movement is not in the asking. It is in the receiving.

You can pray fervently, visualize vividly, and affirm daily. But if your heart remains guarded and your hands still cling to control, all the energy you have stirred has nowhere to land.

Manifestation flows best where surrender is present.

Receiving is often the most misunderstood—and most resisted—part of the journey. We ask with clarity. We hope with passion. But when the blessing knocks, many of us hesitate to open the door.

Why? Because receiving requires vulnerability. Trust. Receptivity. It calls us to open—not just in thought, but in posture. It invites us to let go of striving and sit in the stillness of enough.

This chapter is an invitation to release the grip.
To become a space where divine flow is welcome.
To open your heart and unfasten your hands—so what is already on its way can finally arrive.

Because the gifts of the Universe are flowing like water.
The only question is: Are you open to receiving them?

Hidden Teaching from Ancient Traditions

—Open Hands, Open Heart—Ancient Wisdom on the Sacred Art of Receiving

The act of receiving is not passive—it is a sacred readiness. Every major spiritual tradition recognizes that divine blessing flows not merely to the deserving, but to the open.

To receive is to prepare a space within yourself—an inner sanctuary where grace can dwell. When your heart becomes a vessel and your spirit a willing host, what you have asked for can finally find its way to you.

Let us explore how this truth echoes through the sacred texts and teachings of five ancient traditions.

✧ Christian Faith

In the Christian tradition, receiving is deeply tied to faith and expectation. Jesus did not force miracles—He invited people to open their hearts. He often said, "**According to your faith let it be done to you..**" (Matthew 9:29, NIV), emphasizing that divine blessing meets us at the point of our receptivity.

In 2 Corinthians 9:8, Paul writes, "**And God is able to bless you abundantly, so that in all things at all times, having all that you need, you will abound in every good work**."
The abundance is already available—but we must allow ourselves to receive it, without shame, fear, or resistance.

The widow of Zarephath (1 Kings 17) received a miraculous supply of oil and flour not by striving, but by trusting the prophet's instruction. Her act of openness made space for provision. The principle is clear: *receiving is not the result of earning—it is the fruit of surrender.*

Divine provision is always present. But it enters the life of the one who is willing to say, "*Yes, Lord. I am ready.*"

✧ Jewish Wisdom

In Judaism, the sacred act of receiving is encoded into the very word kabbalah, which means "*to receive.*" Far beyond mysticism, this reflects a posture of life: to become a vessel for divine light.

The Hebrew Scriptures speak often of blessing, but always with the implicit message of readiness. "**Open your mouth wide, and I will fill it**," says (Psalm 81:10, ESV). This is more than a metaphor—it is a divine invitation to trust the abundance waiting to be poured in.

Rabbinic teachings also point to the concept of hakarat hatov—the practice of recognizing the good. To recognize is to receive. Gratitude opens the soul's hands.

The weekly observance of Shabbat is itself a radical act of receiving. No work. No striving. Only presence. It teaches that divine flow comes not from effort, but from surrender.

In Jewish tradition, to receive is to hold space for the holy—and to know that every breath, every gift, and every moment is shefa, a sacred abundance flowing from above.

✧ Islamic Teaching

In Islam, receiving is deeply tied to the concept of tawakkul—trusting in Allah while letting go of control. The believer is not only invited to ask but called to believe that the response is already unfolding.

The Qur'an says, "**And He gives you from where you do not expect**." (Surah At-Talaq 65:3, Sahih International). This verse reminds us that divine provision often bypasses logic. The path to blessing is not always visible—but it is always near to the open heart.

The Prophet Muhammad (peace be upon him) said, "**No fatigue, nor disease, nor sorrow... befalls a Muslim, but that Allah expiates**

some of his sins for it.” (Sahih al-Bukhari 5641). Even struggle becomes a gift when received with trust.

In prayer, Muslims lift their hands upward, palms open—a posture of spiritual receptivity. This is not begging—it is holy readiness.

Receiving in Islam is not a weakness. It is the strength of faith that says, “I do not need to know how... I just need to remain open.”

✧ Buddhist Practices

Buddhism teaches that the Universe is always offering—but the mind must be clear enough to notice. One of the foundational teachings of the Buddha says: “**With an open hand, the wise one gives and receives**.” (Dhammapada, Verse 224). This mirrors the core principle of equanimity—the ability to remain balanced, open, and spacious. To receive is not to grasp. It is to allow.

Zen practices like shoshin—beginner's mind—remind us that receiving happens when we let go of assumptions and stay curious. Every breath, every moment, every sensation becomes a sacred gift when met with awareness.

Thich Nhat Hanh wrote, “**People usually consider walking on water or in thin air a miracle. But the real miracle is not to walk either on water or in thin air, but to walk on earth**.” Receiving is the miracle of presence—welcoming what is here now, as enough.

To receive, in Buddhist wisdom, is to open without attachment and let life fill you—moment by moment, breath by breath.

✧ Hindu Traditions

In Hinduism, receiving is both a physical ritual and a metaphysical posture. The hands are often joined in anjali mudra—a gesture of offering, humility, and readiness. When blessings are given as prasad, they are not taken—they are received with reverence.

The Bhagavad Gita teaches, **"Whatever you do, whatever you eat, whatever you offer or give, do it as an offering to Me."** (Gita 9:27). This means all action becomes sacred when done in devotion. And all receiving becomes sacred when done in surrender.

In the Upanishads, the phrase **"Isha vasyam idam sarvam"** means **"All this is pervaded by God."** (Isa Upanishad 1) There is nothing outside the divine flow. The challenge is not to find the blessing—but to recognize it and receive it.

To receive in Hindu thought is to remember your oneness with the Divine. You are not separate from the source of abundance. When you clear the inner noise, blessings do not have to travel far. They are already within and around you, waiting to be welcomed home.

Across every faith, the sacred invitation is the same: open your hands. The Divine is always pouring—but it flows best into vessels that are empty of resistance, full of trust, and ready to be filled. When you become a sanctuary for the sacred, you do not just receive the blessing—you become the blessing's home.

Wisdom from Contemporary Spiritual Leaders

When it comes to receiving, today's spiritual leaders offer profound reminders that what we allow is just as powerful as what we ask for. Their words cut through the noise of striving and achievement, pointing us back to a deeper truth: that openness is not passivity—it is sacred participation. To receive is to say yes to the good that is already seeking you.

Below are voices that remind us that readiness is not a mood—it's a spiritual posture.

—Louise Hay often said, **"We must be open and receptive to all the good and abundance in the Universe."** She reminded people that the door is always open—but we have to walk through it.

—Abraham Hicks teaches that receiving is a natural result of alignment. **"You don't need to work harder. You just need to stop resisting**." Allowing is the art of letting what you've asked for come in. He reminds us that receiving isn't about effort—it's about releasing resistance and letting alignment do the work.

—Iyanla Vanzant says, **"The capacity to receive is a soul issue**." She teaches that many people self-sabotage because they do not believe they deserve what is trying to reach them.

—Eckhart Tolle frames receiving as presence: **"This moment is complete. The more you honor it, the more open you become to miracles unfolding in the next one**." He reveals that true receiving begins by honoring the now—presence, which is the gateway to unfolding miracles.

—Roy Waugh, **"The universe knocks softly. It is not trying to convince you—only to see if you are home**." Receiving is not about force; it is about readiness. This quote invites you to reflect on the subtle ways blessings arrive—not with fanfare, but with quiet certainty.

Opportunities, answers, and manifestations do not always come loud and obvious. Often, they arrive gently, checking to see if your heart is open, your spirit is listening, and your energy is present. The question is not whether the universe is delivering—it is whether you are willing to hear the knock, open the door, and say yes.

Scientific Perspectives on Openness and Receiving
—How Openness Rewires the Mind and Attracts Reality

Modern science is increasingly affirming what the mystics have long taught: that true receiving is not weakness—it is wisdom. It is not the absence of effort, but the presence of openness. From psychology to neuroscience, from behavioral science to quantum physics, we now understand that being receptive is a measurable state—one that shapes our thoughts, biology, energy, and outcomes.

Below are insights that reveal how the posture of openness prepares the entire system—mind, body, and field—for manifestation.

✦ Psychology and the Receptivity Quotient

Research in positive psychology reveals that individuals who possess a high receptivity quotient—the willingness to allow good into their lives—consistently report greater levels of well-being, success, and satisfaction.

This is not optimism alone. It is a pattern of thought and emotional regulation that allows abundance to enter. People who expect goodness often unconsciously make choices, take actions, and interpret experiences in ways that align with their expectations. This sets into motion a self-reinforcing loop of blessing.

Openness is not wishful thinking—it is a practiced orientation toward possibility.

✦ Neuroscience and the Reticular Activating System (RAS)

The brain has a built-in filter called the Reticular Activating System, or RAS. Its job is to determine what you pay attention to—and what you ignore. When you program your mind with intention and openness, your RAS starts spotlighting alignment: the right conversation, the open door, the gentle nudge. You begin to notice what you were blind to before; changes not just your luck, but your lens.

By staying open, you literally train your brain to see opportunity where others see limitation.

✦ Gratitude and the Nervous System

Gratitude does more than feel good—it opens the body for receiving. Neuroscience shows that practicing gratitude calms the nervous system, lowers cortisol, and activates the parasympathetic response—what we call "rest and receive." When the body feels safe, it becomes receptive. In this state, the mind quiets, the heart opens, and the energy field shifts from contraction to expansion.

Openness is not just a mindset—it is a physiological invitation that says to the Universe: I am ready. I am aligned. I am available.

✧ Quantum Physics and Possibility Collapse

In quantum theory, every possibility exists in an energetic field of potential—until consciousness chooses. The act of "collapsing the wave function" happens when awareness aligns with expectation. And that collapse determines what becomes real. But here is the key: the less you grasp, the more fluid the field remains. Openness does not weaken the outcome—it frees the universe to deliver in the most aligned way.

When you surrender control and hold space with clarity, you allow the quantum field to do what it does best: organize reality around your frequency.

✧ Behavioral Science and Receiving as Identity

Studies in behavioral science reveal that people who identify as worthy and open are far more likely to engage in receiving behaviors. These include accepting help, recognizing opportunities, or allowing joy. Self-concept dictates behavior—and behavior reinforces belief. When you say "yes" to what you desire, even in small ways, you reinforce the identity of someone who receives. That identity then becomes the blueprint that the Universe mirrors. Receiving is not a reward for doing more. It is a natural result of being willing.

Openness is not a soft trait—it is a sacred state. It rewires your brain, soothes your body, and calibrates your energy field to allow in what is already trying to find you. In the dance of manifestation, it is the moment when the music shifts from asking to allowing.

You are not just attracting by what you desire. You are attracting by what you make room for. And the moment you become a match for receiving, the rhythm of your life changes. It softens. It expands. And the gifts you once chased begin to chase you.

Personal Story
—When I Was Not Ready To Receive

My music ministry was one of the greatest moments in my life, but there was a time when everything looked like success from the outside, but—inside, I did not know how to receive.

I had the big shiny tour bus, a talented group of backup singers, a lighting guy, a sound guy—the whole production. I was singing in churches all across the country, and it felt like the vision God gave me was unfolding at full speed.

Somewhere along the way, we stopped at a church where I performed, and I immediately connected with the pastor there. Over time, he became like a second father to me, and before long, my ministry was considered an extension of that church.

It felt like a blessing. I was an independent artist—handling all the advertising, every booking, every radio interview, every television spot by myself, sales, and I performed. It was exhausting. So, when this church offered to take over some of those duties, I accepted with gratitude.

I still never charged a penny to perform, but the church would collect offerings at my concerts, and my ministry would use those funds to pay the singers, the crew, and cover ministry expenses, etc. It was a relief. Or so I thought.

Soon, we were on the road singing seven to eight times a week—sometimes twice on Saturdays or Sundays. This had gone on for at least nine or ten months.

I had become so tired that I did not know what city I was in half the time. I was so worn out; I had to ask someone what state I was in before I stepped on stage.

I called the pastor one night and said, "Pastor, I need to take a break. I'm exhausted. I can not even see straight, I am so tired."

He replied, "Son, you know you have to strike while the iron is hot?"
And I remember saying back, "But Pastor, if I am dead from exhaustion, there will be no iron to strike."

So, against his advice, I made a choice: I called ahead, canceled a week of bookings, rescheduled them, and came home. I slept for three days.

When I woke up, I thought to myself, you know what? I need a few new suits. I had sweated through the ones I had so many times that no dry cleaner could save them any longer.

But when I went to pay, my debit card was declined. I tried again, several times to no avail.

Confused, I called the bank—my heart sank. They told me I was overdrawn by nearly $1,200.

I knew in my spirit that something was very wrong. I had a mental tally of what should've been in that account based on the concert offerings. We sang to audiences of between 1,000 and 5,000 people, plus made sales of quite a few CDs and T-shirts. I should have had close to $1.5 million still in that account.

Instead, I was in the red.

I called the pastor immediately, and he said, "Son, you need to come in. We need to talk."

That conversation changed everything. The pastor had decided to expand the church, and my ministry funds were used to jumpstart the project.

No one told me. No one asked. He had hoped to replace the money before I noticed. That is why he was so adamant about my not coming home so soon.

I trusted that man with my life. I trusted him more than I trusted anyone at the time.

I left that church crushed. I let everyone in my group go. Canceled every future concert, every television appearance. And for a long time, I could not even pass a church without shaking.

My grandmother told me to press charges. But every time I tried to pick up the phone to call the police, I heard a still, small voice whisper, "Vengeance is Mine."

So, I chose surrender.

I told my grandmother, that the money was never mine. It was given to God for His work. And I believe that somehow, He will take care of this.

Scripture says, "...**whatever the locusts have eaten, God will restore**." (Joel 2:25). I held on to that.

A few years passed. I healed. I forgave. I started to sing again.

One night, we sang at a church in West Palm Beach, Florida. After the concert, the pastor mentioned we had five days off before our next stop. A woman from the audience came up to me as I stood at my product table.

She had a peaceful glow about her and said, "You do not need to stay in a hotel. Come stay with me. I have plenty of room for all of you." I hesitated, thinking. I said, "There are seven of us. Are you sure?" She smiled and said, "I'm sure."

We followed her into Palm Beach—past mansions and estates—until we pulled up to a grand compound. I assumed she lived in one of the buildings. But no, the entire complex was hers.
We are going to call her Mary. Mary's husband owned a major fashion label, one you would recognize instantly.

That night, after everyone went to bed, she invited me to sit on the back patio by the pool. She said softly, "I have to confess something. I brought you here with an ulterior motive."

She shared that her daughter had recently gone through a painful divorce, contracted HIV from her husband, and was abandoned by all her friends and most of the family, out of fear. She had fallen into deep depression and stopped taking her medication. Because she had stopped taking her medication, she had been given less than a year to live.

Mary said she had tried everything—doctors, healers, psychologists, psychiatrists, therapists—but nothing worked. "And then I saw you sing tonight," she said, tears in her eyes. "The way you spoke... the way you sang... the love that poured from your spirit... I thought maybe—just maybe—you could be the light she needs."

I told her gently, "I am just a church singer, Mary. I am not trained for something like this."

She said, "I know. But she just needs a friend."

The next morning, I spent time with her daughter, shared a few stories, encouraged her, and spoke life into her. I did the best I could. We connected and became friends.

By the time we left a few days later, she had started taking her medication again.

Every month after that, I sent her something—a note, a flower, a card. I never heard back. For years, nothing.

Then, one day, about six years later, a package arrived at my door from a law office. Inside was a letter. Mary's daughter had passed—but she had left me a sapphire. Not just any sapphire—a nearly 300-carat sapphire. I could not keep it.

I immediately packed it up and sent it to Mary. Mary called me as soon as she received the package. "Why did you do that?" she asked. "That stone was hers, and she wanted you to have it. It is worth millions of dollars; you could have sold it."

I said to Mary, "I would not have sold it, not knowing who it belonged to. But Mary, you could have this—put into a brooch and wear it to every gala in town. If I keep it, it will just sit in a box until I die, and then perhaps be donated to the Smithsonian. That stone deserves to live." She reluctantly accepted.

Years later, another package arrived. This time it was massive. Mary herself had passed away. Inside was Mary's loose gemstone collection— diamonds, rubies, emeralds, sapphires of every color from mines all over the world. A letter from her lawyer said I had been named as the heir to these stones.

I was dumbfounded. I thought to myself, wait, was this restoration? Was this God keeping His promise—not just to return what was lost, but to pour it back in a way I never could have imagined.

More than that—it was the moment I realized that I had finally learned how to receive.

I had been comfortable being the one always giving.

I realized the first time God tried to restore, I was not ready. I sent the sapphire back. I still carried a wound. Still wrestled with whether I was worthy of something so extravagant.

But then, God tried again. And this time, I had healed enough to say yes and receive.

I did not chase it. I did not earn it. I was just—open.

And that is the rhythm of receiving:

Sometimes the blessing does not come until your soul is still enough, and your hands are open enough to hold it.

Practical Applications
—Practicing the Art of Receiving

Before you can fully receive in the spiritual, you often need to make small shifts in the physical. Receiving is not just a concept—it is a practice. It lives in your posture, your habits, your mindset, and even in how you respond to kindness.

These next practices are gentle but powerful ways to open the doors within you. Think of them as tuning your instrument to the frequency of blessing—so when it arrives, you are not just ready, you are in harmony with it.

1. **Say yes to the small things**.
   Let someone treat you to coffee. Accept compliments without deflecting. These small yeses train your nervous system to receive.

2. **Create daily receiving rituals**.
   Each morning, whisper: "I open myself to receive today. I trust what flows to me." Let this be your sacred welcome.

3. **Declutter to make room**.
   Spiritual energy flows where there is space. Clean a drawer, clear your calendar, release an old grudge. Make room.

4. **Soften your body language**.
   Unclench your jaw. Relax your shoulders. Breathe deeply. Receiving begins in the body.

5. **Journal as if it is already here**.
   Write: "I am so grateful that..." and describe your manifestation in present-tense detail. Let your spirit welcome it.

6. **Practice the receiving breath**.
   Inhale with the thought: "I receive." Exhale: "I allow." Do this for two minutes a day.

7. **Be a channel, not a container**.
   As you receive, let energy flow through you. Give, share, bless. The more you circulate, the more you open to receive.

8. **Do not rob someone else's blessing**.
   Sometimes we resist receiving out of pride or discomfort, but saying no to a gift or gesture can block someone else's opportunity to be a blessing. Letting them give, honors their obedience—and keeps the flow of grace moving.

Receiving is not a finish line—it is a frequency you return to, moment by moment, with intention and grace.

These practices are not about perfection. They are about presence. They help you loosen the grip of resistance and open your whole being to divine orchestration.

The more you say yes—to the small, the sacred, the unexpected—the more you align with the rhythm of flow. And in that rhythm, blessings do not just pass by; they recognize you. They see a soul ready, a heart open, and a life that has made room.

So, keep practicing. Keep softening. Keep allowing. Because what is on its way is not just coming to visit—it is coming to stay.

Affirmation

"I am open. I am willing. I am ready to receive. What is mine flows to me with ease, grace, and perfect timing."

Guided Meditation
—Opening to the Flow

Sit still. Breathe softly. Feel your body as a vessel—open, present, steady.

Now, imagine a gentle river of light flowing toward you. This is your answered prayer. Your peace. Your abundance. Your healing.

Let it flow into your hands, your chest, your being. Whisper inwardly, "I receive. I am safe. I am ready." Feel the flow continue—not forced, not grasped—just allowed.

You are open. You are aligned. You are in rhythm with the Universe.

Conclusion

Receiving is not a weakness. It is not passive. And it is certainly not the result of perfection.

It is presence.

It is the holy exhale after you have done your part. It is the sacred stillness where your energy stops striving—and starts allowing.

To receive is not to grasp, chase, or demand. It is to open and remember that you were never meant to carry the weight of manifesting alone. You are a co-creator, yes—but also a divine receiver. And the receiving requires a posture of trust. A rhythm of surrender.

Most people do not miss their blessings because they were not worthy. They miss them because they were unavailable. Closed. Caught in control. They were too busy proving they had earned it instead of simply preparing to hold it.

But the blessings do not disappear. They wait.

They wait for a heart soft enough to recognize them. For hands willing to release what no longer serves. For a soul that says, "*I do not have to do it all. I just have to be open.*"

Because when the energy of your being becomes receptive, the flow returns. The stream of divine provision begins to move again—not because you forced it, but because you finally made space for it.

This is not the end of the manifesting journey; it is its fulfillment. The point where the invisible becomes visible. Where the prayers you once whispered begin to echo back in answered form. Where the light you have been sending out starts making its way home.

And all of it begins with one quiet, powerful shift: When you stop reaching and you start receiving.

You do not have to chase what has already been sent. All you need to do is welcome it. With stillness, with faith, and with readiness.

Because the truth is—what you are waiting for is also waiting for you. And the moment you say yes—not with your lips, but with your life—it finds its way to your door.

Open your heart. Unclench your hands. And receive.

Because anything is possible—if you just allow the blessing to enter.

Chapter 17: The Power of Focus
—Where Attention Goes, Energy Flows

Opening Reflection

"Watch your thoughts, for they become words; watch your words, for they become actions; watch your actions, for they become habits; watch your habits, for they become character; watch your character, for it becomes your destiny."
—Frank Outlaw.

Introduction

Focus is not just about what you look at—it is about what you energize. Your attention is the currency of creation. It is the spotlight that brings ideas into clarity, the magnifying glass that heats desire into action.

Whatever you consistently focus on—whether in thought, word, or emotion—begins to take root in your life. In this way, focus is not only mental—it is vibrational. It determines your frequency. And your frequency shapes your future.

As we pointed out above in the opening reflection, Frank Outlaw once said, "Watch your thoughts, for they become words... watch your character, for it becomes your destiny." He was describing more than habit formation—he was describing **energetic law**. *What you think, you become. What you dwell on, you attract. What you focus on, you vibrate. And that vibration draws matching experiences to you.*

Manifestation is not just about the things you want. It is about what you pay attention to over and over again. The question is not, "Why has it not happened yet?" but "What have I been giving my energy to?"

Most people are unaware of the quiet drift of their focus. One moment, they are visualizing a goal, and within 10 seconds, they are drowning in worry, feeding doubt, or rehearsing worst-case scenarios.

And energy follows.

This chapter is about becoming intentional with your focus—because what you focus on, you feed. And what you feed, grows.

Hidden Teachings from Ancient Traditions
—The Sacred Lens of Focus—How Spiritual Attention Shapes Reality

Across every sacred tradition, the act of focus is not treated as mere mental discipline—it is revered as spiritual power.

In these teachings, attention is a gateway to transformation. Where the eyes of the heart rest, life responds. From Hebrew psalms to Sufi prayers, from yogic meditation to Buddhist mindfulness, the ancient masters understood that what we dwell upon becomes what we manifest.

Focus, in their view, is not just concentration—it is devotion. Not just awareness—but alignment.

Let us look at how these traditions guide us to harness the sacred power of focus as a frequency that shapes reality.

✧ **Christian Faith**

Scripture reminds us in Philippians 4:8, "**Whatever is true, whatever is noble, whatever is right, whatever is pure, whatever is lovely, whatever is admirable—if anything is excellent or praiseworthy —think about such things**." Why? Because your thoughts are not harmless. They are the architects of your reality.

Jesus often redirected focus before performing miracles. When Peter walked on water, he stayed afloat only while his eyes were on Jesus. The moment he looked at the wind and waves, he sank (Matthew 14:30). *The principle is clear: fear entered because focus shifted.*

The psalmist declared, "**I keep my eyes always on the Lord. With Him at my right hand, I will not be shaken..**" (Psalm 16:8). Focus is faith in motion.

Even in the wilderness, the Israelites were instructed to look up at the bronze serpent to be healed (Numbers 21:9). Their healing came not from effort—but from focus.

✧ Jewish Wisdom

In Jewish tradition, focus is a sacred act of remembrance. The Hebrew word zakhor— "to remember"—appears throughout the Torah not merely as a call to mental recall, but as a deep, embodied attentiveness to what is holy. Focus, in this view, is a form of spiritual fidelity.

Proverbs 4: 25–27 teaches, "**Let your eyes look directly forward, and your gaze be straight before you. Ponder the path of your feet; then all your ways will be sure. Do not swerve to the right or to the left; turn your foot away from evil.**" This is more than advice—it is instruction for disciplined presence. Right vision creates the right direction.

Jewish mysticism, particularly in Kabbalah, emphasizes the importance of kavanah—focused intention in both prayer and action. Without kavanah, even sacred rituals can become empty. But with it, the soul aligns with divine will. Rabbi Chaim of Volozhin wrote that "*One word of prayer with true intention can ascend higher than thousands without it.*" (The Soul of Life Vilna, 1824)

The teachings of Rabbi Abraham Joshua Heschel also remind us that "*just to be is a blessing. Just to live is holy.*" (The Insecurity of Freedom: Essays on Human Existence. Farrar, Straus and Giroux, 1966) But we only touch that holiness when we are present enough to notice it.

In Jewish thought, distraction is not simply a lapse in attention—it is a break in relationship. And to focus the heart, the eyes, and the soul on the Divine is to return to wholeness.

✦ Islamic Teaching

The Qur'an says, "**Indeed, in the remembrance of Allah do hearts find rest**." (Qur'an 13:28) Dhikr—remembrance—is not just prayer, but focused awareness of divine names and attributes. The repetition of Allah's names calls the soul into alignment with mercy, peace, strength, and provision.

Salāh (prayer) is a practice of spiritual focus—facing the qibla, quieting the world, entering a sacred rhythm of recitation. Even posture becomes prayer.

The Prophet Muhammad (peace be upon him) taught that the wandering mind during prayer weakens its power. Presence is the portal to nearness. In Islam, focus is not control—it is surrender.

It is trusting that your gaze toward the Divine is enough to bring rest to your heart and alignment to your life.

✦ Buddhist Practices

In Buddhism, the power of focus is not about force—it is about returning. The mind, often likened to a restless monkey, leaps from thought to thought, chasing what is next and missing what is now. But the practice of mindfulness, or sati, is the gentle art of bringing attention back—again and again—to the present moment.

Right concentration (sammā samādhi) is one of the eightfold path's core pillars. It is not suppression. It is spacious, steady awareness. The Buddha taught: "**The mind is hard to control; swiftly and lightly it moves and lands wherever it pleases. It is good to tame the mind, for a well-tamed mind brings happiness**." (Dhammapada 35) Meditation, breath awareness, and shamatha (calm abiding) are practices that train the mind not just to settle, but to see clearly. In that clarity, illusion begins to dissolve, and the practitioner sees the impermanence of all things.

The Zen master Shunryu Suzuki once said, "**The mind of a beginner is empty, free of the habits of the expert, ready to accept, to doubt, and open to all the possibilities**." This shoshin, or beginner's mind, is a sacred focus—not narrowed by attachment, but opened by humility.

To focus in the Buddhist tradition is not to strain—it is to let go of noise. To return to breath. To dwell fully in the only moment that ever truly exists: *now*.

✧ Hindu Insights

In Hinduism, the power of focus is revered as a path to divine union. The word dhyāna—deep, meditative focus—is the heartbeat of spiritual discipline across nearly every yogic path.

The Bhagavad Gita says, "**Whenever the mind wanders, due to its unsteady nature, one should bring it back under the control of the Self**." (Gita 6:26) Focus is not forced—it is remembered.

Hindu sages describe the focused mind as a lamp in a windless place. Undisturbed. Radiant. Clear. This steady gaze pierces illusion (maya) and reveals truth.

The Upanishads declare: "**As one acts and as one conducts himself, so does he become**." (Brihadaranyaka Upanishad 4.4.5) What you think, you become. What you focus on, you radiate.

Focus, in this tradition, is not self-improvement—it is divine remembrance. It is returning your awareness to the truth you never left.

In every sacred path, focus is more than discipline—it is devotion. It is where the eyes of the soul meet the presence of the Divine. When you fix your gaze on peace, you become peace. When you fix your thoughts on possibility, you create a path for miracles. Focus is the sacred lens that shapes reality. And once you choose what to see with your whole heart, the frequency of your life begins to rise in response.

Wisdom from Contemporary Spiritual Leaders

Focus is more than a technique—it is a sacred discipline seen by many spiritual teachers as the doorway to transformation. The great ones remind us that what we fix our gaze upon, we begin to energize with the full weight of our belief. Whether it is science-backed guidance or soul-deep knowing, their wisdom circles back to this truth: your focus is not small. It is a creative force.

Below, we explore insights from thought leaders and spiritual teachers who have taught us—each in their own way—that manifestation begins with choosing what you will see, what you will dwell on, and what you will honor with your attention.

—Dr. Joe Dispenza teaches that "**energy flows where attention goes.**" If you want to shift your life, you must shift your focus—because your focus determines your frequency.

—Abraham Hicks reminds us: "**You get what you think about, whether you want it or not.**" If you focus on the absence of something, you prolong the absence. If you focus on the joy of its arrival, you draw it near.

—Oprah Winfrey has said that one of her greatest lessons was learning the power of focus. "**Whatever you focus on expands. So, focus on what you want, not what you fear.**"

— Iyanla Vanzant teaches; "**Your energy introduces you before you speak—and that energy is shaped by what you have been focusing on all day.**" Our words don't stand alone—they are carried on the frequency of the energy we've cultivated, making our focus throughout the day just as important as the speech that follows.

—Albert Einstein said, "**I am thankful to all those who said no. It is because of them I am doing it myself.**" That is focus turned inward. The ability to fix your eyes on vision, not opposition.

—Dannion Brinkley says, "**What you think is what you are. What you radiate outward in your thoughts, feelings, mental pictures, and words, you draw to you.**" Dannion emphasizes that our inner focus—our thoughts, feelings, and even mental images—act as magnets, attracting matching outcomes into our lives.

—Roy Waugh, "**I have learned that focus is more than just paying attention—it is a sacred lens. Whatever you look at with belief, with intention, with your whole heart, you start inviting into form.**" This quote is not just philosophy—it has lived truth. When I look back on my own journey, I can see how what I focused on—really focused on, with faith and feeling—started to show up in my life. Focus is not just what we see—it is what we honor. And the moment we focus with belief, we start shaping reality.

In the end, every teacher here is pointing to the same revelation: your energy flows where your attention goes. Not by accident, and not by force —but through clarity, consistency, and intention. Focus is not a magic trick. It is the alignment of your inner world with your truest desires. And when that alignment locks into place—when your focus becomes a spiritual yes—the field responds. Reality begins to reorient. What once felt far begins to draw near. What once seemed impossible starts shaping itself in your direction.

All because you finally chose to look—and keep looking—with your whole heart.

Scientific Perspectives on Focus and Energy
—The Physics of Attention — How Focus Shapes Mind, Matter, and Momentum

Science continues to affirm what spiritual teachers have always known: focus is not passive. It is a force. In both the seen and unseen realms, your attention operates like a tuning fork—sending signals to your brain, your body, and the field around you. Whether through the rewiring of neural pathways or the quantum-level shifts in probability, modern research now confirms that where you place your attention does not just change what you notice—it begins to change what is.

Let us explore how neuroscience, physiology, and quantum physics all converge on one truth: your focus holds creative power.

✧ Neuroplasticity and the Architecture of Belief

Your brain is not fixed—it is fluid. Through a process called neuroplasticity, the brain continuously reorganizes itself based on experience and focus. The more you give attention to a thought, a belief, or an intention, the stronger those neural pathways become.

Dr. Joe Dispenza often says, "Neurons that fire together, wire together." That means each time you focus on possibility, peace, or purpose, you are reinforcing the neural patterns that make those states easier to return to. Over time, your focus literally sculpts your internal reality—and that internal blueprint becomes the template for your external world.

✧ The Reticular Activating System: The Brain's Filter of Reality

Inside your brainstem is a small but powerful mechanism known as the reticular activating system (RAS). Its job is to filter the millions of pieces of information you receive every second and show you only what you have told it matters to you.

If you focus on abundance, the RAS highlights opportunities. If you focus on lack, it shows you more reasons to fear.

Your focus trains the system. It creates a feedback loop that either expands your awareness—or narrows it. The RAS does not judge. It just obeys. So, the question becomes: what reality have you been telling it to look for?

✦ Visualization, Performance, and Embodied Belief

Elite athletes, musicians, and performers across disciplines have long used visualization to enhance their craft. Scientific studies confirm that when you mentally rehearse an action with intense focus, your brain activates the same regions as if you were physically performing it.

This is not imaginary play—it is embodied training. The body cannot always tell the difference between real and vividly imagined experiences. So, when your focus is sharp and intentional, you are not just daydreaming—you are imprinting. You are sending instructions to your cells, your muscles, your emotions, and your energy field. Focus becomes rehearsal for reality.

✦ Quantum Physics and the Observer Effect

In the world of quantum mechanics, the act of observation influences the outcome. Known as the observer effect, this principle reveals that subatomic particles exist in a state of probability until they are observed—at which point they collapse into form. Focus, then, becomes a catalyst.

You are not just a bystander—you are a participant. When you fix your attention with belief and clarity, you begin shaping which possibilities take shape. You collapse the wave. You call the form. This is not mysticism—it is physics. The universe responds not just to thought but also to focused thought that is aligned with expectation.

Across disciplines—from the inner workings of the brain to the laws of quantum energy—the evidence is clear: focus creates shifts not just in mindset, but in biology, behavior, and the fabric of reality itself.

Your attention is a sacred instrument—more than just noticing, it is selecting, energizing, and informing what becomes real. Science may use a different language from spirit, but the conclusion is the same: focus is a creative command. And the more aligned your focus becomes with your intention, the more the world begins to mirror your vision—one clear thought at a time.

Personal Story
—The Night The Thermostat Listened

There was a season in college when I was doing everything I could to stay afloat.

My tuition, room, and board were covered—thank God—and I had my little car (that same little car that I tried to run away from home with).
I did not have much else.

Part of my tuition agreement included an on-campus job. Actually, I worked multiple jobs: I was the secretary for the football coach, a yell leader for both the football and basketball teams, and on weekends, I traveled with one of the university's revival teams to sing and minister at churches. I never saw a dollar from it—my wages went straight to the university. So, when anything unexpected came up, there was not much to fall back on.

And then my car started overheating.
At first, it was sporadic. I kept a few gallons of water in the trunk to manage it. I had a hunch it was the thermostat sticking—something I had learned from watching my dad work on engines when I was little. He could fix anything when he wanted to, but he was four hours away, and we did not have a phone at home to call for help. Even if I could have reached him, I knew he could not afford to buy the gas to get to me. It was just me and whatever faith I could muster.

One weekend, we had a long drive for a revival, and I was halfway there when the car started overheating again. The temperature gauge kept creeping into the red. Worse yet, I was on a stretch of highway with no exits, no gas stations, no traffic, and the sun had already gone down. I was completely alone. I kept driving.

Panic hit me fast. My chest was tight. My mind started racing with everything that could go wrong. I began to pray—desperate, pleading prayers. "God, please—please just get me there. I will do anything. Just help me." I cried. I bargained. I begged. I pleaded for what seemed like an hour.

Then something strange happened.

In the middle of that fear, I remembered something I had told a friend not long before: "When you pray, be specific. Do not just ask—focus. See it. Speak it. Believe it." I had preached it to others. But in that moment, it came echoing back to me like a boomerang from heaven.
So, I stopped begging—and I started focusing.
Even with my eyes on the road, I could see the thermostat in my mind, and I saw the exact piece I knew was stuck. I visualized it releasing. I imagined it opening like it was supposed to, but with ease. I did not just think it—I saw it. I felt it. I knew it.

Then something came over me—an energy, a presence, something beyond description. It was like fire in my veins, but not burning—illuminating. My skin felt electric. Without thinking, my voice began to declare out loud:

"I command you to obey."

I spoke it as if I had the authority to change reality with my own voice. Over and over, I repeated it.

"I command you to obey."

I was not shouting—I was channeling. I was locked into a singular, unwavering focus. It was like the failing part of the car's cooling system I needed was floating in front of me like a hologram, and my faith was tuning it in real-time.

Then something shifted.

I felt it inside—like a bomb of release, a letting-go so powerful it was almost physical. My whole body exhaled at once.

And in that exact moment, I looked down at my dashboard and watched— **YES WATCHED**—the temperature gauge move down. Not slowly. Not randomly. But deliberately—like someone was pressing it down with their fingertip.

It slid from red to safe, and I sat there stunned.

I had chills that gave birth to chills. It felt like I was floating. The car was quiet, peaceful. The air felt thick with something divine, almost like there was an invisible cloud in the car.
And I drove the rest of the way without a single problem.

When I arrived at the revival, I did not mention what had happened—part of me wondered if anyone would believe it. *But I knew*. I knew what I had just experienced was not mechanical—it was spiritual. I had not just instantly manifested the repair my car needed. I had learned something life-changing: *Focused belief is spiritual ignition.*

Begging had gotten me nowhere. But the moment I brought my attention, intention, and imagination into alignment—something obeyed. Something responded.

Looking back, that moment taught me one of the most important lessons I have ever learned:

You do not just pray with words. You pray with your entire being. You pray with focus.

You do not just manifest with hope. You manifest with vision. And when your focus becomes as clear as your desire, the universe itself, the laws of life, faith, and energy start moving on your behalf.

Practical Applications
—Training the Power of Focus

Focus is a muscle—and like any muscle, it grows stronger with use. The following practices are designed to help you train your attention, reclaim your energy, and direct your mental spotlight toward what matters most. These are not just habits—they are alignment tools.

As you apply them, you will begin to notice a shift in how you think, how you feel, and what shows up in your life. Remember: *what you focus on, you energize. And what you energize, you attract.*

1. **Morning focus ritual**.
   Before anything else, ask: "What do I want to magnify today?" Choose one quality—peace, courage, clarity—and focus on it throughout your day.

2. **Create a focused environment**. Remove visual clutter. Curate what you consume. Set up physical reminders (quotes, images, objects) that reinforce your vision.

3. **Use a focus mantra**.
   Repeat a phrase like: "Where my focus goes, energy flows." Or: "I choose to see the good, feel the good, and expect the good."

4. **Limit focus leaks**.
   Catch yourself when you are feeding doubt, gossip, or distractions. Gently redirect: "Not that. This." Reclaim your focus.

5. **Set a sacred hour**.
   Designate an hour a day—morning or night—for pure focus on your vision: meditating, writing, affirming, or visualizing.

6. **Use visual anchors**.
   Choose a color, candle, stone, or image that represents your desire. Look at it often. Let it bring your focus back to center.

7. **Breath as focus training**.
   Practice breathwork to train attention. Inhale focus. Exhale distraction. Repeat.

Focus is not just a tool—it is a devotion. Each of these practices is a way of saying to the universe, "This is where I choose to place my energy." When you focus with intention, you stop scattering your power and start gathering your light. Even small shifts in attention create momentum. You begin to notice more, feel more, attract more—not because the world changed, but because your awareness did.

The power was never outside of you. It was always in the lens through which you chose to see. So, focus the lens. Hold your gaze. And watch your reality begin to reflect the clarity of your inner vision.

Affirmation

"My focus is powerful. I direct it with purpose. Where I place my attention, life begins to bloom."

Guided Meditation
—Sharpening the Inner Lens

Find a comfortable space. Simply turn inward.

Breathe in clarity.
Breathe out distraction.

Picture a beam of light at the center of your forehead. This is your focus. Now, place it gently on one vision—one desire that excites your soul. Let the light surround it. Fill it. Energize it. See every detail.

Whisper inwardly: "This is where I place my energy. This is what I choose to grow." Stay there. Let the light deepen. Then return to your breath, carrying that clarity and focus with you.

Conclusion

Focus is not just a mental act—it is a spiritual commitment.

It is the moment you stop scattering your energy and start gathering your power. The moment you stop chasing every noise around you and begin listening for the voice within you. Focus is faith with direction.

It is vision in motion. It is choosing—again and again—to give your energy to what you want to grow, rather than what you fear will happen.

Your life is already reflecting your focus. Look around. What has been growing? What has been fading? That is your energy speaking.

That is your attention at work.

But here is the sacred truth: you can shift it. You can train it. You can reclaim it.

You do not need to force your way into the future—you need only to focus your way forward.

The world will always offer distractions. The mind will always wander. But the soul? The soul knows how to return. To quiet the noise. To fix its gaze. To trust what it sees—before it is seen.

Because when you begin to focus with clarity, speak with conviction, and believe with intensity, the atmosphere begins to rearrange itself in your favor. Sometimes the mountains do not move because you yell at them. They move because you focus long enough to believe they must.

You are already powerful.
You already carry divine potential.

Focus does not give you that power—it reveals it.

So, hold your gaze. Choose your thought. Guard your energy like the sacred instrument it is.

Because the moment you lock into divine alignment—heaven listens.

And sometimes—even a stuck thermostat starts to obey when your frequency becomes too focused to ignore.

Chapter 18: The Power of Persistence
—Holding the Vision When Nothing Seems to Be Happening

Opening Reflection

"Faith and attitude are loud at the beginning. But persistence? Persistence is that quiet voice that keeps nudging you, whispering 'keep going,' even when everything around you goes silent."
—Roy Waugh

Introduction

Persistence is not loud—it is loyal.

It does not burst onto the scene with fanfare. It does not shout like faith or dance like joy. Persistence is quieter than all of that. It is the sacred whisper that rises when the fireworks fade. The gentle nudge that says, keep going—even when the room has emptied, the phone has stopped ringing, and the miracle still has not shown up.

At the beginning of a vision, everything feels electric. Faith surges. Energy pulses. The alignment feels effortless. But what happens when the high wears off? When the signs go silent and all you hear is your own heartbeat echoing in the stillness?

That is where manifestation either dissolves or deepens.

Persistence is not about striving. It is not about pushing harder or doing more. It is about staying anchored. It is about believing, even when nothing looks like it is working. It is the choice to stand in sacred agreement with your vision, even when the world offers you nothing but delay.

This chapter is not about hustle. It is about holy endurance. The kind that holds steady. The kind that does not let go. The kind that keeps showing up to the altar of your dream, even when the skies are quiet.
Because sometimes, the silence is not your enemy—it is your invitation.

Hidden Teachings from Ancient Traditions
—How Persistence Deepens Manifestation Across Spiritual Paths

Persistence is more than endurance. It is sacred devotion in motion. While the modern world often associates manifestation with speed, ancient wisdom speaks of something deeper—faith that holds its ground when the evidence disappears.

Each of the great spiritual traditions teaches that lasting transformation is not born in the moment of inspiration, but in the steady, patient tending of vision through silence, struggle, and delay.

Let us explore how five sacred traditions illuminate the soul-deep power of persistence.

✧ Christian Faith

In Christianity, persistence is not just praised—it is promised a harvest. Galatians 6:9 urges, **"Let us not grow weary in doing good, for at the proper time we will reap a harvest if we do not give up."** It is not the flash of belief that brings the miracle—it is the staying power of faith.

Scripture is rich with stories of holy endurance. Noah continued building the ark with no rain in sight. Genesis 6:13–22 (NIV) Joseph held onto his dream through betrayal and imprisonment. Genesis 37:5–28; 39:20–23; 41:14–16 (NIV) David persisted in worship while hunted by Saul. 1 Samuel 19:1–2; Psalm 59 (NIV) And Jesus shared the story of the persistent widow, whose unyielding petitions brought justice. (Luke 18:1-8)

Each story points to the same truth: persistence does not push God—it positions us. To stay in alignment when heaven is silent is one of the greatest acts of spiritual trust.

✧ Jewish Wisdom

Judaism is a faith forged in the fires of sacred resilience. The name "Israel" itself—given to Jacob after his long night of wrestling with the divine—means *one who wrestles with God.* It represents not just a person or a people, but a spiritual posture: one that holds on when others would let go.

Scripture offers powerful images of this holy perseverance. When Abraham pleaded for Sodom, he persisted in intercession, negotiating boldly with God. Jacob declared, **"I will not let You go unless You bless me**." (Genesis 32:26, NKJV) That stubborn trust earned him both a blessing and a new identity.

Even Jewish prayer life echoes this persistence. Daily blessings are repeated with devotion, and davening—the swaying movement during prayer—mirrors the soul's unwillingness to be still in the face of divine silence.

In Jewish mysticism, time is not linear—it spirals. This means every moment carries the potential to begin again. To persist in the sacred is to recognize that even in delay, you are never starting over. You are circling deeper.

✧ Islamic Teaching

In Islam, persistence flows from the attribute of God known as As-Sabur— The Most Patient. To reflect this divine quality is to embody enduring trust.

The Qur'an declares: **"So be patient. Indeed, the promise of Allah is truth**." (Qur'an 30:60) The life of the Prophet Muhammad (peace be upon him) exemplifies this principle. He faced rejection, exile, and persecution for over two decades, yet remained steadfast in his mission.

Daily prayers (salah), performed five times a day, cultivate spiritual stamina. Ramadan, a month of fasting, teaches delayed gratification and discipline. These are not arbitrary rituals—they are sacred training grounds for the soul.

Persistence in Islam is not ego-driven striving. It is surrender that moves. Endurance that flows. Faith that trusts without a timeline.

✧ Buddhist Practices

In Buddhism, persistence is understood not as force, but as right effort—the quiet courage to keep returning, keep practicing, and keep believing, even when progress feels invisible. It is one of the key teachings of the Noble Eightfold Path and forms the backbone of all spiritual discipline.
The Dhammapada reminds us: "**As a solid rock is not shaken by the wind, wise people falter not amidst blame and praise**." (Dhammapada 6:81) This verse anchors the truth that persistence is not loud—it is steady. It is rooted in internal strength, not external validation.

The Buddha's own journey under the Bodhi tree is a testament to sacred persistence. He vowed not to rise until he reached enlightenment. It was not dramatic action, but unshakable stillness, that carried him across the threshold of awakening.

Daily mindfulness, too, is a form of persistence—the gentle art of returning again and again to presence, to breath, to compassion. And over time, those small returns become a powerful transformation.

In Buddhist practice, spiritual enlightenment is rarely lightning—it is rain. Gentle, consistent, and quietly unstoppable.

✧ Hindu Traditions

In Hindu philosophy, the concept of tapas—inner fire—captures the soul's capacity to stay lit in seasons of darkness. Tapas is not burnout. It is devotion that glows without demanding an outcome.

The Bhagavad Gita speaks to this sacred perseverance: "**Be steadfast in yoga... Perform your duty and abandon all attachment to success or failure**." (Gita 2:47) This is persistence rooted in divine detachment.

Sadhana, the daily discipline of spiritual practice, is persistence in action —chanting, meditating, honoring the divine even when no visible fruit appears.

From epic tales to quiet rituals, Hinduism teaches that manifestation is not a race—it is a rhythm. And those who stay in that rhythm will see the fruit in divine time.

Every path speaks the same silent truth: persistence is not passive waiting —it is active, sacred alignment with what you know is coming. When you stay faithful through silence, you are not just proving your belief—you are becoming the version of you that can hold the miracle when it arrives.

Wisdom from Contemporary Spiritual Leaders

Persistence may not always feel profound. It often shows up not with thunder, but with a whisper that says, "Keep going." When faith feels like a flicker, and vision feels far away, the words of those who have walked the path before us become lanterns in the dark.

These spiritual teachers remind us that breakthrough rarely comes from force—it comes from consistency, from trust, and from the daily choice to hold on when the miracle is still invisible.

—Dr. Joe Dispenza says, "**Your brain is a record of the past, but your mind is a map of the future**." Persistence is what keeps your map active—even when your past screams otherwise.

—Joyce Meyer often reminds people: "**You don't need to feel like it to do it**." Persistence doesn't wait for motivation—it moves with conviction.

—Iyanla Vanzant teaches that transformation is often slow. She says, "**You have to do the work, keep showing up, and trust that the results are coming—even if you don't see them yet**."

—Abraham Hicks explains that staying in the vortex (alignment) over time is more important than trying to force a manifestation through effort. "**Your only job is to stay in the receiving mode. The rest is coming**."

—**Maya Angelou's entire life was a testament to persistence**. Her story, her voice, her poetry—all born from the choice to keep rising.

—Dannion Brinkley says, "**You are a great, mighty, and powerful spiritual being with dignity, direction, and purpose**." This is one of my favorites from Dannion, it reinforces the soul's capacity to persist through darkness and delay. It reminds the reader that persistence is not about forcing outcomes—it is about remembering who you are when nothing seems to be working. In the context of this chapter, it serves as a gentle but powerful affirmation: You are not forgotten. You are powerful. Keep going.

—Roy Waugh, "**Persistence is not loud—it is loyal. It is the quiet agreement between you and God that you are not letting go, no matter how long it takes**." This captures the heart of spiritual endurance—not as striving, but as sacred devotion. Persistence is not about constant motion; it is about inner agreement. It is the decision to keep believing and to keep standing, even when there is no applause or sign. Persistence is not flashy—it is faithful.

These voices remind us that miracles are rarely microwaved. They are slow-cooked in the chambers of time, trust, and tenacity. The ones who manifest the impossible are rarely the most talented—they are the ones who simply refused to stop believing.

Scientific Perspectives on Persistence and Neuroplasticity

—When Consistency Shapes the Brain and Reality Responds

Persistence is more than personal strength—it is a biological strategy. Science shows that the consistent repetition of thought, action, and intention rewires the very fabric of your brain and nervous system. It turns vision into structure.

Over time, what you persist in—mentally, emotionally, and energetically— does not just change your mindset. It reshapes your reality.

Let us explore how neuroscience, psychology, and quantum theory confirm what spiritual teachings have long known: persistence is power in motion.

✧ Neuroplasticity: Repetition Builds Reality

Neuroscience has revealed that the brain is not fixed—it is fluid. This principle, known as neuroplasticity, means that every time you repeat a behavior, belief, or affirmation, you reinforce a neural pathway. Like a trail being worn into a forest floor, the more you walk it, the easier it becomes to travel.

What once felt unnatural becomes automatic. What once required effort begins to flow. The brain quite literally adapts to the pattern you persist in. That is why persistence does not just help you stay on track—it eventually becomes the track.

Dr. Caroline Leaf, a cognitive neuroscientist, teaches that "As you think, you change your brain." Every thought you rehearse becomes a sculptor of your internal landscape.

✦ Grit: The Psychology of Long-Term Success

Psychologist Angela Duckworth coined the term "grit" to describe the blend of passion and perseverance over time. Her groundbreaking research showed that grit—not talent, not IQ—is the greatest predictor of long-term success.

Persistent individuals are not always the fastest starters, but they are almost always the ones who finish. In the context of manifestation, this means holding your vibration, your vision, and your voice steady—even when the results are slow to appear.

Persistence is what builds resilience in the nervous system. It gives the mind a reference point: I have been here before, and I stayed. I can stay again. Over time, this inner stability becomes your spiritual muscle memory.

✦ The Observer Effect: Attention Over Time Creates Form

In quantum physics, the observer effect teaches us that particles behave differently when observed. But it is not just the act of noticing—it is the sustained focus that collapses potential into form.

When you persistently hold a vision in your awareness, you are not just daydreaming—you are collapsing the wave of infinite possibility into the particle of manifested reality.

In this way, persistent focus becomes a spiritual technology. It aligns intention, emotion, and belief long enough for the unseen to become seen.

✧ Persistence as Energetic Calibration

Energetically, persistence signals to the body and the universe: This is real. This matters. I am not letting go. That steady frequency activates coherence between your thoughts, emotions, and physiology.

Studies in heart-brain coherence from the HeartMath Institute have shown that sustained emotional states—like hope, trust, and patience—create measurable changes in immunity, decision-making, and intuition. These shifts do not come from bursts of belief; they come from steady, aligned repetition over time.

In the sacred science of persistence, time is not your enemy—it's your alchemist. It takes your seeds of thought and faith, waters them with repetition, and grows them into form. You are not just waiting—you are wiring. You are not just believing—you are building.

Personal Story
—A Song, A Seed, And A Slap From Heaven

I began singing semi-professionally when I was about sixteen years old. I say "semi-professionally" because, truthfully, I had no idea what I was doing. My grandpa told me that because I was being paid to sing, I was a professional.

It was not planned. I did not grow up thinking I would be a singer. But somehow, through a series of quiet nudges and unexpected doors, God revealed a gift I did not know I had.

My Voice.

It was like God had handed me a gift I did not know I was carrying.
After the very first time I had ever sung in public, I started receiving invitations to sing in small churches—nothing big, nothing flashy, but steady. Word of mouth was my only advertisement. I prayed constantly: "God, what are You doing with this? Is this something YOU are calling me

into, or just something you are trying to teach me, or am I just passing through?"

I had no formal training, no plan, no team—just a voice, a heart full of faith, and a hope that, somehow, this could become a real ministry. I kept showing up. Singing where I could. Driving from church to church in about a 50-mile radius. And all the while waiting.

After several years of it, I felt like I was stuck in spiritual limbo.
I would talk about expanding what I thought was becoming a ministry, but I did not know how. I remember well-meaning people saying, "Maybe you're just meant to be a church soloist. That is a beautiful calling, you know." And I would smile and nod, trying to be gracious. But I also carried a quiet ache inside: Lord, is this it?

But deep inside, there was this stubborn little flame I could not blow out. I knew I was made for something more—I just did not know how to get there.

Then I heard about a Christian artist competition in Estes Park, Colorado —a two-week gathering that included workshops, classes, training, and mentorship from top leaders in Christian music. It was not just a contest. It was a launchpad. A blueprint. And I wanted in—not to compete, but to learn. To finally get the tools I had been praying for.

But I could not afford it.
Between the entry fees, the flight, and lodging, the cost was more than I could even imagine at the time. So, I tucked the dream away, told myself it was not meant to be, and went back to my usual routine.

What I did not know was that while I was quietly trying to let go, God was still working.

A close friend of mine—without telling me—had taken it upon herself to contact churches I had sung in and friends who believed in me. Over several months, she gathered enough donations to pay for my entry fee.

That Christmas, she handed me a big box. Inside was an old microphone and a photo of the Rocky Mountains.

I stared at it, confused.

Then she smiled and said, "You are going. You have been entered. You are going to Colorado."

Tears filled my eyes. I was stunned. Humbled. And terrified.

I still had to raise money for the rest—my plane fare and lodging—but I scraped and saved every penny I could. The day came to leave for Colorado. I had never flown before. My parents drove me to the airport, nervous and proud. My mother was especially afraid to see me step onto that plane. None of us had ever flown before.

When I arrived, I immediately dove into what I came for: the classes. I had notebooks, pens, and a heart hungry to learn. I was not there to win. I did not even prepare a competition song. I just figured I would sing one of my standards, "His Eye Is on the Sparrow," get through the first round, and spend the rest of my time soaking up as much wisdom as I could.

But then something unexpected happened.

I sang, left the stage, and ran straight to a workshop. Later that day, someone came up to me and said, "So, what are you singing tomorrow?" I blinked, confused. "Tomorrow? What do you mean?"

"You made it to the next round."

(Deep breath) I was annoyed.

I had to miss a class I had marked in my schedule during the first round. Now, I would have to miss another one. But I honored the round and sang something else. The next day—same story. Another round. Another missed class.

I came to learn, and these incessant rounds of competition were keeping me from it.

Day after day, I kept advancing. Everyone else was excited for me. I was quietly frustrated. I felt like the very thing I came for was slipping through my fingers.

Until the night before the final round.

That night, I had a dream.

In the dream, an angel entered my room—gliding peacefully down through the ceiling like a breath of light. He walked gently up to the end of my bed and then *slapped the soles of my feet.*

I woke up instantly and sat up, not from fear—but from familiarity.

That was exactly how my grandfather used to wake me up when I stayed at his house. He had passed away a few years earlier, but I knew without question: this was his way of saying, Wake up. Pay attention. Respect this moment.

I did not understand what was going on. But I now trusted that God must know what He is doing.

The next morning, for the final round, I sang "His Eye Is on the Sparrow" again. But this time, I signed the lyrics as I sang—a silent tribute to my mother, who had been born deaf. It was her favorite song.

I poured everything I had into that performance. Not for a trophy. Not for a title. But because I knew I was standing in a holy moment that had taken years to grow into.

And then it happened.

I won Best Male Vocalist.

The prize? Studio time at the studio of one of the most influential Christian Artists in the country.

That project became the launchpad for the next chapter of my life: it opened the doors for me to start opening for some of the biggest names in Contemporary Christian Music, and I stepped onto stages I never even knew existed.

It all began in silence.

In waiting.

And in the frustration of doing everything right—showing up, learning all I could—it felt like the competition was holding me back. Those classes I came for kept slipping through my fingers, and nothing seemed to be moving. At least, that is what I thought.

But God was moving.

He was preparing. Aligning. Planting seeds for the very thing I was trying to manifest, I just did not know it.

And persistence—quiet, patient, weary persistence—is what kept me in position until the door opened.

You see, sometimes the dream does not die. It just goes underground for a while. And if you can hold your ground, hold your belief, hold your vision —even when it looks like nothing is happening. You may just wake up one day and realize everything was growing the whole time.

Practical Applications
—Strengthening Your Spiritual Persistence

Persistence is not always dramatic—it is often quiet, daily, and unseen. It is not about pushing harder, but about standing longer. These next practices are meant to help you stay anchored in what you believe, even when the evidence has not yet caught up. They are not about forcing results—they are about staying available for the manifestation that is still unfolding. Because sometimes, the most powerful thing you can do is simply not give up.

1. **Set a vision anchor.**
   Choose a word, image, or object that represents your desire. Let it remind you to keep going, no matter what.

2. **Track your consistency, not just your results.**
   Celebrate how often you show up, speak life, or stay in alignment—even if the outcome hasn't arrived yet.

3. **Reframe delays as development.**
   Say to yourself: "This isn't a delay. It is a deepening. I am becoming stronger."

4. **Create a spiritual grit journal.**
   Write down moments when you persisted and were rewarded. Let them fuel you during the next stretch.

5. **Let go of the timeline, keep the vision.**
   Detach from "when" and "how." Anchor yourself in "what" and "why.

6. **Develop a comeback phrase.**
   Something short and powerful like: "Still believing.", "I'm not done yet.", or "The seed is still growing."

Persistence is not proven in the grand moments—it is revealed in the quiet ones. When you choose to keep showing up, even without applause, and when you speak life into your vision with no proof in sight, and when you stay aligned long enough for the unseen to catch up with your faith—that is when spiritual persistence becomes divine power.

These practices are not just tools. They are signals. They tell the universe, "I am still here. I still believe." And in time, the universe answers—with a harvest that only endurance could have unlocked.

Affirmation

"I persist in faith. I stand in belief. I hold the vision even when the world is silent. What I planted will bloom in divine time."

Guided Meditation
—The Fire That Keeps Burning

Breathe in slowly.

Picture a small flame in your chest. Not a wildfire—just a steady burn. This is your persistence. It does not flicker. It does not go out.

Imagine yourself walking a path—long, quiet, maybe even dark. But the flame in your chest stays warm. Whisper inwardly: "I believe. I am still here. I am still becoming." With every step, your light glows brighter. Feel the warmth. The resolve.

Let it guide you. Let it steady you. You are still in motion.

Take a deep breath, let the oxygen you are breathing in, nurture that flame. Exhale and be grateful.

Conclusion

Persistence is not glamorous. It does not always look like mountaintops or breakthroughs. More often, it looks like whispering "yes" when no one hears you. It looks like standing when nothing is moving. It looks like praying when you're not even sure anyone is listening.

It is the kind of faith that keeps sowing when the field looks empty. The kind that walks forward without a map. The kind that keeps showing up—not because you feel strong, but because something deeper in you refuses to let go of what you know is promised.

That is persistence.

And if you have ever felt forgotten, delayed, overlooked, or just plain tired, you are not alone. The in-between is where most of us live. It is where the seed sits in silence, where the soil does not speak, where your calling gets tested—not by storms, but by stillness.

But here is the sacred truth:
God does some of His deepest work in the quiet.

The silence does not mean the vision is dead. The delay does not mean the answer's been denied. It may simply mean: not yet. The roots are going deeper; the miracle is maturing, and the doors are aligning behind the scenes.

Because persistence is not about forcing fruit to grow—it is about trusting the process enough to keep watering the soil.

Sometimes, the only thing standing between where you are and what you are trying to manifest is the decision to stay. Stay faithful, stay grounded, and stay available.

You may not feel like you are moving—but the promise still is. You may not hear progress—but heaven has not gone silent. The Universe is still in motion—and it remembers every seed you have ever sown.

So, if today feels quiet, your spirit feels weary, and the wait feels endless, do not walk away. This is sacred ground.

When you persist in the silence, you show the Universe that you are ready to hold the promise when it comes.

And it will come.

Because what you have planted in faith will bloom in divine time.

Chapter 19: Walking in Gratitude

—Living as Though the Prayer Is Already Answered

Opening Reflection

"In the end, life is about how we touch and uplift others—and the gratitude we carry for the chance to do it."
—Dannion Brinkley

Introduction

Gratitude is the key that turns what you have into enough—and what you envision into reality.

In the spiritual language of manifestation, gratitude is not merely a reaction to blessings received. It is a magnetic state of being. It is the bold declaration: "*I trust so deeply in the goodness that is coming, I am already giving thanks for it.*"

Gratitude accelerates manifestation because it tunes your frequency to wholeness, not lack. It says to the universe, to God, to your higher self, "*I see the evidence of goodness. I expect more of it.*"

It dissolves anxiety. Reframes setbacks. Transforms waiting into worship. And, perhaps most powerfully, it becomes a declaration of alignment: *I live as though my prayer has already been answered.*

This chapter is about learning to walk in that posture—not as a technique, but as a lifestyle.

Because gratitude is not a sidebar to manifestation.

It is the road that brings it home.

Hidden Teachings from Ancient Traditions
—Sacred Expressions of Gratitude Across Faiths

Gratitude is not exclusive to any one belief system—it echoes through the sacred texts and practices of every major spiritual tradition. From whispered prayers of thanks to elaborate festivals of appreciation, each path teaches that acknowledging the blessing is part of receiving it. Gratitude, in its truest form, is not just a response—it is a spiritual signal that says, "I recognize the divine at work."

In this section, we explore how ancient traditions across faiths elevate gratitude from sentiment to sacred practice.

✧ Christian Faith

Scripture teaches that gratitude is not only a response—it is a doorway. **"Enter His gates with thanksgiving and His courts with praise."** (Psalm 100:4, NIV) Gratitude ushers us into the presence of the Divine. It is not an afterthought—it is the beginning.

When Jesus fed the five thousand, He gave thanks before the miracle occurred. **"Then Jesus took the loaves, gave thanks, and distributed to those who were seated as much as they wanted."** (John 6:11, NIV) The blessing was multiplied not after the abundance arrived—but when gratitude was spoken for what was already there.

The Apostle Paul echoes this timeless principle: **"Give thanks in all circumstances; for this is God's will for you in Christ Jesus."** (1 Thessalonians 5:18, NIV) Not after circumstances change, but in them.

Gratitude does not require resolution—it requires revelation.

✧ Jewish Wisdom

In Jewish tradition, gratitude is the breath before the day begins. The prayer Modeh Ani— **"I thank You."**—is spoken upon waking, even before the first steps or spoken words. It centers the soul in appreciation before anything else begins.

The Torah commands a rhythm of gratitude woven into daily life: "**You shall eat and be satisfied, and bless the Lord your God for the good land He has given you**." (Deuteronomy 8:10, ESV) This is not just about meals—it is about remembering the Source.

The Talmud teaches: "**A person is obligated to say one hundred blessings each day**." (Menachot 43b) Gratitude is not occasional—it is continuous, a spiritual rhythm meant to be lived.

During Sukkot, a holiday celebrating divine provision during the wilderness journey, Jews give thanks not for perfection but for presence—for God's faithfulness even in the midst of impermanence.

Gratitude here becomes the very heartbeat of resilience.

✧ Islamic Teaching

Gratitude (shukr) is a foundational principle in Islam, and it is directly linked to divine increase: "**If you are grateful, I will surely increase you**." (Qur'an 14:7, Sahih International) Gratitude is not only spiritual—it is causative. It multiplies what is acknowledged.

The Prophet Muhammad (peace be upon him) modeled this with profound devotion. Though free from sin, he would spend hours in prayer and prostration. When asked why, he replied: "**Should I not be a grateful servant**?" (Hadith, Bukhari, and Muslim)

In Islam, gratitude is expressed with every Bismillah ("In the name of God") before action, and every Alhamdulillah ("Praise be to God") after receiving. These words form a sacred cycle—starting with intention, ending with praise.

✦ Buddhist Practice

In Buddhism, gratitude is not demanded—it arises naturally through mindfulness. When one is fully present, everything becomes a gift. The breath. The sky. The silence.

A foundational practice is the gratitude meditation, which includes giving thanks not only for joys but also for suffering—for these, too, are teachers. This non-dual view fosters compassion and equanimity.

The Dhammapada teaches: "**Let us rise and be thankful, for if we didn't learn a lot today, at least we learned a little**." (Dhammapada, Verse 292) Gratitude becomes the path to peace, not its result.

Even in walking meditation, one is instructed to step with reverence. As Zen Master Thich Nhat Hanh said, "Walk as if you are kissing the Earth with your feet." Gratitude is not a word—it is a way of moving through the world.

✦ Hindu Insights

In Hinduism, gratitude is embedded in dharma—the path of rightful living. The Sanskrit word kritajna means "one *who remembers the good.*" This remembering becomes a sacred act.

The Rig Veda sings praises to the elements: the sun, rivers, air, and fire—not just as utilities, but as divine presences worthy of thanks. The gratitude is cosmic.

In the Bhagavad Gita, Lord Krishna teaches: "**Whatever you do, whatever you eat, whatever you offer or give away... do that as an offering to Me**." (Bhagavad Gita 9:27, ESV) This transforms every act—even eating, giving, speaking—into an act of thanks.

Through rituals like puja, which involve offering flowers, incense, or food to the Divine, gratitude is not just remembered—it is enacted. Every small act becomes a bridge to the sacred.

Gratitude may wear different names across traditions, but its essence remains the same: a sacred alignment with Source.

It is the silent thank you whispered in the morning, the song sung before the harvest, the offering made with no expectation in return. Gratitude shifts perception, softens the heart, and multiplies what is good.

When we walk in gratitude, we don't just invite blessing—we recognize that we are already living within one.

Wisdom from Contemporary Spiritual Leaders

Gratitude is more than a spiritual virtue—it is a frequency that some of today's most influential teachers say opens the doorway to healing, alignment, and abundance. Across the spectrum of modern spiritual wisdom, one truth keeps surfacing: when you learn to give thanks before the blessing arrives, you become a magnet for miracles.

The following voices remind us that gratitude is not something you feel after life gets better—it is the way you bring better into your life. Their insights echo what ancient scriptures have long taught: that thankfulness is not just a reaction. It is a sacred initiation.

—Louise Hay said, "**Gratitude brings more to be grateful for**." She taught that every morning should begin with a thank you—and every challenge should be met with one too.

—Oprah Winfrey popularized the gratitude journal, encouraging millions to record five things a day for which they were thankful. She said, "**The more you praise and celebrate your life, the more there is in life to celebrate**." Oprah's gratitude practice reminds us that celebration multiplies—what you honor grows, and joy expands where thanks is given.

—Abraham Hicks teaches that gratitude is one of the highest vibrations. **"Appreciation is the vibration of alignment with who-you-really-are."** Abraham reminds us that gratitude isn't just a feeling—it's a frequency that aligns you with your truest, most powerful self.

—Dr. Joe Dispenza teaches that *gratitude in advance is one of the fastest ways to create new neural pathways—telling the brain,* **"This is already happening."** Then the body begins to experience the future now.

—Maya Angelou said, **"Let gratitude be the pillow upon which you kneel to say your nightly prayer."** For her, thankfulness was not event-based—it was a posture of the soul.

—Roy Waugh, **"Every morning before my feet touch the floor, I say thank you. Gratitude is how I tell the universe I see the blessing all around me—right here, right now, and I am Grateful."** This quote is a reminder that gratitude is how we begin aligning with blessings before the day even starts. Saying "thank you" first thing in the morning signals to the universe—and to your own spirit—that you are aware of the good already around you. It is a simple act, but a powerful shift in energy.

Gratitude is not just how we respond to life—it is how we position ourselves to receive more of it.

What unites each of these teachers is their shared reverence for the power of gratitude not as a concept, but as a way of living. Whether it is spoken through a whispered "thank you" at dawn, or written in a journal under flickering candlelight, gratitude realigns your energy with the truth of abundance. It softens your heart, sharpens your focus, and sends a clear signal to the universe: "I trust. I am ready. I see the gifts all around me."

When you walk in that kind of thankfulness, you do not just change your life—you change your frequency.

Scientific Perspectives on Gratitude and Manifestation

—The Neurobiology of Thanksgiving and the Frequency of Receiving

Gratitude is not just poetic—it is measurable. While spiritual traditions have long understood gratitude as a powerful act of alignment, modern science now confirms what sages and mystics have taught for centuries: living in a state of thankfulness changes the chemistry of your body, the wiring of your brain, and the electromagnetic signals you emit into the world.

Gratitude is more than a positive feeling—it is a biological frequency that shifts your entire being into receptivity. And when you learn to live as though the prayer is already answered, your mind, body, and energy field begin responding accordingly.

✧ Neuroscience and Gratitude: Rewiring for Joy

Neuroscientists have found that practicing gratitude stimulates activity in the brain's prefrontal cortex—the region associated with decision-making, empathy, and future planning. Gratitude also activates the brain's reward circuitry, increasing the production of dopamine and serotonin—neurotransmitters that promote joy, calm, and motivation.

In a widely cited study by Emmons & McCullough (2003), participants who wrote daily gratitude lists reported significantly better sleep, increased optimism, and fewer physical symptoms of illness. Over time, gratitude was shown to rewire the brain for emotional resilience and overall well-being.

Repeated expressions of thanks—even in the absence of outward change—train the nervous system to expect good. This expectation primes the body for healing, clarity, and trust.

✧ Gratitude and the Law of Frequency

From a metaphysical standpoint, everything in the universe emits a frequency—including your thoughts and emotions. Gratitude, as measured through heart coherence studies by the HeartMath Institute, generates one of the most harmonious electromagnetic fields the human body can produce. When you feel deep appreciation, your heart rhythm becomes smooth and synchronized, sending a coherent signal to the brain —and to the world around you.

This coherence is not just inward—it is communicative.
The Law of Frequency teaches that you attract what resonates with your dominant vibration. Gratitude places you in a frequency that matches abundance, peace, and joy. And like a tuning fork, it draws experiences into your field that match the energy you are radiating.

✧ Quantum Theory and the Energy of Thankfulness

Quantum physics suggests that at the subatomic level, observation collapses possibility into form, and where you place your focus matters. When you focus on gratitude, even in advance of your manifestation, you are not merely thinking optimistically—you are creating an energetic agreement with your desired outcome.

Dr. Joe Dispenza refers to this as *"firing and wiring"* the brain to believe the future has already happened. The body begins to live in the reality of the prayer fulfilled—and the energy you carry starts aligning with that fulfilled state.

Gratitude becomes more than emotion—it becomes embodiment. And embodiment is the bridge between the invisible and the visible.

To live in gratitude is to train your mind to see what is working, your body to feel what is good, and your energy to align with what is possible. It is not blind optimism—it is biological alignment with divine expectation.

When you give thanks before the miracle, you are telling your brain, your cells, and the universe: "I trust that what I've asked for is already on its way." You begin to resonate with answers not yet seen, and you step into a posture of energetic receiving.

Gratitude is not a soft gesture—it is a sacred signal.
And when you send that signal clearly, the universe listens.

Personal Story
—Because That Is What My Mom Taught Me

I learned as a very young child how to be grateful.
Not from books. Not from church pews. I learned it because life required it and because my mom lived it.

My mother was only 18 when I was born. So, in many ways, we kind of grew up together. She was born completely deaf, and though she could speak a little, her voice sounded different—so different that people stared. Some laughed. Others did not know how to respond. Eventually, she made the heartbreaking decision to stop speaking altogether in public, afraid someone might make fun of her.

And from that moment on, I became her voice.

Everywhere we went—the grocery store, the doctor's office, the bank—I was her mouthpiece. I did not get to just be a kid. I became her interpreter before I even knew how to spell the word. I learned how to read a room before I knew how to read. I learned how to speak for her, explain for her, reword things for her so she could understand and carry her presence into places where her sound could not go.

But if I ever felt sorry for myself, my mom never let me stay there.
She taught me that gratitude is not about what you are given—it is about how you carry what you have. She was a stickler for cleanliness and order. Everything had its place, and every belonging, no matter how small, had to be taken care of.

She used to say, "If you can't take care of the small stuff, how will you ever be able to take care of the big stuff when it comes?"

That lesson stuck.

Most of what we owned came from neighborhood yard sales or thrift stores. My shoes had already walked in someone else's story before they ever made it to mine. But you better believe she had me shine them, line them up, and treat them like they were brand new. Because they were mine now, and that mattered.

There was a time when we went to the bank to get change for a twenty-dollar bill. The teller gave us four fives—but accidentally handed back the original twenty as well. We did not notice until we got home.

The moment we opened the envelope, my mom's eyes widened, "We have to go back. Right now," she signed urgently. Even though we needed money desperately, she said, "That money isn't ours."

Back in the car we went, straight to the bank.

When I explained to the teller what had happened, she broke down in tears. She said she would have had to pay the missing twenty out of her own paycheck—or worse. That small moment could have cost her a lot.

But my mom did not return it for credit or praise. She returned it because it was right.

That is who she was.

If we had a little extra food, she made sure we took it to the elderly woman down the street, whom she knew was struggling too. She would have given her last dime to help someone else if she could.

Even in silence, my mom's light entered a room before she ever did.
She could not hear my voice, but she always felt my heart. She could not sing with me, but she sure knew how to dance to the vibrations she felt with her feet on the floor.

And in her quiet way, she taught me the rhythm of gratitude—not as a reaction, but as a way of life.

I remember coming home from school one day after a kid pointed out the holes in my worn-out shoes. I had not said a word, but she saw it on my face. She did not lecture me. She just pulled off my shoes, wrapped my feet in a warm towel fresh from the dryer, and smiled.

Then she said something I will never forget: "These feet are going to take you places. And we are going to continue to take care of them until then."

And I believed her.

Years later, when I was boarding my first flight to Estes Park for the Christian Artists Competition—a trip that had once seemed impossible—I thought about that moment.

I thought about those shoes. That towel. That warm-handed love.

And I whispered, "Thank you."

Because gratitude did not come after the blessing, it came through the struggle. Through the silence. Through the small acts of dignity that shaped my soul before the spotlight ever touched me.

Now, every morning, before my feet touch the floor, I still say thank you. Not because my life is perfect. But because every single moment is sacred.

Gratitude is not just something I feel—it is something I walk in. It is the breath I take. The story I carry. The grace I inherited from a woman who taught me how to see the light—without ever needing to open your eyes.

Because at the end of the day, I walk in gratitude because that is what my mom taught me.

Practical Applications
—Living as If the Prayer Is Already Answered

Gratitude is not just a feeling—it is a frequency we choose to live in. It is easy to give thanks when life feels full, but the real transformation happens when we learn to walk in gratitude before the breakthrough, before the blessing, and even in the midst of the unknown.

These practices are simple ways to shift your perspective and your energy —to anchor you in the vibration of trust, expectation, and joy. Because when you live like the prayer is already answered, life begins to echo it back to you.

1. **Gratitude in advance**.
   Start each day by thanking God, the Universe, or Life for what is coming. Speak it like it is already here.

2. **Create a thank you ritual**.
   Light a candle and say three "thank yous" out loud before bed—one for the past, one for the present, one for the future.

3. **Use the 5-senses practice**.
   What can you see, hear, smell, taste, and touch that brings you gratitude right now? This grounds you in embodied appreciation.

4. **Write a letter to your future self**.
   Begin with: "Thank you for receiving..." and describe your manifestation as if it is already yours.

5. **Walk in gratitude**.
   Take a walk while repeating: "Thank You, Thank You, Thank You" in rhythm with your steps. Let it become a moving meditation.

6. **Bless the in-between**.
   Say: "Thank you for what is forming.", "Thank you for what's aligning.", and "Thank you for the unseen."

Gratitude shifts the atmosphere long before the answer arrives. When you choose to live in thankfulness—not just for what you see, but for what you trust is unfolding—you align yourself with the very frequency of fulfillment. Every "thank you" plants a seed in the unseen. Every word of gratitude waters what is becoming. And soon, what you once thanked God, the Universe, or Life for in faith will meet you in form.

Affirmation

"I walk in gratitude. I live in the vibration of answered prayer. My thankfulness is the bridge to more."

Guided Meditation
—Living the Thank You Now

Take a slow, deep breath. And another. Feel your heart center expand.

Now imagine standing in the life you have prayed for—your manifestation realized. Picture it clearly. Feel it deeply. See yourself smiling, breathing, thriving.

From that place, begin to say thank you. Not to get—just to recognize. Whisper it again: "Thank You. Thank You. Thank You." Let it rise from your chest. Let it soften your shoulders. Let it tune your whole being to joy.

Now, walk in gratitude.

Because everything you can see with your eyes, hear with your ears, and smell with your nose, even the air that you are breathing, is a gift.

Conclusion

Gratitude is more than a polite "thank you." It is a posture. A way of being. A spiritual stance that says, "Even if I don't see it yet—I trust that it's already on the way."

We often wait until the prayer is answered to celebrate. We wait for the confirmation email, the check in the mail, the healing report, and the closed deal. Then we give thanks.

But gratitude, in its highest form, does not wait. It leads.

It walks ahead of the answer.

It sets the table before the guest arrives.

It makes room in your heart while the blessing is still forming.

That is what walking in gratitude really means.

It is not denying the struggle—it is choosing to find the beauty in it. It is saying, "Thank you," not just when the door opens, but while you are still knocking. It is wiping your feet on the welcome mat of faith and trusting that the threshold you are standing on leads to something good.

My mom taught me that.

She did not just give thanks when things were going well. She gave thanks in the struggle, in the silence, in the sacrifice. She showed me that the real power of gratitude is not found in what you have—it is found in how you carry what you have been given.

And when I think back on those quiet moments—shoes too small, fridges nearly empty, a warm towel and a soft smile—I see now that gratitude was the thread holding it all together.

It was the music under the noise. The calm in the chaos, and the proof that God was still present, even when the manifestation of miracles was still on the way.

So, if you are waiting for the answer, if you are still in the middle of the story, if the breakthrough has not come yet—start saying thank you anyway.

Say it while the page is still turning.

Say it in the hallway before the door opens.

Say it before your feet hit the floor in the morning.

Because that simple act of gratitude may be the very thing that tells The Universe: **"I'm ready**."

And maybe—just maybe—that is when the blessing starts walking toward you, too.

Chapter 20: Inspired Action
—Moving in Alignment with What You've Asked For

Opening Reflection

"Faith by itself, if it is not accompanied by action, is dead."
—James 2:17 (NIV)

Introduction

There comes a moment when belief must walk, when vision must rise from the page of your journal and take a step into the world.

Manifestation is not about wishful thinking alone—it is about partnership. It is about a sacred dance between the inner and the outer, the invisible and the seen, the spiritual and the practical. And that bridge between the two? Inspired action.

Not frantic hustle. Not forced movement. But action born of alignment. The kind of movement that flows from clarity, trust, and divine impulse.

This chapter is an invitation to tune your heart to the rhythm of your calling—and then move with it. Because while the universe is always conspiring for your good, it moves through your willingness to say yes, take the step, and answer the nudge.

Faith activates the power. Action invites the manifestation.

Hidden Teachings from Ancient Traditions
—When Spirit Moves, So Must You

Across the world's sacred traditions, action is not separated from belief— it is the fulfillment of it. Whether in ancient texts or oral traditions, we find a consistent truth: faith becomes real when it moves. Divine intention becomes manifestation when aligned action is taken. These timeless teachings invite us to listen for the prompt—and then respond with our hands, our feet, our lives. Because sacred power is not just something we hold, it is something we express.

✧ Christian Faith

Scripture reminds us that divine power often flows through physical obedience. In James 2:17, we read: "**Faith by itself, if it is not accompanied by action, is dead.**" This is not a rebuke—it is a revelation. Action is not a substitute for faith; it is its expression.

Jesus frequently asked those seeking healing to do something: "**Stretch out your hand,**" "**Take up your mat,**" "**Go and show yourself.**" (Mark 3:5, John 5:8, Luke 17:14). Their movement was not a condition—it was a catalyst.

Even the miracle of water into wine required action: "**Fill the jars with water.**" (John 2:7).

To act in faith is to place your steps where your spirit already believes the ground will meet you.

✧ Jewish Wisdom

In Jewish tradition, action is at the heart of spiritual life. The Torah is not just a book of beliefs—it is a book of practices. As the Israelites stood at Sinai, they declared: "**Na'aseh v'nishma**"— "**We will do, and we will understand.**" (Exodus 24:7). In Judaism, doing precedes knowing. You grow into wisdom by walking it out.

The mystical Kabbalah teaches that divine light is made manifest through vessels, and those vessels are formed by righteous deeds. Each act becomes a container for blessing.

As it is written in Proverbs 16:3: "**Commit your actions to the Lord, and your plans will succeed.**" Not your thoughts alone—your actions.

✧ Islamic Teaching

Islam weds faith to movement with unwavering clarity. The Qur'an says: **"Indeed, those who believe and do righteous deeds—Paradise will be theirs**." (Qur'an 18:107). Belief is the seed, but action is the cultivation.

The Prophet Muhammad (peace be upon him) said, **"Trust in Allah, but tie your camel**." In other words, spiritual trust does not exempt us from practical responsibility. Inspired action is not opposition to faith. It is how faith walks.

Even the five pillars of Islam are movement-based: faith, prayer, fasting, giving, pilgrimage—all sacred steps. Each act grounds divine intention in lived expression.

✧ Buddhist Practices

In Buddhism, the path to awakening is walked through Right Action, part of the Noble Eightfold Path. The Buddha taught that good intentions without good deeds remain incomplete. Compassion must move.

The Dhammapada states: **"An idea that is developed and put into action is more important than an idea that exists only as an idea**." (Dhammapada 20:1)

Whether it is mindful speech, ethical livelihood, or walking meditation, each act becomes a doorway to presence. Even enlightenment is not static —it is a practice embodied in the ordinary. Chop wood. Carry water. Move with purpose.

✧ Hindu Insights

Hindu philosophy reveres action as a sacred offering. The concept of karma yoga teaches that right action, when done without attachment, becomes a path to liberation.

In the Bhagavad Gita, Lord Krishna says: "**You have a right to perform your prescribed duties, but you are not entitled to the fruits of your actions**." (Gita 2:47). This speaks to the heart of inspired action—movement born from surrender, not outcome.

To act in alignment with one's dharma (soul's purpose) is to live in spiritual harmony. Even the simplest deed, when done as an offering to God, becomes divine.

When Spirit Moves, So Must You.

These ancient traditions agree: your faith is not proven by how long you wait—it is proven by how well you walk. Inspired action is not striving. It is sacred participation. It is the moment your belief steps into the world and says, "I'm ready." And when your steps align with divine timing, manifestation begins to move with you.

Wisdom from Contemporary Spiritual Leaders

Throughout modern spiritual teachings, one truth rings clear: manifestation is not magic—it is movement. Vision becomes reality when belief is paired with motion.

The spiritual leaders below remind us that action is not just about doing more—it is about doing what flows from alignment, clarity, and trust. Inspired action is not frantic effort. It is sacred participation. And when your movement matches your faith, the path begins to rise to meet your feet.

—Abraham Hicks reminds us that when you are truly aligned, action feels inspired—not like effort, but like flow. "**When action is inspired by alignment, it is always joyful**." Real momentum begins in alignment —when you're tuned in, action flows with joy, not strain.

—Iyanla Vanzant teaches that spiritual maturity is revealed in what you do, not what you claim. "**If you want to manifest something different, do something different**." Iyanla reminds us that transformation isn't declared—it's demonstrated; real change begins with aligned action.

—Joyce Meyer has long preached, "**Do not wait until you feel like it. Obedience is doing the right thing whether you feel like it or not**." True obedience isn't led by emotion—it's the choice to act in alignment, even when it's hard.

—Dannion Brinkley often says, "**You are a great, mighty, and powerful spiritual being with dignity, direction, and purpose**." Dannion's words awaken the truth that you're not here by accident— you're a powerful soul, born with purpose and direction.

—Dr. Joe Dispenza teaches that elevated emotions must be paired with clear intention—and then repeated action—to create lasting change. He says, "**You can't just think greater. You must also act greater**." Dr. Joe reminds us that true transformation begins when inspired thoughts move our feet—change happens when emotion fuels action.

—Roy Waugh, "**The moment you take a step in faith, you're not chasing the blessing anymore—you're walking beside it**." This quote is here to remind you: the blessing you are waiting for is already in motion—and when you take a step in alignment, you are no longer waiting on it from a distance. You are partnering with it. Each step forward is a signal that you are ready, willing, and available for the answer to find you.

Do not wait for everything to be perfect. Just move with trust. Because sometimes, the very moment you act is the moment the breakthrough begins, walking right beside you.

In every tradition—ancient or modern—manifestation is not passive. It is alive. It moves. These spiritual voices echo a sacred truth: the energy of belief must be carried into motion. When you walk in alignment with your calling, the universe does not just observe—it responds. The blessing you are seeking is not standing still. It is waiting for your yes.

Scientific Perspectives on Action and Alignment
—How Science Confirms the Power of Inspired Steps

Manifestation does not just live in vision boards and prayers—it lives in movement. The bridge between belief and reality is often built one step at a time. And while ancient wisdom has always spoken of the sacred power of aligned action, science is now catching up, offering a clear and measurable affirmation: when you act in harmony with your inner truth, everything changes—mind, body, energy, and outcome.

Let us explore how neuroscience, behavioral psychology, and quantum physics each confirm what spiritual traditions have long known: that inspired action is not just a nice idea—it is a necessary force.

✧ Neuroscience: The Spark Before the Step

Before your body takes a single step, something happens in your brain called an action potential—a burst of electrical activity that signals motion. That moment is where thought becomes intention, and intention prepares to become form. But without movement, the signal fades. In spiritual terms, it is the moment the Divine nudges you. And your response? That is what keeps the spark alive.

Studies also show that repeated action builds neural pathways. When you step toward a goal consistently, your brain begins to expect success. Over time, you're not just hoping you can do it—you believe it. That belief becomes embodied.

✧ Psychology: Action Builds Confidence

Behavioral psychologists teach us that action doesn't just come from belief—it creates belief. When you take even a small aligned step, it signals your subconscious that you're moving forward. This breaks paralysis and builds what's known as self-efficacy—your internal trust in your own ability to create change.

The Zeigarnik Effect further explains that uncompleted actions create tension in the brain. That's why taking just one step can offer relief, clarity, and renewed momentum. The act of doing—even just a little—clears space for more doing.

✧ Quantum Physics: Energy Requires Engagement

In quantum theory, the observer effect tells us that intention affects outcome. But intention alone is only the beginning. It's interaction that collapses possibility into reality. In other words, attention activates the field—but action engages it.

Everything is energy, including your vision. But energy needs a conductor. Just like electricity cannot flow without a wire, your manifestation cannot move without your step. Inspired action becomes that conductor—the channel through which energy flows into form.

When science and Spirit both point to the power of motion, we begin to see action not as striving, but as sacred agreement. A single step, taken in faith, aligns your body, your brain, and your vibration with the reality you've asked for. It's not about effort—it's about embodiment. Because the moment you move, the field responds.

Personal Story
—The Step I Was Not Ready For

When my first recording project was finally finished, you would think I would have been celebrating.

I had worked for that moment for years—praying, scraping together resources, dreaming of what it could become. The songs were recorded. The CD was in my hands. The dream I had carried quietly for so long had taken form.

But what I felt was not triumph.

It was terror.

Because now came the question that had been lurking in the background the whole time:

Now what?

I did not have a manager. I did not have a tour schedule. I did not have a marketing plan. And I definitely did not have the money to fund the vision that was growing in my heart—a full-scale ministry with backup singers, a sound crew, a tour bus, and the infrastructure to carry this message far beyond my hometown.

I had the dream, yes. But the next steps?

No clue.

It was like I was standing at the edge of a vast river, holding a boat I did not know how to row. And yet—I felt it deep in my spirit: It is time to go.

And then—right on time—an unexpected door opened.

Just as the last CD came off the press, I was invited to audition for a national touring musical based on the life of King David. I did not go looking for it. It found me. And in a matter of weeks, I was cast in the lead role—as David himself.

I packed my bags, not fully understanding what I was walking into. All I knew was that I had asked God for a path, and this opportunity had shown up at my feet, seemingly overnight.

What I could not have known then is that this was the bridge between the studio and the stage. Between vision and manifestation.

You see, the very cast members I worked with on that tour—fellow singers, musicians, even some of the crew—became my first support system. The backup singers and sound guy for my new ministry were not found through auditions or expensive ads. They were walking beside me already. Traveling across the country with me. Watching me grow into my own voice while playing David by night and selling my CDs after the show.

I remember standing behind the product table the night after our very first show—feeling humbled, nervous, and wide open. My first CDs were there, lined up in neat rows. I had no idea if anyone would stop. No idea if people would buy them. But I smiled, opened my mouth, and introduced myself anyway.

And people came. And people bought. And people shared stories of how the music was reaching them.

I realized: This is it. This is how it starts. Not with a perfect plan. Not with a multimillion-dollar launch. But with one step. One faithful yes. One open hand holding a CD that had me cost everything to make.

There were nights I went to sleep wondering how I would pay for fuel. There were moments I stood in a dressing room asking God, "Is this really what You had in mind?" But every time I showed up—God did too.

The equipment came. The singers committed. The doors kept opening. One step led to the next. And somehow, piece by piece, it all began to form.

I did not know how to start a ministry. But I started anyway. I did not know how I would pay for it all. But I walked forward anyway.

And I learned something sacred in that season: *The way does not appear before the step. The way appears because of the step.*

Practical Applications
—Moving in Alignment with Your Vision

Taking inspired action doesn't mean you charge forward with a five-year plan. Often, it begins with a whisper. A nudge. A quiet yes that no one else hears but you. The universe doesn't ask you to have it all figured out—it just asks for your willingness to move with what you already know. These practices are designed to help you lean into that sacred movement. To make the invisible vision visible. To respond to your soul's own timing with trust, alignment, and motion.

These are not about proving your worth or performing your faith. They're about becoming available to the life that's already calling your name—one step at a time.

1. **Ask, "What is the next aligned step?"**
   Not the whole plan. Just the next thing that feels clear and aligned. Then do it.

2. **Do not wait for perfect clarity**.
   Sometimes clarity comes after the step, not before it. Movement reveals more than stillness.

3. **Act "as-if" daily**.
   What would someone who already has your vision do today? Speak that way. Walk that way. Make decisions that match.

4. **Honor small actions**.
   Call it sacred. A small step, done in alignment, is more powerful than a big movement done in fear.

5. **Create a daily movement ritual**.
   Even 10 minutes a day of inspired action—writing, calling, researching, planning—moves the energy.

6. **Name your step, then take it**.
   Each morning, write down one action that would bring your desire closer. Say it aloud. Then do it.

7. **Detach from immediate results**.
   Action is not a vending machine. Trust that every step sends a signal —and that return is coming.

Alignment is not about giant leaps—it's about steady, intentional steps that honor the vision planted within you. Every time you act from a place of trust instead of fear, you are casting a vote for the future you believe in. These daily movements, however small, create momentum. And momentum is what turns vision into reality. When you walk in alignment, you are not chasing your destiny—you are meeting it step by sacred step.

Affirmation

"My steps are sacred. I move in alignment. I walk with vision and act with faith. My actions call my dreams into form."

Guided Meditation
—Walking into the Vision

Take a slow, deep breath.

Now imagine standing at the edge of your vision. You can see it—clear, vivid, alive. Now take a step toward it. In your mind, see your feet moving. Hear them. Feel your body in motion.

As you walk, speak inwardly: "I move in faith. I act with clarity. I align with what I have asked for."

Each step brings it closer. Each breath deepens your trust. You are walking with purpose now. Carry this rhythm into your day.

Conclusion

There will always be a reason to wait.
To pause.
To gather just a little more confidence.
To pray a little longer.
To plan a little tighter.

But eventually, faith must rise from the journal and step into your feet.
Because manifestation doesn't live in theory—it lives in motion.
You can believe with all your heart, but if your feet never move, you'll never know what was waiting just beyond your willingness to act. Inspired

action isn't reckless or rushed—it's responsive. It's born in stillness, but it moves with courage. It listens for the whisper that says, "This is your moment," and then dares to follow.

No, it doesn't have to be dramatic. It doesn't have to be big.
It just has to be true.

You don't need the whole map—only enough light for the next step. And when you take it, something shifts in the atmosphere. Heaven takes notice. Resources align. The right people appear. Doors that looked bolted shut begin to move. Not because you forced them—but because you finally matched their frequency.

That step sends a signal:
"I'm not just hoping for this—I'm ready for it."

So make the call.
Write the song.
Send the email.
Take the class.
Step on the stage.
Launch the dream.
Say the yes.

Because one soul-aligned action can pull an entire miracle into motion.

You are not waiting to become powerful—you already are.

You were created with dignity, direction, and divine purpose. When you remember that truth, your actions stop coming from pressure and start flowing from identity.

Inspired action begins when you stop striving to become—and start moving from who you already are.
Let that truth guide your next step.
Not forced. Not frantic.

But aligned. Purposeful. Sacred.

Don't just wait for the blessing.

Walk like it's already on the way.

Because anything is possible—when your faith finds its feet.

Alignment Before the Arrival
—The End of Part II

Well, here we are again.

The end of Part II—and the crossing of another sacred threshold.

If you are reading this, take a moment and breathe that in.

What you've just walked through is more than the middle of a book—it is the middle of a becoming. It is the place where belief deepens into knowing. Where asking begins to give way to receiving. Where the foundation becomes embodiment.

You have not just learned new things; you have become something new.

Part II was not about waiting—it was about aligning. It was about clearing the static, sharpening the vision, and preparing your frequency to hold the very things you've been calling in.

And quietly—something deeper has been happening:

You've been removing the inner barriers you didn't even know were there; The silent fears, the buried doubts, and the unspoken unworthiness.

In their place, something ancient and holy has been rising.

The power within you.

Not borrowed, not earned, but Awakened. You've moved from thinking about manifestation to living it.

✧**You've learned to walk in gratitude before the answer arrives**.

✧**You've discovered the quiet power of persistence**.

✧**You've practiced focus as a magnetic force**.

✧**You've redefined what it means to receive**.

✧ **You've started taking aligned, inspired steps**.

And perhaps most powerfully of all, you are realizing that alignment is not about perfection. It is about resonance. It is about flow.
It is about walking in tune with what you already carry in your spirit.
You are no longer just visualizing the promise. You are becoming the version of you who can hold it.

Pause, let that sink in.

Let your nervous system absorb what your spirit already knows: You are readying yourself to receive what's already been written in your name.
Because the space between belief and becoming is not empty—it's sacred.
And your faith in that space is everything.

Take a deep breath.

Honor what you've just completed.

Bless the ground you're standing on.

The next part of this book isn't about effort—it's about embodiment. It's not about chasing the vision—it's about living as though it's already yours.

You don't have to strive for worthiness, you only have to remember the power that's already within you and let it rise.

Now, take a deep breath, and when you are ready, turn the page.

Part III — Becoming the Manifestation

—Living the Miracle

This final section is not about doing more. It is about being more.

Part III is where the journey turns inward and upward—where you no longer chase the dream, because you are embodying it.

These chapters invite you into deeper trust, sacred rest, vivid imagination, and radical self-alignment.

You will learn to release limiting beliefs, tune into divine timing, and live from a place of fulfillment rather than striving.

This is where your frequency stabilizes—where what you once visualized becomes the atmosphere you live and breathe.

You are no longer manifesting from the outside in.
You're manifesting from the inside out.

This is the becoming.

This is the integration.

This is your frequency, your power igniting and resonating with the very vibration of your heart's desire—echoing the essence of The Manifestation Frequency.

Chapter 21: Trusting Divine Timing
—Surrendering to the Rhythm of When

Opening Reflection

"For I know the plans I have for you," declares the Lord, "plans to prosper you and not to harm you, plans to give you a future and a hope."
— Jeremiah 29:11

Introduction

You have prayed. You have visualized. You have believed.

But still you wait.

There is a silence that sits between the asking and the arrival. A space of not yet. A hallway where the door has not opened, and you are tempted to walk away. This is where many abandon the vision—not because it is impossible, but because it is delayed.

But divine timing is not denial.

What feels like a pause may be protection. What seems like resistance may be refinement. And what appears to be silence might be the sacred sound of preparation—of things aligning in a way you cannot yet see. Sometimes the answer is, "Not Yet."

This chapter is about trusting divine timing. The art of surrendering not just the outcome, but the when. It is about learning to live with deep-rooted peace even when the manifestation hasn't arrived—knowing that the universe, God, Source, is never late.

Only right on time.

Hidden Teachings from Ancient Traditions
—The Sacred Pace of Patience—Wisdom on Divine Timing Across Faiths

Throughout every sacred tradition, we find a deep and resounding truth: timing is not just practical—it is spiritual. Divine timing is not an afterthought. It is a force. A rhythm. A language of love written into the soul of the universe. When you learn to trust its pulse, you begin to live not by deadlines, but by divine design.

✧ Christian Faith

In the Christian tradition, divine timing is often woven through the tension between promise and fulfillment. Ecclesiastes 3:1 reminds us, **"To everything there is a season, and a time to every purpose under heaven."**

Scripture is filled with stories of waiting—David, anointed as king, waited years before taking the throne. (1 Samuel 16:12–13, 2 Samuel 5:4) Joseph held prophetic dreams but endured betrayal and prison before stepping into his destiny. (Genesis 37:5–11, 39:20-23, 41:39-41) Jesus Himself waited 30 years before beginning His public ministry. (Luke 3:21–23)

Galatians 4:4 speaks of perfect timing: **"But when the set time had fully come, God sent His Son."** Not early. Not late. God's timing was—and is—flawlessly intentional.

The waiting seasons are not wasted; they are where character is shaped, faith is refined, and spiritual maturity is born.

✧ Jewish Wisdom

In Jewish spirituality, time is sacred, not linear. It moves in spirals through the Hebrew calendar, bringing return and revelation with each cycle. The word mo'ed refers to "appointed times"—spiritually significant moments set by God. Some blessings require sacred alignment before they can unfold.

Psalm 31:15 affirms this beautifully: "**My times are in Your hands**." This verse reflects a deep surrender to divine orchestration. The timing of your life is not random—it is held, guided, and watched over.

The Talmud teaches that *even delays can be divinely appointed*. When the building of the Holy Temple was postponed, it was not rejection—it was divine readiness in progress. (Talmud Bavli, Berakhot 3a)

The principle of hashgacha pratit (personal divine providence) teaches that every detail of life, even waiting, is part of a divinely orchestrated plan.

To the Jewish heart, time is not something to conquer—it is something to honor.

✧ Islamic Teachings

In Islam, divine timing is a foundational expression of tawakkul—trust in God's wisdom. The Qur'an offers this assurance: "**Indeed, Allah is never late in fulfilling His promise**." (Qur'an 3:9) Timing belongs to God, and each delay is viewed not as punishment, but as protection or preparation.

The Prophet Muhammad (peace be upon him) endured over a decade of persecution before migrating to Medina, where his mission flourished. That waiting refined his strength and deepened the reach of his message. Even du'a (prayer) is offered with surrender, trusting that if the answer is "*not now*," it is because something better or more aligned is unfolding.

The faithful Muslim does not just wait—they wait with worship. (Lings, Martin. Muhammad: His Life Based on the Earliest Sources. Islamic Texts Society, 1983. See Chapters 10–17, especially Chapter 17: "The First Pledge of 'Aqabah" and Chapter 18: "The Hijrah")

✧ Buddhist Practices

Buddhism teaches patience (kshanti) as a virtue and pathway to peace. Within the Six Paramitas, patience is not passive, but powerful—it is the grace to endure without agitation. Zen wisdom echoes: "**When the fruit is ripe, it will fall**." (Zen proverb) There is no rushing of enlightenment, only presence.

Mindfulness trains the practitioner to trust the now. To detach from urgency and sit gently in the unfolding. The lotus does not bloom because it is pushed—it blooms when its roots are deep enough. So too does wisdom. So too does manifestation. Divine timing, in Buddhist thought, is not about the external world catching up—it's about your inner world becoming ready.

✧ Hindu Traditions

In Hindu philosophy, divine timing is inseparable from karma (action) and dharma (purpose). The Gita teaches: "**Perform your duty without attachment to the results**." (Bhagavad Gita 2:47) This reveals a deep truth: your job is to act in alignment—*outcomes belong to the Divine.*

Ishvara pranidhana, or surrender to God's will, encourages trust that even setbacks and delays are part of sacred alignment. Time (kāla) itself is viewed as a divine force—creative, cyclical, and governed by the sacred intelligence of the universe. Nothing is random. Everything unfolds exactly as it should. And what is meant for you cannot be lost—it can only be delayed until your soul is ready to receive it.

When seen through the lens of sacred wisdom, delay is no longer punishment—it is preparation. Waiting is not a void—it is a sacred vessel being filled. Trusting divine timing is not weakness; it is the deepest kind of strength. The kind that whispers, "I may not see it yet... but I know it's already mine."

Wisdom from Contemporary Spiritual Leaders

There's a universal thread running through the voices of today's most influential spiritual teachers: timing matters—but trust matters more. When your desire feels delayed, it's easy to spiral into self-doubt or urgency.

These teachers remind us that waiting is not wasted time. It's alignment in motion. Whether rooted in energetic theory, faith, or inner peace, their wisdom offers comfort and perspective. What's meant for you won't miss you—but sometimes, it takes time to get everything (and everyone) in place.

—Louise Hay wrote, "**The Universe loves me and always wants to bring me the highest good, at the right time**." Louise taught that life is always orchestrating your highest good—even when you can't see it. Her words remind us to lean into the belief that delay isn't rejection, but divine protection, working behind the scenes to bring about what serves us best.

—Abraham Hicks teaches that urgency is a sign of misalignment, not readiness. "**When you feel peace—even in the waiting—you are allowing**." This quote reminds us that when we chase after what we want, we disrupt the flow. But when we settle into peace and trust, we become magnets for manifestation—proving that allowance is a form of alignment.

—Iyanla Vanzant says, "**Delay is not denial. It's preparation. Sometimes God is setting you up for more than you asked for**." Iyanla reframes waiting as sacred preparation. What looks like a detour is often a divine setup. Her wisdom teaches that what feels like a pause may be the exact space needed to grow into the fullness of what you've prayed for.

—Joyce Meyer reminds us, "**You may not be where you want to be, but thank God you are not where you used to be. Keep walking. God's timing is always right**." Joyce calls us to celebrate progress, not just perfection. Her message is grounded in hope: even if you can't see the destination yet, you're already further than you were—and God hasn't forgotten where you're going.

—Dr. Joe Dispenza teaches that "**Gratitude for what has not arrived yet brings it faster. Why? Because the body responds to vibration—not the clock**." Dispenza's work blends science and spirit, showing us that when we emotionally align with the future we desire, we draw it closer. Gratitude becomes a tool of quantum resonance, syncing our inner state with unseen outcomes.

—Roy Waugh, "**Delay does not mean no... it just means sometimes the answer is, 'not yet.'**" Sometimes we take silence as rejection. We assume if it hasn't happened yet, it won't happen at all. But the truth is—"not yet" is still an answer. Delay is often divine protection, divine preparation, or divine realignment. When you don't see movement, it doesn't mean nothing is happening—it means things are being arranged behind the scenes in a way you could not orchestrate on your own. Trust that the pause has a purpose. Timing is not just about when the blessing is ready—it's also about when you are. And when all of it aligns, the "yes" will arrive without resistance, right on time.

In every tradition, and from every teacher, the truth rings clear: waiting is not weakness—it's wisdom. You are not being overlooked. You are being orchestrated. Stay the course. The rhythm of your "yes" is already unfolding.

Scientific Perspectives on Timing and Surrender
—How Science Supports the Sacred Power of Trusting the Process

The art of waiting well is not often celebrated in a world that prizes instant gratification. But manifestation doesn't always move at the speed of desire. Sometimes, it unfolds at the pace of alignment. And as ancient wisdom teaches the necessity of trust, patience, and surrender, modern science is quietly confirming something astonishing: waiting—when done with faith—rewires your mind, heals your body, and prepares your energy for what's to come.

Let us explore how neuroscience, psychology, and quantum physics each validate what spiritual traditions have long known: that divine timing is not passive—it's a precise, active preparation for arrival.

✧ **Neuroscience: The Brain Prefers Now—But Thrives in Not Yet**

Studies in intertemporal choice show that your brain holds two competing systems when faced with waiting: one craves immediate gratification, the other governs future-focused wisdom. Researchers at Princeton and Stanford found that delayed rewards activate the brain's prefrontal cortex, the same region responsible for planning, wisdom, and self-control (McClure et al., 2004).

This means that when you trust divine timing, you are not suppressing your desire—you are activating a higher, more evolved part of your consciousness. You are choosing coherence over impulse.

Waiting becomes not a sign of weakness, but of neurobiological strength.

✧ **Neuroscience: Patience Reshapes the Brain**

Every time you choose to stay grounded during a delay, you activate and strengthen the prefrontal cortex—the part of the brain responsible for decision-making, impulse control, and long-term planning. Practices like meditation and breathwork—which promote calm in the face of uncertainty—actually change the brain's structure over time, increasing your capacity to stay present, even in the in-between.

In spiritual language: when you trust divine timing, you're not "doing nothing." You're building the neurological pathways that can hold your future with wisdom and grace.

✧ **Quantum Physics: Alignment Over Arrival**

In quantum theory, all possible outcomes exist as energetic potential until one is observed or engaged. This is known as the observer effect. But here's what many overlook: it is not simply desire that activates a result—it's alignment.

Your thoughts initiate vibration. Your emotions stabilize it. But your energetic alignment—your readiness to receive—collapses possibility into reality. And readiness cannot be rushed. Just like a flower does not bloom before its time, your manifestation arrives when your frequency matches its form.

Surrender, then, becomes a kind of sacred conductivity. It is the quiet signal to the field: I am available for the blessing. I am not pushing—I am prepared.

When science meets Spirit, we begin to see surrender not as passivity, but as presence, not as delay, but as divine design. Because timing is not just a matter of the calendar—it's a matter of coherence. And coherence happens when your mind, body, and spirit say yes—all at once.

So, if you are still waiting, don't assume you're behind. You may simply be aligning with what is already on its way. And when it comes—because it will—you'll realize it wasn't about the waiting.

It was about who you became—while the waiting was shaping you.

Personal Story
—The Seeds I Saved For Someday

I cannot tell you how many decades I have had an ember burning in my spirit to write a book.

Not just any book. **This book**.

A place where I could gather all the lessons, revelations, trials, and miracles I have lived through and offer them as light to someone else's path.

For years, I felt that pull in my chest—one day, I am going to write this all down. But "one day" kept slipping further away. It is not that I did not want to write. I did. Desperately. But something in me always whispered, "Not yet."

Years passed, and life moved fast. Ministries evolved. Doors opened, closed, reopened. I traveled, I sang, I poured myself into other people's healing. But in the quiet in-between moments, I kept collecting breadcrumbs—little pieces of wisdom that marked my journey.

Some were teachings that changed me.

Some were phrases I heard in my spirit.
Some were hard-earned truths I only learned through tears.

And I would scribble them down—sometimes on napkins, envelopes, whatever was nearby—and slide them into the pages of my Bible like *tiny sacred seeds*. I did not know when I would use them. I just knew they were meant to live.

That collection became a secret archive of my heart.

I thought maybe someday, when I was older or had more time, or more clarity, then the writing would begin. But the truth is, I never really knew when it would be time. I just trusted that I would know.

And then one morning, I woke up different.

There was no lightning bolt or a dramatic moment. Just a quiet, undeniable fire in my heart. I felt it in my bones: **Now**, **it is time**.

There was no reason. No explanation. Just divine urgency—like something had shifted in the invisible, and the gates had opened.

I did not know how to write a book. I did not have a plan. I just started organizing the little pieces of paper. Then I realized, as I was organizing, that some of them went together really well. So, I wrote a paragraph with that bit. Then another. Before I knew it, I started writing. And then I rewrote it. And I rewrote some more. And I sorted, prayed, rearranged.

What began as a journal turned into a teaching. What started as personal reflection became spiritual guidance. What I thought might be a memoir slowly bloomed into something so much more—a multi-faith, Spirit-rooted blueprint for manifesting, healing, and remembering who you really are.

And you know what?

I could not have written this any sooner.

If I had tried five or ten years ago, I would have written from the wound instead of the wisdom. I would have forced what now flows. I would have taught what I had not yet fully lived.

But now—now I write from the other side. Not because I have all the answers, but because I have walked through enough to share what I have learned with clarity, humility, and power.

This book did not come because I pushed for it. It came because I waited with faith. I trusted the ember to grow on its own time.

And when the season said yes, I said yes too.

So, if you are holding a dream that feels delayed, if you have been carrying ideas in the folds of your spirit, waiting for your green light.
Let me tell you: when the time is right, you will not have to force it.
You will feel it. You will know. And you will move—not with panic, but with peace.

Because sometimes the "not yet" isn't a punishment. It's just divine choreography, waiting for your cue. And when it finally comes? It will feel just like this book is for me, like writing your life into being.

Practical Applications
—Trusting the Timing of Your Life

Trusting divine timing is one of the most challenging and beautiful parts of the manifestation journey. It asks you to release your grip on the clock and trust that the unseen is still working—even when nothing looks like it's moving. It is not passive. It is not giving up. It is a sacred posture of faith that says, "Even here—even now—I believe something good is forming."

These practices are here to help you hold that faith through the waiting. They are invitations to live with more ease, to find peace in the pause, and to recognize that the in-between is not a delay—it's preparation. Every breath you take in trust is part of your becoming.

1. **Release the clock.**
   Stop measuring your life by the world's timeline. Say: "I trust divine timing more than deadlines."

2. **Bless the future.**
   Instead of saying, "Why isn't it here?" try: "Thank you for what's forming, even if I can't see it yet."

3. **Track the seeds, not just the harvest.**
   Keep a journal of small alignments, nudges, and growth. Celebrate progress, not just outcome.

4. **Practice waiting with wonder.**
   Replace anxiety with curiosity. Ask: "I wonder what is being arranged for my highest good?"

5. **Affirm: It is already on the way.**
   Speak daily: "Everything is unfolding perfectly for me. I do not chase —what is mine arrives in peace."

6. **Visualized without clutching.**
   See the vision, then let it breathe. Trust that it knows when to arrive.

7. **Anchor in past proof.**
   Remember when you waited—and were amazed. Use that evidence to build trust again.

The space between asking and arrival is holy ground. And how you walk through it matters. You don't need to have all the answers. You just need to keep your heart open, your spirit grounded, and your trust anchored in something greater than time.

These small but intentional acts of faith are not wasted—they're planting seeds in unseen soil. One day soon, you'll look back and realize: the waiting was not empty. It was sacred. And every moment you spent trusting was a step closer to the divine, yes, already on its way.

Affirmation

"I trust divine timing. What is meant for me flows to me easily and arrives right on time. I wait with peace, purpose, and presence."

Guided Meditation
—Resting in the Timing

Take a deep breath.

Imagine your life as a garden. Some seeds are sprouting. Others are still beneath the soil. You cannot rush them—but you can trust them.

Picture your hands releasing control, opening to the sky. Whisper: "I trust the process. I release the pressure. I am aligned with perfect timing."

Feel the peace wash over you. Your part is done. The rest is unfolding. Rest here. Breathe here. Receive here.

Conclusion

I have learned that divine timing has a rhythm all its own. And you cannot rush it, bargain with it, or bend it to your will.

Believe me—I've tried.

But here's what I've come to understand: Just because what you're trying to manifest hasn't happened yet doesn't mean it won't. It simply means it's still being prepared—and so are you.

Sometimes what looks like a delay is actually a setup for something greater than you even asked for.

Sometimes God isn't just answering your prayer—the Universe is expanding it. Adding layers to it. Protecting it. Perfecting it.

And sometimes, the waiting is simply this: giving you time to grow into the version of yourself who can actually carry what you've asked for.

That doesn't mean the waiting is easy. I've stood in front of closed doors for so long that I started to question the vision altogether.

I've mistaken silence for rejection—convinced myself I missed it, that I was too late, that maybe I dreamed too big. But every single time when I look back, I see it clearly now.

God wasn't saying no. He was saying, "Not yet... because I love you too much to let you settle for less."

And when the time finally came—when the thing I was waiting for arrived —it didn't come with chaos or confusion. It came with peace. It felt like home. It felt like, "*Ah... this is what I was really waiting for.*"

So, if you're in that middle place right now—between the asking and the arrival—take heart. You are not behind. You are not forgotten. And you are not off course. You are right on schedule for something more beautiful than you can imagine.

So, breathe.

Trust.

And walk in the rhythm of "not yet" with grace.

Because one day soon, what you've been waiting for will come. And it will arrive so gently, so perfectly, that you'll understand: It was never just about the answer, it was about who you became while you were waiting for it.

And when that moment comes, something in you will know—without question— It was worth the wait.

Chapter 22: The Kingdom Within
—Awakening the Temple of Manifestation Inside You

Opening Reflection

"You are not separate from the Divine—you are a living extension of it. A spark of the infinite wrapped in breath, blood, and bone. Your body is not merely a vessel; it is the sacred temple where Divine power dwells and moves through you."
—Roy Waugh

Introduction

So much of manifestation is talked about as an outward act—send the signal, speak the word, take the step.

But at its deepest level, manifestation is not about reaching out. It's about returning inward. The Kingdom is not in the clouds or on some far-off mountaintop. It's not waiting in the next chapter of your life. It is already here—within you. Dormant, maybe. But present. Whole. Sacred.

And when you begin to see yourself as the very dwelling place of Divine power, your relationship with manifestation changes. You stop striving for it. You start awakening it.

This chapter is a call to the inner sanctuary.

To recognize your own body, your own breath, your own being as the sacred vessel through which creation flows.

Because you are not separate from the Source.

You are the soil it grows through.

Hidden Teachings from Ancient Traditions
—The Sacred Within—Discovering the Divine Dwelling in Every Faith

Across nearly every spiritual path, there is a quiet but profound truth: the Divine is not distant. It lives within. The idea that God, Source, or the Higher Power chooses to dwell inside us is not new—it is ancient.

These teachings remind us that the journey of manifestation doesn't begin by reaching into the heavens, but by awakening what is already encoded in our own being. From temples to tabernacles, from chants to sacred texts, each tradition has whispered the same message in its own tongue: You are the dwelling place. The temple. The spark of creation in motion.

Let's explore how the great wisdom traditions reveal this inner kingdom.

✧ Christian Faith

Jesus said, "**The kingdom of God is within you**." (Luke 17:21, KJV) He was not referring to some distant afterlife. He was pointing to a divine realm that already lives inside each of us—a place of faith, connection, and creative power.

Paul echoed this in his letter to the Corinthians: "**Do you not know that your body is the temple of the Holy Spirit, who is in you...?**" (1 Corinthians 6:19, NKJV) Here, the body is not just a shell. It is a holy dwelling—a sacred place where Spirit lives and breathes.

And in 1 Kings 19:12, when Elijah searches for God, the voice does not come in fire or wind—but in a still, small whisper.

The kingdom within is not loud. It is present. Patient. Waiting to be noticed.

✧ Jewish Wisdom

In Jewish tradition, the construction of the Mishkan (the portable sanctuary) was deeply symbolic—it represented not just a physical temple, but the indwelling presence of God within the soul. The divine instruction was: "**Let them make Me a sanctuary, that I may dwell among them**." (Exodus 25:8, JPS Tanakh)

The mystical branch of Judaism, Kabbalah, teaches that divine sparks are hidden in all things—especially within human beings. When we awaken to our inner sacredness, we lift these sparks back to the Source.

And the Shema, the foundational prayer of Jewish faith, calls for full-body devotion: "**Love the Lord your God with all your heart, and with all your soul, and with all your might**." (Deuteronomy 6:5, JPS)
The message is clear: the inner world is not separate from holiness—it is where it begins.

✧ Islamic Teachings

In Islam, the path to God is not external—it is deeply internal. The Qur'an speaks directly to this inner access: "**And [know] that Allah comes in between a person and his heart**..." (Qur'an 8:24, Sahih International) This verse affirms that God is not distant or removed—He is intimately present within the very core of your being. The heart, in Islamic thought, is more than an organ—it is the spiritual center, the seat of divine connection.

The concept of fitrah teaches that every soul is born in pure alignment with its Creator. This purity is not something to be earned—it is something to be remembered. When we go inward, we return to that original design.

The Prophet Muhammad (peace be upon him) often retreated into silence, not to escape the world but to enter more fully into that inner connection. His example of inward reflection, especially through practices like khalwa (solitude) and dhikr (remembrance), reveals that the sacred is not above you—it is within you. (As preserved by Ibn Hisham. The Life of Muhammad: A Translation of Ibn Ishaq's Sirat Rasul Allah, trans. A. Guillaume. Oxford University Press, 1955. (See pp. 106–107)

Even acts like wudu (ritual cleansing) and salah (prayer) serve not only as external rituals but as pathways inward—reminders that the body is a holy trust, a vessel for divine expression.

The Kingdom of God, in the Islamic tradition, is not something you must chase.

It is something you awaken—right where you are, right inside your soul.

✧ **Buddhist Practices**

Buddhism teaches that the path to enlightenment is not a journey outward—it is a return inward to the truth already present within. You do not need to climb mountains or leave the world to find peace. You only need to go home to yourself.

The Buddha said: "**Within this very body... lies the world, the origin of the world, the cessation of the world, and the path leading to the cessation of the world.**" (Samyutta Nikaya, SN 12.20) This scripture is among the most powerful affirmations of inner divinity found in Buddhist teaching. It tells us that the entire path to liberation—the full cycle of suffering and freedom—can be discovered by turning inward. The body is not a distraction from awakening. It is the doorway to it.

Mindfulness practices like Vipassana (insight meditation), anapanasati (breath awareness), and walking meditation are not just disciplines—they are invitations to dwell in your inner kingdom. Breath becomes the bridge. Stillness becomes the temple. Presence becomes the portal.

You do not need to escape the body to find the sacred.
You need to inhabit it—fully, reverently, and with compassion.

✧ **Hindu Traditions**

In Hinduism, the body is not seen as an obstacle to the Divine—it is seen as a temple.

The Isha Upanishad opens with this powerful truth: "**The Lord is enshrined in the hearts of all**." (Isha Upanishad, verse 1) This echoes the belief that Brahman, the Supreme Reality, expresses through the atman, the soul within.

Practices like yoga, pranayama, and mantra are not just disciplines—they are pathways to remember what has always been true: the Divine is already within.

The Bhagavad Gita teaches: "**The Supreme Person is situated within the heart of all living entities**." (Bhagavad Gita 18:61, ESV)
Liberation (moksha) comes not from escaping the body—but from recognizing its holiness.

The ancient texts have always known: You are not just a seeker of the Divine. You are a sanctuary for it. In every faith, the message is clear: the kingdom is not beyond your reach—it is already within your breath, your bones, your being.

Manifestation begins not with striving—but with remembering. Not by calling down heaven—but by awakening the heaven that has been quietly alive inside you all along.

Wisdom from Contemporary Spiritual Leaders

Throughout time, spiritual teachers have reminded us that the search for divinity does not begin outside—it begins within. This section gathers voices from today's most influential thought leaders, each echoing the same sacred truth: you are not separate from the Source—you are the sanctuary.

These are not just teachings; they are invitations to return to yourself, your center, your breath, your body—where the Kingdom truly lives.

—Eckhart Tolle teaches: "**The power for creating a better future is contained in the present moment: you create a good future by creating a good now**." He reminds us that the doorway to transformation isn't in the past or the distant future. It is right here, in the stillness of now. Your inner presence is the gateway to divine power.

—Dr. Joe Dispenza explains: "If your **body is emotionally conditioned to the past, your mind will think from the past— and you'll create more of the same**." To access divine potential, he teaches that we must recondition the body with the energy of the future. When we align internally, we become the temple through which new realities emerge.

—Esther Hicks (Abraham) emphasizes: "**Your inner being is always calling you toward the fulfillment of everything you desire**." This teaching reframes manifestation as an inside-out process. When your inner alignment is strong, your outer life responds in kind. Your inner being holds the blueprint.

—Denise Woods, master voice coach, says: "**Your voice is a reflection of your spirit. When you free your voice, you free yourself**." She teaches that voice is not just sound—it is soul. When you reconnect to your breath, you reconnect to truth. And when your truth is expressed, your inner kingdom expands.

—Rev. Michael Bernard Beckwith teaches: "**You are not here to get anything from the world, but to bring something through you into it**." This shifts the idea of manifestation from external acquisition to divine transmission. The kingdom is not something we extract—it's something we reveal through our being.

—Marianne Williamson writes: "**We were born to make manifest the glory of God that is within us**." She reminds us that the Divine doesn't just dwell around us—it lives within us, waiting to be remembered and expressed. The more we own this truth, the more we embody light.

—Roy Waugh, "**You are not reaching for the frequency—you are remembering it. The Kingdom isn't coming from outside. It's rising from within**." This truth calls you to stop striving and start remembering. The Kingdom isn't something you chase—it's something you carry. When you quiet the noise and return to your center, you don't find the frequency. You realize you are the frequency.

These teachers all say the same thing, though in different words: The temple is not a building. It is your breath. Your mind. Your stillness.

The voice of God is not only heard in thunder. Sometimes, it is heard when you listen inward. Because the truth you've been seeking has been living within you all along.

Scientific Perspectives on the Inner World and Manifestation
—How Modern Research Confirms the Temple Within

Modern science is beginning to catch up with what sacred traditions have always known: your body is not simply a vessel—it is a temple. A dynamic, intelligent, and responsive container of thought, energy, spirit, and transformation. While ancient texts spoke in terms of soul, spirit, and breath, science now offers language like neuroplasticity, coherence, and quantum resonance—but they are describing the same truth.

Let's explore how today's scientific insights affirm the sacred power already living inside of you.

✧ The Vagus Nerve and Inner Harmony

Often called the "soul nerve," the vagus nerve is a major conduit between your brain, heart, and gut. It regulates your body's ability to move between stress and peace. When activated through practices like deep breathing, meditation, and prayer, it brings the nervous system into coherence—reducing anxiety, increasing clarity, and enhancing your capacity to receive intuitive insight.

In spiritual terms, it quiets the world so you can hear the divine within.

✧ Heart-Brain Coherence

Research from the HeartMath Institute shows that when your heart and brain are in sync—through emotions like gratitude, love, and compassion—the body enters a state of harmony that radiates far beyond you. This is not just an internal feeling. It creates a measurable electromagnetic field that can influence others and alter the energy of the space around you.

When you align from within, your entire reality begins to resonate with that same frequency.

✧ Neuroplasticity and the Rewiring of Identity

Your brain is not fixed. It is moldable—designed to rewire based on what you repeatedly think, believe, and feel. Every time you affirm a truth, meditate on your divine worth, or choose presence over panic, you are reshaping your neural architecture.

This is not just cognitive. It is sacred remodeling—retraining the body to live from the temple within, rather than reacting to the chaos without.

✧ Quantum Consciousness and Inner Influence

Quantum physics has revealed that at the most fundamental level, the observer affects the outcome. This means your inner state—what you focus on, how you feel, and what you believe—interacts with the very fabric of reality. You are not a bystander in your life. You are a participant.

When your internal frequency aligns with sacred intention, you begin to collapse possibility into form.

✧ Embodiment as Energetic Transmission

Studies in psychoneuroimmunology and epigenetics now confirm that your emotional state influences your biology. Joy strengthens immunity. Stress weakens it. Peace enhances heart function. Resentment constricts it. The way you inhabit your body—your breath, your posture, your thoughts—is not just about wellness. It is about energetic stewardship.

Your temple is broadcasting constantly. The question is: what are you transmitting?

When you begin to honor your body as the sacred technology it is—not just a shell, but a sanctuary—you reclaim your role as the divine architect of your reality.

Science is not here to diminish mystery. It is here to reveal its design. And every study, every discovery, every breakthrough continues to affirm what Spirit has always whispered: You are not outside the power. You are the place where it resides. You are the temple. And the Divine dwells within.

Personal Story
—Waking Up From Within

For most of my life, I did not fully understand the sacredness of my body. I knew how to honor God with my gifts, but I did not yet realize the full truth: that I was the dwelling place. That I did not need to reach upward to find God; I needed to return inward.

Growing up in hardship, there was never much time to reflect on the body as anything other than functional. I was the oldest of six children. The interpreter for my mom. The one who had to hold it all together. I did not know what it meant to sit still in my own skin. I knew how to perform, how to pray upward, how to sing outward, but not how to go inward.

When my music ministry began, I finally felt like a fish in water. Being on stage felt like home—like I was doing what I was born to do. But even then, I knew it was not just me up there. I always felt like a vessel—like God, the Universe, the Divine, was channeling something through me.

It is hard to explain, but I used to imagine it.

I would visualize a beam of white light coming down from the center of The Universe or from the Throne of God, piercing right into the crown of my head—pure, focused, like a laser. It would then bounce off my heart, and then as I opened my mouth to sing, that light would burst out like a rainbow, flooding the room. It would wash over every person—touching ears, hearts, souls. Not just heard, but felt.

And I was grateful for that. I was proud to be used in that way. I understood I was being trusted as a conduit for something greater than myself.

But over time—and especially after walking through some painful physical challenges—I started to realize there was more. I had spent so much of my life visualizing God outside of me. I would shoot my prayers into the sky, into space, hoping to catch His attention like I was placing an order and waiting on a delivery.

One day, after recovering from yet another surgery that had forced me to slow down, I found myself sitting in complete stillness. I was not asking for anything. I just placed my hand over my heart and whispered, "Are YOU here?"

And in the silence that followed, I felt something stir. A warmth. A presence. A holy stillness that did not come from above—but from within. It was as if God leaned forward, right inside my chest, and whispered, "I've been here all along."

That moment broke something open in me.

It finally hit me—not just as a concept, but as a revelation: I am not separate from the Creator. I am an extension of Him. I am a living piece of the Divine.

I thought to myself, "Oh, that is what Jesus was saying when He said, 'The kingdom of God is within you."

That truth had been there all along. This body I have carried, this voice I have used, this breath I have taken for granted—it is all sacred. It is all a temple. Not because I said so, but because that is what it was designed to be.

And everything changed from that point forward.

I began treating myself differently. Treating my breath differently. Treating my silence differently. I did not just sing to inspire others anymore—I sang from a place of divine inhabitation. I was not just a vessel God used—I was the sanctuary He chose to dwell in.

And when I began to see myself that way, manifestations came with more clarity, peace, and alignment. I did not have to strive to "reach" God. I just had to return to myself.

Because the Kingdom? It was never far. It was never out there. It was here all along, waiting for me to come home.

Practical Applications
—Awakening the Kingdom Within

Manifestation doesn't begin in the ethers—it begins in the sanctuary of your own being. When you understand that the Divine does not reside in the clouds but within your very breath and bones, everything changes.

These practices are not about striving—they are about stewarding. They are sacred invitations to return to your center, to tend to the temple within, and to manifest not from longing, but from alignment. Because once you awaken the kingdom inside, the outside world starts to follow.

1. **Start your day inward**.
   Before you check your phone, check in with your spirit. Place a hand on your heart and ask, "What do I need today?"

2. **Treat your body as a temple**.
   Hydrate. Nourish. Move. Rest. Speak to yourself as you would a sacred altar because you are one.

3. **Use breath as a portal**.
   Three conscious breaths throughout the day can realign your nervous system and return you to the inner now.

4. **Create an inner sanctuary**.
   Set up a physical space—however small—for reflection. A chair, a cushion, a candle. Let it be a symbol of your inner kingdom.

5. **Use mirror practice**.
   Look into your own eyes. Speak gently. Say, "You are sacred. You are a vessel of divine power." Watch how your inner world responds.

6. **Anchor with mantras**.
   Choose a phrase like: "The Kingdom is within me.", "I am aligned with the Source.", or "My body is a temple."

7. **Practice deep listening**.
   When unsure of a decision, go inward. Ask, "What does my spirit say?" Then wait for the whisper.

You do not have to ascend a mountain to find the Divine. You are the mountain. You are the sanctuary. You are the sacred ground where Spirit and self meet.

These practices are not small acts of self-care. They are acts of sacred remembrance—daily invitations to live as if the Creator truly dwells within you because it does.

When you honor your body, you honor the Builder. When you trust your breath, you align with the Source of life itself. And when you listen inwardly, you awaken the deepest truth of all: *You are not looking for the Kingdom, You are the Kingdom—awakening, aligning, and becoming.*

Affirmation

"I am the temple. I am the vessel. I am aligned with divine power. Everything I need is already within me."

Guided Meditation
—Entering the Inner Kingdom

Sit comfortably. Breathe slowly.

Now picture a radiant light within your chest. This is your inner sanctuary.

Let it expand with each inhale. Let it glow with peace.

Whisper inwardly: "I return to the Source within."

With each breath, feel the light growing. Feel the stillness rising. Feel yourself coming home.

In this space, ask: "What truth lives in me today?" Listen. Trust.

You are already connected, already worthy, and already whole.

Conclusion

You have never been separate from the Source. Not even for a heartbeat.

The Divine has never needed a building to dwell in. It chose you. And not by accident—but by design.

You were not created to be a bystander to holiness. You were created to be a carrier of it. Your hands. Your voice. Your breath. Your beating heart. All of it—crafted to hold light and to radiate power.

And yet for so long, we were taught to look up, to reach out, to cry toward the sky as if God were far away.

But the truth is this: The power you're looking for, the wisdom you're chasing, the presence you're praying for; It's been with you all along. Closer than your next breath. Alive in your very cells.

When you begin to treat yourself as holy ground—when you nourish your body, honor your breath, and listen to your spirit—you don't just shift your mindset. You realign with your true identity. You stop begging for miracles and start embodying them. You stop chasing the light and realize you are the prism.

Yes, speak your vision, walk in faith, and dream big dreams.

But never forget—The power you are trying to manifest is not just something you call down from above. It's something you wake up within yourself.

So, rise. Breathe with reverence. Move like a temple in motion. Speak with the knowing that your voice is an echo of the Divine.

Because you are not a vessel waiting to be filled. You are already filled. Not because you earned it. But because you were born to carry it.

When that truth settles deep in your bones, when you finally stop searching and start remembering, the world around you begins to change.

Because the Kingdom within you has come alive.

Chapter 23: Letting Go of Limiting Beliefs
—Uprooting What No Longer Serves

Opening Reflection

"Old beliefs can't hold new blessings. Any belief that dims your vision doesn't belong in your spirit."
—Roy Waugh

Introduction

Every seed you plant—every thought, word, and belief—sets something in motion. The beliefs that live beneath the surface of your life either nurture your vision or quietly strangle it. They either shine light on your vision or cast shadows over it. They draw your dream closer—or keep it out of reach.

Limiting beliefs are not just ideas. They are energetic contracts—agreements we made in fear, in trauma, in survival. And unless we uproot them, they will keep designing a life that does not match the destiny we were born to manifest.

This chapter is about clearing the soil. It is about identifying the beliefs that were planted by pain, shame, or scarcity—and choosing to plant something new. Something true.

Because you cannot manifest a harvest of blessings while clinging to the roots of lack.

If you want a new future, you must give your voice to a new truth. And it starts here.

Hidden Teachings from Ancient Traditions
—Uprooting What No Longer Serves Across Sacred Wisdom

Across every sacred tradition, there is a shared understanding: what we believe shapes what we experience. Whether it's called faith, karma, alignment, or inner purification, each path speaks to the unseen forces that govern our lives from within. Limiting beliefs are not part of the soul's divine blueprint—they are distortions, often born from pain or passed down through generations. But what was learned can be unlearned. What was planted can be uprooted. And what was lost can be restored.

Let us turn now to the ancient voices that remind us: you are not the story you inherited. You are the truth you choose to embody.

✧ Christian Faith

Jesus often spoke in parables about seeds and soil because He understood that transformation begins beneath the surface. In the parable of the sower, the same seed was scattered across many types of ground—but only the good soil produced lasting fruit. "**But the seed falling on good soil refers to someone who hears the word and understands it. This is the one who produces a crop**." (Matthew 13:23, NIV). The seed wasn't the problem—it was the soil.

Paul echoes this inner transformation when he writes: "Do **not conform to the pattern of this world, but be transformed by the renewing of your mind**." (Romans 12:2, NIV). Limiting beliefs—especially those rooted in fear or unworthiness—can become strongholds.

But the promise remains: "**The weapons we fight with are not the weapons of the world. On the contrary, they have divine power to demolish strongholds**." (2 Corinthians 10:4, NIV).

In the Christian walk, healing is not just about changing behavior—it's about allowing God to rewrite what you believe at the root.

✧ Jewish Wisdom

In Judaism, the divine worth of every person is foundational. We are created b'tzelem Elohim—in the image of God (Genesis 1:27). This means that inherent value is not earned; it is embedded into our very being.

Yet life often buries this truth. The journey of teshuvah—commonly translated as repentance—also means "return." Not just returning to God, but returning to your true self. The rabbis teach that teshuvah is a form of spiritual remembering.

In Kabbalistic teaching, the soul is filled with divine sparks, but limiting beliefs act like veils that cover the light. The work is not to become someone new—but to remove the layers that hide who you've always been.

When Moses doubted his calling and said, **"Who am I, that I should go to Pharaoh?"** (Exodus 3:11, ESV), God didn't argue his qualifications. He simply answered, **"I will be with you."** (Exodus 3:12, ESV).

The Divine doesn't wait for you to feel worthy—only for you to be willing.

✧ Islamic Teachings

The Qur'an affirms human dignity with unwavering clarity: **"We have certainly created man in the best of stature."** (Surah At-Tin, 95:4, Sahih International). And yet, so many carry beliefs that deny this divine truth. The internal whisper of unworthiness, shame, or self-rejection is not from God—it is a distortion of truth.

Islam teaches the concept of tazkiyah—the purification of the soul. This is a lifelong practice of uncovering falsehoods and restoring the heart to its original fitrah—its natural, God-given state.

The Prophet Muhammad (peace be upon him) said, **"Seek knowledge from the cradle to the grave."** Hadith, Sunan al-Bayhaqi), encouraging believers to question inherited ideas that no longer align with truth.

Letting go of limiting beliefs is not rebellion—it is restoration. It is removing the rust from the mirror of the soul so that it can reflect the light of the Divine once again.

✧ Buddhist Practices

Buddhism teaches that suffering arises from attachment—not only to things, but also to false ideas about ourselves. We become attached to the belief that we are unworthy, broken, or separate from joy. And these beliefs build a cage around the spirit.

The Buddha said, "**Believe nothing, no matter where you read it or who has said it, unless it agrees with your own reason and your own common sense.**" (Kalama Sutta, AN 3.65). *The spiritual path is not about blind belief—it is about waking up.*

Through mindfulness and compassionate inquiry, Buddhism invites us to observe our thoughts without judgment. When we stop identifying with them, they lose their power. As Thich Nhat Hanh teaches, "**To be beautiful means to be yourself. You don't need to be accepted by others. You need to accept yourself.**" (True Love, 1997).

You do not need to destroy the old. You only need to stop feeding it.

✧ Hindu Traditions

In Hindu philosophy, the mind is both the creator of bondage and the instrument of liberation. The Upanishads teach, "**You are what your deep, driving desire is. As your desire is, so is your will... so is your destiny.**" (Brihadaranyaka Upanishad, 4.4.5). Belief is the seed of destiny.

The Bhagavad Gita echoes this truth: "A **person is made by their belief. As they believe, so they become.**" (Bhagavad Gita, 17:3). Limiting beliefs are known as avidya—false knowledge that clouds the light of the Atman, the divine Self within.

Jnana Yoga—the path of wisdom—calls us to examine our inherited stories, question illusion (maya), and return to the truth that we are not our wounds or weaknesses. We are divine consciousness, temporarily wearing a human form.

Letting go of limiting beliefs is not striving to become something more. It is remembering what you already are.

Wisdom from Contemporary Spiritual Leaders

Before a person can walk in power, they must first question the stories that told them they weren't allowed to. Every generation has been given teachers—voices raised in divine timing to remind us that we are not our wounds, our past, or our conditioning. We are not what the pain said. We are not what fear taught.

These spiritual leaders help us remember: the world outside of us begins with the world within us. If we want to change our lives, we must start with what we believe about who we are.

—Dr. Joe Dispenza teaches, "**Your personality creates your personal reality**." That means the identity you carry—the thoughts you rehearse, the emotions you dwell in, the beliefs you embody—becomes the blueprint for your life. You cannot create a future from the energy of your past. When you rewrite the inner script, the outer scene changes too.

—Abraham Hicks reminds us, "**A belief is just a thought you keep thinking**." This simple teaching breaks the illusion that beliefs are permanent. They're just ideas we've repeated—some for so long they've become invisible. But the moment we stop rehearsing the thought, its power begins to fade. And a new thought—a new truth—can take root.

—Louise Hay said, "**You have been criticizing yourself for years, and it has not worked. Try approving of yourself and see what happens**." We are so quick to shame ourselves into change. But shame cannot grow miracles—only love can. Self-approval is not arrogance; it's alignment. When you speak kindly to yourself, you begin to build a life that reflects that kindness.

—Oprah Winfrey has shared, "**You don't become what you want. You become what you believe**." Manifestation doesn't begin with desire—it begins with identity. If you believe you are unworthy, your vision will always feel out of reach. But when you believe you were born for abundance, wholeness, and divine connection—life rises to meet you there.

—Iyanla Vanzant declares, "**You have to meet yourself where you are. Not where you wish you were, or where you used to be.**" Releasing limiting beliefs begins with radical honesty. You can't heal what you won't name. But when you tell the truth about the lies you've believed, you take your power back—one revelation at a time.

—Dannion Brinkley once said, "**We are great, powerful, and mighty spiritual beings with dignity, direction, and purpose.**" Most people don't struggle because they are broken—they struggle because they have forgotten who they are. Limiting beliefs shrink us into roles we were never meant to play. But the truth of who you are is divine, whole, and radiant. And once you begin to believe that, you rise differently. You speak differently. You live from the inside out.

—Roy Waugh; "**A lie believed too long becomes a life too small. But the moment you replace it with truth, you don't just shift your thinking—you shift your entire destiny**. Limiting beliefs don't just cloud the mind—they shape the life. But once you begin speaking truth into the places where shame used to live, everything begins to change. Your voice returns. Your vision expands. And the version of you that's been waiting on the other side of healing finally gets to rise.

Each of these voices echoes the same sacred truth: you were never the lie. You were never the fear, the failure, or the label. You were simply someone who forgot their light for a moment. But now you remember. And in that remembering, something holy begins to rise.

Scientific Perspectives on Rewriting Belief
—How the Brain Unlearns the Lie

What we believe doesn't just live in the mind—it lives in the body. It informs our posture, our choices, our emotional patterns, and even the chemistry of our cells. Science has confirmed what spiritual traditions have long taught: our inner world shapes our outer reality. But here's the good news—beliefs are not set in stone. They are patterns, and patterns can be reprogrammed.

✧ Neuroplasticity and the Power to Rewire

Neuroscience confirms that the brain is not fixed—it is changeable. This concept, called neuroplasticity, reveals that each time you challenge a limiting belief and replace it with a new one, you are literally rewiring your brain. Repeated thoughts create stronger neural pathways, like grooves in a trail.

The more you walk a new mental path—one rooted in truth, not fear—the more natural it becomes.

✧ Cognitive Behavioral Therapy (CBT)

Cognitive Behavioral Therapy is based on this core principle: when you change your thoughts, your feelings and behaviors follow. CBT helps uncover subconscious beliefs that influence patterns of fear, procrastination, low self-worth, and anxiety.

By identifying distorted thought patterns and reframing them, people experience measurable improvements in well-being, relationships, and confidence.

✧ Subconscious Belief and Inner Programming

The subconscious mind governs approximately 95% of our daily thoughts and actions, meaning most of what drives us is happening below conscious awareness. Limiting beliefs often live here—picked up in childhood, through trauma, or inherited messaging.

But practices like meditation, affirmations, hypnosis, and journaling have been shown to open access to the subconscious, offering a doorway to rewrite old programming.

✧ Energy Psychology and Emotional Frequencies

Emerging fields like energy psychology suggest that every belief carries a measurable frequency. Limiting beliefs tend to vibrate at lower frequencies, often linked to emotions like guilt, shame, fear, or lack. Empowered beliefs—such as "I am worthy" or "I am aligned"—register higher.

These shifts in frequency affect not only your emotional state but your magnetic field, attracting different outcomes into your life.
Our brains were designed to evolve.

Our thoughts were never meant to stay stuck. Every time you speak a new truth, you don't just create a better day—you create a new neurological map, a new frequency of being. And in time, that frequency becomes your future.

Personal Story
—Who Was I To Speak?

For the longest time, I wrestled with the weight of where I came from.

I was the son of a deaf mother, abused and trapped, and a father caught up in addiction. We did not grow up with much money, stability, or confidence. There were no family vacations. No guidance counselors to map out college plans. We did not talk about dreams. We talked about surviving the month.

We had love, but we also had lack.

And I carried that lack into adulthood like a hidden chain. I did not even know I was doing it. I just thought this is the way life works for people like me.

So even when I started singing—when doors began to open and people invited me to stand on stages, share my voice, speak hope—I still had that nagging thought in the back of my mind: "Who are you to tell anyone about blessings?" — "Who are you to talk about faith and possibility?" —

"You are just a kid from nowhere." — "You are just a nobody with a broken family and nothing but trauma in your rearview mirror."

And over time, I did not just think that—I believed it. And that belief made decisions for me.

I passed on opportunities. I held back my gifts. I made safe choices. I stayed in the background, not because I was not called—but because I did not feel worthy to show up.

I thought I was being humble, but really, I was just afraid.

Then one night, after a concert, someone handed me a note. I wish I remembered their face, but I don't. I just remember the words:
"You gave me hope tonight—because you didn't just sing, you really opened your heart, and you let us see YOU. Your pain. Your grace. Your scars. And it hit me if light can shine through you, maybe it can shine through me too."

I stood there, speechless.

It was not the polished parts of me that touched people—it was the pieces I tried to hide. The cracks I covered were the very places where the light poured through.

That was what people were feeling in my voice when I sang—it was not just music. It was my truth, breaking through.

That night, I sat down with one of my old journals. The pages were full of prayers, questions, and scribbled song lyrics, but this time, I wrote something different.

I wrote the lie I had believed for years: *"I'll never reach greatness because of where I come from." And then I crossed it out.*

Underneath, I wrote: *"I come from strength. I come from survival. I come from grace. My story does not disqualify me—it empowers me."*

I let that permeate my spirit as I cried. Through those tears, I was able to release that old weight that had held me back for so long.

I thought about all the times I had said no when I should have said yes. All the times I let fear make the call. I was not mad at myself—I just felt sad. Sad for how long I had carried something that never belonged to me.

Then, I did something I had never done before: I blessed my own beginning.

I thanked the struggle that made me empathetic.
I thanked the silence that taught me how to listen.
I thanked the ache that made room for so much joy.

And I even thanked the shame—because it helped mold and make me into the person that I am today.

Since then, I have walked differently. I have spoken differently. I have stopped apologizing for my story—and started honoring it.

Because now I know, I was not too broken to be used. I was born for this.

I was made for this.

Practical Applications
—Uprooting and Replacing Limiting Beliefs

Letting go of limiting beliefs is not about pretending they never existed—it's about recognizing they no longer have permission to shape your life. These inner agreements, often formed in pain or survival, may have once felt protective, but now, they are simply too small for who you've become.

The following steps aren't just mental exercises—they are sacred tools for reclamation. They invite you to examine your inner soil, uproot what no longer serves, and plant new truth with intention. Because once you change the belief, you change the blueprint. And from there, anything is possible—if you just believe.

1. **Name the belief**.
   Ask: "What is one belief I hold that is limiting my vision?" Write it down.

2. **Ask, "Is this absolutely true?"**
   Challenge the belief. Where did it come from? Is it a universal truth— or just a painful story?

3. **Find the fruit**.
   What has this belief produced in your life? What has it cost you?

4. **Plant a new seed**.
   Write a new belief that aligns with your vision: "I am enough.", "I deserve to thrive.", "I release fear and embrace trust."

5. **Affirm it daily**.
   Say the new belief out loud every morning. Let your voice reshape your inner world.

6. **Track the shift**.
   Notice how your thoughts, emotions, and results begin to change. Your life will start to mirror your new root.

7. **Be gentle in the process**.
   You are not failing if the old belief shows up again, just do not feed it. Return to truth and water the new seed.

Every time you choose truth over an old story, you reclaim a piece of your power. Uprooting limiting beliefs is not a one-time act—it is a daily tending of your inner garden. Some weeds try to grow back, but with each return to your new belief, their hold weakens. Remember, the life you long for cannot grow in the soil of doubt. It flourishes where faith, clarity, and self-worth are planted. Keep watering the seeds of truth, and soon your life will bear the fruit of what you now dare to believe.

Affirmation

"I uproot what no longer serves me. I plant truth in its place. My inner world is fertile ground for miracles."

Guided Meditation
—Releasing the Old, Welcoming the New

Breathe in. And again.

Picture yourself standing in a garden. You see a plant that no longer serves you. You kneel and gently, you dig around the roots and you lift it out of the soil. You bless it for what it taught you.

And now, you release it.

In its place, you plant a new seed.

You whisper into the soil: "I am enough. I am ready. I am aligned." Water it with light.

Breath in, feel the shift.

Now, you are free and you are clear of the old beliefs that no longer serve you.

Conclusion

There comes a moment in every soul's journey when the lies we've carried begin to feel heavier than the truth we've been running from.

Maybe you've felt it too—that quiet ache beneath the surface that whispers, "You're not enough. You'll never get there. Who do you think you are?"

I've felt it. I've lived it. For years, I let that voice shape my choices, shrink my posture, and dim my light. I thought my past had marked me permanently. I believed that where I came from meant I could never rise too far.

The truth is, we all inherit beliefs we never asked for.

Some are passed down like family recipes—seasoned with fear, shame, and survival. Others are handed to us in moments of heartbreak, rejection, or silence. We take them in when we are young, not knowing better. Not knowing they would root themselves deep inside us. And before we realize it, we've built entire identities on stories that were never even ours.

But just because something was planted, doesn't mean it has to stay. Letting go of limiting beliefs isn't only about clearing space—it's about reclaiming power. It's about reaching into the soil of your spirit and asking, "Does this still belong here?" And if the answer is no, then it's time to pull it—gently, honestly, with compassion.

Because you're not just weeding a garden. You're making room for a new harvest.

And yes, it may feel tender because even the lies gave us something to hold.

But here's the sacred truth: you don't have to live in the shadow of who you used to be. Not anymore.

The voice that told you you weren't enough? *It was never yours.*

The shame that said your past disqualified you? *That was never the voice of truth.*

The doubt that whispered, "Who do you think you are?" *That was never the voice of the Divine.*

This is the season of release. Release the old labels. Release the inherited shame. Release the false ceilings that told you to stay small, stay quiet, or dim your light.

Because the soil of your spirit is sacred, and it's time to plant something worthy of who you are now.

So, speak the truth boldly. Live it loudly. And water it with belief until it grows tall, and strong, and undeniable.

Because when you pull out the root of a lie, you make space for a miracle.

And that miracle is YOU.

Chapter 24: Receiving Through Rest
—The Sacred Stillness of Manifestation

Opening Reflection

"Sometimes the most powerful thing you can do... is nothing at all."
—Roy Waugh

Introduction

In a world that constantly rewards doing, rest can feel like falling behind. But in the deeper work of manifestation, rest isn't weakness—it's wisdom. It's not giving up—it's leaning in. Rest is a choice to trust the process. To believe that what's meant for you is already in motion, even if you can't see it yet.

When you pause, you stop pushing. And when you stop pushing, you start allowing. That's when the energy can shift. Because in the spiritual realm, insistence creates resistance. The more you try to force it, the more it slips away.

Because when you insist, you're often insisting that the manifestation unfold your way—on your timeline, through your limited understanding. But that kind of control closes off other doors. It blocks the flow. It shuts down the very possibilities the Universe is trying to align and deliver on your behalf.

This chapter is about redefining rest—not as something you earn after doing enough, but as something essential to the creative process itself. It's about softening into the space between intention and outcome, and letting your energy do the work you can't force.

Because the seed grows in silence.
The body restores in stillness.

And the breakthroughs? They often show up not when you're pushing forward—but when you simply let go.

Hidden Teachings from Ancient Traditions
—The Sacred Pause Across Faith: Trusting the Wisdom of Rest

Rest is not a modern luxury—it is an ancient spiritual discipline woven into the fabric of sacred wisdom across every tradition. Whether it's a day of stillness, a posture of prayer, or a rhythm of reflection, the message is clear: we were never meant to live in constant motion. The soul, like the soil, needs time to breathe.

In the teachings that follow, we'll explore how rest is not just a break from life—it is a return to the divine rhythm within life. A rhythm that trusts, surrenders, and opens to receive.

✧ Christian Faith

From the very beginning, rest was modeled as divine. In the creation story, God worked for six days and then rested—not because He needed to, but to show us that rest is holy. **"By the seventh day God had finished the work he had been doing; so on the seventh day he rested from all his work."** (Genesis 2:2, NIV). That rest wasn't about exhaustion—it was about completion. It was a pause that sanctified the rhythm of creation itself.

Jesus also embodied this rhythm. He withdrew from the crowds to restore His spirit and modeled the balance between giving and receiving. **"Very early in the morning... Jesus got up, left the house and went off to a solitary place, where He prayed."** (Mark 1:35, NIV). Even in moments of chaos, Jesus rested. When a storm raged around the disciples, He was asleep in the boat. The peace they were begging for was already present—within Him.

Rest, in the Christian faith, is not the absence of action. It is the presence of deep trust.

✧ Jewish Wisdom

In Judaism, rest is not optional—it's a covenant. Shabbat, the weekly Sabbath, is a sacred pause from Friday sundown to Saturday nightfall. It's a time when striving stops, when the world slows, when the soul remembers.

"You shall remember that you were a slave in the land of Egypt, and the Lord your God brought you out... therefore the Lord your God commanded you to keep the Sabbath day.**"** (Deuteronomy 5:15, ESV). Rest is not just a ritual—it's a declaration of freedom. A way of saying, I am no longer enslaved to endless doing.

Even the land was given rest. The Shemittah year, every seventh year, allowed the earth to lie fallow—a reminder that everything, even the soil, needs time to recover and renew.

Jewish mysticism teaches that Shabbat isn't just physical rest—it is soul elevation. In that stillness, the Divine spark within is rekindled. Rest becomes sacred resistance to a world that tells you your worth is tied to your productivity.

✧ Islamic Teachings

In Islam, rest and rhythm are woven into daily spiritual practice. The five daily prayers serve not as interruptions but as recalibrations—intentional pauses that anchor the heart and body back to divine presence.

The Prophet Muhammad (peace be upon him) taught his followers the value of balance. He said, **"Your body has a right over you**.**"** (Sahih Bukhari 5199), which includes the right to rest, replenish, and restore. Islam honors the body as a sacred trust.

During Ramadan, rest becomes a spiritual necessity. Fasting slows the pace, quiets the ego, and makes space for remembrance (dhikr). In that softening, the believer is invited to listen, to feel, to align.

And through it all, the heart is central. "**Verily, in the body is a piece of flesh which, if it is sound, the whole body is sound... indeed, it is the heart**." (Sahih Bukhari 52). Rest in Islam is not passivity—it is a tuning of the heart to divine frequency.

✧ Buddhist Practices

In Buddhism, rest is not the absence of motion—it is the presence of awareness.

Thich Nhat Hanh wrote, "**Sometimes the most important thing in a whole day is the rest we take between two deep breaths**." (Peace Is Every Step: The Path of Mindfulness in Everyday Life, Bantam, 1992) That breath—that pause—is a return to stillness.

Mindfulness itself is a sacred form of rest. It pulls us out of compulsive doing and places us gently into the moment. Walking meditation teaches us that we don't need to be still to rest—we simply need to be present.

The Buddha encouraged retreat—not as escape, but as reconnection. In silence and solitude, the mind clears, the heart opens, and the soul remembers what is enough.

Rest in Buddhist teaching is not about checking out—it's about tuning in. It's where effort dissolves, and awareness expands.

✧ Hindu Traditions

In Hinduism, rest is woven into the very cycle of life. The Bhagavad Gita teaches harmony through balance: "**He who is temperate in eating, sleeping, working, and recreation can mitigate all sorrows by practicing the yoga which destroys pain**." (Gita 6:17, Eknath Easwaran translation). Stillness is not seen as passive—it is sacred. In yoga nidra, or "*yogic sleep*," the body is completely at rest while the mind remains conscious. This deep state allows for profound healing, restoration, and spiritual awakening.

Even in chanting Om, the silence between the sounds is revered. That gap, that stillness, is not emptiness—it is the presence of the Divine.

Hindu wisdom teaches that rest is not what you do when you're done being spiritual. *Rest is the practice.* It's how you return to the Self—Atman—the divine spark within.

Rest has never been a sign of failure. Across every path, it is taught as holy ground. A time to release the grip of striving and fall back into divine rhythm. These sacred traditions agree: you were not created to run on empty. You were created to receive. And sometimes the most faithful thing you can do is to stop. Breathe. Trust that what you're waiting for is already on its way.

Because when you sit alone in silence, in stillness, whether in meditation or simply being present with yourself, something happens.

At first, the mind resists. It clings to noise. It recycles worry. But stay with it. After a few minutes, the mind begins to quiet. The noise softens. The spinning slows. And in that stillness, something sacred stirs.

That's when you begin to hear it—that small, still voice inside. The one that was there all along, waiting for space to speak. This is where the answers come. This is where new ideas, unexpected guidance, and even visions begin to rise. Not because you chased them, but because you made room.

Stillness is not empty. It's full of everything you've been asking for. And it arrives when you finally sit still enough to receive it.

Wisdom from Contemporary Spiritual Leaders

Before the body breaks down or the spirit burns out, rest begins whispering. But we're often too busy to hear it. That's why every generation is given voices—messengers who remind us that rest isn't laziness or weakness. It's alignment. It's wisdom. It's how the soul opens back up to receive.

These teachers have all spoken to the deeper truth behind rest: that stillness doesn't stop the flow—it activates it.

—Louise Hay wrote, "**Rest when you need to. Your body is a precious vessel. Honor it**." Louise reminds us that rest isn't selfish—it's sacred. The body is not a machine to be pushed to the limit. It's a living altar. And when we honor it, it responds with healing and grace.

—Abraham Hicks teaches, "**The rule of thumb is, you never get it done and you can't get it wrong. So rest. Take a nap. Let the universe do the heavy lifting**." This teaching reminds us that rest isn't a disruption to manifestation—it's part of it. When you stop trying to control every outcome and just let go, you make space for the Universe to do what you couldn't have orchestrated on your own. When resting, you stop chasing alignment and start receiving it.

—Dr. Joe Dispenza says, "**You can't create a new future while you're living in a survival mode. You have to get beyond the analytical mind and enter the operating system of the subconscious**." Rest and meditation help shift us out of survival and into creation. When the brain slows down, the door opens to deeper change—where intention becomes integration.

—Oprah Winfrey has said, "**The greatest discovery of all time is that a person can change their future by merely changing their attitude**." And often, the shift in attitude comes in rest. Oprah shows us that clarity doesn't always come through doing more. Sometimes it comes when you finally pause long enough to hear what's been inside you all along.

—Iyanla Vanzant shares that rest is a form of self-love. "**You cannot serve from an empty vessel. Rest is how you refill**." Iyanla brings us back to the truth that you can't pour from depletion. Rest is not an interruption—it's preparation. It's how we serve from overflow, not burnout.

—Albert Einstein once said, "**I think 99 times and find nothing. I stop thinking, swim in silence, and the truth comes to me**." Even a mind like Einstein's knew the power of pause. Truth doesn't always arrive through effort. Sometimes it emerges from the space between thoughts.

—Roy Waugh: "**Rest is not what happens after the work is done— rest is the crescendo of the work. It's where everything you've planted gets permission to rise**." When you rest, you're not stepping away from alignment—you're stepping deeper into it. Rest resets your frequency, clears the static, and reconnects you to divine flow.

When you look at these voices together, a pattern appears: *rest is not a break from the journey—it's part of the divine rhythm of creation itself.* When at rest, the soul speaks. The body listens. And the energy aligns.

So, if you're tired, don't push harder. Pause.
If nothing's moving, stop forcing. Make space.
Because in that stillness, the answer often arrives.

Scientific Perspectives on Rest and Receiving
—What the Body Knows Before the Mind Catches Up

Rest is not a luxury—it is biological intelligence. The body and brain were not designed for constant motion or output. In fact, the systems most responsible for healing, intuition, emotional balance, and even creative insight become fully accessible only when we allow ourselves to slow down.

Science confirms what ancient wisdom has always taught: you are most magnetic, most receptive, and most energetically aligned when you are at peace.

✧ **Neuroscience of Brainwave States**

The brain operates on different wave frequencies depending on our level of alertness or relaxation. In waking life, we spend much of our time in high-frequency beta waves—ideal for decision-making but also linked to stress and overthinking. However, during states of alpha (relaxed awareness) and theta (deep rest, meditation, and light sleep), the brain becomes far more receptive to new ideas, insights, and inner transformation.

Theta, in particular, is associated with deep subconscious access. This is where affirmations take root and visualizations imprint more powerfully. Rest isn't just a pause—it's a portal.

✦ Autonomic Nervous System / Parasympathetic Activation

Your autonomic nervous system governs your body's unconscious processes, and it has two main settings: sympathetic (fight or flight) and parasympathetic (rest and digest). When you're constantly active, your sympathetic system dominates—keeping your body in a mild state of emergency.

Rest activates the parasympathetic system. Heart rate slows, cortisol drops, and digestion improves. Inflammation lowers. Immune function strengthens. This is not passive healing—it is the body doing exactly what it was designed to do: recover, balance, and prepare to receive.

✦ Default Mode Network and Insight Generation

The default mode network (DMN) is a network of brain regions that activates when you are at rest—not focused on a task, but daydreaming, reflecting, or simply being. It's responsible for introspection, memory consolidation, and intuitive breakthroughs.

Scientific studies show that many of our most creative ideas, sudden solutions, and spiritual insights arise when the DMN is active. That's why so many people report "downloads" during showers, nature walks, or quiet moments before sleep. Rest doesn't switch the brain off—it switches a higher intelligence on.

✦ Bioenergetics and Coherence in Stillness

From an energy science perspective, rest creates measurable shifts in your electromagnetic field. Research from the HeartMath Institute reveals that during deep rest, the heart enters a state of coherence—a rhythm of balance between the nervous system and emotional state. This heart-brain coherence not only improves well-being but is believed to enhance the body's receptivity to external energy fields.

When you are at rest and in resonance, your energetic signature becomes more coherent. You are not just relaxed—you are magnetic. You attract not by force, but by frequency.

You were not created to manifest from burnout.

The biology of belief, the frequency of healing, and the intelligence of your own nervous system all point to one truth: rest is not the opposite of progress—it is a condition for receiving. When you rest, you stop striving. When you stop striving, you open. And when you open, what you've been calling in finally knows where to land.

Personal Story
—When David Had to Sit Down

At the height of our national tour for David: A Man After God's Own Heart, I was performing the lead role—fully choreographed, vocally demanding, and emotionally rich. The production lasted nearly three hours, and I was on stage for all but twenty minutes of it. Night after night, we brought to life the journey of a shepherd boy destined for greatness, and I poured every part of myself into that story—body, voice, energy, and spirit.

Over the course of the first 30 performances on our nationwide tour, I poured out everything I had—and still had 67 shows ahead of me. At the start, I'd been given a special pair of dancing sandals: thin leather soles that covered only the ball of my toes and ball of my feet, which helped me move with ease across glossy stages while maintaining the look of being barefoot. But somewhere around the twentieth show, those sandals were accidentally left behind at a venue—and they were never recovered.

From that point on, the barefoot dancing on slick, hard surfaces began to wear on me. My ankles ached. The pain crept in slowly but grew louder with every performance. At first, I ignored it. I smiled, I sang, I leapt across the stage. I whispered small hopes to myself that I could keep going. I convinced myself this was what strength and commitment looked like.

But deep down, I could feel it—my body was calling for rest. My spirit too.

Still, I stayed quiet.

I did not want to let down the cast or disrupt the flow of the tour. I told myself, "Just keep going. Do not let anyone down."

But beneath that voice, another one began to rise—quiet at first, but persistent: "Even great stories need an intermission. You need rest."

Eventually, the pain became impossible to hide. Every step felt like a signal—one I could no longer ignore. So, I finally spoke up. I asked the tour director if we could pause for a few days to give my body time to recover.

I'll never forget what the director said in response: "We were waiting for you to say something."

It stunned me.

I had been so focused on holding everything together, I did not realize that by resisting rest, I was withholding what I truly needed—not just physically, but energetically. I had been performing the role of David, yes —but in the silence of those few days of rest, something deeper unfolded.

I stopped pushing. I gave myself permission to pause. I rested.
And in that rest, something shifted. I found my center—not just in the role, but in myself. I felt more grounded, more connected, more present. I stopped trying to control the performance and instead let it move through me.

When I returned to the stage, I was not just playing David; I was channeling the essence of David and his journey. His vulnerability. His resilience. His transformation. It became less about delivering lines or hitting marks, and more about transmitting something honest. Something alive.

And the audiences felt it. The cast felt it. I felt it.

Because sometimes, the very thing we think we cannot afford to do—rest —is the thing that realigns us with our deepest power.

The moment I stopped striving was the moment everything began to flow again.

That is when I truly learned: Sometimes, the greatest breakthroughs do not come from pushing harder. They come from letting go and letting grace take the lead.

Practical Applications
—Receiving Through Rest

We have been taught to measure progress by motion, and to equate stillness with stagnation—but in the realm of manifestation, rest is its own sacred movement. In this next section, you will find practices designed to help you realign with the natural rhythm of receiving.

These tools are not about doing more—they are about allowing more. By creating space, softening your energy, and honoring the wisdom of pause, you open the door for miracles to meet you without force. Because sometimes, the most powerful action is the one you do not take.

1. **Schedule sacred stillness**.
   Even 15 minutes a day of intentional rest—no phone, no input—can recalibrate your energy.

2. **Practice guided rest meditation**.
   Use body scan meditations to invite your body into peace. Let your muscles relax. Let your mind drift.

3. **Honor the sabbath principle**.
    Pick one day—or part of a day—to cease striving. No agendas. No productivity. Just rest.

4. **Replace guilt with gratitude**.
    When you rest, instead of saying, "I should be doing more," say, "I'm grateful to be receiving."

5. **Notice what emerges**.
    Pay attention to ideas, solutions, and insights that arise in rest. Write them down. These are often divine downloads.

6. **Affirm before you rest**.
    Say: "I receive while I rest. I am safe to pause. My soul is still working, even in silence."

7. **Treat sleep as sacred**.
    Let your bedtime be a ritual. Cleanse your energy. Speak peace over yourself. Invite divine alignment in dreams.

Rest is not where the work ends. Rest is where the work takes root. Every pause you honor sends a signal to the Universe: "I trust. I'm ready. I receive."

In stillness, you realign. In silence, you hear. And in that gentle space of non-doing, everything you've been calling in finally has room to arrive.

Affirmation

"I receive while I rest. I trust the divine flow. I am open, surrendered, and aligned. All that is mine finds me with ease."

Guided Meditation
—The Sacred Stillness of Receiving

Breathe in slowly. Breathe out fully.

Let your shoulders drop. Let your jaw soften.

Now imagine a warm light around you—a soft cocoon of peace expanding out from the inside. Nothing is required of you right now. Nothing must be earned. You are already aligned.

Whisper inwardly: "I am safe to rest. I am open to receive. I am held in grace." Let this stillness hold you. Let your breath carry you deeper. Here, in this quiet, the blessing arrives.

Conclusion

Rest is not what happens when everything else is finished. Rest is the very fabric of trust.

It is the holy exhale that tells the Universe: **"I've done my part… now I release**."

In a world that glorifies hustle, that urges us to keep pushing, proving, producing—choosing rest can feel rebellious. But it is not rebellion, it is a declaration of trust.

Because when you truly believe your blessing is already on its way, you stop chasing and start receiving.

We were never meant to live in constant output.

Even the earth takes a season to lie in rest.
Even the tides know when to retreat and return.
And your soul, your beautiful, intuitive soul, remembers how to be still.

Rest is not a weakness. It is quiet power. It is the sacred space where healing breathes, where energy recalibrates, and where divine guidance whispers what it couldn't say through noise.

Part of that power is the posture you take; the posture of open hands, of unclenched faith, of a heart wide enough to welcome what is next.

And maybe—just maybe—rest is where the real work happens. The invisible kind. The sacred kind. The kind that aligns your frequency so purely that everything you were chasing finally knows how to find you.

So, trust the divine rhythm.

And the next time you feel the urge to press, strive, or force—pause. Because sometimes, the greatest leap forward is the moment you finally sit still.

Chapter 25: Faith Over Fear
—Choosing to Believe Anyway

Opening Reflection

"Faith isn't the absence of fear—it's the courage to keep moving while fear watches you do it."
—Roy Waugh

Introduction

There's always that moment. The one where you're standing at a fork in the road, and fear is loud. It's shouting worst-case scenarios and dragging up every disappointment you've ever faced. You can feel it in your chest, in your breath, in that tight little knot in your gut.

And then—there's faith. Not loud. Not pushy. Just a quiet nudge. A whisper in your spirit that says, "But what if this time... it works?"

Fear will always try to protect you. It'll say, "Let's not get our hopes up." But faith? Faith dares you to believe again. To dream bigger. To move forward even if your knees are shaking, your voice is trembling, and your hands are sweaty.

When it comes to manifestation, there will always be a moment—usually right before something breaks through—when you have to choose. Will fear lead or will faith?

This chapter is about choosing faith. Not just once, but again and again. Not just when life is calm, but when everything inside you wants to run and hide. It's about believing—not because it's easy, but because deep down you know you were made for more.

Faith doesn't need perfection. It just needs one open-hearted yes.

And the moment you say it—everything begins to shift.

Hidden Teachings for Ancient Traditions
—Ancient Wisdom and Choosing Faith Over Fear

There's a sacred thread that runs through every faith tradition—one that recognizes fear as a natural human emotion, but calls the soul to something greater. Whether it's a trembling step into the Red Sea, a still breath beneath the Bodhi tree, or a whispered surrender in the desert, every spiritual path has faced fear and walked forward anyway.

This section gathers the timeless truths from across the world's great traditions, reminding us that faith is not the absence of fear—it's the sacred choice to move forward in the presence of it.

✧ Christian Faith

Throughout Scripture, fear often shows up just before the miraculous. The invitation is not to deny fear, but to choose a deeper truth.

When the angel appeared to Mary, she was "*greatly troubled.*" Yet the angel said, "**Do not be afraid, Mary; you have found favor with God**." (Luke 1:30, NIV). That moment changed history—but it began with fear and a choice to trust.

Peter stepped out of the boat while a storm raged. As long as his eyes stayed on Jesus, he walked on water. But when fear entered, he began to sink (Matthew 14:29–30). Faith kept him afloat. Fear pulled him under.

Paul reminds the early church, "**We walk by faith, not by sight**." (2 Corinthians 5:7, KJV). That means choosing truth over circumstance. Spirit over statistics.

Faith in the Christian tradition is not about certainty—it's about courage rooted in divine promise. It is the determination that says, "Even if I can't see the outcome, I will still take the step."

✧ Jewish Wisdom

In Judaism, faith and fear often coexist—but it is emunah, the deep-rooted trust in God, that guides the path forward.

When Joshua prepared to lead the Israelites into the Promised Land, God said, **"Be strong and very courageous. Do not be afraid; do not be discouraged, for the Lord your God will be with you wherever you go**." (Joshua 1:9, NIV). The task was daunting. But the promise was presence.

The Psalms offer soul-anchoring truths in fearful moments. **"When I am afraid, I put my trust in You**." (Psalm 56:3, ESV). Not if—but when. Fear is assumed. Trust is chosen.

The Talmud teaches, **"All is in the hands of Heaven, except the fear of Heaven**." (Berakhot 33b). In other words, fear of circumstance is optional. Awe of the Divine is transformational.

Faith here is not passive acceptance—it's active remembrance. A return to the truth that God walks with us into the unknown.

✧ Islamic Teachings

Islam honors the realness of fear while calling the believer into surrender and trust.

When the Prophet Muhammad (peace be upon him) was fleeing persecution, he and Abu Bakr hid in a cave. Abu Bakr feared for their lives, but the Prophet said, **"Do not be afraid. Indeed, Allah is with us**." (Qur'an 9:40). That presence changed everything.

The Qur'an teaches: **"Indeed, those who have said, 'Our Lord is Allah' and then remained steadfast—there will be no fear concerning them, nor will they grieve**." (Qur'an 46:13). Fear may come, but it does not get to stay.

Tawakkul, the deep trust in God, does not mean ignoring fear—it means handing it over.

And in that handoff, the believer receives something greater: a calm that does not come from outcomes, but from nearness to the Divine.

✧ **Buddhist Practices**

In Buddhist teaching, fear is not a flaw—it is an invitation to awaken.
The Buddha taught that fear arises from clinging—clinging to outcomes, identities, control. But he also taught, **"There is no fear for one whose mind is not filled with desires**." (Dhammapada, verse 39). Fear begins to dissolve when attachment loosens.

Meditation offers the practitioner a way to sit with fear, not run from it. In doing so, fear often softens. It becomes energy that can be observed, understood, and released.

One powerful teaching from The Buddha says, **"Those who are mindful do not fear**." (Paraphrased from Udana 4.4) This is not because fear is absent, but because awareness creates space between the stimulus and the self.

Faith in the Buddhist sense is a trust in the now—a grounded presence that says, "This moment is safe. This breath is enough."

✧ **Hindu Traditions**

Hindu wisdom teaches that fear is born of illusion—of forgetting who you truly are.

In the Bhagavad Gita, Arjuna is frozen with fear at the edge of battle. Krishna says to him, **"Do not yield to this degrading impotence. Arise, O chastiser of the enemy**." (Bhagavad Gita 2:3, ESV). The call was not to deny fear, but to rise in divine identity.

The Upanishads declare, "**Where there is duality, there is fear**." (Brihadaranyaka Upanishad 1.4.2). Fear arises when we forget our oneness with the Source.

Even the deity Hanuman, known for immense courage, once said to Lord Rama, "**When I forget who I am, I serve You. When I remember who I am, I am You**." Faith, in the Hindu tradition, is a remembering. A return. A reconnection to the truth that the same Divine spark lives within you—and nothing can threaten that light.

Fear may look different in each tradition, but the sacred response remains the same: remember who you are and remember who walks with you.

These ancient teachings do not deny the trembling—they dignify it.

They show us that fear has always been a part of the journey, but so has faith. And every time faith is chosen, something sacred is set in motion. A step. A shift. A miracle. Even if the outcome is uncertain, the path is clear: *believe anyway.*

Wisdom from Contemporary Spiritual Leaders

In the face of fear, the voices of wisdom throughout history have offered more than comfort—they have offered strategy. They remind us that fear may be part of the human journey, but it does not have to be the driver.

The following voices—some ancient, some modern—offer insights on how to shift from panic to peace, from doubt to direction. Let their words anchor you in a deeper truth: you are not powerless in the presence of fear. You are powerful beyond it.

—Dr. Joe Dispenza says, "**Your body believes what your brain tells it. If you rehearse fear, you will live it. If you rehearse faith, you will manifest it**." His teachings bridge neuroscience and spirituality, showing that when you wire your mind for belief, your body follows—and your reality transforms.

—Abraham Hicks teaches, "**When you're in alignment, fear cannot stay**." Fear is not an enemy—it is an indicator. According to this teaching, the more you return to emotional alignment, the less room fear has to live.

—Iyanla Vanzant boldly proclaims, "**Fear is false evidence appearing real. Faith is feeling assured in the heart**." She reminds us that while fear distorts, faith clarifies. It brings us back to inner knowing, even when the external feels uncertain.

—Louise Hay reminded readers, "**I am safe. All is well**." Instead of wrestling fear to the ground, she taught us to gently replace it with affirmations of truth. Safety is not just a condition—it is a consciousness.

—Oprah Winfrey has said, "**Every time you state what you want or believe, you're the first to hear it. It's a message to both you and the universe**." For her, faith was never the absence of fear—it was what gave her the courage to leap anyway.

—Albert Einstein believed, "**The most important decision we make is whether we believe we live in a friendly or hostile universe**." Fear says life is against you. Faith says life is conspiring with you. That belief changes what you see—and what you receive.

—Roy Waugh, "**Faith doesn't silence fear—it just stops giving it the microphone**." Fear might still be in the room, whispering its doubts and what-ifs—but faith is the one holding the mic. When you stop giving fear the final word, something shifts. You no longer wait for fear to disappear—you just decide it does not get to lead. Faith steps in, steady and clear, and starts rewriting the script.

Each of these voices calls you to the same invitation: let faith have the final word. Whether you are quoting a scientist, a spiritual guide, or your own inner wisdom—the message is clear. Fear may be loud, but faith is stronger. And when you align with that strength, the impossible starts to move.

Scientific Perspectives on Fear and Faith
—How Belief Shifts Biology and Reshapes Reality

Fear is not just emotional—it is chemical, neurological, and physiological. It hijacks the body and rewires the brain.

But here is the miracle: just as fear leaves a footprint in your biology, so does faith.

✦ Neuroscience of Fear and Faith

When fear is triggered, the amygdala—the brain's alarm center—fires rapidly, activating a cascade of stress hormones like cortisol and adrenaline. These chemicals heighten alertness, but they also suppress creative thinking, impair memory, and flood the body with tension. This is survival mode.

But faith—the calm conviction that something good is coming—engages a different system entirely. Research shows that practices like prayer, meditation, and visualization activate the prefrontal cortex, the brain's center for rational thought, empathy, and decision-making. It is as though faith gives your brain permission to rise above survival, and into alignment.

✦ Biology of Belief

Dr. Bruce Lipton, a cell biologist, famously wrote, "**The moment you change your perception is the moment you rewrite the chemistry of your body.**" Belief is not abstract—it is biological. If you constantly anticipate disaster, your cells respond with stress. But if you hold steady in faith, your biology begins to mirror that internal trust.

The heart rate stabilizes, breathing deepens, and hormones shift. You become a vessel of peace, not panic.

✧ Psychology of Courage and Resilience

In psychology, the concept of self-efficacy—a belief in your ability to affect outcomes—is one of the strongest predictors of success. Even when fear is present, those with high self-efficacy take action. They do not wait to feel fearless—they act from belief. And over time, belief becomes their new baseline.

Cognitive Behavioral Therapy also teaches that fear-based thoughts create avoidance. But when you interrupt those patterns—when you reframe the story—you literally create new neural pathways. That is faith in motion.

✧ Energetics of Fear vs. Faith

From an energetic standpoint, fear is dense and contractive. It lowers your vibration, narrows your field, and repels aligned outcomes. But faith is expansive. It lifts your frequency and opens the channel between you and the divine. As Abraham Hicks teaches, **"You cannot be a vibrational match for fear and alignment at the same time."**

Quantum physics echoes this, suggesting that observation affects outcome. *The mindset you carry—whether fear or faith—actually alters how matter organizes itself around you.*

Fear may be natural, but faith is transformational. It is not about denying what is hard—it is about choosing a perspective that partners with possibility. Your body listens. Your cells adapt. And your life responds.

So, whether it is through breath, belief, or a whispered prayer in the dark —every time you choose faith, you shift your biology, your brain, and your future.

Personal Story
— When I Chose to Believe Anyway

I do not think anything has tested my faith more than the moment I realized I might not survive what was ahead.

But to understand the depth of that moment, you have to go back with me —back to a dusty gravel road in front of our old family house.

I was just four years old. My dad, who was on the other side of the street, had asked me to run inside and grab a pen. And I did. I remember putting my little toes right at the edge of the gravel, just like I had learned from the children's program I watched: "Stop, look, and listen before you cross." So, I did. Nothing was coming. And then I stepped out.

Halfway across, something sparkly in the rocks caught my eye. (If you know me, you are already laughing—I have always had a thing for sparkly rock and still do.) I reached down to grab that shimmering rock, completely forgetting what I was doing.

That is when I heard it—the crunch of gravel under tires.
I turned just in time to see a bumper coming straight at me. I turned away from the car, tensed my body, and raised my little fists to my face. And then—nothing.

I do not remember the impact. But my mom saw the whole thing from the kitchen window. She said my legs disappeared under the car while my upper body slammed into the grill, and my head and neck bent backward off the top of the hood. Then, my body flung through the air before I hit our mailbox.

But somehow—I survived.

No broken bones. No spinal damage. Just a miracle that still leaves me in awe.

Fast forward many years.

You have read in this book how, at around the age of 21, I bent over to pick up a tray of mail and heard a sudden pop—could not walk, could not stand, could not move much from the waist down. Gratefully—I recovered.

Now fast forward again—to age 49.

We had just moved into a new home in a brand-new city, and I was in full nesting mode. Unpacking like a madman, breaking down boxes, making everything beautiful. I felt great.

That is, until a few weeks later, I started tripping over things that were not there. Then cups and glasses started slipping right out of my hand, smashing on the floor.

I brushed it off. New city. New surroundings. I told myself I was just distracted, being clumsy.

But then I could not swallow.

Food would get stuck halfway down, and my throat would spasm violently —above and below the blockage—like it did not know what to do. It was some of the worst pain I have ever experienced in my life.

My husband took me to the hospital. They ran reflex tests—no reflexes in my knees or ankles, not good. Then came the Babinski test. When they scraped the bottom of my foot, my toes shot straight toward the sky instead of curling down. That is when the doctor's face changed. That response meant I have a major spinal cord issue.

An MRI was ordered. A couple of days later, I was called in to see the orthopedic surgeon.

He sat me down and said, "We found the problem."

At the top of my spine, in my neck, in the canal of cervical vertebra number two— that was supposed to be about 18mm wide, allowing my 12mm spinal cord to move freely—was only 5mm. My spinal cord was being crushed.

He looked me straight in the eye and said, "We need to do emergency surgery. And until we do—no stairs, no car rides unless absolutely necessary. Do not sneeze. Do not jar your neck in any way. One wrong move and you could be paralyzed or worse."

I was stunned. In less than a week, I was in a surgical waiting room. On the other side of that door was a full team, scrubbed in, waiting for my insurance company to green-light the procedure. The moment the call came, they rushed me in. IVs in one arm, arterial line in the other, and spinal cord monitors being pinned to my limbs.

I could barely breathe, let alone process what was happening.

The surgeon came in and explained everything. "We will be removing the bone on the backside of your vertebrae from C2 to T2 (almost my tire neck), inserting rods and screws, and fusing your neck. We will do our best—but I have to tell you, there is a chance we could nick the nerve in the front of our spinal cord. If that happens, your heart could stop, and we would not be able to save you."

That is when it hit me.

I felt a gray, heavy curtain fall over me. It was fear—thick, suffocating fear. I thought I may not wake up from this.

So, I did the only thing I could do.
I closed my eyes. Took a long, slow breath. And whispered in my heart, God, I am in your hands. Let Your will be done.
Tears streamed down my face. My body started to tremble.
And then—something happened.

Suddenly, it felt like a warm, electric wave poured over my head and flowed through my body. The only way I can describe it is as invisible light —like liquid energy. It made that heavy curtain of fear scatter and lift, immediately and completely.

And I knew, I had a choice.

I could choose to be afraid. Or I could stand in the truth I had told others for years: **_Anything is possible—if you just believe_**.

So, even though it did not look good, I decided to _believe anyway_.

I woke up nearly ten hours later. The first thing I thought was: "Wait, my eyes are open. I'm still here."

The surgery was a success. No more stumbling. No more spasms. My reflexes had returned. I did have to wear a rather "fancy" neck brace for a while—one that my friends jokingly threatened to bedazzle just to keep things interesting.

Every day, I walked a little stronger.

At my follow-up, the doctor explained something we had not known before: the damage to my spine had started decades earlier. That car accident when I was four did not break any bones—but it did something else. It altered the growth of my spine. Over the years, scar-like bone formations grew inside my spinal canal, silently narrowing the space for my spinal cord.

It is called spinal stenosis, and in my case, it was severe.

The other accident I spoke of earlier in this book- the sudden injury at 21, the walking issues, the lost reflexes—was all connected.

What I faced was terrifying. But it taught me the most powerful truth I have ever known: Faith is not the absence of fear. It is the decision to move forward anyway.

And sometimes, faith begins not with a shout, but with a whisper that says; I chose to believe anyway.

Practical Applications
—Living from Faith, Not Fear

Fear may show up uninvited, but you do not have to let it take the lead. These next practices are designed to help you move through fear with clarity, courage, and spiritual grounding. They are not about pretending you are not afraid—they are about choosing faith anyway. Step by step, breath by breath, these tools will help you realign with truth, calm your nervous system, and move forward in the direction of your highest belief because the power is not in being fearless. It is in being willing.

1. **Name the fear**.
   Bring it into the light. Say, "I'm afraid that..." Then ask, "Is this absolutely true?" Challenge the fear's authority.

2. **Reverse the question**.
   If fear says, "What if it doesn't work?"—ask instead, "What if it does?"

3. **Create a faith anchor**.
   Choose a quote, verse, or phrase to repeat when fear rises. Something like; "I trust what's unfolding.", or "I choose faith."

4. **Practice the breath of trust**.
   Inhale peace. Exhale fear. Repeat for two minutes. Reset your nervous system through breath.

5. **Act from belief**.
   Take one small action that reflects your desired outcome—not your current fear.

6. **Speak what you want to see**.
   Even if your voice trembles, speak from vision. Say, "I am capable. I am supported. I am ready."

7. **Rehearse the best outcome**.
   Visualize things going right. Feel it. See it. Let faith become your dominant script.

Each time you choose faith over fear, no matter how small the step, you rewire your inner world to expect goodness. You shift your posture from defense to trust, from contraction to expansion.

These practices are not about pretending fear does not exist—they are about remembering who you are when fear tries to speak louder than truth. And when you move from that place—even trembling—you move in alignment with divine power.

Fear may visit, but it does not get to lead. Faith does.

Affirmation

"I choose faith over fear. I believe, even when I cannot see. I am safe. I am led. I am aligned with divine power."

Guided Meditation
—Breathing Through Fear Into Faith

Take a slow breath. Now another.

Imagine the word "fear" as a grey cloud in front of you.

Gently, with your breath, begin to blow it away. Watch it dissolve.

Now see a golden light forming in your chest. This is faith. It glows with quiet but almighty power. It warms you from within.

Whisper inwardly: "I believe anyway."

Let that belief expand. Let it steady your breath. Let it lead your next step.

You are no longer ruled by fear. You walk in faith.

Conclusion

Fear will always try to knock. It will whisper old stories, stir up your past, question your worth, and play out the worst-case scenario like it is a fact.

But just because fear knocks, does not mean you have to open the door. Faith does not mean you will not feel fear. It just means fear does not get to be the one driving the car.

There will be moments—real ones—when your body feels unsure, when courage feels like a distant echo, and the unknown grows louder than your certainty.

You might feel the tension in your chest, the unease in your gut, the hesitation in your step.

But even in those fragile spaces, I want you to remember this: *The same Spirit that ignited galaxies into being lives in you.* And that divine presence is never shaken, never rushed, never afraid.

I have seen what fear can do. I have felt how it can paralyze, how it steals your breath, sleep, and peace.

But I have also seen what faith can undo. I have been in a surgical gown, not knowing if I would make it through. I have sat in dark rooms with an empty wallet and a full heart. I have faced the unknown more times than I can count. And still—I chose to believe.

Why?

Because belief has never let me down, even when I did not get what I asked for, I always got what I needed. Even when nothing looked certain on the outside, something shifted on the inside.

That is the thing about faith—it does not need perfect conditions to work. It just needs your "yes."

Faith speaks even when your voice trembles. It walks forward even when the path is foggy. It dares to hope when everything says "don't."

So, if you are standing at the edge of something right now—uncertain, afraid, unsure—do not shrink back. Do not let fear decide who you are.

You were made to believe. You were made to be bold. And your next breakthrough? It might not be waiting for everything to be perfect. It might be waiting on you to just say yes.

Now, take a breath. Lift your chin.

And if you need to say it out loud, go ahead: **"I choose to believe anyway**."

Then watch what happens when faith takes the lead.

Chapter 26: The Power of Imagination
—Where Heaven Meets the Mind

Opening Reflection

"Imagination is everything. It is the preview of life's coming attractions."
—Albert Einstein

Introduction

Before anything ever shows up in the physical world, it first walks through the doorway of imagination.

As Einstein said, it is not a fantasy or illusion—it is a preview. A glimpse into what your spirit is already reaching for.

Imagination is not a detour from reality—it is the architecture of it. It is the quiet sanctuary where vision begins to breathe, where the invisible starts to take shape. Every miracle ever witnessed, every breakthrough ever born, began first as a thought—nurtured in stillness, shaped by belief, carried forward by courage.

But somewhere along the way, many of us learn to silence that sacred part of ourselves. We are told to be practical, to keep our feet on the ground, to stop daydreaming and "face reality." Imagination gets dismissed as childish, unrealistic, even foolish. But what if that inner vision you were told to keep quiet was never a distraction at all?

What if it was a divine signal—whispering from above, rising from within —showing you what is possible before it is visible?

This chapter is about reclaiming imagination as more than wishful thinking. It is about remembering that when you dare to visualize your deepest desires with clarity and conviction, you are not escaping reality— you are designing it. You are stepping into a divine rehearsal. You are aligning your frequency with the future you were made for.

Imagination is not child's play—it is spiritual strategy. It is a holy invitation to co-create with the unseen.

And the pictures you dare to paint in your mind may become the very portals through which your destiny arrives.

Hidden Teachings from Ancient Traditions
—How Imagination Shapes Reality Across Faiths

From the earliest scrolls to the deepest mystical teachings, the sacred traditions of the world have long honored the imagination as more than idle daydreaming. It is seen as a divine instrument—an invisible brush painting the outline of what is to come. Whether in visions, parables, symbolic prayers, or contemplative visualization, imagination has always been part of the spiritual blueprint. It is the seedbed of belief, the gateway to manifestation, and the meeting place between the human soul and divine possibility.

Let us explore how each tradition holds and honors this sacred gift.

✧ Christian Faith

The Bible is saturated with dreams, symbols, and holy imagination—often used by God as the first invitation into destiny.

When God gave Abraham the promise of future generations, He did not hand him a scroll. He gave him the stars. "**Look now toward heaven, and count the stars... so shall your offspring be.**" (Genesis 15:5, NKJV)

When Joseph was called into purpose, it began with vivid, symbolic dreams. "**Listen to this dream I had: We were binding sheaves of grain... and suddenly my sheaf rose and stood upright, while your sheaves gathered around mine and bowed down.**" (Genesis 37:6–7, NIV). His brothers saw arrogance—but God saw preparation. That dream became the first glimpse of a future calling to leadership and deliverance.

Jesus used imagination as a teaching tool. His parables bypassed intellect and entered the soul—using imagery like seeds, pearls, nets, and hidden treasures to describe the unseen Kingdom.

Paul writes, "**Now unto Him who is able to do exceedingly abundantly above all we ask or imagine...**" (Ephesians 3:20, NIV). Imagination, then, is not the limit—it is the launching point.

And in Romans 12:2, we are reminded: "**Be transformed by the renewing of your mind**." That renewal often begins by replacing fear-driven inner movies with images rooted in faith and creative alignment. In scripture, imagination is not fantasy—it is a form of faith made visible.

✧ **Jewish Wisdom**

In Judaism, imagination is not merely allowed—it is honored. It plays a central role in prayer, storytelling, and spiritual awakening.

The Hebrew word ḥazon, often translated as "vision," carries a sacred weight. Proverbs 29:18 says, "**Where there is no vision, the people perish**." (Proverbs 29:18, KJV) This is not just about seeing with your eyes—it is about seeing with your spirit. Without divine vision, direction is lost. But when you imagine a world rooted in peace, wholeness, and sacred purpose, you participate in creating it.

The mystical practice of kavanah—deep spiritual intention during prayer —requires more than words. It invites the full participation of the heart, the emotions, and the imagination. To pray with kavanah is to see with inner eyes what your soul longs for, and to hold that vision before the Divine.

Jewish mysticism, especially in the Kabbalah, speaks of sacred images— internal blueprints that reflect divine realities. Visualizing light, healing, or redemption is not wishful thinking; it is a co-creative act.

Rabbi Nachman of Breslov taught his students to "imagine redemption"— not only for the world, but for their own souls. Through imagination, he believed, a person could ascend to higher states of connection with the Divine.

Even the physical rituals of Judaism reflect this imaginative practice. The Shabbat table is set with beauty, abundance, and peace—not simply as tradition, but as a reflection of inner joy. It is a tangible expression of an inner, imagined wholeness.

In Jewish tradition, imagination is not fantasy—it is a sacred rehearsal. A way to align your heart with the world as it could be, and to call it into being.

✧ Islamic Teachings

In Islam, imagination plays a subtle but deeply sacred role in cultivating trust and spiritual perception.

The Prophet Muhammad (peace be upon him) often received guidance through dreams—symbolic, powerful, and spiritually instructive. These dreams offered direction, eased fears, and confirmed divine timing.

Imagination, in this tradition, is not illusion—it is illumination.

The Qur'an uses vivid imagery to stir the soul, not for entertainment, but for awakening. Descriptions of Paradise—gardens beneath which rivers flow, fruits like dates and pomegranates, pure light, and eternal peace—are not mere poetic flourishes. They are visual invitations, expanding the heart's capacity to believe in divine beauty and bounty.

Islam also emphasizes tafakkur, or deep reflection—a contemplative practice that activates inner vision. As the Qur'an says, "**It is not the eyes that are blind, but the hearts in the chests that grow blind.**" (Qur'an 22:46). This sacred verse reminds us that true sight is not just with the physical eye but with the awakened heart. To imagine with faith is to see with the soul.

Muslim mystics and Sufi poets like Rumi describe imagination as the lamp of the heart—a way to connect with the divine and perceive unseen realities. The practice of visualizing the names and attributes of God—Al-Rahman (The Merciful), Al-Nur (The Light), Al-Fattah (The Opener)—becomes a meditative act that infuses one's inner world with divine presence.

To imagine, in Islam, is not to escape—it is to remember. And to envision good while trusting in the unseen is to embody tawakkul—deep reliance on divine wisdom.

✧ Buddhist Practices

In Buddhism, imagination is not escapism—it is a spiritual art form that transforms the inner world.

In metta bhavana (loving-kindness meditation), practitioners envision themselves and others surrounded by love, repeating phrases like *"May you be happy. May you be free from suffering."* The visualization becomes embodied. The imagined becomes real.

Tibetan Buddhism uses deity visualization as a path of self-realization—not to inflate ego, but to help the practitioner embody enlightened qualities.

The Buddha taught, "**With our thoughts we make the world**." (Dhammapada 1:1) This is more than philosophy—it is energetic truth.

Imagination, when tethered to mindfulness, becomes not illusion—but insight.

✧ Hindu Traditions

In Hinduism, imagination is not secondary to spirituality—it is central to divine creation.

The Rig Veda speaks of the universe's origin, not from action—but from desire and thought: **"There was neither existence nor non-existence... but then desire arose in That, the first seed of**

mind." (Rig Veda 10.129.1) This seed—imagination—is sacred. It is the spark of manifestation.

In yogic practice, sankalpa (a soul-driven intention or vow) begins with visualization. One imagines the desired state—peace, health, purpose—and then begins to live into it.

Deities like Vishwakarma, the divine architect, represent the power of sacred imagination to shape reality.

And the Upanishads echo the creative sequence of inner to outer: "**As is your desire, so is your will. As is your will, so is your deed. As is your deed, so is your destiny.**" (Brihadaranyaka Upanishad 4.4.5) Imagination, then, is not child's play. It is divine participation in the unfolding of the world.

Across every faith, imagination is not dismissed as fantasy—it is revered as divine language. Whether through dreams, visions, sacred visualization, or contemplative prayer, the world's wisdom keepers have always known this truth: *what we dare to see within becomes the blueprint for what unfolds without.*

Your imagination is not a detour from spiritual practice—it is part of the path. It is where divine possibility meets human willingness. And when you engage that sacred inner canvas with reverence, clarity, and faith, you are not just dreaming.

You are co-creating with the Divine.

Wisdom from Contemporary Spiritual Leaders

Imagination is not just a tool for artists or dreamers—it is a divine faculty, and many of today's spiritual leaders and visionaries recognize it as one of the most powerful forces behind transformation. From metaphysical teachers to modern mystics, the message is clear: when you dare to see something within, you begin to call it into being.

The following voices echo that truth—reminding us that imagination is not idle wandering, but sacred rehearsal.

—Dr. Joe Dispenza teaches that imagination is where you rehearse a new future. **"If you can see it in your mind and feel it in your body, you'll move toward it like a magnet**." He reminds us that the body responds not just to what is, but to what is imagined with conviction. Visualization becomes preparation.

—Abraham Hicks affirms that the act of imagining is one of the highest vibrations. **"What you visualize consistently, you begin to live vibrationally—and life meets you there**." Imagination, then, is not fantasy—it is energetic alignment. What you dwell on inwardly begins to shape your reality outwardly.

—Oprah Winfrey has said, **"Create the highest, grandest vision possible for your life, because you become what you believe**." She reminds us that vision is not just a dream—it is a declaration. What we dare to imagine sets the tone for what we become.

—Iyanla Vanzant says, **"The vision always comes before the victory**." She teaches that your inner image must rise before your outer circumstance does. It is a call to lead from within—to let the mind and spirit create the path before the feet ever step forward.

—Albert Einstein, whose scientific genius was rooted in a deeply intuitive vision, famously said, **"Imagination is more important than knowledge**." Because knowledge tells you what is. Imagination tells you what could be. He saw imagination as the blueprint for all advancement— personal, spiritual, and collective.

—Roy Waugh, **"I've learned this much: I don't have to know how it will happen. I just have to dare to see it—and keep showing up like it's already mine**." Because what we see within—when held with faith—starts to shape how we walk, speak, trust, and show up. Imagination leads us forward.

Imagination is the soul's compass. The teachers who walked before us did not just speak truth—they saw it, lived it, envisioned it before it arrived. And that is your invitation now. To let your inner picture rise above your current circumstances. To hold the vision, even when nothing around you confirms it yet. Because the moment you honor what you see within the world around you, you begin to lean in and listen.

Scientific Perspectives on Imagination and Manifestation
—Training the Brain to Believe

Imagination may seem like a soft skill—an inner daydream or playful distraction—but science reveals something much deeper: imagination changes your brain. When you visualize something vividly and emotionally, your neurons begin to rewire. Your body reacts. Your beliefs adapt. And your reality starts to lean in the direction of what you repeatedly envision.

In this section, we will explore how modern neuroscience, psychology, and mind-body research all confirm what spiritual teachers have long taught: your inner vision becomes your outer experience.

Each of the following insights reveals a scientific lens through which we can understand imagination not as fantasy, but as a bridge between belief and manifestation.

✧ Neuroplasticity and Mental Rehearsal

The human brain is constantly changing. This ability—called neuroplasticity—means that your thoughts and mental images can literally reshape your neural pathways. Studies show that when you repeatedly imagine a skill, an experience, or even a healing, your brain lights up in the same regions as it would during the real thing.

One landmark study had participants mentally practice piano for two hours a day without touching a keyboard. After just five days, their motor cortex showed nearly identical growth to that of those who physically practiced. In my own life, I have found this to be true—whether rehearsing a song, preparing for a major talk, or visualizing healing, I have seen that what you run in your mind, your body begins to believe.

Mental rehearsal is not a game. It is a neurological signal that prepares the body to receive what the spirit has already seen.

✧ Psychophysiology and Emotional Response

What you imagine does not just stay in your head—it floods your system. Psychophysiology is the study of how mental and emotional processes affect the body, and when it comes to imagination, the effects are powerful. If you imagine something frightening, your body will respond with a spike in cortisol, your heart rate may rise, and your muscles might even tense.

But the same is true in the other direction. If you visualize peace, joy, or gratitude, your body releases dopamine, oxytocin, and serotonin. These are not just pleasant feelings; they are chemical confirmations that the body is aligning with the inner vision.

When I was healing after surgery, I imagined myself walking again, laughing again, fully alive. And I could feel something shift—not just in my hope, but in my chemistry. Science confirms what many of us have felt intuitively: when you imagine with emotion, you signal to the body, "This is happening."

And the body listens.

✧ Cognitive Psychology and Goal Imagery

Cognitive psychology teaches that visualization enhances motivation, decision-making, and perseverance. In essence, your mind creates an internal "goal image," and that image begins to shape how you act and respond in the world.

Research has shown that people who engage in detailed mental imagery—especially when paired with action—are more likely to achieve their goals.

Visualization helps encode these goals more deeply in the brain, creating what some scientists call "pre-experiencing."

This explains why elite athletes, actors, musicians, and entrepreneurs often visualize their performance or outcome before it happens. For me, even long before I had a stage or an audience, I would see myself connecting with people through music. I did not need proof—I had a picture. And that picture pulled me forward.

When your mind is clear on where you are going, your choices begin to align with that vision—even when you do not realize it.

✧ Belief Formation and Memory Reconsolidation

Much of what we believe about ourselves—our limitations, fears, and potential—is stored in implicit memory. However, neuroscience has discovered that these old beliefs are not fixed. Through a process called memory reconsolidation, we can revisit and reimagine old experiences, thereby softening their emotional charge and rewriting the story.

Imagination plays a key role in this. When you visualize a new version of yourself—confident, free, capable—you are giving your brain new evidence. You are rehearsing a different outcome. Over time, those visualizations can begin to override limiting beliefs and shift your identity from the inside out.

I have seen this firsthand. When I have struggled with feelings of inadequacy or fear, I have used imagination—not to escape, but to reframe. I would imagine what it would feel like to believe I was enough, to walk into the room with my shoulders back and my spirit steady. And little by little, that imagined self began to feel like the real me.

Because when you consistently show your brain a new image, it eventually stops arguing—and starts agreeing.

Imagination is not just a personal tool—it is a physiological force. What you see inside your mind, when paired with emotion and repetition, becomes the architecture your brain builds upon. Science now affirms what the soul has always sensed: if you can hold it in your inner world, you can move toward it in the outer one.

So, do not dismiss the visions that rise when you are quiet. Do not downplay the scenes that stir your heart. They are not silly. They are not foolish. They are formative.

Because every time you dare to see yourself healed, whole, worthy, and thriving—your brain gets the message. And one day, your life will too.

Personal Story
—The Inner Stage

I don't think I realized it until now—but imagination has always been my companion. Not as a game or an escape, but as a quiet kind of knowing. A whisper from within. Long before I ever learned the language of manifestation or vision boards or energy alignment, I was already practicing it—instinctively.

When I was a kid, growing up in the kind of home that left you more acquainted with survival than safety, I didn't have the tools to change my world. But I had one sacred tool I did not know was sacred: my imagination.

I could close my eyes and see something better. A life where things were not so heavy. Where I did not feel responsible for everyone. Where laughter was not rare and love didn't have to be earned. I didn't tell anyone about it—I just let myself visit that place in the quiet. It was my internal sanctuary. And now I understand: I was not escaping. I was previewing a possible future.

When I was hit by a car at age four, I do not remember the impact—but I remember the moment before. The sparkle of a stone on the road. And somehow, even in the aftermath, I recall lying in bed, imagining myself back outside, running, laughing, whole again. That picture in my mind gave me peace. I didn't know it then, but that was energy work. That was frequency. That was alignment.

As life unfolded, and I ran away from home at fifteen, I did not have a clear destination. But I had a deep inner picture. A sense that something more was waiting. I couldn't explain it, but it was always there like a faint image in the fog. A better life. A future that felt safer, freer, more alive. That image became a lighthouse I did not know I was steering toward.

Later, when I began singing semi-professionally and questioning how to move forward, I would let myself imagine things. Not grand stages—but connections; faces that lit up, hearts that were changed, and people feeling moved—a life that mattered. That vision helped pull me through the plateaus, through the doors that didn't open, and into the ones that finally did.

Even when I traveled to the International Christian Artists Competition in Colorado, I was not there to win. I entered as a contestant because I had to in order to attend the workshops—but what I really wanted was to learn. To understand the path of ministry. How to build something real, something lasting? But still, in the quiet of my hotel room, or sitting in the back of a teaching session, I would catch glimpses—images of myself on stage in larger places, singing before a crowd, something flowing through me, not from me. That was not ego. That was vision. I was not chasing a spotlight. I was aligning with a calling.

When I toured as David in David: A Man After God's Own Heart, I was not just acting. Before every performance, I would stand in stillness, close my eyes, and let myself become the role. I would visualize the spirit of David—not as a character, but as a frequency—flowing through me. I was not performing. I was embodying. And people could feel it. That was not performance energy. That was alignment.

Years later, when I had physical issues again and I received the terrifying diagnosis of severe spinal stenosis, imagination became my lifeline. I was lying in a hospital bed, moments away from emergency surgery. The risks were overwhelming—paralysis, cardiac failure, worse. Fear hovered like a storm cloud.

But I closed my eyes. I took a breath. And I saw something different.

I imagined waking up. I imagined walking without stumbling. I saw myself healed, laughing, whole again. I imagined being on the other side of it all—grateful, grounded, alive.

That image became my anchor.

And when I woke up from that ten-hour surgery, blinking into the recovery room lights, I realized: I had made it. And not just because of medicine or luck—but because I chose to believe the vision within me was possible. I aligned with it before it arrived.

Even now, writing this book—something I have dreamed about for decades—I realize I have been creating it piece by piece, moment by moment, with every imagined teaching, every inner whisper scribbled on scraps of paper tucked into my Bible. I thought I was waiting for the right time. But the truth is, I was already painting the picture.

This book existed long before the first chapter.

Because I imagined it.

And that is the lesson I carry now: **When I had no map, imagination drew one. When I had no voice, imagination gave me one. When the world said, "Be realistic," imagination said, "Be ready."**

So, if you ask me how I've made it this far? I would tell you—I saw it first.

Practical Applications
—Activating Imagination with Intention

Imagination is more than play—it is the prelude to creation. The inner pictures you nurture shape the outer reality you experience. However, moving from casual daydreaming to conscious visioning requires presence, clarity, and intention. In the following practices, you'll learn how to harness your imagination as a co-creative force.

These tools will help you see your desires vividly, feel them fully, and align your energy with the life you are calling into being. Because when you dare to see it—consistently, clearly, and boldly—you give it permission to begin forming.

1. **Create a vision theater.**
   Let your mind become a movie screen. Step inside the story. What does your best life look like, feel like, sound like?

2. **Daydream with purpose.**
   Allow yourself to drift. Then, with gentleness, shape the direction. Ask, "What if this were possible?"

3. **Journal in the future tense.**
   Write your life as if it's already unfolding. Use the phrase: "I am so grateful now that..."

4. **Mirror visualization.**
   Speak your vision aloud while looking at yourself. Imagine yourself already living it.

5. **Anchor with symbolic objects.**
   Place a visual reminder of your dream where you'll see it daily. Let it stir your inner vision.

6. **Rehearse graceful outcomes.**
   Visualize yourself navigating challenges with poise. See yourself calm, clear, victorious.

7. **Bless your inner movies.**
   When imagination plays scenes of your desired future, don't downplay them. Whisper: "I receive that. Thank you."

Your imagination is not a waste of time—it is a sacred rehearsal. Each time you dare to see yourself thriving, healed, aligned, or free, you are planting a spiritual seed in the soil of the unseen. These practices are not about escaping the present—they are about preparing your energy to receive what is coming.

So, give yourself permission to dream on purpose. To imagine with boldness. To paint with the colors of possibility. Because what you continue to imagine with faith and feeling is already looking for you in return.

Affirmation

"My imagination is a sacred space. I see clearly. I dream boldly. I envision a life aligned with purpose, peace, and power."

Guided Meditation
—The Canvas of Your Mind

Take a slow, steady breath.

Envision a blank canvas stretched wide before you. Slowly, you begin to paint—colors of your joy, the shape of your dreams, the glow of your becoming.

Feel yourself inside the image. Let it surround you.

Whisper inwardly: "This is real. This is forming. This is mine."

Rest in the beauty. Trust in the vision. You have created it, and now it is coming to you.

Conclusion

Imagination is not an escape—it is an entrance. A threshold. A sacred doorway where unseen realities begin to take form.

Throughout your life—in the shadows of your hardest moments and the peaks of your highest dreams—imagination has quietly walked beside you. Not as fantasy, but as a faithful companion. A flicker of light in the dark. A whispered invitation from the future saying, "Come see who you really are."

When you were hurting, it showed you healing. When you felt invisible, it painted you in places where your presence mattered. When fear pressed in, it offered you another picture—one of freedom, wholeness, and becoming.

That was not just daydreaming. That was divine rehearsal.

You were aligning with the truth already living inside you—even if you did not have the words for it yet. Because imagination, at its most sacred level, is not about pretending. It is about remembering. Remembering what is possible. Remembering who you are.

It is the soul's way of pointing to what is real before it shows up in form. And the more you visit that inner world with reverence and curiosity, the more the outer world begins to take shape in its image.

So, honor the visions that rise in stillness. Do not rush past them. Do not call them foolish or too far off. They are messages. Blueprints. Glimpses of what is already on its way.

Trust the movie that plays when your eyes are closed and your heart is wide open.

Because what you dare to imagine today may become the world you wake up in tomorrow.

You are not just a dreamer. You are a creator. And your imagination is where the Divine whispers and the Universe meet, in your mind.

Chapter 27: The Details Matter
—Manifesting with Intention and Clarity

Opening Reflection

"The clearer your intention, the more divine forces can move in your favor. The universe doesn't respond to confusion—it responds to precision."
—Dannion Brinkley (paraphrased)

Introduction

The Manifestation Frequency does not respond to confusion—it responds to clarity.

Your thoughts send out a signal. Your vision becomes a blueprint. And the more clearly you can see that vision, the more powerfully it begins to take form.

Every time you imagine with intention, you are placing a sacred request into the field. But if that request is vague, the response will be too. The universe does not move with uncertainty—it moves with precision.

As Dannion Brinkley said, "You have to be specific when you ask God for something. The universe does not do vague." He is right. Clarity sharpens your frequency. It tells the Divine you are serious, that you are ready.

This chapter is an invitation to get clear—not just in what you want, but in how it feels, looks, sounds, and lives. Because when your vision is specific, your intention becomes focused. And focused intention is magnetic.

A dream without detail may stir the soul, but it is the details that give it breath.

Hidden Teachings from Ancient Traditions
—The Sacred Power of Specificity Across Faiths

Across the world's sacred traditions, detail is not seen as a distraction—it is seen as devotion. Specificity is a spiritual act, a way of honoring the divine through clarity, focus, and intention. Whether it is the dimensions of an ark, the steps of a ritual, or the shape of a prayer, ancient texts and practices remind us: what we do with precision, we do with reverence.

When the vision is clear, the spiritual current flows stronger. Let's explore how these spiritual paths honor the sacred power of getting specific.

✧ Christian Faith

Scripture is filled with examples of divine specificity.
When God gave Noah instructions for building the ark, they were not vague or symbolic. "**Make yourself an ark of gopher wood. Make rooms in the ark, and cover it inside and out with pitch.**" (Genesis 6:14). The design was detailed. The materials were named. Every part was intentional.

We see the same divine clarity in the construction of the Tabernacle. From the color of the curtains to the arrangement of sacred objects, each detail was given by divine instruction (Exodus 26). Sacred spaces were not thrown together—they were crafted with precision.

Even the calling of individuals came with specificity. When God called Jeremiah, He said, "**Before I formed you in the womb I knew you, before you were born, I set you apart; I appointed you as a prophet to the nations.**" (Jeremiah 1:5, NIV). His identity was not random—it was named, chosen, and declared.

And in Habakkuk 2:2, we are reminded: "**Write the vision. Make it plain on tablets...**" When your vision is clear, your steps become steady. In every line of scripture, we find this truth: the Divine does not move through chaos, but through clarity. And manifestation flows through the same path.

✧ Jewish Wisdom

In Judaism, the sacred is often found in the specifics—not as a burden, but as a blessing. The Hebrew concept of kavanah, or holy intention, reminds us that every word, gesture, and ritual becomes more powerful when aligned with conscious focus.

The Passover Seder is a vivid example. Every bite of food, every recited word, every symbolic gesture is chosen with meaning. Together, these details do not just tell a story—they become the story, turning an ordinary meal into a portal of memory and liberation.

When the Israelites were instructed to build the Mishkan (Tabernacle), God did not just say, "Build me a place." The instructions were exact—down to the cubits and the colors. "**See that you make them according to the pattern shown to you on the mountain**." (Exodus 25:40, Tanakh). That verse is often quoted to underscore the importance of following divine design with care and reverence.

Even the garments worn by the priests were not left to chance—they were detailed by divine wisdom, crafted "**for glory and for beauty**" (Exodus 28:2). Why so specific? Because in Jewish tradition, form shapes focus. The vessel determines the flow.

The Zohar, a foundational mystical text, teaches that divine light flows best through vessels formed with intention. Specificity, then, becomes more than precision—it becomes a spiritual container.

Jewish wisdom invites us to ask not just "What am I doing?"—but "Why? For whom? With what spirit?" Because God, in this tradition, meets us most deeply in the details.

✧ Islamic Teachings

In Islam, the concept of niyyah—clear, inward intention—shapes the value of every act.

The Prophet Muhammad (peace be upon him) said: "**Actions are judged by intentions, and every person will receive according to what they intended**." (Sahih al-Bukhari 1). Even before prayer, the believer performs wudu—a ritual washing done in detailed steps. Each motion is a preparation of the soul.

When Muslims pray du'a (supplication), they are taught not to be vague. Ask for what you truly want—healing for your child, wisdom for a decision, or peace in a situation.

The Qur'an also models specificity through its vivid imagery. It does not just describe paradise—it paints it: "**Gardens of perpetual residence beneath which rivers flow...**" (Qur'an 9:72). These are not random images. They are designed to stir belief.

The more detailed your intention, the more intimate your connection becomes.

✧ Buddhist Practices

Buddhism teaches that mindfulness begins with attention to detail—the breath, the step, the sip of tea. Every act becomes a doorway to presence when met with intention.

In loving-kindness meditation (metta), practitioners do not just send out a vague feeling of peace—they focus their compassion on specific individuals: a dear friend, a stranger, even someone they find difficult.

The practice becomes more than a mental exercise; it becomes a precise energetic offering.

Tibetan visualization practices also reflect this sacred attention. Deities are not simply figures of worship but vivid expressions of enlightened qualities. Practitioners are taught to visualize every detail—color, clothing, posture, radiance—until they begin to embody the energy themselves.

The Buddhist path constantly calls us back to this truth: how you hold your thoughts is how you shape your life.

As the Dhammapada says: "**All that we are is the result of what we have thought: it is founded on our thoughts, it is made up of our thoughts**." (Dhammapada, Verse: 1) That one line holds the entire architecture of manifestation. It reminds us that creation begins not in the world around us, but in the mind within us. And when your thoughts are focused, intentional, and lovingly detailed—your life begins to mirror that same energy.

So, in the Buddhist tradition, detail is not about control—it is about deep, sacred presence. A form of reverence. A way of becoming fully available to the now, and to what is still becoming.

✧ Hindu Traditions

In Hinduism, creation itself is rooted in specific thought.
The Rig Veda declares: "**Then even nothingness was not, nor existence... but then desire arose in That, the first seed of mind**." (Rig Veda 10.129). That first seed was not vague—it was pointed. Specific desire birthed all of creation.

The concept of sankalpa—a sacred intention—requires a person to mentally and spiritually define what they are calling forth. Not just "*I want peace,*" but "*I intend to live in harmony with my body, my family, and my soul's calling.*"

When Hindus invoke deities like Vishwakarma (the divine architect), they do so in detail—imagining form, tools, and purpose. These inner images shape the outer world.

The Bhagavad Gita reminds us: "**You become what you believe yourself to be**." (Bhagavad Gita 17:3). And belief begins with vision—clear, vivid, heart-centered vision.

In this tradition, to dream in detail is to walk the first step of destiny.

From sacred blueprints to symbolic meals, from visualized meditations to whispered prayers, the ancient traditions agree: there is power in the details. Specificity is not about control—it is about clarity. It is about aligning your heart, mind, and soul with a vision that can be felt, described, and lived into. When you name your intention with reverence and precision, you step into the divine rhythm that echoes through every sacred text: what is clear becomes sacred, and what is sacred begins to take shape.

Wisdom from Contemporary Spiritual Leaders

Clarity is not just a mental tool—it is a spiritual signal. Over and over again, those who teach the art of manifestation echo one truth: the more specific your vision, the more powerful your results.

These leaders, each in their own voice and tradition, remind us that the Universe isn't vague. It listens to frequencies. It reads your intention through the details you dare to name.

Below, you will find insights from some of today's most influential spiritual teachers—each offering a unique angle on the sacred power of specificity.

—Abraham Hicks teaches, **"The Universe responds not just to general wishes, but to vibrational alignment—and clarity sharpens that alignment**." When your desire is vague, your vibration is scattered. But when your vision is specific, your frequency becomes like a laser beam. Abraham reminds us that the Universe is not guessing—it is matching your energy. Get clear, and life will meet you there.

—Louise Hay encouraged readers to write affirmations that were detailed: **"I live in a spacious, light-filled home with warm wood floors, a peaceful garden, and sunlight pouring in**." That vision magnetizes more than "I want a house." Louise taught us that the soul listens through imagery. The more sensory-rich your affirmations, the more your body, mind, and spirit begin to agree. Her approach was not just about words— it was about painting the scene until it came to life.

—Dr. Joe Dispenza explains. **"When we visualize with rich sensory detail, our brain and body begin to believe it is happening. The more real it feels, the faster it manifests**." Dr. Joe brings the science behind the sacred. He reminds us that the brain does not know the difference between a vividly imagined experience and a real one. So, when you add texture, sound, emotion, and movement to your vision, you literally begin rehearsing your future.

—Oprah Winfrey has shared that she wrote down her vision of success in great detail—and reviewed it often. "**I didn't just say I wanted to be successful. I knew where I wanted to live. What kind of conversations I wanted to have. Who I wanted to become**." Oprah did not manifest success by accident. She shaped it with deliberate clarity. She teaches us that when you honor your dream with detailed attention, it becomes more than a fantasy—it becomes a plan your spirit can walk toward.

—Iyanla Vanzant tells her students: "**Don't just ask the universe for cake. Say what kind. What flavor. What size. The universe doesn't work off vague orders**." Leave it to Iyanla to say plainly. She reminds us that the Universe is like a divine kitchen—it is waiting for your order, but it needs more than just "Something sweet." Give it your flavor, your texture, your preference. That is how specificity becomes sacred.

—Roy Waugh likes to say: "**What you name with precision, you magnetize with power**." This is not just a phrase—it is a lived truth. Every time I have named a vision clearly and fully, something in the atmosphere responded. Clarity does not just direct your focus—it tunes your energy. The more precise your vision, the more powerful its pull.

These teachings are clear across the board: do not just hope—hone. Do not just wish—write. Do not just speak—specify. When you give form to your vision, you give it weight. You give it energy. You give it life. Whether you are writing an affirmation, visualizing a new chapter, or praying for a breakthrough, let your details be bold.

Let your vision be vivid. Because when you dare to be specific, you are not just calling something in—you are showing the Universe that you are ready to receive it.

Scientific Perspectives: The Brain and the Blueprint
—Training the Brain to Believe in Specifics

Something remarkable happens when you stop imagining vaguely and start visualizing precisely. Your brain does not just sit back and watch—it adapts. It begins organizing thoughts, directing focus, and rewiring itself to bring that vision to life. This is not just "mind over matter." It is biology. It is the sacred wiring of a mind-body system that was built to collaborate with the Universe.

The clearer your inner picture becomes, the more your brain leans in. With every repetition, it forms new grooves. With every emotion you attach, it responds more deeply. What you see inside—when practiced consistently and vividly—begins shaping how you show up outside.

✧ **Embodied Simulation — Rehearsing the Future Before It Arrives**

Your brain does not always distinguish between something real and something vividly imagined. Thanks to a mechanism called embodied simulation, when you picture yourself in a specific scene—stepping onstage, walking through your new home, or holding the keys to your dream car—your brain activates the same regions it would if it were actually happening.

You are not pretending. You are preparing.

Your body begins producing the chemicals of confidence, the emotional state of fulfillment, and even subtle motor memory. This is why athletes visualize before a race, why musicians rehearse silently before playing.

And why you, too, can become the energy of your future self simply by seeing it clearly and often.

✧ **Premotor Cortex Activation — Practicing the Move Before You Make It**

The premotor cortex is the part of your brain that helps plan and prepare physical movement. But here is the beautiful part: it does not wait for reality. It activates even when you only imagine the action.

So, when you see yourself walking into that dream opportunity—speaking, shaking hands, smiling with ease—your premotor cortex is firing as if it is already in motion. The more clearly you see it, the more fluently your body rehearses it. By the time the real moment arrives, your brain has already practiced. And what once felt like a stretch now feels natural.

✧ Neuroplasticity — Wiring Your Vision into Reality

Neuroplasticity is your brain's capacity to change—literally rewiring itself —based on thought, repetition, and experience. When you visualize something vividly over time, especially when emotion is involved, your brain begins carving out new neural pathways.

These are not just mental images—they become a blueprint your nervous system follows.

Each time you repeat the vision, the path gets clearer. Specificity accelerates the process. A vague hope barely registers, but a richly imagined dream lights up your brain like a signal tower. You're not just thinking about your future—you are building it. One intentional image at a time.

✧ Hebbian Learning — What You Repeat, You Strengthen

According to Hebbian theory, "neurons that fire together wire together." Translation? Repetition creates reality. The more you focus on a specific, detailed outcome—and especially if you feel it while you do—the stronger the associated neural circuits become.

Eventually, this inner rehearsal starts influencing your default thoughts, your emotions, and your behavior. It becomes your norm. And over time, your outer world starts reflecting that inner pattern. In short, the more clearly and consistently you imagine, the more you become a match for the life you are envisioning.

✧ Mental Time Travel — How the Brain Pre-Experiences Desired Outcomes

Scientists call this episodic future thinking—your brain's ability to simulate experiences that have not happened yet. This capacity is more than a fun daydream. It is your brain's built-in rehearsal system.

When you imagine a scene in detail—how it feels, who is with you, what you are wearing—you activate dopamine pathways, lower anxiety, and actually improve the likelihood of following through. You have seen it, so your body trusts it. The imagined becomes emotionally real, and you begin acting in alignment with it.

There is no mystery here. There is no guesswork. The science of the brain is aligning with this spiritual truth: what you focus on becomes your frequency. And what you imagine in detail becomes the blueprint from which your biology starts building.

So, use your vision like a sculptor uses a chisel. Not once. Not vaguely. But with repetition, clarity, and heart.

Because every time you see it clearly, your brain starts believing it is already yours. And that belief becomes the doorway. That precision becomes the path.

Personal Story
—When the Details Became the Story

For years, this book lived in pieces. Not chapters. Not outlines.

But pieces.

There were scraps of hotel notepads tucked into Bibles, torn corners of old church bulletins with phrases scribbled sideways, voice memos whispered into phones at three in the morning, and notebooks I had long forgotten, filled with half-sentences, prayers, quotes, and lyrics that had no clear home.

I did not realize it then, but I was writing this book before I even knew it existed.

I was living it—collecting it in fragments, one sacred detail at a time. Some of those fragments were written in joy, some in heartbreak, and some in hotel rooms and hospital beds. And for a long time, they just sat there— quiet, scattered, and waiting.

I would stumble across them now and then. A line would tug at me. A phrase would glow. And I would whisper, "That belongs somewhere." But I did not know where. Or what it belonged to.

I thought I had to be more organized. More certain. More ready.

So, I waited for clarity to strike like lightning. But it did not.

What finally shifted was this: When I asked.
When I stopped trying to control the process and simply asked the Universe: "Help me write the book I'm meant to write."

Not just any book.

This book.

The one hidden in those paper scraps. The one buried in old journals and voice memos. The one that had been quietly gathering itself over years of real life.

So, I did something simple. I began gathering the pieces.

I grouped scraps of paper that shared the same energy, intent, or idea. I clipped together quotes and themes that seemed to echo each other. I shaped a few into short paragraphs—just to make sense of it all. To give myself a clearer path forward.
And that is when I noticed something. They already belonged together, almost word for word in some cases. They made more sense than I ever realized.

What I thought were random scribbles were actually revelations. What I thought were scattered ideas were scenes. Moments. Truths. Pieces of my life, my story, and my dream of creating something meaningful—quietly forming right in front of me.

It was as if the vision had been there all along, just waiting for me to catch up.

The fragments started speaking. The scribbled notes were not just leftovers; they were the blueprint. The scattered pieces were not in the way; they were the way. They were the book.

Every quote I had saved, every memory I had jotted down, every phrase I could not shake—these were not just ideas. They were the architecture. The bones and breath of what I was meant to write.

Once I committed—once I said "Yes"—it was as if the book rose up to meet me.

A sentence would unlock a theme. A dream would become a chapter. A phrase I had written on the back of a receipt five years ago would suddenly feel like gold. I would rename sections, rewrite entire pages, revisit stories I thought were too small—and find they were holding the whole message.

What I thought were fragments turned out to be the foundation.
And the more I honored the details, the more I stopped asking for "a book" and started honoring this book—the more it flowed. Not all at once, but faithfully.

Looking back now, I see it clearly: The vision was never missing. It was just waiting to be named. Clarity did not arrive fully formed—it arrived through the doing.

And every step I took made the next one visible.

This was not about chasing brilliance. It was about listening to what had already been given.

Because a dream without detail is like a prayer without a voice; it lives, but it cannot lead.

But when you start giving shape to the vision—when you gather the fragments and dare to name them—something powerful happens: What was once only imagined comes to life.

In the end, it was not just belief that brought this book forth. It was the scraps. The scribbles. The details.

The details were the book.

And the more clearly I saw them, the more they began to see me back.

Practical Applications
—Visualize It Specifically, Live It Fully

When it comes to manifestation, clarity is your compass. Specificity is the language the universe listens to.

This next section offers tools to help you shape your desires with precision —refining your vision so that it's not just seen, but felt, known, and magnetically alive. The clearer your picture, the more powerfully it pulls your future into the now.

1. **Be specific with your vision**.
   Do not just say "I want success." Define it. "I want to speak on global stages, write books, and work three days a week doing what I love."

2. **Intend everything you do.**
   From brushing your teeth to applying for a job, set an inner intention. "I do this in love. I do this in alignment."

3. **Write it down in vivid detail**.
   Journal your vision like it already exists. Describe your ideal day, from waking to sleeping. Include colors, people, spaces, moments.

4. **Name the Dream**.
   Instead of saying, "I want a house," say, "I am manifesting a three-bedroom home with tall ceilings, golden light, and a fireplace that feels like peace."

5. **Bless the Details**.
   When you notice a small part of your vision unfolding, name it and give thanks. "This is part of it. I see it. I bless it."

Clarity is not about control—it's about alignment. When you dare to name the details of your dream, you're not just fantasizing; you're giving the universe a blueprint to build with. Every word you write, every image you hold, every intention you set is a thread weaving your future into the fabric of today. The more specifically you see it, the more fully you can live it now. And when you live as if it already belongs to you, the universe has no choice but to echo it back.

Affirmation

"My vision is clear. My details are sacred. I set my intention with purpose, and I manifest with clarity and confidence."

Guided Meditation
—The Vision in Vivid Detail

Take a gentle breath.

Picture the life you desire—clearly, richly.

Walk through your dream home. What color are the walls? How many rooms? What does it smell like inside? Imagine the table where you drink tea, the floor beneath your feet, the sunlight on your skin.

Speak to this vision: "I see you. I welcome you. I align with you."

Let each detail imprint into your heart. Let your spirit say yes.

Conclusion

Clarity is not just about clean lines and perfect plans—it is about reverence. It is a way of honoring the dream you carry, the story you have lived, and the truth that has been waiting inside you all along.

Because when you begin to name your desire in detail, you are not just crafting a goal—you are giving language to your becoming.

Sometimes we are afraid to get specific because it feels risky, like we are setting ourselves up for disappointment.

But I have learned that when we avoid the details, we dilute the power. Vague hope can only take you so far. But when you dare to define the vision—when you start shaping it with feeling, precision, and intent—that is when the magic starts to move.

Because the Universe does not respond to maybe, it responds to meaning.

And no, it does not always show up the way we first imagined. But that's okay. The process itself transforms us.

Every time we clarify, rewrite, or speak it out loud, we become more aligned. More available. More rooted in who we really are and what we are truly here to create.

So, do not rush the vision. Do not be afraid of the edits. And don't dismiss the tiny notes you have tucked away—they may be the very blueprint for your next miracle.

Because in the end, you are not just naming a dream. You are naming yourself.

And that's where manifestation begins.

Chapter 28: Divine Timing
—Trusting the Unfolding

Opening Reflection

"Delays are sometimes detours—gentle redirections guiding you to what the universe has already arranged as a divine appointment."
—Roy Waugh

Introduction

We live in a world that celebrates immediacy. Same-day delivery, instant messages, overnight miracles. We are conditioned to expect quick answers and rapid results.

However, manifestation does not operate within the timeline of modern convenience. It unfolds by divine orchestration.

Sometimes what we call a delay is actually a redirection—an unseen alignment guiding us into a moment we could not have scheduled, but was perfectly appointed for us all along.

There is a sacred rhythm beneath every detour and pause. And when we learn to trust it, we realize that waiting does not mean we've been forgotten. It means the universe is setting the stage for something exquisitely timed:

Not just a blessing, but a **Divine Appointment**.

In this chapter, we will explore what it really means to trust divine timing —not as a passive waiting room, but as an active alignment with something higher. You will discover how patience can become power, how pauses can carry purpose, and how life often arranges itself with more wisdom than we could ever plan. You will learn how to stay present, stay ready, and stay aligned—so that when your moment comes, you do not miss it.

Hidden Teachings from Ancient Traditions
—The Appointed Hour—Timing, Delay, and Divine Alignment

There is a rhythm moving beneath the surface of every spiritual tradition —an unspoken agreement between the soul and the Divine that timing is holy. Though human desire often pleads for immediacy, sacred texts remind us that delay is not denial. Instead, delay is often designed. It is in the pauses and detours that character is shaped, wisdom is gained, and the stage is set for something far greater than we could have orchestrated ourselves.

Each tradition below offers a glimpse into how divine timing is not just a concept—it is a spiritual discipline.

✧ Christian Faith

The Bible is full of stories about when waiting preceded the miracle. Divine timing was not rushed, yet always right.

"And the Lord visited Sarah as He had said, and the Lord did for Sarah as He had spoken. For Sarah conceived and bore Abraham a son in his old age, at the set time of which God had spoken to him." (Genesis 21:1–2 NKJV) Abraham and Sarah waited decades for their promised child. The delay was not punishment—it was preparation. And when Isaac arrived, it was clear the miracle was not man-made but divinely orchestrated.

David was anointed king as a teenager, yet he waited years through hardship, exile, and obscurity before ascending the throne. **"So he sent and brought him in. Now he was ruddy, with bright eyes, and good-looking. And the Lord said, 'Arise, anoint him; for this is the one!"** (1 Samuel 16:12 NKJV)

Then years of trials followed—his flight from Saul, hiding in caves, and seasons of apparent delay. **"Then all the tribes of Israel came to David at Hebron and spoke, saying, 'Indeed we are your bone and your flesh.' ... Also, in time past, when Saul was king over us, you were the one who led Israel out and brought them in.**

And the Lord said to you, 'You shall shepherd My people Israel, and be ruler over Israel.' Therefore, all the elders of Israel came to the king at Hebron, and King David made a covenant with them before the Lord. And they anointed David king over Israel." (2 Samuel 5:1–3 NKJV) His detours were not wasted; they shaped the heart of a leader who could carry the weight of the crown.

Even Jesus, the Son of God, lived thirty hidden years before His public ministry began. Luke 2:52 says, **"And Jesus grew in wisdom and stature, and in favor with God and man**." Timing was never off—it was sacredly unfolding.

As Ecclesiastes 3:1 declares, **"To everything there is a season, and a time to every purpose under heaven**." Faith is not just about what we believe—it is about when we are willing to believe it, even in the silence.

✧ Jewish Wisdom

In Judaism, time itself is understood as sacred. The Hebrew word z'man implies that every moment carries divine purpose.

The story of the Exodus is a powerful lesson in appointed time. Though Moses was chosen to lead the Israelites out of Egypt, deliverance did not come immediately. It followed plagues, rejection, and resistance. And yet, **"at the end of the 430 years... all the hosts of the Lord went out from the land of Egypt**." (Exodus 12:41, ESV) Not early. Not late. Right on time.

Shabbat, the weekly day of rest, is a lived ritual of surrendering to divine timing. Sundown arrives, and no matter what is unfinished, the heart enters sacred pause—trusting that the world keeps spinning even when we stop.

Rabbi Abraham Joshua Heschel wrote, **"Shabbat is not about doing— it is about being. It is a cathedral in time**." (The Sabbath: Its Meaning for Modern Man, Farrar, Straus and Giroux, 1951) To embrace the appointed moment, one must also honor the sacred stillness that precedes it.

✧ Islamic Teachings

Divine timing is central in Islam, woven into daily life and spiritual posture.

The Qur'an reassures believers again and again to trust in the unseen process: "Indeed, Allah is with those who patiently endure." (Qur'an 8:46)

The Prophet Muhammad (peace be upon him) did not receive revelation all at once. *It came over 23 years—at the exact times it was needed.* His migration to Medina, after years of persecution, opened the way for his mission to flourish. Timing was not passive—it was divinely orchestrated. The concept of tawakkul—complete trust in Allah—teaches that while effort is ours, timing is God's.

As the Qur'an affirms: "**Verily, with hardship comes ease**." (Qur'an 94:6)

Imam Al-Ghazali once said, "**Never have I dealt with anything more difficult than my own soul, which sometimes helps me and sometimes opposes me**." The soul's surrender to divine timing is what transforms hardship into harvest.

✧ Buddhist Practices

In Buddhism, patience is not a passive state—it is active spiritual mastery. Kshanti, or patient endurance, is one of the Six Paramitas (perfections) required for enlightenment. It is a reminder that rushing leads to restlessness, but presence leads to peace.

The lotus, a cherished symbol in Buddhism, grows slowly in muddy waters before it ever blooms. Its timing is not dictated by external pressure but by the inner ripening of readiness.

The Dhammapada states, "**A mind unruffled by the vagaries of fortune, from sorrow freed, from defilements cleansed, from fear liberated—this is the greatest blessing**." (Dhammapada, verse 331) Meditation itself is an exercise in divine timing. You do not force stillness—you return to it. You do not chase insight—you make space for it to rise in its own time.

In the Buddhist path, the wait is not empty—it is enlightened.

✧ **Hindu Traditions**

Hinduism treats time as divine. The Sanskrit word kāla means not only time but also destiny and divine intelligence.

The Bhagavad Gita teaches this surrender clearly: "**Whatever happened, happened for the good. Whatever is happening, is happening for the good. Whatever will happen, will also happen for the good**." (Bhagavad Gita 2.47–2.48, paraphrased)
This is not spiritual apathy—it is soulful trust. The universe moves in cycles, and the wise do not try to control them. They align with them.

Karma deepens this lesson: every action has its appointed consequence, which unfolds when the time is ripe. Just as a seed will bloom only when its inner conditions meet the external season, destiny also reveals itself through the right timing.

As Swami Sivananda once said, "**Put your heart, mind, and soul into even your smallest acts. This is the secret of success**." (Bliss Divine: A Book of Spiritual Essays on the Lofty Purpose of Human Life. 10th ed. Rishikesh: The Divine Life Society, 1996) Success is not rushed—it is readied.

Across all sacred paths, we are reminded that divine timing is not a passive delay—it is a sacred rhythm. Whether through the waiting of prophets, the patience of lotus blossoms, or the unfolding of karma, spiritual wisdom teaches us that life is always moving toward alignment—even when it seems still.

The appointed moment is not something you chase. It is something you become ready to receive. And when it arrives, you recognize it—not because it is loud, but because it fits.

Wisdom from Contemporary Spiritual Leaders

Sometimes the most profound reminders come from voices we have grown to trust—those who have walked through waiting seasons and still chose to believe. Divine timing is not just a spiritual principle; it is a lived experience.

These leaders, each in their own way, teach us that waiting is not a sign of absence, but of alignment. Their words remind us that the pause is purposeful, and the unfolding is divine.

—Joyce Meyer teaches, "**God's timing is always right. He is never late—though He seldom comes early**." There is something comforting about that kind of honesty. Joyce doesn't sugarcoat the process. She acknowledges the ache of waiting but anchors it in trust. Divine timing may not follow our preferences, but it always fulfills our purpose.

—Dr. Joe Dispenza explains, "**When we try to force outcomes, we lock ourselves into predictable futures. But when we release the grip of 'how', and 'when' the universe begins to respond in ways far more creative than we could have imagined**." His teachings remind us: surrender is not giving up—it is giving over. When we let go of the calendar, we give space for the miraculous.

—Abraham Hicks often says, "**What you want is already in your vibrational escrow. It is ready. Are you**?" This question flips the waiting game on its head. It is not about delay—it is about readiness. Divine timing is not the universe stalling—it is the universe syncing with our alignment.

—Louise Hay reminded readers, "**I trust the process of life. Everything I need comes to me in the perfect time and space sequence**." Louise's gentle wisdom brings peace to the soul. She invites us to trust the current even when we cannot see the shore. That trust becomes a bridge between longing and fulfillment.

—Maya Angelou once said, "**Ask for what you want and be prepared to get it. But do not try to dictate how and when**." Leave it to Maya to speak truth with elegance. Her words remind us: clarity is our job. Timing is not. Our task is to be prepared, not to be in charge.

—Roy Waugh, "**Divine timing isn't a delay—it's a dance. You're not late. You're being led**." In the moments we feel left behind, this truth brings us back home. We are not lost. We are being invited to move in rhythm with something greater than us. And that rhythm always knows the way.

When we stop trying to outrun the wait and instead begin to walk with it, something shifts. We do not just learn patience—we learn presence. Divine timing teaches us to stop chasing the moment and start becoming the moment. And when we do, what we were waiting for often walks in— right on time.

Scientific Perspectives: Timing, Surrender, and the Invisible Shift
—How Science Reveals the Power of Perfect Timing

There are seasons in life when everything feels still—like nothing is moving, nothing is changing. But science tells us a different story.

Beneath what appears to be silence, a profound reordering is taking place. The human brain, quantum fields, and biological systems all reflect a hidden truth: transformation often happens before it becomes visible. What we call "waiting" is often just the necessary space for realignment and integration.

Here is what science is revealing about the sacred unseen shift.

✧ Neuroscience — Latent Learning and Hidden Integration

In the realm of neuroscience, latent learning is the process by which the brain absorbs new information without immediately demonstrating it. Just because you do not see the result does not mean your system is not changing. This explains why repeated visualization, affirmations, or spiritual rituals may feel slow to take effect—but later lead to sudden clarity or breakthroughs. The prefrontal cortex, responsible for planning and decision-making, lights up with new patterns even when you are not consciously aware of it.

Neuroscientist Dr. Andrew Huberman has noted that neuroplasticity—the brain's ability to rewire itself—is most active when paired with focus, emotion, and rest. So, while you may feel like nothing is happening, the mind is preparing for transformation behind the scenes. The silence is not absence—it is integration.

✧ Quantum Physics — Holding Frequency Until Collapse

Quantum physics has shown that energy does not always move in linear ways. In fact, energy exists in states of superposition—multiple potential realities—until it collapses into one outcome through observation and resonance. This supports the idea that our energy, intention, and attention co-create reality.

A phenomenon called quantum coherence shows how separate particles can suddenly shift into alignment once a threshold is reached. In manifestation terms, this means that holding your vibration long enough can cause a seemingly "sudden" breakthrough—because your internal field has finally aligned with a larger energetic pattern.

Waiting, then, is not passive. It is holding the field steady enough for the shift to occur.

✧ Developmental Psychology — Incubation and Creative Insight

In cognitive psychology, creative problem-solving often follows a 4-stage cycle: preparation, incubation, illumination, and verification. The incubation phase—the one most overlooked—is a quiet, nonlinear period when the brain steps back and allows ideas to percolate unconsciously. Psychologist Graham Wallas coined this model in the early 20th century, and modern studies confirm that the brain continues to solve problems beneath conscious awareness. This is why many breakthroughs come after we stop trying so hard. The timing of insight is not random—it arrives when we are mentally and emotionally prepared to receive it.

✧ Chronobiology — The Sacred Timing of Biological Rhythms

Even the body teaches us about divine timing. Chronobiology, the study of natural biological cycles, shows that cells regenerate, hormones release, and healing processes unfold according to internal clocks—called circadian rhythms and ultradian rhythms. You cannot force your liver to detox faster, or your skin to regenerate in an instant. The process unfolds by design.

Just like a seed takes time to sprout, your manifestations often require internal seasons of rest, integration, and gestation. When we override these rhythms with constant effort, we disrupt natural timing. But when we trust the body's wisdom, healing and transformation unfold more gracefully.

✧ Systems Theory — Emergence and the Tipping Point

Systems theory teaches that complex changes do not always happen incrementally. Sometimes, a system reaches a tipping point—where multiple small shifts accumulate until a sudden large transformation occurs.

This is known as emergence.

Your life is a system. And even when you do not see movement on the surface, small consistent actions—meditations, visualizations, mindset shifts—are creating invisible momentum. What feels like stillness may actually be critical mass building in silence. When the moment is right, the shift comes all at once.

What science confirms again and again is what the soul has always known: timing matters. Not because the universe is testing us—but because we are being prepared. Every pause, every quiet season, every stretch of silence is working with you, not against you. The invisible work is still work. Your alignment is still creating. Trust the unseen processes.

Because when everything finally converges—when the brain, energy, heart, and soul sync—you will not just see results.

You will feel the sacred precision of a universe that was never late.

Personal Story
—Rocks in a Box

There are moments in life when something is placed in your hands that makes no earthly sense—but feels too sacred to ignore.

That is exactly how I felt the day I inherited a large box of loose gemstones from a woman whose husband had once owned an international clothing brand. Inside were hundreds of stones, each carefully bagged and labeled —white and colored diamonds, rubies and emeralds, sapphires of every shade, lustrous pearls, and rare minerals shaped into radiant gems. It wasn't a jewelry collection. It was a galaxy of light.

And I had no clue as to what to do with it.

I lovingly referred to them as my "rocks in a box." I kept them locked away in a safety deposit vault because of who they came from; they were too precious to sell and too mysterious to understand. I prayed over them, asking God, the Universe—whoever was listening— "What is this? Why me? What am I supposed to do with these?" But for years, no answer came.

So, I just sat on them like a bird on a nest, trusting that there was a reason for me to have received these stones, even if I could not see it. I did not know it then, but that was divine timing in its purest form: a sacred pause, a holding pattern for destiny.

Years passed.

Then one afternoon, seemingly out of nowhere, my husband said, "Why don't you have a ring made from one of those stones that woman gave you?" I laughed. "A ring? I would not know where to start." And he just smiled and said, "You're an artist. Just draw it. Design the ring the way you want it to look.

So, I did. I took my time. I opened that safety deposit box like it was a treasure chest and slowly sifted through each tiny bag, holding the stones up to the light one by one.

Then I saw it—a magnificent 10-carat white diamond. It sparkled with a clarity that stopped me in my tracks. And in that instant, it took my breath away.

It sparkled just like the little rock I picked up from the middle of the road when I was four years old—right before that car hit me.

That memory rushed back in a flash of light. The innocence of that moment. The shimmer of something beautiful in an unexpected place.

And now here it was again—another sparkle, another still point in time, catching my attention and whispering: This is important.

I asked the stone to tell me what it wants its house to look like.

And in my imagination, the stone began to speak. It told me it wanted to live in something royal—something worthy of a king.

So, I drew it just as I thought it might look: a bold, detailed ring that looked like it had stepped out of ancient nobility.

When I was done, I took the sketch and the stone to a local jeweler I had never visited before. I had no idea if they would even be able to help.

The shop owner took one look and said, "Oh, this is what we do—custom pieces." She called up her goldsmith. And that—is when the magic began.

Up walked a man with bright eyes and a kind smile. His visor was pushed back on his forehead, and his apron was still dusted from his work. There was something about him—a light, a joy, a warmth that felt like a blessing in human form. The kind of person you just want to get a hug from. He looked at the drawing, then looked at me. "Where did you get this design?" he asked. "I drew it," I replied.

His eyes widened. "You drew this?" He studied it again. "Son, if you drew this, you could make this."

I blinked. "What do you mean?"

"I mean, I'm looking for an apprentice," he said. "Why don't you let me teach you how to make this ring yourself? Do you want to become my apprentice?"

And just like that, the divine appointment revealed itself.

I told him I still traveled to sing and perform concerts, and that my schedule was unpredictable. He smiled. "Then just come when you can. Let me know the night before, and I will have a space ready for you."

For the next ten years, on and off, I studied at his side. I learned to melt gold and shape it. I discovered how adding different elements to pure gold could create green, rose, or even blue gold. I carved wax models, set stones, and finished designs. I created beauty with my own hands—things I never dreamed I would be able to make.

Those "rocks in a box" were not just stones. They were assignments. They were soul gifts. And the waiting was not a waste—it was a womb.

Now, years later, I have not sold a single one of those stones. But I have given many away—to honor special moments, to bring light where it was needed, to turn something beautiful into something meaningful. That box of gemstones became more than an inheritance.

It became a calling.

Today, I am a jewelry designer. I have had the privilege of creating extraordinary pieces—some that now live in museums, others that have become legacy heirlooms to be passed down through generations. Rings, pendants, and bracelets that hold not just value, but story, memory, and energy.

I have made treasures for matriarchs of families who wanted to mark a life well-lived. I have crafted symbols of healing, of celebration, of rebirth. Each design begins as a whisper in the spirit—a vision that forms first in the imagination before it ever touches gold.

And I believe, with all my heart, that sometimes we are the ones that God uses to be His hands to deliver blessings. Through our hands. Through our gifts. Through our willingness to wait, listen, and create.

Because what starts as a mystery often reveals itself as a mission.

And maybe those rocks in a box are not just waiting for me.

Maybe they are waiting for someone else's divine appointment.

Practical Applications
—Living Aligned with Divine Timing

Trusting divine timing is not just a spiritual concept—it is a daily practice. It requires you to stay present, surrender your urgency, and keep preparing even when the outcome is not visible yet.

These next steps will help you align your inner posture with the unfolding of divine order—so that when your appointed moment arrives, you will not only be ready for it, you will recognize it. Because alignment is often what turns waiting into receiving.

1. **Release the urgency**.
   Repeat: "I do not need to rush what is mine. It is already aligning with me."

2. **Stay ready**.
Do not pause your preparation. Just because the delivery is delayed does not mean the destination has changed.

3. **Track progress beyond results**.
Look for subtle shifts: new ideas, fresh peace, chance encounters. These are signs the manifestation is forming.

4. **Use the waiting season to refine**.
Ask: "How can I become even more aligned with what I'm calling in?"

5. **Visualize with patience**.
Do not force the outcome. Instead, gently return to the vision daily with love, not pressure.

6. **Trust the detours**.
Bless closed doors and redirected steps. They are often the clearest evidence of divine guidance.

7. **Speak the season you want to see**.
"I may not see it yet, but I trust that it is coming in perfect timing, in the best way."

Every moment you choose presence over pressure, trust over control, and preparation over panic—you bring yourself into deeper alignment with what has already been written for you. These small daily shifts are not insignificant; they are the quiet yeses that whisper back to the universe, "I'm ready when it's ready."

Divine timing does not ask you to force the unfolding—it simply asks you to stay in rhythm with it. Because when you live in tune with the unseen, you do not just wait for your destiny; you meet it.

Affirmation

"I trust divine timing. I release the need to control. What is mine is making its way to me—right on schedule, perfectly aligned, and filled with grace."

Guided Meditation
—Trusting the Flow of Time

Breathe. Feel your chest rise and fall.

Imagine a golden river flowing beside you—steady, strong, and full of promise.
This river is divine timing. You do not need to push. You do not need to paddle upstream. You float. You allow. You trust.

In the distance, you see your vision waiting—glowing, calm, already prepared.

Whisper inwardly: "I trust the unfolding. I am in rhythm. I am in sync."

Rest in this knowing. Let the current carry you.

Conclusion

Divine timing is not a delay—it is a design. A sacred unfolding that draws every piece into place at exactly the right moment.

We may not always see it while we are in it. We may question the silence, the slowness, the curve in the road. But every step, every pause, every detour is part of the choreography of grace.

There are moments in life when the doors swing open instantly. But more often, the most profound blessings are the ones we waited for. The ones that found us not when we expected them, but when we were finally aligned enough to hold them with reverence.

I have lived long enough to see that what feels like uncertainty is often just a sacred gestation. A masterpiece is being formed behind the curtain.

Like the box of gemstones I inherited—mysterious, precious, and without explanation—I did not understand their purpose at first. I only knew they were meaningful. So, I waited. I listened. I honored the mystery. And in time, clarity revealed itself through the quiet unfolding of purpose.

That is how divine appointments work. They do not rush. They do not beg for attention. They arrive like whispers at the perfect moment, when your hands are open and your heart is finally ready to receive.

This chapter is a reminder that you are not behind. You are not being punished. You are being positioned.

The universe is not ignoring you. It is preparing something so aligned, so radiant, that if it had come any sooner, you might have missed its fullness.

So, take heart in the pause. Breathe in the now. Stay faithful in the preparation.

Because what is meant for you has already been assigned.

And when it arrives, it will not just fit your life—it will feel like it has been waiting for you too.

Chapter 29: Embody the Vision
— Becoming What You Believe

Opening Reflection

"You do not manifest what you wish for—you manifest what you walk like, speak like, and live like before it ever arrives. Because the moment you begin to live as if it is already yours, the universe starts responding like it is."
—Roy Waugh

Introduction

There comes a moment in every journey when it is no longer about learning more—but about living differently.

You have visualized, written, and spoken the words, prayed the prayers, and aligned your energy. You have waited through the silence and surrendered to divine timing.

But manifestation does not respond to hope alone. It responds to embodiment.

Because, as the opening reflection says: You do not manifest what you wish for—you manifest what you walk like, speak like, and live like before it ever arrives.

This chapter is about stepping into the version of yourself who already has it—not someday, but now. It is about understanding that the life you are calling in is not waiting for permission to arrive. It is waiting for alignment. Waiting for you to show up as the person who can carry it, sustain it, and take care of it with grace.

Because the moment you begin to live as if it is already yours, the world starts responding like it is.

Hidden Teachings from Ancient Traditions
—Becoming the Reflection of What You Believe to Be True

Throughout sacred traditions, the act of embodying what one believes is not an afterthought—it is the doorway. Faith is not meant to remain internal. It is lived out in words, actions, postures, and presence. Across every spiritual path, there is an invitation to become what you seek, to move as if your prayers are already answered, and to align your life with the energy of what you believe is possible.

This is the sacred practice of embodiment—the bridge between inner truth and outer experience.

✧ **Christian Faith**

In the Bible, transformation always preceded elevation.

Before David became king, he carried the identity of one. He honored God in the field, cared for sheep with leadership, and spoke to Goliath as if he already knew the victory was his. When he stood before the giant, he declared with fearless faith: "**You come to me with a sword, with a spear, and with a javelin. But I come to you in the name of the Lord of hosts... This day the Lord will deliver you into my hand...**" (1 Samuel 17:45–46, NKJV). That was not the voice of a shepherd boy—it was the voice of someone already walking in the calling before the crown.

Jesus, too, healed countless people by activating their identity—not just their faith. "**Your faith has made you whole**." (Mark 5:34, KJV). He called people out of paralysis, not by changing their conditions, but by inviting them into a new way of seeing themselves: "**Rise, take up your bed and walk**." (John 5:8, NKJV).

Romans 4:17 describes God as the One who "**calls those things which do not exist as though they did**." (Romans 4:17, NKJV). And as His reflection, so do we.

You must begin to speak, move, and live from the version of yourself who already is what you are calling in.

Because identity precedes reality.

✧ Jewish Wisdom

In Judaism, the inner and outer worlds are deeply intertwined. Emunah—faith—is not static belief. It is an active, lived trust.

Faith is made visible through daily rhythm and ritual. From the way prayers are spoken aloud and accompanied by movement, to how the Shema is recited daily—"**Hear, O Israel: The Lord is our God, the Lord is one**" (Deuteronomy 6:4)—every practice is a call to embody the oneness of God with wholeness of self.

Even the Passover Haggadah does not say, They were slaves in Egypt. It says You were—reminding each generation to live as though they themselves walked through the Red Sea.

Embodiment is not metaphor—it is memory carried in the body and lived in the present.

✧ Islamic Teachings

In Islam, the connection between belief and embodiment is non-negotiable. Iman (faith) must be expressed through word and deed.

The Prophet Muhammad (peace be upon him) did not just speak about compassion, integrity, or discipline—he lived it. His every action reflected alignment between inner knowing and outer living. He said, "**Verily, Allah does not look at your appearance or wealth, but rather He looks at your hearts and your deeds**." (Sahih Muslim 2564)

The Qur'an echoes this in saying: "**Indeed, those who have said, 'Our Lord is Allah,' and then remained steadfast—upon them will descend angels...**" (Qur'an 41:30). That steadfastness, istiqama, is spiritual embodiment—walking your prayer until it becomes your path.

✧ Buddhist Practices

In Buddhism, the path is not merely studied—it is lived through practice and presence.

The Noble Eightfold Path is a guide not for thinking, but for being: Right intention. Right speech. Right action. Right livelihood. It is an invitation to bring spiritual awareness into every breath and every choice.

Embodiment is taught in walking meditation, where each step is sacred, and in metta (loving-kindness), where compassion is first directed inward before being shared outward.

As the Dhammapada teaches: **"We are what we think. All that we are arises with our thoughts. With our thoughts, we make the world**." (Dhammapada, verse 1)

To embody your vision is to become the vibration of what you wish to see —not someday, but now.

✧ Hindu Traditions

In Hinduism, embodiment is the expression of dharma—your sacred purpose made manifest through action.

The Bhagavad Gita teaches: **"It is better to live your own dharma imperfectly than to live another's well**." (Bhagavad Gita 3:35) This is a call to authenticity, not imitation. You were not created to perform someone else's dream. You were designed to walk your own with devotion and boldness.

Through yoga, mantra, mudra, and seva (selfless service), the spiritual life is lived—not theorized. Every movement becomes a message to the universe: I am living what I believe.

When the external begins to mirror the internal, embodiment becomes the evidence of belief. You do not wait for the vision to arrive—you arrive in it.

In every tradition, the message is clear: faith without embodiment is incomplete. It is not enough to hope or wish or wait. You must begin to move, speak, and carry yourself as though what you believe is already true. Not out of performance—but out of resonance.

Because what you embody, you attract. What you live, you amplify. And what you walk in, you eventually witness.

Wisdom from Contemporary Spiritual Leaders

The journey from vision to manifestation is not merely about believing—it is about embodying. And some of the greatest spiritual voices of our time have echoed this truth: that what you seek does not come because you wish for it, but because you become the version of yourself who can carry it.

This section brings together timeless insights from teachers who have reminded us that alignment is not a passive state—it is a lived energy. When you begin to walk, speak, and live from your future self, life begins to mirror back your inner transformation.

—Dr. Joe Dispenza teaches: "**To change your personal reality, you must change your personality**." In other words, who you are being right now must reflect the version of you that already has what you are calling in. Your thoughts, your emotions, your habits, they become the energetic framework for your future reality.

—Abraham Hicks says: "**You have to become a vibrational match to what you want**." Your manifestation does not find you through effort—it finds you through resonance. When your frequency aligns with your vision, you do not chase it. You attract it.

—Louise Hay would often ask: "**If you believed you were worthy, how would you act today**?" It is a profound invitation to walk in worthiness now. Because the universe does not respond to self-doubt—it responds to self-honoring action.

—Joyce Meyer reminds us: **"You can't be pitiful and powerful at the same time"**. This is a truth that stings a little, but frees a lot. If you want to live in your divine authority, you have to let go of the identity that is still rehearsing powerlessness.

—Neale Donald Walsch, in his Conversations with God series, writes: **"You are already doing it. You are already being it. Now own it."** Ownership is a spiritual act. It says, *"I trust that what I carry is real, even before the evidence appears."* That is where manifestation begins to take root.

—Eckhart Tolle teaches: **"You are not waiting for something. You are it"**. When you stop placing your fulfillment in a future event and bring it into the present moment, everything changes. Embodiment starts with now.

—Roy Waugh: **"Embodiment is not performance—it is permission. The moment you let yourself live the life you've envisioned, you give the universe something to agree with."** There is a shift that happens when you stop trying to earn your future and start inhabiting it. This is not about pretending. It is about saying: I *trust myself enough to live like it is already real.* That kind of alignment becomes an invitation—one the universe cannot ignore.

The wisdom here is simple but transformative: stop rehearsing your vision and start living it. You are not preparing for who you are becoming —you are already carrying that version within you. These teachings do not ask you to wait for permission. They ask you to give it. To yourself.

Because the moment you do, everything around you begins to rise to match your new frequency.

Scientific Perspectives on Identity and Action
—When You Become It, the Brain Believes It

Manifestation does not just require vision—it requires integration. The bridge between desire and reality is often built not by force, but by frequency. And science continues to affirm what many spiritual traditions have long known: when you begin to act like it, live like it, and feel like it, your brain, your body, and your energy begin to respond as if it were already real.

This section explores how identity is shaped and solidified through action, emotion, and embodiment—offering compelling evidence from neuroscience, psychology, and behavioral science that supports the spiritual truth: you manifest what you are, not just what you want.

✧ Psychology — Identity Drives Behavior

From a psychological perspective, your sense of identity is the compass of your behavior. You do not act out of discipline alone—you act from what you believe is true about who you are.

When you begin to see yourself as someone who is abundant, healed, whole, or chosen, you naturally begin to make choices in alignment with that belief. And the more those actions repeat, the more they reinforce your identity, forming a virtuous cycle of embodiment.

This is why inner change precedes outer change: because behavior follows belief, energy follows intention, and reality follows identity.

✧ Behavioral Neuroscience — The 'As-If' Principle

The As-If Principle, supported by embodied cognition research, shows that acting as if something is already true can create the emotional and physiological conditions to support it. Smile, and you feel happier. Stand tall, and you feel stronger. Move like you are free—and your brain begins to believe you are.

"We do not laugh because we are happy," wrote psychologist William James, "**we are happy because we laugh**."

This principle directly affirms your power to co-create reality by choosing not just how you think—but how you carry yourself, even before the evidence appears.

✧ Cognitive Science — Enclothed Cognition

In a fascinating study from Northwestern University, participants who wore lab coats believed to belong to doctors showed increased focus, confidence, and attention to detail—even though they were not doctors.

The phenomenon, known as enclothed cognition, suggests that what you wear can shape how you think and feel—because it activates the identity associated with the clothing.

This echoes a deeper truth: when you dress like your future self, you begin to think like them, speak like them, move like them. And energy responds to what you are being—not just what you are hoping for.

✧ Motor Simulation Theory — Rehearsing Creates Readiness

Studies in motor simulation theory show that imagining yourself performing an action (like walking onto a stage, giving a talk, or living your future life) activates the same regions of the brain as actually doing it.

This means visualization is not just mental—it is neurological training.

The more you imagine yourself embodying your future, the more your body becomes familiar with it. So, when the real moment arrives, you are not just wishing—you are ready.

✧ Social Psychology — The Pygmalion Effect

The Pygmalion Effect shows that expectation shapes reality. Originally studied in educational settings, it reveals that when teachers expected more from certain students, those students consistently outperformed peers—not because of ability, but because of belief.

Now used in coaching and leadership psychology, this effect demonstrates that when you expect more from yourself, your actions will begin to rise to meet that expectation. You do not wait to become—you expect to become, and in doing so, you embody the prophecy.

These studies all point to the same sacred truth: embodiment creates reality. You do not wait for confirmation to become—you become, and the confirmation follows. Science affirms what the soul already knows: when you live in alignment with the identity of your future self, the universe begins to mirror that alignment back to you.

So, speak it, wear it, walk it, believe it.
The moment you start showing up as who you truly are, the Universe starts showing up to match.

Personal Story
—When I Became What I Believed

As I have shared earlier in this book, when it came to music, ministry, or writing, I had no idea what I was doing in the beginning. I just knew that once I discovered I had a gift, I could not keep it hidden. I could not bury it under fear or wait until I had it "figured out." I had to share it. I had to start somewhere.

That is what led me to places like the Christian Artists Seminar in the Rockies. I was not trying to win anything—I was trying to learn. I wanted to know how to take this flame inside of me and turn it into something that could light up a room.

How did people become those kinds of singers—the ones whose songs moved people to tears or shifted something in a struggling heart? How did speakers pour words like water into thirsty souls? Where did you even begin?

I remembered something from my childhood—a little show I used to perform for my mom. I had a knack for imitation. I could mimic voices, gestures, and mannerisms. And though my mom could not hear me, she could read my lips, see my expression, and feel the energy. And oh, how she would laugh. I lived for that laughter.

It taught me that connection was not always about words—it was about energy. About presence.

So, I took that idea with me.

What if I could learn by embodying what I saw in others? What if, instead of just watching someone perform or speak, I stepped into the feeling of being them? Imitated them? Felt their energy? Walked in their emotion?

So, I did.

I mimicked how they moved, how they breathed before a note. How they looked into a crowd like they were looking into someone's soul.

At first, I was just pretending—playing the part. But something strange and beautiful happened: eventually, it stopped feeling like imitation and started feeling like me.

I began to refine my own performances. My own voice. My own message. And the more I did it, the more opportunities arrived—bigger platforms, brighter stages, television appearances, concerts opening for some of the greatest names in Contemporary Christian Music. And I did not take a second of it for granted.

I became a sponge around those people. I soaked up everything I could. I asked questions. I studied how they carried themselves—not just professionally, but energetically.

I found that being near those who were walking in their purpose changed something in me. Just being in the same space began to shift my frequency.

There is a phenomenon in physics called sympathetic resonance. If you place two pianos in the same room and strike a note on one, the same string on the second piano will begin to vibrate on its own. No one touching it—it simply responded to the energy. And that is what I felt happening to me.

By opening myself up—by being teachable, by aligning with people who were already walking in the energy I longed for—something in me began to resonate. My spirit began to vibrate in harmony with a higher version of myself.

I was not chasing the dream anymore. I was becoming it.

I stepped into the frequency of who I was called to be. And over time, the dream began to step toward me. The stages came. The lights came. But more importantly, I had become what I had long believed for—in my heart, in my thoughts, and in the silent language of my meditations.

And that—is the sacred intersection where belief, reality, and the energy of the universe combined—and became my manifestation.

Practical Applications
—Embodying Your Manifestation Now

You have envisioned the life. You have prayed the prayer. You have done the inner work. Now it is time to embody it. This section is about bringing your inner vision into your outer reality—through action, energy, and alignment.

These practices are designed to help you step into the frequency of your future self now. Because the more you live as though it is already done, the more effortlessly the universe will reflect it back to you. You do not need to chase the dream. You just need to become the person who already lives it.

1. **Wear the vision you believe in**.
   Wear what aligns with how you want to feel. Power, grace, joy—let it show on the outside.

2. **Speak it before you see it**.
   Say things like: "This is who I am becoming." "This is already happening." Use identity-based language.

3. **Use detailed visualization**.
   Do not just imagine the thing—imagine being the one who holds it. What is your posture? What is your energy? What are your habits?

4. **Make micro-decisions in alignment**.
   Every choice—food, emails, bedtime—can reflect who you are becoming. Let your future self guide today's steps.

5. **Set the tone each morning**.
   Ask: "What would the version of me who already has it do first today?"

6. **Practice vibrational integrity**.
   Do not speak against your own vision. Do not doubt out loud. Speak in the energy of certainty.

7. **Walk as though it is already done**.
   Carry yourself with the weightlessness of one who knows: it is already unfolding.

When you live as though it is already done, something within you begins to shift—and the world around you starts shifting too. Embodiment is not about pretending; it is about aligning with the deepest truth of who you already are. Each small decision becomes a declaration. Each act of alignment becomes a magnet.

You are not just calling in the vision—you are becoming the vessel that can carry it. And when your outer life begins to echo the frequency of your inner knowing, manifestation is no longer a matter of if—it becomes a matter of now.

Affirmation

"**I do not just believe—I align, I radiate, I receive. I am no longer waiting; I am embodying what I once imagined**."

Guided Meditation
—Walking as the One Who Already Is

Take a moment. Picture your highest self standing before you—radiant, strong, fulfilled.

Step into that image. Feel your higher self's posture, peace, and clarity.

Let it fill you from the inside. Walk through your day with this energy.

Let every breath affirm: "I am already becoming what I once only dreamed."

Conclusion

There comes a moment in the journey where you stop chasing the vision and start becoming it.

Not in theory. Not in concept. But in posture. In presence. In power.

It is the moment when you realize: you have prayed the prayers, spoken the affirmations, done the inner work, and called the future forth with every ounce of your faith. Now the question is no longer, Will it come?

The question is: Can I hold it? Can I walk in it? Can I embody what I have dared to believe?

Because manifestation is not about convincing the universe, it is about calibrating your spirit.

When you embody the vision, something profound begins to happen.

Your energy shifts. Your choices sharpen. Your voice carries more weight. You stop begging for signs and start breathing as the sign. You begin to walk like the door is already open. You dress like your future is already here. You speak like someone who knows they have already touched what they used to only imagine.

And that shift? It is magnetic.

It draws resources, relationships, divine appointments, opportunities, and realities to match the frequency you have stepped into.

Energy does not lie. The universe listens not just to your desire, but to your alignment.

So, walk tall. Live loud. Move with intention. Let your outer life mirror the sacred vision you carry within.

You do not have to be perfect. But you do have to be present. Present to your power. Present to your purpose. Present to the version of you that already knows how to rise.

Because that version? That future self you have dreamed of; that person has been waiting for you to remember.

And when you finally align with who you already are at your highest level, when you choose to embody the truth instead of just imagining it, and when you let your energy walk into the room before your words do—that is when the divine moves.

That is when the shift happens.

That is when manifestation becomes motion.

And that—is the sacred intersection where belief, reality, and the energy of the Universe itself combine—and become your manifestation.

Chapter 30: Living The Frequency
—Manifestation In Motion

Opening Reflection

"You are not merely a reflection of God—You are a vessel of Divine essence, radiating light into form. Every word you speak echoes the Divine voice within. You are the living, breathing frequency of what God, Yahweh, Allah, or the Universe manifested you to be—the embodiment of what this book has revealed: The Manifestation Frequency—in motion."
—Roy Waugh

Introduction

This is not the end of a book. It is the beginning of your embodiment.

You have walked through sacred truths, ancient wisdoms, and the unveiling of your own divine design. This journey was never about acquiring more knowledge—it was about remembering who you already are. And now, the invitation is clear: not just to believe it, but to become it.

You are not simply carrying the light—you are the light.
You are not waiting for a sign—you are the sign.

And this truth has been written into your very breath.

From the very beginning, you were already speaking the Divine. In the Hebrew tradition, the sacred name of God—YHWH—is composed only of breath sounds. Rabbis and mystics have taught that this Name cannot truly be spoken in ordinary language; it can only be breathed. The inhale whispers "Yah," the exhale sighs "weh." Your first cry at birth carries it. Your final breath releases it. Every moment in between is marked by the living rhythm of God's name on your lips, whether you realize it or not.

This is the mystery of frequency: you are not waiting to align with the Divine—you are already resonating with it. Each breath is a prayer. Each inhale and exhale is proof that you are a living echo of the Source. Manifestation, then, is not about forcing or striving—it is about remembering. Remembering that your very life is a vibration of that sacred Name, moving through you in every moment.

You are not separate from the Divine voice—you are its echo, its vessel, its vibration. More than that, YOU are the manifestation of the Divine itself—God, Yahweh, Allah, the Universe—breathing, moving, and becoming—through you.

This is what it means to live the frequency—not as theory, but as daily embodiment. This final chapter is about integration, where truth becomes lifestyle and alignment becomes devotion.

Because you were not created to only witness miracles.
You were created to become one.

Hidden Teachings from Ancient Traditions
—A Final Teaching

Before these truths were written in books or spoken on stages, they lived in breath, in silence, in firelight circles and whispered prayers. They traveled across deserts, through temples, over oceans—carried in the hearts of seekers and saints.

And now, having walked through every chapter of this journey, you carry them too. These ancient truths are not distant—they are alive within you.

What follows is not new information—it is ancient wisdom remembered.

Let this be your final blessing from the sacred lineages that have always known: **You were never separate from the Divine, you were simply waiting to awaken to it**.

From the Bible, we were shown:
"You shall decree a thing, and it will be established."

You are not just a servant of miracles—you are a co-creator with God himself.

From the Torah, we remember:
You were made b'tzelem Elohim—in the image of God.
Your worth was never in question.

From the Qur'an, we recall:
"With hardship comes ease."
You were never forgotten. Waiting was your preparation.

From the Buddhist path, we were taught:
"The mind is everything. What you think, you become."
Presence is power. Stillness is sanctuary.

From the Hindu tradition, we learned:
The Atman within you is one with Brahman.
The whole cosmos shifts when you speak your truth.

So, whether you chant or whisper, kneel or dance, meditate or pray, whether you seek your alignment in a temple or in your kitchen—know this: **You carry the hidden teachings now**—etched not just in books, but in the way you now breathe, love, and live. Woven from every lineage, every truth, every light-filled step you have taken.

My hope is that this helps you realize who you really are.

And just as wisdom once passed from scroll to soul, from teacher to seeker—you are now the living continuation of that sacred knowing.

Now is your time—not just to remember these sacred truths, but to become them, and to speak boldly, live fully, and pass this knowledge forward with sincere intentions.

The Practice of Awakened Living
—Daily Application and Integration for a Manifested Life

This book was never just meant to be read. It was meant to be practiced and lived.

Because manifestation isn't a one-time miracle; it's a rhythm— a rewiring, a daily remembering of who you truly are.

Neuroscience has shown us that what you practice, you strengthen. Repetition reshapes your brain. New thoughts create new pathways. Your body learns to harmonize with the identity you embody most often.

This is the invitation of awakened living—not to wait for transformation to arrive, but to become it through consistency, intention, and alignment.

Carry it forward by weaving it into your morning breath, your midday choices, your evening thoughts.

You speak like someone who believes.
You walk like someone who knows.
You return, again and again, to the vibration of your vision—until it feels like home in your body.

This is not a checklist—it is a sacred guide, a daily resonance recalibration; a gentle reminder that your thoughts emit frequency, your emotions encode meaning, and your body carries the blueprint of your belief.

You do not have to do it perfectly.
You only have to do it on purpose.

Because the awakened life is not a destination—it is a sacred devotion, a lived frequency, an embodied remembering.

Let this be your guide as you begin.

Live It Forward
—Daily Anchors for an Awakened Life

At Dawn — Align Your Breath.
1. Begin with stillness. Whisper an affirmation.
2. Envision your day flowing in peace and clarity.
3. Ask: What energy will I embody today?

At Midday — Return to Presence.
1. Pause between tasks. Breathe yourself back to center.
2. Check your posture, your tone, your thoughts.
3. Speak kindly—to yourself and others.
4. Ask: Am I moving from faith or from fear?

At Evening — Rest in Gratitude.
1. Scan your day gently, without judgment.
2. Celebrate the smallest wins; release what is heavy.
3. Whisper: I did my best today. Tomorrow I align even more deeply.

Weekly Rhythm — One Truth at a Time.
1. Choose one principle—trust, clarity, surrender.
2. Live it fully for seven days.
3. Write what awakens in you.

Sacred Reset — When You Forget.
1. Light a candle. Breathe slowly.
2. Speak a scripture, affirmation, or mantra aloud.
3. See yourself step back into alignment with grace and power.

Conclusion
—The Seed Remains

If you have reached this final page, then something in you has already begun to shift. Not just to believe—but to embody.

This book was never meant to entertain.

It was written soul-first, breath by breath, with one intention:

To ignite your divine frequency.

You are not just a seeker—you are a creator.
Not separate from the Divine, but a vessel of it.

Every story, every scripture, every reflection here was not only mine—it was a mirror. A reminder that you were meant for more.

This is the moment when these teachings stop being words on a page and start becoming your rhythm, your walk, your signature frequency.

So the question is no longer: What do you believe?
It is: What will you now embody?

Because you are not waiting on destiny—you are living it.
You are not hoping for a sign—you are the sign.
You are not dreaming of miracles—you are the miracle.

Every page has been a seed.
Now the seed is in you.
Not all bloom at once, but each is alive, vibrating with the power to become.
They know what to do. And so do you.

So breathe. Align. Speak. Create.
And let your life become the prayer.

You are the light.
You are the frequency.
You are the miracle.

Closing Breath Practice & Affirmation

(Sit quietly. Place one hand on your heart, the other on your belly.)

Inhale slowly and whisper:
"Yah..."

Exhale gently and whisper:
"...weh."

Feel the sacred Name move through you.

✧ **Every breath a prayer**.
✧ **Every inhale a receiving**.
✧ **Every exhale a becoming**.

Affirm aloud:

✧ **I am the light**.
✧ **I am the frequency**.
✧ **I am the miracle**.

Carry this rhythm with you.

Let each breath remind you:

✧ **You are never separate**.
✧ **You are always aligned**.
✧ **You are manifestation in motion**.

With every breathe, creation is listening—so go, speak, live and become...

Any thing is possible—if you just believe.

Thank you for walking this journey with me. If these pages have spoken to your heart, I invite you to let them keep speaking—by sharing them. Tell a friend, a loved one, anyone who needs to remember their own divine frequency. Together, we can help this message travel farther, touch more hearts and help others to awaken their own lives across the world.

Your voice *is the bridge that carries this frequency farther than I ever could alone."*

Share the frequency. Awaken the world.
Thank you — Roy Waugh

ACKNOWLEDGMENTS

To the Higher Power I call God—known by many names and felt in many ways—THANK YOU for the breath, the light, the vision, and the grace that carried every word of this book into being. You are the pulse beneath each page, the spark behind every sentence.

To my beloved spouse—thank you for your unwavering love, wisdom, and support. Your belief in me has been the steady hand at my back, your presence a reflection of answered prayer, and your partnership a gift I cherish with my whole being.

Thank you to my family—the family I was born into and the chosen family I found along the way. To those who held space for me, loved me into healing, and walked beside me in light when the road was dark, your presence became a kind of home I never knew I needed. I am grateful to stand where I can give back in love and strength.

To my readers—you are not here by accident; this journey was written with you in mind. Thank you for daring to believe that more is possible, and for allowing these words to awaken something profound, divine, and alive within you.

To the child I once was—thank you for holding on, believing in the unseen, and listening to the whisper in the dark; this is the life you dreamed of, and we have become it.

To every sacred voice that lent its light to this book—your wisdom helped illuminate the path and deepen the truth:

Maya Angelou, Denise Woods, the Dalai Lama, Oprah Winfrey, Louise Hay, Joyce Meyer, Neale Donald Walsch, Esther Hicks (Abraham), Eckhart Tolle, Rhonda Byrne, Elizabeth Gilbert, Iyanla Vanzant, Tara Brack, Albert Einstein, Dr. Wayne Dyer, Marianne Williamson, Deepak Chopra, Howard Thurman, Neville Godard, Margaret Thatcher, Michael Bernard Beckwith, Dannion Brinkley. And to the eternal wisdom found in the sacred texts of the Bible, the Qur'an, the Torah, the Dhammapada, the

Bhagavad Gita, the teachings of Buddha, and every spiritual tradition that echoes the truth of our oneness,

Thank you

Your words did more than inspire—they became part of the living fire that now lights the way for others.

This book was never written for applause—it was written to awaken. And if even one soul remembers who they are because of it, every word will have been worth it

With deepest gratitude,
Roy Waugh

ABOUT THE AUTHOR

Roy Waugh is a nationally recognized singer, motivational speaker, jewelry designer, and spiritual teacher, and performer whose life stands as a living testimony to the power of faith, resilience, and divine alignment. Shaped by hardship, perseverance, and an unshakable belief in what is possible, Roy's journey has inspired thousands to rise into their own light.

As a professional vocalist, Roy has graced stages across the country in the Contemporary Christian genre, opened for some of the most celebrated names in music, and has had numerous appearances on national television. But his true gift lies not just in his voice—but in the frequency behind it. Whether performing, speaking, or writing, Roy carries a signature energy—rooted in lived experience, spiritual depth, and a calling to awaken others to their inner power.

His story defies odds. At just four years old, Roy was struck by a car in a traumatic accident that should have ended his life—but instead became the spark of his first miracle. Years later, after self-funding his gymnastics training and pursuing an Olympic dream, a catastrophic spinal injury ruptured discs in his lower back. Doctors said he would never walk again.

But Roy did not surrender to limitation. Through a combination of unshakable belief, daily affirmations, spiritual alignment, years of recovery, and surgical intervention, he rose again.

Born into poverty and raised in a home marked by addiction, silence, and survival, Roy was unfamiliar with spirituality until his teenage years. His spiritual journey began not in doctrine—but in a raw, desperate cry for help. That moment of surrender became the first step into a lifelong walk of healing, awakening, and service.

Alongside his music and ministry, Roy became a goldsmith—turning a box of inherited loose gemstones into legacy pieces filled with story, light, and intention. Like his message, his artistry is a reflection of Divine creation—transformed through love and given as a gift.

As a speaker and teacher, Roy is known for his emotional depth, spiritual clarity, and rare ability to translate sacred truth into everyday life. His teachings draw from the Bible, the Qur'an, the Torah, the Dhammapada, the Bhagavad Gita, Buddha, and the voices of contemporary spiritual leaders—reminding us that the Divine speaks many languages, and every soul carries a spark of that voice.

The Manifestation Frequency: *Hidden Ancient Secrets Revealed to Awaken the Power Within* is more than a book. It is a sacred culmination of Roy's life—his scars, stories, breakthroughs, and his song—woven into an invitation for others to rise into their own frequency and remember who they truly are.

Roy's message is simple—but powerful:

"Anything is possible, if you just believe."

Sources

Chapter 1

Opening Reflection

Roy Waugh: "Every word you speak becomes a seed, a seed of infinite potential. When given the power of your intention, truth to root it in, time—and a touch of love—the harvest is inevitable."
(Original quote)

Wisdom from Contemporary Spiritual Leaders

- **Joyce Meyer**: "Words are containers for power; you choose what kind of power they carry."
  Source: Me and My Big Mouth! (Harrison House, 1997)

- **Deepak Chopra**: "Intention is the starting point of every dream."
  Source: The Seven Spiritual Laws of Success (New World Library, 1994)

- **Esther Hicks**: (Abraham-Hicks) "You are the creator of your own reality, and so you are the initiator of the vibration that creates it."
  Source: Ask and It Is Given by Esther and Jerry Hicks (Hay House, 2004)

- **Iyanla Vanzant,** "Words are the voice of the heart. Speak with intention, because every word you utter plants a seed in the world—and in you."
  Source: In the Meantime: Finding Yourself and the Love You Want (New York: Simon & Schuster, 1999)

- **Roy Waugh**: "Every word you speak becomes a seed—planted in the soil of your reality. If you want a sacred harvest, you must speak with sacred intent."
  (Original Quote)

Scientific Perspectives

✧Neuroscience of Thought

- Neuroplasticity: Repetition strengthens neural pathways.
  Source: Doidge, Norman, The Brain That Changes Itself (Penguin Books, 2007)

✧ Epigenetics and Belief

- "Your perception controls your biology."

- Source: Lipton, Bruce H., The Biology of Belief (Hay House, 2005)

✧ Quantum Physics and Attention

- The double-slit experiment shows that observation affects particle behavior.

- Source: Greene, Brian, The Fabric of the Cosmos (Knopf, 2004)

✧ Vibrational Effects on Matter

- Masaru Emoto's water crystal experiments showed the effects of words on water molecule formation.

- Source: Emoto, Masaru, The Hidden Messages in Water (Atria Books, 2004)

Chapter 2

Opening Reflection

Henry Ford: "Whether you think you can, or whether you think you can't—you're right."

Source: Hill, Napoleon. Think and Grow Rich. (Cleveland: The Ralston Society, 1937) (Paraphrased)

Wisdom from Contemporary Spiritual Leaders

- **Maya Angelou**: "I believed that I was born to do something. That belief has made all the difference."
  Source: Quoted in Rainbow in the Cloud: The Wisdom and Spirit of Maya Angelou (Random House, 2014)

- **Iyanla Vanzant**: "You cannot expect to live a positive life with a negative mind."

- Source: Frequently quoted across her media appearances and books; widely attributed with no single published origin

- **Rhonda Byrne**: "When you truly believe that you are worthy of receiving, and feel it as your truth, you become magnetic to the manifestation."

- Source: The Secret (Atria Books, 2006)

- **Roy Waugh**: "Belief isn't just a mindset—it's the spiritual DNA of everything you're manifesting."

- (Original Quote)

Scientific Perspectives

✧ **Neuroscience of Belief**

- Repetition of belief strengthens neural pathways (neuroplasticity). Source: Doidge, Norman, The Brain That Changes Itself (Penguin Books, 2007)

✧ **Confirmation Bias**

- The brain filters reality to confirm existing beliefs.

- Source: Nickerson, Raymond S., "Confirmation Bias: A Ubiquitous Phenomenon in Many Guises." (Review of General Psychology, vol. 2, no. 2, 1998, pp. 175–220)

✧ **The Placebo Effect**

- Belief can trigger real healing responses in the body. Source: Benedetti, Fabrizio, Placebo Effects: Understanding the Mechanisms in Health and Disease (Oxford University Press, 2009)

✧ **Belief as Energy**

- Vibrational frequency linked to thought and emotional alignment (resonance principle). Note: Metaphysical interpretation; aligns with teachings.

- Source: Lipton, Bruce H., The Biology of Belief (Hay House, 2005)

Chapter 3

Opening Reflection

"By the word of the Lord the heavens were made, their starry host by the breath of His mouth."

Source: Psalm 33:6 (JPS Tanakh)

Wisdom from Contemporary Spiritual Leaders

- **Iyanla Vanzant**: "Your words create your world."
  Source: Common teaching across her books and appearances; notably in Acts of Faith (Simon & Schuster, 1993)

- **Oprah Winfrey**: "You become what you believe, not what you want."
  Source: The Life You Want Tour (2014), media appearances, and What I Know for Sure (Flatiron Books, 2014)

- **Denise Woods**: "Your voice carries more than words—it carries your energy."
  Source: The Power of Voice: A Guide to Making Yourself Heard (HarperOne, 2021)

- **Abraham Hicks**: "When you speak your desires aloud with conviction, you align your vibration with the reality you seek."
  Source: The Law of Attraction: The Basics of the Teachings of Abraham (Hay House, 2006)

- **Roy Waugh**: "Your words are like a boomerang. Be careful what you throw out there—it might come back and hit you in the blessings... or in the forehead."
  (Original Quote)

Scientific Perspectives

✧ Cymatics and Sound Vibration

- Cymatics shows how sound shapes matter.
  Source: Jenny, Hans, Cymatics: A Study of Wave Phenomena and Vibration (MACROmedia Press, 2001)

✧ Neuroscience and Self-Talk

- Positive affirmations and repeated speech activate neuroplasticity.
  Source: Doidge, Norman, The Brain That Changes Itself (Penguin Books, 2007) Quote: "Nerve cells that fire together, wire together."
  Source: Hebbian principle, Dr. Joe Dispenza, Breaking the Habit of Being Yourself (Hay House, 2012)

✧ Quantum Physics and the Observer Effect

- Language and intention influence perception and observed outcomes.
  Source: Greene, Brian. The Fabric of the Cosmos (Knopf, 2004); general commentary on observer effect in quantum physics

✧ The Biological Impact of Spoken Intention

- Spoken affirmations affect the nervous system, heart rate, and stress levels.
  Source: Seppälä, Emma, "The Science of the Voice." Scientific American Mind, vol. 26, no. 5, 2015; also supported in studies by Dr. Herbert Benson (The Relaxation Response, HarperTorch, 2000)

Chapter 4

Opening Reflection

Albert Einstein: "Everything in life is vibration."
Attribution to Albert Einstein is widely cited, though no primary source confirms he said this verbatim. Used as a popular paraphrase.

Wisdom from Contemporary Spiritual Leaders

- **Esther Hicks**: "You are a vibrational being in a vibrational universe."
  Source: The Law of Attraction by Esther and Jerry Hicks (Hay House, 2006)

- **Dr. Joe Dispenza**: "The moment you feel abundant and worthy, you are generating wealth."
  Source: Becoming Supernatural (Hay House, 2017)

- **Louise Hay**: "What I give out comes back to me."
  Source: You Can Heal Your Life (Hay House, 1984)

- **Albert Einstein**: "Everything is energy, and that's all there is to it. Match the frequency..."
  Popular paraphrase; not directly traceable to a verified written or recorded source. Commonly attributed but disputed in academic circles.

- **Roy Waugh**: "If your energy is off, it doesn't matter how gorgeous your vision board looks—you're just sending glittery desperation into the universe."
  (Original Quote)

Scientific Perspectives

- ✧**Quantum Physics and the Frequency Field Quantum mechanics**
  All matter is energy vibrating at frequencies.
  Source: Greene, Brian, The Fabric of the Cosmos (Knopf, 2004); Einstein's paraphrase widely referenced, but not verified in his writings

✧ The Heart's Electromagnetic Power

- The heart's electromagnetic field is up to 60x stronger than the brain's.
  Source: HeartMath Institute, McCraty, Rollin, "The Energetic Heart: Bioelectromagnetic Communication Within and Between People."
  (HeartMath Research Center, 2003)

✧ Neuroscience and Emotional Conditioning

- Neuroplasticity and emotional states.
  Source: Lipton, Bruce, The Biology of Belief (Hay House, 2005)

- Quote: "The moment you change your perception is the moment you rewrite the chemistry of your body."
  Source: Lipton, Bruce H., The Biology of Belief: Unleashing the Power of Consciousness, Matter & Miracles (Santa Rosa, CA: Mountain of Love/ Elite Books, 2005), p. 111.

✧ Energy Psychology and Embodied Resonance

- Somatic therapies confirm that vibration affects immune and hormonal systems.
  Source: Fred Gallo, Energy Psychology (CRC Press, 2002)

- Source: Psalm 34:5 – "Those who look to Him are radiant; their faces are never covered with shame." (NIV)

Chapter 5

Opening Reflection

"...Faith is the substance of things hoped for, the evidence of things not seen."
Source: Hebrews 11:1 (KJV)

Wisdom from Contemporary Spiritual Leaders

- **Joyce Meyer**: "Faith is not believing that God can—it's knowing that He will."
  Source: Joyce Meyer Ministries; often cited in her teachings and devotionals such as Battlefield of the Mind (Warner Faith, 2002)

- **Rhonda Byrne**: "Faith is trusting in the unseen and being certain of what you hope for."
  Source: Paraphrased from The Secret (Atria Books, 2006); aligns with Hebrews 11:1 interpretation

- **Eckhart Tolle**: "Faith is the substance of surrender."
  Source: Paraphrased from Tolle's teachings; similar phrasing appears in The Power of Now (New World Library, 1999)

- **Iyanla Vanzant**: "Faith is the light that guides you through the darkness—not away from it, but through it."
  Source: Paraphrased teaching consistent with Acts of Faith (Simon & Schuster, 1993)

- **Roy Waugh**: "Faith is not crossing your fingers—it is opening your heart to what has not yet arrived..."
  (Original Quote)

Scientific Perspectives

✧ The Placebo Effect

- Mind-body healing based on belief.
  Source: Benedetti, Fabrizio. Placebo Effects: Understanding the Mechanisms in Health and Disease (Oxford University Press, 2009)

✧ Neuroscience: Predictive Processing and Expectation

- The brain anticipates based on belief and prepares bodily responses.
  Source: Clark, Andy. "Whatever Next? Predictive Brains, Situated Agents, and the Future of Cognitive Science." Behavioral and Brain Sciences, vol. 36, no. 3, 2013

✧ Cognitive Bias and Selective Attention

- Confirmation bias: Belief filters perception and attention.
  Source: Nickerson, Raymond S. "Confirmation Bias: A Ubiquitous Phenomenon in Many Guises." Review of General Psychology, 1998

✧ Quantum Observation

- Observer effect suggests consciousness influences quantum behavior.
  Source: Rosenblum, Bruce & Kuttner, Fred. Quantum Enigma: Physics Encounters Consciousness (Oxford University Press, 2011)

Chapter 6

Opening Reflection

Roy Waugh: "Your heart knows the way. Run in that direction."
Source: Often attributed to Rumi. (Paraphrased)

Wisdom from Contemporary Spiritual Leaders

- **Abraham Hicks**: "Desire is the beginning of all new creation."
  Source: Esther Hicks, Ask and It Is Given, Hay House, 2004

- **Oprah Winfrey**: "Every right decision I've ever made has come from my gut."

Source: Oprah Winfrey, interview in O, The Oprah Magazine (various issues); public keynote speeches.

- **Elizabeth Gilbert**: "Your curiosity is a clue. Follow it."
  Source: Elizabeth Gilbert, Big Magic: Creative Living Beyond Fear (Riverhead Books, 2015)

- **Deepak Chopra**: "The desire to improve your life, to grow spiritually, to love more deeply—is a divine impulse."
  Source: Deepak Chopra, teachings in The Seven Spiritual Laws of Success (New World Library, 1994)

- **Roy Waugh**: "The desire that will not let go of you—that quiet pull that returns in your stillest moments—is not a distraction. It is direction."
  (Original Quote)

Scientific Perspectives

✧ Psychological Research

- Self-Determination Theory.
  Source: Edward L. Deci and Richard M. Ryan, Intrinsic Motivation and Self-Determination in Human Behavior (Springer, 1985)

✧ Neuroscience of Desire

- Dopaminergic Pathways and Motivation.
  Source: Berridge, Kent C. & Robinson, Terry E., "Parsing reward" (Trends in Neurosciences, Vol. 26, No. 9, 2003).

✧ Quantum Perspective

- Energy and Vibrational Field Theory.
  Source: Dispenza, Joe. Becoming Supernatural: How Common People Are Doing the Uncommon (Hay House, 2017)

✧ Heart Coherence and Electromagnetic Field

- HeartMath Institute Research.
  Source: McCraty, Rollin et al., "The Energetic Heart: Bioelectromagnetic

Communication Within and Between People" (HeartMath Research Center, 2003)

Chapter 7

Opening Reflection

"Do you not know that your bodies are temples of the Holy Spirit, who is in you...?"
Source: 1 Corinthians 6:19 (NIV)

Wisdom from Contemporary Spiritual Leaders

- **Dr. Joe Dispenza**: "When you change your internal state, you change your external reality."
  Source: Dr. Joe Dispenza, Breaking the Habit of Being Yourself (Hay House, 2012)

- **Joyce Meyer**: "You cannot have a positive life and a negative mind."
  Source: Joyce Meyer, Battlefield of the Mind (FaithWords, 1995)

- **Maya Angelou**: "Nothing can dim the light that shines from within."
  Source: Maya Angelou, Letter to My Daughter (Random House, 2008)

- **Tara Brach**: "The sacred pause is the first step in the dance of intimacy."
  Source: Tara Brach, Radical Acceptance (Bantam Books, 2003)

- **Roy Waugh**: "You do not need to go mountain climbing to find God. Sometimes the holiest place is the quiet corner of your own mind—right between your last doubt and your next breath.
  (Original Quote)

Scientific Perspectives on the Inner State

✧ Neuroscience

- Reticular Activating System. (RAS)
  Source: Baars, Bernard J., In the Theater of Consciousness: The Workspace of the Mind. (Oxford University Press, 1997)

- Neuroplasticity.
  Source: Doidge, Norman, The Brain That Changes Itself. (Viking Penguin, 2007)

✧ Quantum Physics

- Observer Effect in Quantum Mechanics.
  Source: Rosenblum, Bruce & Kuttner, Fred. Quantum Enigma: Physics Encounters Consciousness, (Oxford University Press, 2006)

✧ Heart-Based Research

- HeartMath Institute.
  Source: McCraty, Rollin et al., "The Energetic Heart: Bioelectromagnetic Communication Within and Between People" (HeartMath Research Center, 2003)

Chapter 8

Opening Reflection

Roy Waugh: "Gratitude is the bridge between your desire and its arrival. Give thanks as if it is already yours, and the Universe has no choice but to respond."
Inspired by Abraham Hicks. (Original Quote)

Wisdom from Contemporary Spiritual Leaders

- **Dr. Joe Dispenza**: "Gratitude is the ultimate state of receivership."
  Source: Becoming Supernatural. (Hay House, 2017)

- **Oprah Winfrey**:— "Be thankful for what you have; you'll end up having more."
  Source: What I Know for Sure. (Flatiron Books, 2014)

- **Louise Hay**: "The universe loves gratitude. The more grateful you are, the more goodies you get."
  Source: You Can Heal Your Life. (Hay House, 1984)

- **Esther Hicks**: (Abraham) "Appreciation in advance brings everything you want to you."
  Source: The Law of Attraction. (Hay House, 2006)

- **Deepak Chopra**: "Gratitude opens the door to...the power, the wisdom, the creativity of the universe."
  Source: The Seven Spiritual Laws of Success. (New World Library, 1994)

- **Albert Einstein**: "There are only two ways to live your life. One is as though nothing is a miracle. The other is as though everything is a miracle."
  Source: Often attributed; widely cited in The World As I See It. (Citadel, 2006)

- **Roy Waugh**: "When you say thank you before the blessing shows up, you are not pretending—it is prophecy."
  (Original Quote)

Scientific Perspectives

✧ Neuroscience

- Gratitude activates the prefrontal cortex, releases dopamine, and serotonin.
  Source: Fox, G.R. et al., Neural correlates of gratitude. (Frontiers in Psychology, 2015)

- Reticular Activating System (RAS) Filters for focused awareness. Source: Heath, R., Exploring the RAS and goal setting. (Educational Leadership, 1996)

✧ Epigenetics

- Gratitude downregulates inflammatory genes and upregulates immune function.
  Source: Fredrickson, B.L., Grewen, K.M., Coffey, K.A., Algoe, S.B., Firestine, A.M., Arevalo, J.M., Ma, J., & Cole, S.W., Proceedings of the National Academy of Sciences of the United States of America (PNAS), 110(33), 13684–13689 (National Academy of Sciences 2013)

✧ Psychophysiology / Heart-Brain Coherence

- Gratitude induces heart-brain coherence, measurable electromagnetic shifts.
  Source: McCraty, R., & Childre, D., The Appreciative Heart: The Psychophysiology of Positive Emotions and Optimal Functioning. (HeartMath Institute 2004)

Chapter 9

Opening Reflection

Roy Waugh: "When you want something, the universe conspires to deliver it. But it is not your wanting that unlocks the flow—it is your alignment. When your heart, mind, and energy say yes in harmony, manifestation becomes motion." Inspired by Paulo Coelho's The Alchemist.
(Original Quote)

Wisdom from Contemporary Spiritual Leaders

- **Abraham Hicks**: "You cannot have what you are not willing to become."
  Source: Ask and It Is Given (Hay House, 2004)

- **Iyanla Vanzant**: "You must master you, before you can master manifestation."
  Source: Widely attributed; included in her teachings and public talks (e.g., Fix My Life, OWN Network)

- **Dr. Joe Dispenza**: "When your thoughts and feelings are out of sync, you send mixed signals to the universe."
  Source: Becoming Supernatural (Hay House, 2017)

- **Maya Angelou**: "When you know better, do better."
  Source: Oprah's Master Class, OWN, also attributed in Maya Angelou: The Legacy of Style

- **Roy Waugh**: "You can't manifest what your mouth says yes to if your spirit keeps whispering no. Alignment isn't performance—it's permission."
  (Original Quote)

Scientific Perspectives

✧ Neuroscience and Alignment

- Neuroplasticity and alignment — Joe Dispenza emphasizes that sustained thought-emotion coherence rewires the brain.
  Source: Dispenza, J., Becoming Supernatural (Hay House, 2017)

✧ Heart-Brain Coherence

- HeartMath Institute research — Heart coherence created through gratitude and calm emotional states.
  Source: McCraty, R., & Childre, D., The Appreciative Heart. (HeartMath Institute, 2004)

✧ Epigenetics and Internal Agreement

- Gene expression influenced by belief — Bruce Lipton.
  Source: Lipton, B.H., The Biology of Belief. (Hay House, 2005)

✧ Psychophysiology of Resonance

- Coherence and tuning fork metaphor.
  Source: Childre, D., & Martin, H., The HeartMath Solution, (HarperOne, 1999)

- Human biofield coherence and resonance research.
  Source: McCraty, Rollin, and Dana Tomasino, Coherence: Bridging Personal, Social, and Global Health. Global Advances in Health and Medicine 3, no.2 56-64. (SAGE Publications on behalf of the Academic Consortium for Integrative Medicine and Health, 2014)

Chapter 10

Opening Reflection

"For I know the plans I have for you," declares the Lord, "plans to prosper you and not to harm you, plans to give you a future and a hope."
Source: Jeremiah 29:11 (NIV)

Wisdom from Contemporary Spiritual Leaders

- **Joyce Meyer**: "God is never late, but He's also rarely early. He is always right on time."

Source: Joyce Meyer Ministries, Teaching Broadcasts & Books (e.g., Trusting God Day by Day, FaithWords, 2012)

- **Rhonda Byrne**: "When you believe, you know. You are calm, you are at peace."
  Source: The Power. (Atria Books, 2010)

- **Eckhart Tolle**: "Realize deeply that the present moment is all you ever have."
  Source: The Power of Now. (New World Library, 1997)

- **Iyanla Vanzant**: "Everything that happens is exactly what needs to happen to bring us into the next moment of our evolution."
  Source: Widely quoted from lectures and appearances; consistent with Vanzant's themes in One Day My Soul Just Opened Up. (Fireside, 1998)

- **Roy Waugh**: "Trust that God knows what He is doing. He sees the whole map—we are just staring at the next hill..."
  (Original Quote)

Scientific Perspectives

✧ The Neuroscience of Delay and Reward

- Prefrontal cortex and self-regulation — Related to delayed gratification and resilience.
  Source: Mischel, Walter, Yuichi Shoda, and Monica L. Rodriguez, "Delay of Gratification in Children." Science 244, no. 4907: 933–938. (American Association for the Advancement of Science [AAAS] 1989)

- Cognitive and attentional mechanisms in delay of gratification.
  Source: Journal of Personality and Social Psychology. Mischel, Walter, Ebbesen, Ebbe B., and Raskoff Zeiss, Antonette. Journal of Personality and Social Psychology 21, no. 2: 204–218. (American Psychological Association, 1972)

- The Marshmallow Experiment: Mastering Self-Control.
  Source: Mischel, W., The Marshmallow Test. (Little, Brown and Company, 2014)

✧ Quantum Possibility and Divine Delay

- Observer effect in quantum physics — Observing affects the outcome.
  Source: Heisenberg, W., Heisenberg's Uncertainty Principle. (Springer-Verlag 1927)

- Quantum Physics for a General Audience.
  Source: Greene, Brian, The Fabric of the Cosmos: Space, Time, and the Texture of Reality. (Vintage Books, a division of Random House, 2004)

- Conceptual Application in Spirituality.
  Source: Goswami, A., The Quantum Doctor: A Physicist's Guide to Health and Healing.(Hampton Roads, 2004).

✧ Chronobiology and Rhythmic Alignment

- Chronobiology and circadian rhythm — Biological timing and wellness.
  Circadian Rhythms: Basic Neurobiology and Clinical Applications.
  Source: Moore, R.Y. Circadian Rhythms: Basic Neurobiology and Clinical Applications. Annual Review of Medicine 48, no. 1: 253–266. (Annual Review of Medicine, 1997)

- Melatonin and the Mammalian Pineal Gland.
  Source: Arendt, J., (Chapman & Hall, 1995)

Chapter 11

Opening Reflection

Roy Waugh: "You were never meant to beg for what is already in your spiritual inheritance. You were born worthy. The moment you believe it... the gates open."
(Original Quote)

Wisdom from Contemporary Spiritual Leaders

- **Louise Hay**: "You've been criticizing yourself for years, and it hasn't worked. Try approving of yourself and see what happens."
  Source: You Can Heal Your Life. (Hay House, 1984)

- **Iyanla Vanzant**: "Your willingness to look at your darkness is what empowers you to manifest your light."

Source: One Day My Soul Just Opened Up (Fireside/Simon & Schuster, 1998)

- **Abraham Hicks**: "You are worthy because you exist. You don't need to prove or earn—it is your birthright."
Source: Ask and It Is Given, Esther and Jerry Hicks. (Hay House, 2004)

- **Denise Woods**: "Your voice is shaped by your self-perception."
Source: The Power of Voice. (Harper One, 2021)

- **Roy Waugh**: "You're not waiting on the blessing—the blessing is waiting on you to remember who you are."
(Original Quote)

Scientific Perspectives

✧ Neuroscience of Self-Worth

- Neural correlates of social exclusion during adolescence: Understanding the role of the ventrolateral prefrontal cortex.
Source: Masten, C.L., Eisenberger, N.I., & Pfeifer, J.H., Developmental Science, 12(5), 847–861., (Wiley-Blackwell [on behalf of the Society for Research in Child Development] 2009)

- Mindset: The New Psychology of Success.
Source: Dweck, C.S. (Random House, 2006)

✧ Self-Fulfilling Prophecy and Cognitive Bias

- Source: Rosenthal, R., & Jacobson, L., Pygmalion in the Classroom. (Holt, Rinehart & Winston, 1968) Aronson, E., Wilson, T.D., Akert, R.M., Social Psychology. (Pearson, 2010)

✧ Heart-Brain Coherence and Receptivity

- Science of the Heart: Exploring the Role of the Heart in Human Performance."
Source: McCraty, R., Atkinson, M., & Tomasino, D., HeartMath Research Center. (Institute of HeartMath, 2001)

- The effects of emotions on short-term power spectrum analysis of heart rate variability."
Source: Rein, G., McCraty, R., & Rollin, M., Journal of Advancement in Medicine, 10(4), 87–105, (Mary Ann Liebert, Inc. 1995)

Chapter 12

Opening Reflection

Maya Angelou: "Words mean more than what is set down on paper. It takes the human voice to infuse them with deeper meaning."
Source: Maya Angelou, I Know Why the Caged Bird Sings (New York: Random House, 1969)

Wisdom from Contemporary Spiritual Leaders

- **Howard Thurman**: "There is something in every one of you that waits and listens for the sound of the genuine in yourself. It is the only true guide you will ever have."
Source: (The Sound of the Genuine, 1980 lecture)

- **Oprah Winfrey**: "You have the ability to change somebody's life with your words."
Source: Oprah Winfrey, What I Know for Sure (Flatiron Books, 2014)

- **Iyanla Vanzant**: "Your words are your wand. They create your reality."
Source: Popularized in modern teaching by Iyanla Vanzant. Florence Scovel Shinn, The Game of Life and How to Play It (Brentano's, 1925)

- **Dannion Brinkley**: "Every thought and word is energy. Once released, it continues to exist. Words can heal or harm, uplift or destroy."
Source: Dannion Brinkley with Kathryn Peters-Brinkley, Secrets of the Light: Lessons from Heaven (Hampton Roads, 2008)

- **Roy Waugh**: "Silence holds potential, but speech activates creation. What you dare to speak, you give permission to exist."
(Original Quote)

Scientific Perspectives

✦ Neuroscience: The Brain on Words

- Source: Andrew Newberg and Mark Robert Waldman, Words Can Change Your Brain: 12 Conversation Strategies to Build Trust, Resolve Conflict, and Increase Intimacy (Hudson Street Press, 2012).

✦ Psychology: The Pygmalion Effect

- Source: Robert Rosenthal and Lenore Jacobson, Pygmalion in the Classroom: Teacher Expectation and Pupils' Intellectual Development (Holt, Rinehart and Winston, 1968).

✦ Health and Medicine: Words as Healing Agents

- Source: James W. Pennebaker, Opening Up: The Healing Power of Expressing Emotions (Guilford Press, 1997).

✦ Quantum Linguistics: Language Shapes Perception

- Source: Benjamin Lee Whorf, Language, Thought, and Reality: Selected Writings of Benjamin Lee Whorf, ed. John B. Carroll (Cambridge, MA: MIT Press, 1956).

Chapter 13

Opening Reflection

Roy Waugh: "Anything is possible... if you just believe."
(Original Quote)

Wisdom from Contemporary Spiritual Leaders

- **Dr. Joe Dispenza**: "To change your life, you have to change your beliefs."
  Source: Breaking the Habit of Being Yourself (Hay House, 2012)

- **Abraham Hicks**: "A belief is just a thought you keep thinking."
  Source: Ask and It Is Given by Esther and Jerry Hicks (Hay House, 2004)

- **Iyanla Vanzant**: "The only thing keeping you from your next level is what you believe you can't have."
  Source: Acts of Faith (Simon & Schuster, 1993)

- **Louise Hay**: "I am open and receptive to all the good and abundance in the Universe."
  Source: You Can Heal Your Life (Hay House, 1984)

- **Maya Angelou**: "I believed I could speak truth and that it would matter. And so, I did."
  Source: Paraphrased from various interviews and public speeches; closest attribution: (Maya Angelou interview with Oprah Winfrey, 1997) No official publication title available.

- **Roy Waugh**: "Your voice does not just describe your life—it designs it."
  (Original Quote)

Scientific Perspectives

✧ The Placebo Effect: Belief as Medicine

- Source: Benedetti, Fabrizio. Placebo Effects: Understanding the Mechanisms in Health and Disease. (Oxford University Press, 2008)

✧ Neuroplasticity: Rewiring Your Reality

- Source: Doidge, Norman. The Brain That Changes Itself. Viking (Penguin, 2007)

✧ Quantum Mechanics: The Observer Effect

- Source: Rosenblum, Bruce, and Fred Kuttner. Quantum Enigma: Physics Encounters Consciousness. (Oxford University Press, 2006)

Chapter 14

Opening Reflection

Roy Waugh: "The weight you carry was never yours. Let go—and the path will rise to meet you."
(Original Quote)

Wisdom from Contemporary Spiritual Leaders

- **Louise Hay**: "I do not fix problems. I fix my thinking. Then problems fix themselves."
  Source: You Can Heal Your Life. (Hay House, 1984)

- **Esther Hicks**: (Abraham) "Manifestation becomes effortless when we stop 'efforting.'"
  Source: The Vortex: Where the Law of Attraction Assembles All Cooperative Relationships. (Hay House, 2009)

- **Oprah Winfrey**: "I let go and trusted that life would unfold as it was meant to."
  Source: What I Know For Sure. (Flatiron Books, 2014)

- **Dr. Wayne Dyer**: "Let go and let God."
  Source: Commonly attributed phrase used throughout Dyer's works, e.g., You'll See It When You Believe It, HarperOne, 2001.

- **Joyce Meyer**: "You can't cast your cares on God and keep worrying about them at the same time."
  Source: Battlefield of the Mind. (Warner Faith, 1995)

- **Roy Waugh**: "Letting go is not losing... it is making space for what is already yours."
  (Original Quote)

Scientific Perspectives

✧ **Neuroscience of Letting Go**

- Dr. Judson Brewer — Research on mindfulness and the brain's default mode network.
  Source: The Craving Mind. (Yale University Press, 2017)

✧ **Flow State and Peak Performance**

- Mihaly Csikszentmihalyi — Concept of "Flow".
  Source: Flow: The Psychology of Optimal Experience. (Harper & Row, 1990)

✧ Heart-Brain Coherence

- HeartMath Institute — Studies on emotional coherence and nervous system regulation.
  Source: Science of the Heart. (HeartMath Institute, 2016)

✧ Quantum Observations and Allowing

- Observer Effect — A Scientific principle from quantum mechanics.
  Source: General quantum theory, often referenced in works like The Quantum Enigma by Bruce Rosenblum and Fred Kuttner. (Oxford University Press, 2011)

✧ The Biology of Trust

- Dr. Bruce Lipton — "Belief controls biology" concept.
  Source: The Biology of Belief. (Hay House, 2005)

Chapter 15

Opening Reflection

Roy Waugh: "Don't wait to receive it. Become the energy of what you've asked for, and let your life rise to match the frequency of your desire." (Original Quote)

Wisdom from Contemporary Spiritual Leaders

- **Dr. Joe Dispenza**: "The body must experience it as real now. The future is drawn to the one who already feels it."
  Source: Becoming Supernatural. (Hay House, 2017)

- **Neville Goddard**: "Assume the feeling of the wish fulfilled."
  Source: The Power of Awareness. (DeVorss & Company, 1952)

- **Esther Hicks**: (Abraham) — "You must become a vibrational match to what you want."
  Source: Ask and It Is Given. (Hay House, 2004)

- **Louise Hay**: "What you think and what you believe will create your reality."
  Source: You Can Heal Your Life. (Hay House, 1984)

- **Maya Angelou**: Embodied her teachings through lived presence and grace.
  Source: Drawn from public interviews and memoirs, such as " A Letter to My Daughter. (Random House, 2008)

- **Roy Waugh**: "Become the vibration of your vision, and the universe will respond—echoing your frequency back to you in the same form." (Original Quote)

Scientific Perspectives

✧ Neuroscience and Mental Rehearsal

- Dr. Joe Dispenza — "Nerve cells that fire together wire together."
  Source: Breaking the Habit of Being Yourself. (Hay House, 2012)

✧ Embodiment and the Nervous System

- Dr. Candace Pert — Research linking emotions to physiological changes through neuropeptides.
  Source: Molecules of Emotion. (Scribner, 1997)

- Psychoneuroimmunology studies on cortisol and DHEA regulation.
  Source: American Journal of Psychiatry, various authors, ongoing research field.

✧ Quantum Physics and Resonance

- Bruce H. Lipton — "The energy you broadcast is the energy that returns to you."
  Source: The Biology of Belief. (Hay House, 2005)

✧ Behavioral Science and Embodied Identity

- Daryl Bem — Self-Perception Theory (1972).
  Source: (Journal of Personality and Social Psychology, Vol. 7(1), 1972, pp. 183–200)

Chapter 16

Opening Reflection

Roy Waugh: "When the heart is open and the hands release control, the gifts of the universe flow like water."
(Original Quote)

Wisdom from Contemporary Spiritual Leaders

- **Louise Hay**: "We must be open and receptive to all the good and abundance in the Universe."
  Source: Louise Hay, You Can Heal Your Life. (Hay House, 1984)

- **Abraham Hicks**: "You don't need to work harder. You just need to stop resisting. Allowing is the art of letting what you've asked for come in."
  Source: Esther and Jerry Hicks, The Amazing Power of Deliberate Intent. (Hay House, 2006)

- **Iyanla Vanzant**: "The capacity to receive is a soul issue."
  Source: Iyanla Vanzant, Acts of Faith. (Simon & Schuster, 1993)

- **Eckhart Tolle**: "This moment is complete. The more you honor it, the more open you become to miracles unfolding in the next one."
  Paraphrased from: Eckhart Tolle, The Power of Now. (New World Library, 1997)

- **Roy Waugh**: "The universe knocks softly. It is not trying to convince you—only to see if you are home."
  (Original Quote)

Scientific Perspectives

✧ **Psychology**

- Receptivity Quotient — Based on positive psychology studies of well-being and openness.
  Source example: Barbara Fredrickson, "The Role of Positive Emotions in Positive Psychology," (American Psychologist, 2001)

✧ **Neuroscience**

- Reticular Activating System (RAS) — Focuses attention and filters for relevance based on beliefs and expectations.

Source: Mark Waldman & Andrew Newberg, Words Can Change Your Brain. (Hudson Street Press, 2012)

✧ Gratitude & Nervous System

- Gratitude activates the parasympathetic nervous system and lowers cortisol.
Source: Glenn R. Fox et al., "Neural Correlates of Gratitude." (Frontiers in Psychology, 2015)

✧ Quantum Physics

- Wave function collapse — Based on the observer effect in quantum mechanics.
Source: Amit Goswami, The Self-Aware Universe. (Tarcher, 1995)

✧ Behavioral Science

- Identity influences receiving behavior and abundance perception.
Source: James Clear, Atomic Habits. (Avery, 2018)

Chapter 17

Opening Reflection

Frank Outlaw: "Watch your thoughts, they become words; watch your words, they become actions; watch your actions, they become habits; watch your habits, they become character; watch your character, for it becomes your destiny."
Source: The original publication source is unknown; it has been widely circulated since at least the 1970s.

Wisdom from Contemporary Spiritual Leaders

- **Dr. Joe Dispenza**: "Energy flows where attention goes."
Source: Becoming Supernatural (Hay House, 2017)

- **Abraham Hicks**: "You get what you think about, whether you want it or not."
Source: Ask and It Is Given by Esther and Jerry Hicks (Hay House, 2004)

- **Oprah Winfrey**: "Whatever you focus on expands."
  Source: The Wisdom of Sundays (Flatiron Books, 2017)

- **Iyanla Vanzant**: "Your energy introduces you before you speak."
  Source: Acts of Faith: Daily Meditations for People of Color. (Simon & Schuster, 1993)

- **Albert Einstein**: "I am thankful to all those who said no. It is because of them I'm doing it myself."
  Note: Widely attributed, but no scholarly record confirms it as his. Considered apocryphal.

- **Dannion Brinkley**: "What you think is what you are…"
  Source: Saved by the Light (HarperOne, 1994)

- **Roy Waugh**: "Focus is more than paying attention—it is a sacred lens…"
  (Original Quote)

Scientific Perspectives

✧ Neuroscience

- Neuroplasticity.
  Source: Dr. Joe Dispenza, Breaking the Habit of Being Yourself (Hay House, 2012)

✧ Behavioral Neuroscience

- Reticular Activating System. (RAS)
  Source: The Power of Your Subconscious Mind by Joseph Murphy (TarcherPerigee, 2001 edition)

✧ Performance Psychology

- Visualization and neural activation.
  Source: Pascual-Leone et al., "The Plastic Human Brain Cortex." (Annual Review of Neuroscience, 2005)

✧ Quantum Physics

- Observer Effect.
  Source: Richard Feynman, The Feynman Lectures on Physics (Addison-Wesley, 1964)

Chapter 18

Opening Reflection

Roy Waugh: "Faith and attitude are loud at the beginning. But persistence? Persistence is that quiet voice that keeps nudging you, whispering 'keep going,' even when everything around you goes silent."(Original Quote)

Wisdom from Contemporary Spiritual Leaders

- **Dr. Joe Dispenza**: "Your brain is a record of the past, but your mind is a map of the future."
  Source: Joe Dispenza, Breaking the Habit of Being Yourself: How to Lose Your Mind and Create a New One. (Hay House, 2012), p. 34.

- **Joyce Meyer**: "You don't need to feel like it to do it."
  Source: Meyer, Joyce. Battlefield of the Mind: Winning the Battle in Your Mind. (FaithWords, 2002)

- **Iyanla Vanzant**: "You have to do the work, keep showing up, and trust that the results are coming—even if you don't see them yet."
  Source: Vanzant, Iyanla. Trust: Mastering the Four Essential Trusts. (Hay House, 2015)

- **Abraham Hicks**: "Your only job is to stay in the receiving mode. The rest is coming."
  Source: Hicks, Esther and Jerry. Ask and It Is Given: Learning to Manifest Your Desires. (Hay House, 2004)

- **Maya Angelou**: (No direct quote used—summary of her embodiment of persistence)

- **Dannion Brinkley:** "You are a great, mighty, and powerful spiritual being with dignity, direction, and purpose."
  Source: Dannion Brinkley, Saved by the Light. (HarperOne, 1995)

- **Roy Waugh**: "Persistence is not loud—it is loyal. It is the quiet agreement between you and God that you are not letting go, no matter how long it takes."
(Original Quote)

Scientific Perspectives

✧ Neuroscience

- Neuroplasticity – Repetition reinforces neural pathways.
Source: Doidge, Norman. The Brain That Changes Itself: Stories of Personal Triumph from the Frontiers of Brain Science. (Viking, 2007)

- Dr. Caroline Leaf – "As you think, you change your brain."
Source: Caroline Leaf, Switch On Your Brain. (Baker Books, 2013)

✧ Psychology / Behavioral Science

- Source: Angela Duckworth – Grit: The Power of Passion and Perseverance. (Scribner, 2016)

✧ Quantum Physics

- Observer Effect – Observation collapses probability into form.
Source: Rosenblum, Bruce, and Fred Kuttner. Quantum Enigma: Physics Encounters Consciousness. (Oxford University Press, 2006)

✧ Energetic Studies

- HeartMath Institute – Research on heart-brain coherence and sustained emotional states.
Source: Rollin McCraty et al., "The Science of the Heart." (HeartMath Institute, 2015)

Chapter 19

Opening Reflection

Dannion Brinkley: "In the end, life is about how we touch and uplift others —and the gratitude we carry for the chance to do it."
Source: Secrets of the Light, Dannion Brinkley and Kathryn Brinkley. (Heart Light Productions, 2008)

Wisdom from Contemporary Spiritual Leaders

- **Louise Hay**: "Gratitude brings more to be grateful for."
  Source: You Can Heal Your Life. (Hay House, 1984)

- **Oprah Winfrey**: "The more you praise and celebrate your life, the more there is in life to celebrate."
  Source: O, The Oprah Magazine, May 2003.

- **Abraham Hicks**: (Esther Hicks) "Appreciation is the vibration of alignment with who-you-really-are."
  Source: Ask and It Is Given. (Hay House, 2004)

- **Dr. Joe Dispenza**: "Gratitude in advance is one of the fastest ways to create new neural pathways...".
  Source: Breaking the Habit of Being Yourself. (Hay House, 2012)

- **Maya Angelou**: "Let gratitude be the pillow upon which you kneel to say your nightly prayer."
  Source: Wouldn't Take Nothing for My Journey Now. (Random House, 1993)

- **Roy Waugh**: "Every morning before my feet touch the floor, I say thank you. Gratitude is how I tell the universe I see the blessing all around me —right here, right now, and I am Grateful."
  (Original Quote)

Scientific Perspectives

✧ Neuroscience

- (Emmons & McCullough, 2003) Study: "Counting Blessings Versus Burdens: An Experimental Investigation of Gratitude and Subjective Well-being in Daily Life"
  Source: Journal of Personality and Social Psychology, Vol. 84, No. 2, 377–389 (Emmons & McCullough 2003)

✧ Vibrational Studies

- HeartMath Institute — Research on heart-brain coherence and gratitude's impact on the electromagnetic field.

Source: Rollin McCraty, "The Energetic Heart: Bioelectromagnetic Interactions Within and Between People." (HeartMath Institute, 2003)

✧ Quantum Physics

- Joe Dispenza — Teaching on "firing and wiring" the brain through gratitude.
  Source: Becoming Supernatural. (Hay House, 2017)

Chapter 20

Opening Reflection

"Faith by itself, if it is not accompanied by action, is dead.
Source: James 2:17 (NIV)

Wisdom from Contemporary Spiritual Leaders

- **Abraham Hicks**: "When action is inspired by alignment, it is always joyful."
  Source: Esther Hicks, Ask and It Is Given. (Hay House, 2004)

- **Iyanla Vanzant**: "If you want to manifest something different, do something different."
  Source: Iyanla Vanzant, Acts of Faith. (Fireside/Simon & Schuster, 1993)

- **Joyce Meyer**: "Do not wait until you feel like it. Obedience is doing the right thing whether you feel like it or not."
  Source: Joyce Meyer, Battlefield of the Mind. (Warner Faith, 2002)

- **Dannion Brinkley**: "You are a great, mighty, and powerful spiritual being with dignity, direction, and purpose."
  Source: Dannion Brinkley, Saved by the Light. (HarperOne, 1994)

- **Dr. Joe Dispenza**: "You can't just think greater. You must also act greater."
  Source: Joe Dispenza, Becoming Supernatural. (Hay House, 2017)

- **Roy Waugh**: "The moment you take a step in faith, you're not chasing the blessing anymore—you're walking beside it."
  (Original Quote)

Scientific Perspectives

✧ **Neuroscience**

- Action Potential — Basic neurobiology of how electrical signals initiate motion.
  Source: Kandel, Eric R., James H. Schwartz, and Thomas M. Jessell. Principles of Neural Science. 4th ed. (McGraw-Hill, 2000)

- Neuroplasticity and habit formation.
  Source: Doidge, Norman. The Brain That Changes Itself: Stories of Personal Triumph from the Frontiers of Brain Science. (Viking Penguin, 2007)

✧ **Psychology**

- Self-efficacy theory.
  Source: Albert Bandura, Self-Efficacy: The Exercise of Control, W.H. (Freeman, 1997)

- Zeigarnik Effect.
  Source: Zeigarnik, Bluma. "Über das Behalten von erledigten und unerledigten Handlungen." (Psychologische Forschung 9, no. 1, 1927) (English translation: "On Finished and Unfinished Tasks")

✧ **Quantum Physics**

- Observer Effect.
  Source: Rosenblum, Bruce, and Fred Kuttner. Quantum Enigma: Physics Encounters Consciousness. (Oxford University Press, 2006)

- Action as conductor for energy collapse.
  Source: Dispenza, Joe. Becoming Supernatural: How Common People Are Doing the Uncommon. (Hay House, 2017)

Chapter 21

Opening Reflection

"For I know the plans I have for you," declares the Lord, "plans to prosper you and not to harm you, plans to give you a future and a hope."
Source: Jeremiah 29:11 (NIV)

Wisdom from Contemporary Spiritual Leaders

- **Louise Hay**: "The Universe loves me and always wants to bring me the highest good, at the right time."
  Source: You Can Heal Your Life. (Hay House, 1984)

- **Abraham Hicks**: "When you feel peace—even in the waiting—you are allowing."
  Source: Hicks, Esther (Abraham). The Law of Attraction: The Basics of the Teachings of Abraham. (Hay House, 2006)

- **Iyanla Vanzant**: "Delay is not denial. It's preparation. Sometimes God is setting you up for more than you asked for."
  Source: Acts of Faith. (Fireside, 1993)

- **Joyce Meyer**: "You may not be where you want to be, but thank God you are not where you used to be…".
  Source: Battlefield of the Mind. (Warner Faith, 1995)

- **Dr. Joe Dispenza**: "Gratitude for what has not arrived yet brings it faster. Why? Because the body responds to vibration—not the clock."
  Source: Breaking the Habit of Being Yourself. (Hay House, 2012)

- **Roy Waugh**: "Delay does not mean no… it just means sometimes the answer is, 'not yet."
  (Original Quote)

Scientific Perspectives

✧Psychology and Neuroscience

- Intertemporal Choice and Future-Oriented Thinking.
  Source: McClure, Samuel M., David Laibson, George Loewenstein, and Jonathan D. Cohen. "Separate Neural Systems Value Immediate and Delayed Monetary Rewards." Science 306, no. 5695 (2004): 503–507. (American Association for the Advancement of Science, 2004 [AAAS])

✧Neuroscience

- Activation of the prefrontal cortex through patience, meditation, and impulse control.
  Source: Tang, Yi-Yuan, Posner, Michael I., and Rothbart, Mary K."Short-Term Meditation Induces White Matter Changes in the Anterior Cingulate." Proceedings of the National Academy of Sciences of the United States of America (PNAS) 107, no. 35 (National Academy of Sciences, 2010): 15649–15652.

- Brain plasticity linked to breathwork and calm presence during uncertainty.
  Source: Zeidan, Fadel, et al. "Mindfulness Meditation Improves Cognition: Evidence of Brief Mental Training." Consciousness and Cognition 19, no. 2 (Elsevier, 2010): 597–605.

✧ Quantum Physics

- Observer Effect — Alignment collapses energetic potential into form.
  Source: Rosenblum, Bruce, and Fred Kuttner. Quantum Enigma: Physics Encounters Consciousness. (Oxford University Press, 2006)

- Emphasis on resonance and coherence rather than urgency.
  Source: Dispenza, Joe. Becoming Supernatural: How Common People Are Doing the Uncommon. (Hay House, 2017)

Chapter 22

Opening Reflection

Roy Waugh: "You are not separate from the Divine—you are a living extension of it. A spark of the Infinite wrapped in breath, blood, and bone. Your body is not merely a vessel; it is the sacred temple where Divine power dwells and moves through you."
(Original Quote)

Wisdom from Contemporary Spiritual Leaders

- **Eckhart Tolle**: "The power for creating a better future is contained in the present moment…"
  Source: The Power of Now. (Namaste Publishing, 1997)

- **Dr. Joe Dispenza**: "If your body is emotionally conditioned to the past, your mind will think from the past..."
  Source: Breaking the Habit of Being Yourself. (Hay House, 2012)

- **Esther Hicks**: (Abraham) "Your inner being is always calling you toward the fulfillment of everything you desire."
  Source: Ask and It Is Given. (Hay House, 2004)

- **Denise Woods**: "Your voice is a reflection of your spirit. When you free your voice, you free yourself."
  Source: The Power of Voice. (HarperOne, 2021)

- **Michael Bernard Beckwith**: "You are not here to get anything from the world, but to bring something through you into it."
  Source: Spiritual Liberation. (Atria Books, 2008)

- **Marianne Williamson**: "We were born to make manifest the glory of God that is within us."
  Source: A Return to Love. (HarperOne, 1992)

- **Roy Waugh**: "The Kingdom of God is within you... It has been living within you all along."
  (Original Quote)

Scientific Perspectives

✧ Vibrational Studies / Neuroscience

- Vagus Nerve & Inner Harmony — Deep breathing and meditation activate the vagus nerve to reduce anxiety and improve heart-brain communication.
  Source: Stephen W. Porges, The Polyvagal Theory. (Norton, 2011)

✧ Heart-Brain Coherence

- The HeartMath Institute — Studies show alignment between heart and brain enhances emotional stability and intuitive clarity.
  Source: Science of the Heart. (HeartMath Institute, 2016)

✧ Neuroplasticity

- Rewiring Identity — Repetition of belief reshapes neural architecture.
  Source: Dr. Joe Dispenza, You Are the Placebo. (Hay House, 2014)

✦ **Quantum Physics**

- Observer Effect — Inner alignment collapses possibility into form.
  Source: Fred Alan Wolf, The Spiritual Universe. (Simon & Schuster, 1996)

✦ **Epigenetics / Psychoneuroimmunology**

- Emotions influence biology — Joy boosts immunity; stress impairs it.
  Source: Dr. Bruce H. Lipton, The Biology of Belief. (Hay House, 2005)

Chapter 23

Opening Reflection

Roy Waugh: "Old beliefs can't hold new blessings. Any belief that dims your vision doesn't belong in your spirit."
(Original Quote)

Wisdom from Contemporary Spiritual Leaders

- **Dr. Joe Dispenza**: "Your personality creates your personal reality."
  Source: Breaking the Habit of Being Yourself. (Hay House, 2012)

- **Abraham Hicks**: (Esther Hicks) "A belief is just a thought you keep thinking."
  Source: Ask and It Is Given. (Hay House, 2004)

- **Louise Hay**: "You have been criticizing yourself for years, and it has not worked. Try approving of yourself and see what happens."
  Source: You Can Heal Your Life. (Hay House, 1984)

- **Oprah Winfrey**: "You don't become what you want. You become what you believe."
  Source: Commonly quoted by Oprah in multiple interviews; earliest documented in The Life You Want Class (2014).

- **Iyanla Vanzant**: "You have to meet yourself where you are. Not where you wish you were, or where you used to be."
  Source: Yesterday, I Cried. (Simon & Schuster, 1998)

- **Dannion Brinkley**: "We are great, powerful, and mighty spiritual beings with dignity, direction, and purpose."
  Source: Saved by the Light. (HarperOne, 1994)

Scientific Perspectives

✧ **Neuroscience**

- Concept: Neuroplasticity — The brain is capable of change through repeated thought patterns.
  Source: Norman Doidge, The Brain That Changes Itself. (Penguin, 2007)

✧ **Psychology / CBT**

- Concept: Cognitive Behavioral Therapy (CBT) — Changing thoughts changes behavior and emotion.
  Source: Judith S. Beck, Cognitive Behavior Therapy: Basics and Beyond. (Guilford Press, 2011)

✧ **Subconscious Belief and Programming**

- Statistic: ~95% of daily behavior stems from the subconscious.
  Source: Bruce Lipton, The Biology of Belief. (Hay House, 2005)

✧ **Energy Psychology**

- Concept: Beliefs have emotional frequencies affecting vibration.
  Source: David R. Hawkins, Power vs. Force. (Hay House, 1995)

Chapter 24

Opening Reflection

Roy Waugh: "Sometimes the most powerful thing you can do... is nothing at all.
(Original Quote)

Wisdom from Contemporary Spiritual Leaders

- **Louise Hay**: "Rest when you need to. Your body is a precious vessel. Honor it."
  Source: You Can Heal Your Life. (Hay House, 1984)

- **Abraham Hicks**: "The rule of thumb is, you never get it done, and you can't get it wrong. So rest. Take a nap. Let the universe do the heavy lifting."
  Source: Ask and It Is Given. (Hay House, 2004)

- **Dr. Joe Dispenza**: "You can't create a new future while you're living in a survival mode. You have to get beyond the analytical mind and enter the operating system of the subconscious."

- Source: Breaking the Habit of Being Yourself. (Hay House, 2012)

- **Oprah Winfrey**: "The greatest discovery of all time is that a person can change their future by merely changing their attitude."

- Source: O Magazine (attributed widely)

- **Iyanla Vanzant**: "You cannot serve from an empty vessel. Rest is how you refill."

- Source: Acts of Faith, Fireside/Simon & Schuster, 1993

- **Albert Einstein**: "I think 99 times and find nothing. I stop thinking, swim in silence, and the truth comes to me."

- Source: Attributed widely; no definitive publication — included as attributed aphorism.

- **Roy Waugh**: "Rest is not what happens after the work is done—rest is the crescendo of the work. It's where everything you've planted gets permission to rise."

- (Original Quote)

Scientific Perspectives

✧ Neuroscience of Brainwave States

- Alpha and Theta Brainwaves. Alpha Brainwaves — Relaxed Alertness and Receptivity.

- Source: Gruzelier, John H., "EEG-neurofeedback for Optimising Performance. I: A Review of Cognitive and Affective Outcome in Healthy Participants." Neuroscience & Biobehavioral Reviews 44: 124–141. (Elsevier, 2014)

- Theta Brainwaves — Subconscious Access and Deep Rest.

- Source: Klimesch, Wolfgang. "EEG Alpha and Theta Oscillations Reflect Cognitive and Memory Performance: A Review and Analysis." Brain Research Reviews 29, no. 2–3: 169–195. (Elsevier, 1999)

✧ Autonomic Nervous System / Parasympathetic Activation

- Sympathetic vs. Parasympathetic: Stress vs. Restoration.

- Source: Thayer, Julian F., and Richard D. Lane. "A Model of Neurovisceral Integration in Emotion Regulation and Dysregulation." Journal of Affective Disorders 61, no. 3: 201–216. (Elsevier, 2000)

- Parasympathetic Activation Lowers Cortisol and Inflammation.

- Source: Pace, Thaddeus W.W., et al. "Effect of Compassion Meditation on Neuroendocrine, Innate Immune and Behavioral Responses to Psychosocial Stress." Psychoneuroendocrinology 34, no. 1: 87–98. (Elsevier, 2009)

- General Review: Parasympathetic Activation Supports Immune Function and Healing.

- Source: Kemeny, Margaret E., "The Psychobiology of Stress."Current Directions in Psychological Science 12, no. 4: 124–129. (SAGE Publications, 2003)

✧ Default Mode Network and Insight Generation

- Rest Is Not Idleness: Implications of the Brain's Default Mode for Human Development and Education.

- Source: Immordino-Yang, Mary Helen, Joanna A. Christodoulou, and Vanessa Singh. Perspectives on Psychological Science 7, no. 4: 352–364. (SAGE Publications, 2012)

❖ **Bioenergetics and Coherence in Stillness**

- Heart-brain coherence enhances emotional and energetic alignment. Source: The HeartMath Solution by Doc Childre & Howard Martin (HarperOne, 1999)

Chapter 25

Opening Reflection

Roy Waugh: "Faith isn't the absence of fear—it's the courage to keep moving while fear watches you do it."

(Original Quote)

Wisdom from Contemporary Spiritual Leaders

- **Dr. Joe Dispenza**: "Your body believes what your brain tells it. If you rehearse fear, you will live it. If you rehearse faith, you will manifest it." Source: Becoming Supernatural: How Common People Are Doing the Uncommon. (Hay House, 2017)

- **Abraham Hicks**: "When you're in alignment, fear cannot stay." Source: Ask and It Is Given, Esther and Jerry Hicks. (Hay House, 2004)

- **Iyanla Vanzant**: "Fear is false evidence appearing real. Faith is feeling assured in the heart." Source: Until Today! Daily Devotions for Spiritual Growth and Peace of Mind. (Simon & Schuster, 2000)

- **Louise Hay**: "I am safe. All is well." Source: You Can Heal Your Life. (Hay House, 1984)

- **Oprah Winfrey**: "Every time you state what you want or believe, you're the first to hear it…" Source: The Wisdom of Sundays. (Flatiron Books, 2017)

- **Albert Einstein**: "The most important decision we make is whether we believe we live in a friendly or hostile universe."
Source: Common attribution; confirmed in The Spiritual Universe by Fred Alan Wolf. (Simon & Schuster, 1999)

- **Roy Waugh**: "Faith doesn't silence fear—it just stops giving it the microphone."
(Original Quote)

Scientific Perspectives

✧ Neuroscience

- Fear response — amygdala activation, cortisol/adrenaline release (survival state) Faith response — activates prefrontal cortex, improves reasoning and empathy.
Source: Andrew Newberg, How God Changes Your Brain. (Ballantine Books, 2009)

✧ Biology of Belief

- Dr. Bruce Lipton: "The moment you change your perception is the moment you rewrite the chemistry of your body."
Source: The Biology of Belief. (Hay House, 2005)

✧ Psychology

- Self-efficacy — belief in one's ability predicts success (Albert Bandura). CBT principle — rewiring fear-based thoughts creates new neural patterns.
Source: Albert Bandura, Self-Efficacy: The Exercise of Control. (Freeman, 1997)

✧ Energetics / Quantum Theory

- Fear is contractive; faith is expansive (energetic principle). Observer effect: the mind influences how reality unfolds.
Source: The Field, Lynne McTaggart. (HarperCollins, 2002)

Chapter 26

Opening Reflection

Albert Einstein: "Imagination is everything. It is the preview of life's coming attractions."
Source: Parade Magazine, March 18, 1976 (interview with Viereck)

Wisdom from Contemporary Spiritual Leaders

- **Dr. Joe Dispenza**: "If you can see it in your mind and feel it in your body, you'll move toward it like a magnet."
  Source: Becoming Supernatural. (Hay House, 2017)

- **Abraham Hicks**: "What you visualize consistently, you begin to live vibrationally—and life meets you there."
  Source: The Law of Attraction. (Hay House, 2006)

- **Oprah Winfrey**: "Create the highest, grandest vision possible for your life, because you become what you believe."
  Source: What I Know For Sure. (Flatiron Books, 2014)

- **Iyanla Vanzant**: "The vision always comes before the victory."
  Source: Acts of Faith. (Simon & Schuster, 1993)

- **Albert Einstein**: "Imagination is more important than knowledge."
  Source: Einstein, Albert. Cosmic Religion and Other Opinions and Aphorisms. (Covici-Friede, 1931)

- **Roy Waugh**: "I've learned this much: I don't have to know how it will happen. I just have to dare to see it—and keep showing up like it's already mine."
  (Original Quote)

Scientific Perspectives

✧ Neuroscience – Neuroplasticity and Mental Rehearsal

- Modulation of Muscle Responses Evoked by Transcranial Magnetic Stimulation During the Acquisition of New Fine Motor Skills.
  Source: Pascual-Leone, A., Nguyet, D., Cohen, L.G., Brasil-Neto, J.P., Cammarota, A., & Hallett, M., Science 270, no. 5234: 1792–1796.
  (American Association for the Advancement of Science [AAAS] 1995)

✧ Psychophysiology – Emotional and Somatic Response to Visualization

- Molecules of Emotion.
  Source: Dr. Candace Pert demonstrated how emotions trigger biochemical responses via imagery and belief. (Scribner, 1997)

✧ Cognitive Psychology – Goal Imagery and Visualization

- Visualization of successful outcomes improves motivation and increases the likelihood of goal achievement.
  Source: Taylor, Pham et al., UCLA. (Journal of Personality and Social Psychology, 1998)

✧ Belief Formation – Memory Reconsolidation and Identity Shaping

- Discusses how imagination and conscious visualization can alter implicit beliefs through memory reconsolidation.
  Source: Ecker, Ticic, Hulley, Unlocking the Emotional Brain. (Routledge, 2012)

Chapter 27

Opening Reflection

Dannion Brinkley (paraphrased): "The clearer your intention, the more divine forces can move in your favor. The universe doesn't respond to confusion—it responds to precision."
Source: Secrets of the Light. (Heart Light Productions, 2004)

Wisdom from Contemporary Spiritual Leaders

- **Abraham Hicks**: "The Universe responds not just to general wishes, but to vibrational alignment—and clarity sharpens that alignment."
  Source: Hicks, Esther and Jerry. Ask and It Is Given. (Hay House, 2004)

- **Louise Hay**: "I live in a spacious, light-filled home with warm wood floors..."
  Source: Hay, Louise. You Can Heal Your Life. (Hay House, 1984)

- **Dr. Joe Dispenza**: "When we visualize with rich sensory detail, our brain and body begin to believe it is happening."
  Source: Becoming Supernatural. (Hay House, 2017)

- **Oprah Winfrey**: "I didn't just say I wanted to be successful…".
  Source: Winfrey, Oprah. The Path Made Clear. (Flatiron Books, 2019)

- **Iyanla Vanzant**: "Don't just ask the universe for cake. Say what kind…".
  Source: Vanzant, Iyanla. Acts of Faith. (Fireside/Simon & Schuster, 1993)

- **Roy Waugh**: "What you name with precision, you magnetize with power."
  (Original Quote)

Scientific Perspectives

✧ Neuroscience

- Embodied Simulation — Visualization activates the same brain regions as real experience.
  Source: Jeannerod, Marc. "Neural Simulation of Action: A Unifying Mechanism for Motor Cognition." NeuroImage 14, no. 1: S103–S109. (Academic Press (now part of Elsevier) 2001)

- Premotor Cortex Activation — Mental rehearsal engages movement centers of the brain.
  Source: Lotze, Martin & Halsband, Ulrike. "Motor Imagery." (Journal of Physiology – vol. 99, 2006)

- Neuroplasticity — Repeated, emotional visualization reshapes brain circuits.
  Source: Doidge, Norman. The Brain That Changes Itself. (Viking Press, 2007)

✧ Cognitive Psychology

- Hebbian Learning — "Neurons that fire together wire together."
  Source: Hebb, Donald O., The Organization of Behavior. (Wiley, 1949)

- Mental Time Travel / Episodic Future Thinking.
  Source: Schacter, Daniel L. & Addis, Donna Rose. "The Cognitive Neuroscience of Constructive Memory." (Philosophical Transactions of the Royal Society B, vol. 362, 2007)

Chapter 28

Opening Reflection

Roy Waugh: "Delays are sometimes detours—gentle redirections guiding you to what the universe has already arranged as a divine appointment."
(Original Quote)

Wisdom from Contemporary Spiritual Leaders

- **Joyce Meyer**: "God's timing is always right. He is never late—though He seldom comes early."
  Source: Enjoying Where You Are on the Way to Where You Are Going. (Warner Faith, 1996)

- **Dr. Joe Dispenza**: "When we try to force outcomes, we lock ourselves into predictable futures..."
  Source: Breaking the Habit of Being Yourself. (Hay House, 2012)

- **Abraham Hicks** (Esther Hicks) "What you want is already in your vibrational escrow. It is ready. Are you?"
  Source: Ask and It Is Given (Hay House, 2004)

- **Louise Hay**: "I trust the process of life. Everything I need comes to me in the perfect time and space sequence."
  Source: You Can Heal Your Life. (Hay House, 1984)

- **Maya Angelou**: "Ask for what you want and be prepared to get it. But do not try to dictate how and when."
  Source: Conversations with Maya Angelou, by Jeffrey M. Elliot. (University Press of Mississippi, 1989)

- **Roy Waugh**: "Divine timing isn't a delay—it's a dance. You're not late. You're being led."
  (Original Quote)

Scientific Perspectives

✧ **Neuroscience**

- Latent learning; neuroplasticity during rest and emotion.
  Source: Huberman, Andrew. "How to Learn Skills Faster —
  Neuroplasticity Explained." Huberman Lab Podcast, Episode 20, May
  31, 2021. Produced by Scicomm Media.

✧ **Quantum Physics**

- Superposition, observer effect, quantum coherence.
  Source: Gribbin, John. In Search of Schrödinger's Cat: Quantum Physics
  and Reality. (Bantam Books, 1984)

✧ **Developmental Psychology**

- Graham Wallas — Four Stages of Insight. (Preparation, Incubation,
  Illumination, Verification)
  Source: The Art of Thought. (Harcourt Brace, 1926)

✧ **Chronobiology**

- Circadian and ultradian rhythms; cellular regeneration aligned to
  timing.
  Source: Lloyd, David, and Ernest L. Rossi. "Ultradian Rhythms in Life
  Processes: An Inquiry into Fundamental Principles of Chronobiology
  and Psychobiology." (The Journal of Interdisciplinary Cycle Research 19,
  no. 1: 1–29, 1988)

✧ **Systems Theory**

- Tipping point and emergence.
  Source: Foundational Text: Thinking in Systems by Donella Meadows.
  (Chelsea Green Publishing, 2008)

Chapter 29

Opening Reflection

Roy Waugh: "You do not manifest what you wish for—you manifest what
you walk like, speak like, and live like before it ever arrives. Because the

moment you begin to live as if it is already yours, the universe starts responding like it is."
(Original Quote)

Wisdom from Contemporary Spiritual Leaders

- **Dr. Joe Dispenza**: "To change your personal reality, you must change your personality."
  Source: Breaking the Habit of Being Yourself. (Hay House, 2012)

- **Abraham Hicks**: "You have to become a vibrational match to what you want."
  Source: Ask and It Is Given. (Hay House, 2004)

- **Louise Hay**: "If you believed you were worthy, how would you act today?"
  Source: Paraphrased teaching from You Can Heal Your Life. (Hay House, 1984)

- **Joyce Meyer**: "You can't be pitiful and powerful at the same time."
  Source: Battlefield of the Mind. (FaithWords, 1995)

- **Neale Donald Walsch**: "You are already doing it. You are already being it. Now own it."
  Source: Conversations with God: Book 1. (Putnam, 1995)

- **Eckhart Tolle**: "You are not waiting for something. You are it."
  Source: Paraphrased concept from The Power of Now. (New World Library, 1997)

- **Roy Waugh**: "Embodiment is not performance—it is permission..."
  (Original Quote)

Scientific Perspectives

✧ Psychology

- Identity drives behavior.
  Source: Bem, Daryl J., "Self-Perception Theory." In Advances in Experimental Social Psychology, vol. 6, edited by Leonard Berkowitz, 1–62. (Academic Press, 1972)

✦ Behavioral Neuroscience

- The As-If Principle. Concept: Acting "as if" rewires emotional and physiological states.
  Source: James, William. The Principles of Psychology. Vol. 2. (Henry Holt and Company, 1890)

✦ Cognitive Science

- Enclothed Cognition. Clothing associated with specific roles can shift cognitive performance.
  Source: Adam Hajo and Adam D. Galinsky, Northwestern University. (Journal of Experimental Social Psychology, Vol. 48, Issue 4, 2012)

✦ Motor Simulation Theory

- Mental rehearsal activates the same neural circuits as physical action.
  Source: Jeannerod, Marc. "The Representing Brain: Neural Correlates of Motor Intention and Imagery." Neuropsychologia 32, no. 11: 1413–1425. (Pergamon Press [now part of Elsevier] 1994)

✦ Social Psychology

- The Pygmalion Effect.
  Source: Rosenthal, Robert, and Lenore Jacobson. Pygmalion in the Classroom: Teacher Expectation and Pupils' Intellectual Development. (Holt, Rinehart and Winston, 1968)

Chapter 30

Opening Reflection

Roy Waugh: "You are not merely a reflection of God—You are a vessel of Divine essence, radiating light into form. Every word you speak echoes the Divine voice within. You are the living, breathing frequency of what God, Yahweh, Allah, or the Universe manifested you to be—the embodiment of what this book has revealed: The Manifestation Frequency—in motion." (Original Quote)

Introduction

- "YHWA" As breath. Kushner, Lawrence. The Book of Words: Talking Spiritual Life, Living Spiritual Talk. Woodstock, VT: Jewish Lights Publishing, 1993.